• At-A-Glance Phone Numbers •

Veterinarian ____________________

Back-up Veterinarian ____________________

Closest Surgery Center ____________________

Farrier ____________________

Insurance Company ____________________

Policy Number(s) ____________________

____

____

____

HORSE & RIDER's

HANDS-ON HORSE CARE

The complete book of equine first aid

By Karen E. N. Hayes DVM, MS

Edited by Thomas C. Bohanon, DVM, MS
and Sue M. Copeland

Printed in U.S.A.

COWLES
Enthusiast Media

President: Philip L. Penny
Group V.P./Publishing Director: Stephen F. Norton
Executive Editor: Sue M. Copeland

Author: Karen E.N. Hayes, DVM, MS
Editors: Thomas C. Bohanon, DVM, MS, Diplomate, American College of Veterinary Surgeons, and Sue M. Copeland
Art Director: Lauryl Suire Eddlemon
Business Managers: Tom Carpenter, Steven Hallem
Managing Editor: William B. Jones
Marketing Coordinator: Lua Oas Southard
Publisher: Pat Eskew
Print Production: Dave Austad, Kim Gerber, Pam Grimm-Hamilton, Steven Hoy
Photography: Cappy Jackson, how-to shots and cover; toxic plant images supplied by Mitsuko Williams, veterinary medicine librarian and associate professor of library administration, the University of Illinois, and Robert D. Linnabary, DVM, MS, associate professor, the University of Tennessee College of Veterinary Medicine.
Illustrations: Kip Carter, MS, CMI
Proofreading: Marilee B. Nudo
Special thanks to Gary Carpenter and the American Association of Equine Practitioners.

T
Trafalgar Square Publishing

Distributed by Trafalgar Square Publishing Company
Howe Hill Road, North Pomfret VT USA 05053

Printed on American paper by Quebecor Printing
00 99 98 97 / 5 4 3 2 1

Library of Congress Cataloging-in-Publication Data

Hayes, Karen E.N.
Horse & rider's hands-on-horse care : the complete book of equine first-aid / by Karen E.N. Hayes : edited by Thomas Bohanon.
p. cm.
Includes bibliographical references and index
1. Horses--Wounds and injuries. 2. Horses--Diseases. 3. First aid for animals. I. Bohanon, Thomas. II. Title.
SF951.H327 1997
636.11'0896025--dc21 97-38656
CIP

ISBN 0-86573-861-0

To my horses, Bandanna, Zydeco, and Charmin, the hands-on stewardship of whom provided the inspiration for this book. And to my husband, Rick, for his unconditional support of and interest in all things horse.

—Sue M. Copeland
Editor, *Horse & Rider* Magazine

Acknowledgements

• AAEP past president Terry Swanson, DVM, for his unfailing support of and confidence in this project. Thanks.
• Gary Carpenter and Julie Kimball of the AAEP, for their valuable time and input.
• Lua Oas Southard, for her tireless efforts to see this project to fruition.
• *Horse & Rider* Associate Editor Jennifer J. Denison, Senior Editor Marilee B. Nudo, Managing Editor Rene E. Riley, Editor-At-Large Juli S. Thorson, and Executive Art Director Lisa Wrigley, for keeping the magazine on course through the duration of book production.
• Bill Jones, Cowles Enthusiast Media creative director, for skillfully organizing a geographically diverse book team.
• Kip Carter, MS, CMI, master medical illustrator, for his collaboration on the illustrations and spot art in this book, and his undying support of team *H&R*.
• Jane E. Tyrie, veterinary assistant to Midge Leitch, VMD, for so ably organizing and demonstrating the how-to photography in Section II, and to Jackie Lesniczak for being her official horse holder during that photo shoot.
• The staff at *Southwest Art* Magazine, for graciously allowing us the space and equipment for book production.
• Mitsuko Williams, veterinary medicine librarian and associate professor of library administration, the University of Illinois, for digging into her slide collection and providing many of the toxic plant photos in Section II.
• Robert D. Linnabary, DVM, MS, associate professor, the University of Tennessee College of Veterinary Medicine, for also sharing his toxic plant slide collection.

Table of Contents

SECTION II: HANDS-ON HORSEKEEPING SKILLS

SECTION III: REFERENCE INFORMATION

SECTION IV: RECORDS

Forward

Equine health care has become an increasingly complex and specialized field over the past 20 years. Huge amounts of new information covering diseases and treatments are available for both veterinarians and horse owners. As a result, the relationship between you and your veterinarian has also become more complex, requiring a common knowledge base that's much more sophisticated than ever before.

It's toward the goal of expanding this foundation of knowledge that *Hands-On Horse Care* is written. I hope it will give you a basic understanding of normal equine physiology, behavior, and physical parameters. Recognizing and understanding what's normal is paramount to detecting and describing abnormal situations in your horse. Clear and accurate communication between you and your veterinarian regarding history, clinical signs, and physical exam findings is essential.

This book is not intended to replace or circumvent regular veterinary care, and should not be used as such. Rather, it will hopefully provide a knowledge base for you that will help you recognize when your horse has a problem and when veterinary attention is indicated. Variability in horses, clients, veterinarians, and the circumstances that bring them together will continue to prevent standardization of techniques in the diagnosis and treatment of equine maladies. In addition to detailed knowledge of hard science, factors such as good judgment, experience, intuition, adaptability, creativity, and art have always been important aspects of the skills that can't be passed on through texts. They're the reasons you'll continue to solicit veterinary care in order to obtain the best for your horse.

I'm confident that *Hands-On Horse Care* contains the information and guidance to make a positive contribution toward a goal that we all share: to assure the health and well-being of the horse.

Thomas C. Bohanon, DVM, MS
Diplomate, American College of Veterinary Surgeons
Centennial Valley Equine Hospital
Broomfield, Colorado

How To Use This Book

Hands-On Horse Care is like having your own personal veterinary consultant—someone who can ask the right questions, give you an action plan based on your answers, and be the liason between you and your veterinarian. Your horse will be the prime beneficiary, but you and your veterinarian will benefit too: Potentially dangerous signs you might have missed or minimized will get attention early, to give your horse the best shot at a fast, seamless recovery. This means less worry and expense for you, and fewer after-hours calls for your veterinarian.

This book is organized into three sections:

1 In **ACTION PLANS**, you'll find just about every sign your horse might exhibit in the course of his adult life. Each signpost is listed just as you'd describe it yourself: If your horse has a weepy eye, look up *Weeping Eye* in the Table of Contents. If he's got dry, brittle hooves, look up *Dry, Brittle Hooves*. (All symptoms can be found in the Index at the back of the book, too.) Turn to the page for your horse's symptom, where you'll be asked a series of yes-or-no questions based on your observations. Your answers will lead you through a flow chart to an action plan that best suits your horse's individual needs, along with a brief explanation of what the problem might be. If veterinary care is needed, the action plan will tell you when to call your vet, and why. If there's something you should do until he or she arrives, it's detailed in *While You Wait*. If home treatment is recommended, it's described in a clear, step-by-step fashion.

2 Use the **HANDS-ON HORSEKEEPING** section as a guideline for basic, preventive horse care. Wondering whether your horse's ration is rational? Check the *Prevention Diet*. Do you want to develop a more critical eye, so you can detect problems early? See *Baseline Behavior*, where you'll learn to interpret subtle clues your horse may give. Need to know how to pull a loose shoe, bandage a wound, treat a troubled eye, or administer a prescription medication? It's all here, in photographic, step-by-step form. And if a home treatment is recommended in Section 1, odds are you'll find that treatment procedure described here, in detail.

3 The **GLOSSARY** section will give you a quick rundown on terms you'll hear around the barn, at the veterinary clinic, and will see in this book. If your horse is diagnosed with a condition you've never heard of, look it up here. If you want to know more about a procedure your veterinarian has recommended, you'll probably find it in this section.

Note: Each section is cross-referenced in the other two sections, using page numbers to provide you with flip-to-it ease.

SECTION I

FIRST-AID ACTION PLANS

CHAPTER 1

How to handle WOUNDS

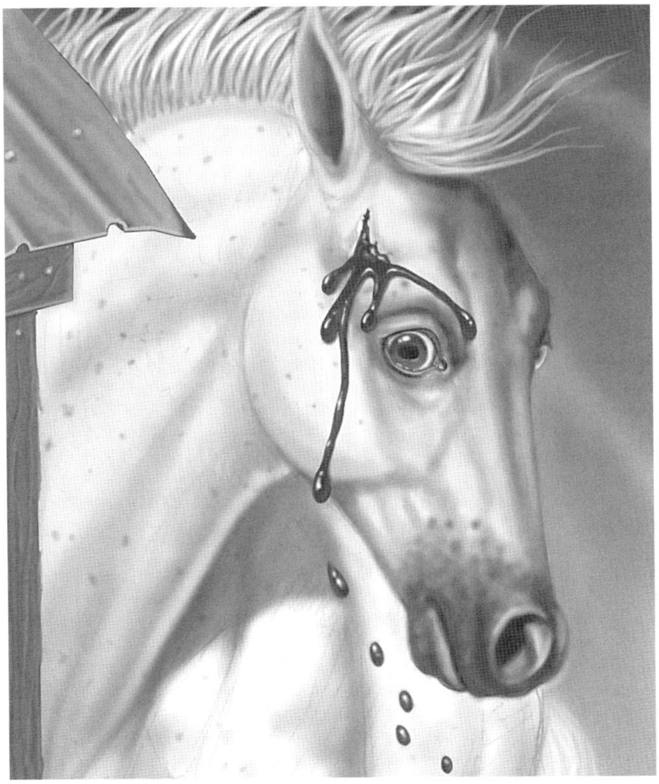

What you see: A torn or jagged cut through your horse's skin. There's dried blood adhered to its margins, and/or fresh blood spilling from the wound, making it difficult to see if tissues beneath the skin are lacerated too.

1-A

THE CUT

(Laceration)

What this might mean: If it involves only the skin and the cushion of fat beneath it, without disturbing major bleeders or vital structures such as tendons, joints, nerves, and ligaments, then it's mainly cosmetic: It might result in a scar or a blemish of proud flesh[G], but your horse will be fine. However, if vital structures are involved, the cut can cause serious—maybe permanent—damage. Proper treatment will help you achieve the best possible outcome.

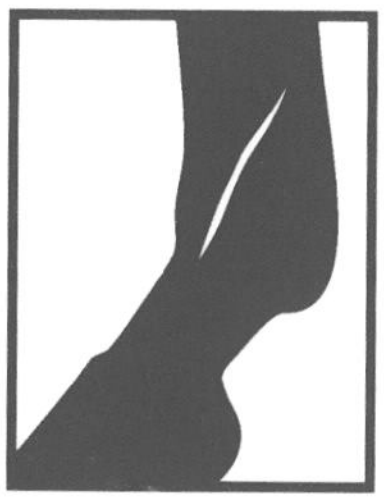

ACTION PLAN:

Is it bleeding profusely (1/4 cup or more per minute)?

YES → Call your veterinarian *NOW*—it might need stitches to stop the bleeding. Go to **While You Wait #1,** opposite page.

NO ↓

Are tissues near the wound drooping? If the wound is on a leg, is the leg buckling or non-weight-bearing?

YES → Call your veterinarian *NOW* if you answer yes to either query—nerves or supporting structures (bone, tendon, or ligament) may be damaged.

NO ↓

Can you see white tissue in the wound?

YES → Call your veterinarian *NOW*—it could be exposed bone, tendon, or ligament.

NO ↓

Are the skin edges gaping or easily pulled apart? Is the wound near enough to a joint to gape when the joint moves? Is the wound on a lower leg, below the knee or hock joint? Has it created a flap of tissue?

YES → Call your veterinarian *NOW* if you answered yes to any of these queries—it may require stitches to stabilize edges, minimize scarring, and/or prevent proud flesh, Go to **While You Wait #2,** opposite page.

NO ↓

Is the wound located over or near a joint? Do you see amber-colored fluid coming from it, or white streaks dried on your horse's coat below the laceration?

YES → Call your veterianarian *NOW* if you answered yes to either query—the wound may have entered a joint or tendon sheath.

NO ↓

Does the wound involve your horse's face and/or eye(s)?

YES → Call your veterinarian *NOW*—the wound may need immediate help to avoid scarring and to help minimize damage to vital tissues. Go to **While You Wait,** page 79.

NO ↓

ACTION PLAN (CONTINUED):

Is there sufficient swelling to obscure your view of the wound? Is there an opaque, white-yellow discharge, or "spoiled" odor? **YES** → Go to **page 24.**

NO ↓

Will he allow you to treat the wound? **YES** → Apply **Home Treatment,** next page.

NO ↓

Call your veterinarian *TODAY.*

WHILE YOU WAIT #1:

1. *Calm your horse.* If he's excited, his heart will pump harder and his blood will run faster. If possible, have a helper hold his halter and soothe him as you work.

2. *Apply direct pressure.* Forget about whether that blood's coming from an artery or a vein—the treatment's the same: Apply pressure over the site with a clean pad of sufficient size to cover the wound and its margins. A folded cloth, disposable diaper, or a 1-inch thick stack of gauze sponges will make a suitable pad. If an ice pack is immediately available, sandwich it between the pad's layers to further stem the bleeding. (For how hard to press, see "How Much Pressure," page 16, this chapter.)

Resist the temptation to lift the pad again to check bleeding—you'll only disturb tentative clots that've formed, undoing the good you've done. If your pad becomes saturated with blood, don't replace it. Keep pressing for a minimum of 5 minutes without moving it.

If there's so much blood you can't tell where it's coming from, press hard for 5 seconds to blanch the site, then briefly lift the pad to find the blood source. Center your pressure there.

Unless instructed to do so by your vet, NEVER administer a sedative or tranquilizer to a horse that's excited or frightened, or that's been exercising during the past half hour. Doing so could depress his heart and/or respiratory systems and cause fainting. If your horse requires chemical restraint, leave the decision to your vet.

3. *Apply a pressure bandage.* After 5 to 10 minutes of pressure, and if the bleeding is coming from a location that lends itself to bandaging, apply a pressure bandage. (See page 279.) Otherwise, just keep pressing in 5-minute shifts. If a bandage becomes saturated with blood, simply add a layer on top of it.

4. *Confine your horse.* Keep him still to prevent a rise in blood pressure, and to restrict movement that might disturb tentative clots.

WHILE YOU WAIT #2:

1. *Ice the wound.* Select an ice pack (see page 262) large enough to extend at least 2 inches beyond the wound's margins. Slip it between layers of a clean cloth, center it over the wound, and hold it there. Follow this icing schedule: ice on for 5 minutes. Ice off: 15 minutes. Repeat this cycle 3 more times times or until your veterinarian arrives, whichever happens first. ➤

YOUR VET MAY NEED TO:

Sedate or anesthetize your horse, and/or numb the tissues, in order to fully determine the depth and extent of the injury and to help facilitate the best possible repair.

HOW MUCH PRESSURE?

Try this midway up your own thigh: squeeze or press until you can feel the contours of the bone within. That's the amount of pressure you need to apply to your horse's bleeding wound. Your effectiveness will depend less on the amount of pressure and more on your ability to hold it consistently, without shifting or letting up, for a minimum of 5 minutes.

2. *Apply pressure.* During ice-off sessions, use clean cloths, sanitary napkins, or 1-inch stacks of gauze pads to firmly press the tissues.

3. *Bandage the wound.* If the injured area lends itself to bandaging (e.g., a lower limb), adjust the cut edges into their correct positions and apply a pressure bandage (for how-to instructions, see page 279).

HOME TREATMENT:

(See ***Action Plan,*** *page 14, to determine whether home treatment is appropriate for your horse's laceration. If at any time during home treatment, your answers on the action plan change for the worse, call your vet.)*

Avoid using antibiotic powders, sprays, or ointments without consulting your veterinarian. Indiscriminate use of antibiotics in any form can favor the growth of tougher, antibiotic-resistant bacteria.

Step 1. *Ice the wound.* Slip an ice pack (see page 262) between layers of clean cloth. Lay the covered pack over the wound, making sure there are no large clumps in the bag that might cause discomfort. Hold it firmly in place, either manually or with a wrap, for 5 minutes.

Step 2. *Clean the wound.* (For in-depth instruction, see page 258.) Irrigate the wound with cold hose water or a trigger-type spray bottle filled with homemade saline solution (see page 242). Spray for 1 full minute or until the wound appears visibly clean, whichever takes longer.

Step 3. *Bandage the wound.*

A. If it's in an area that lends itself to bandaging and if environmental conditions make it likely to get contaminated with dirt, dust, and flies unless covered, press a non-stick pad such as Telfa® or Release® directly over the wound. Choose a pad that's large enough to extend an inch or more past the wound's margins. Secure with bandage materials appropriate for the location. (See page 267.)

B. If the wound is in an area that doesn't lend itself to bandaging, and if environmental conditions make it likely to get contaminated with dirt, dust, and flies unless covered, use a clean gauze pad or your finger to apply a thin layer of a non-antibiotic dressing, such as povidone iodine ointment (see page 238). This will act as a barrier against contamination. If flies are a problem, apply a second layer of Swat®, a repellant for use on open wounds.

C. If contamination and flies aren't a problem, leave the wound open to air.

Step 4. *Review/renew* tetanus immunization. (See page 211.)

Step 5. *Keep it up.* Repeat steps 1 through 3 once or twice daily, depending on how gooey, dirty, and crusty the wound and bandage become. Begin by changing the bandage twice daily to assess the wound; reduce to once daily if the wound and bandage become only slightly moist. (If the wound becomes slimy or off-smelling, consult your veterinarian about using an antibiotic dressing.) Continue until the wound remains clean and uncrusted between cleanings (about 2 to 3 weeks).

What you see: A flesh wound in which layers of your horse's skin and subcutanous tissue have been scraped away. Droplets of blood and/or clear, amber-colored fluid are oozing from or drying on the wound's surface.

What this might mean: It's potentially serious, depending on the depth and breadth of skin involved and whether the injured tissue is embedded with foreign material, such as gravel. As a rule of thumb, the larger and more contaminated the abrasion, the more vulnerable it will be to infection. Deep abrasions can damage hair follicles and skin cells, which can result in scarring. Hair may grow in white or fail to regrow at all because of follicle damage. Attending to these wounds can be dangerous to you, because your horse's skin is packed with pain-sensing nerve endings, making abrasions very painful for him.

1-B

THE SCRAPE

(Abrasion)

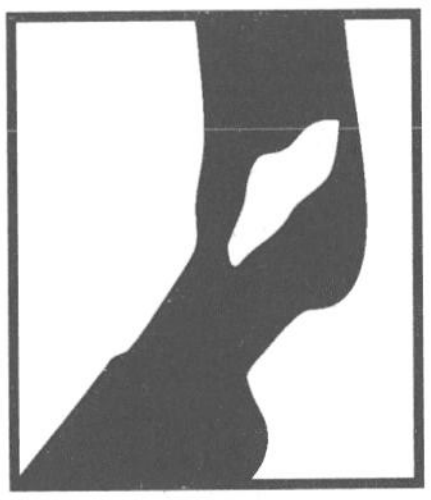

ACTION PLAN:

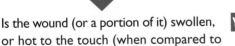

Is your horse lame as a result of the injury? **YES** → Go to **page 89.**

NO ↓

Does the abrasion involve more than 15 percent of your horse's skin (roughly enough to cover one entire side of his rump)? **YES** → Call your veterinarian *NOW*—it might require treatment to prevent excessive fluid loss and infection.

NO ↓

Can you see white tissue in the wound? Is the abrasion over or near a joint? **YES** → Call your veterinarian *NOW*—the abrasion may be deep enough to reach bone, tendon, or ligament, or it may have damaged a tendon sheath or joint tissues.

NO ↓

Is there foreign material embedded in the wound that you can't entirely remove (e.g., gravel, dirt, splinters)? **YES** → Call your veterinarian *NOW*—to avoid infection, all debris must be removed.

NO ↓

Is the wound (or a portion of it) swollen, or hot to the touch (when compared to adjacent tissue)? Is it "spoiled" smelling, blackened, or draining white or yellowish pus? **YES** → Call your veterinarian *NOW* if you answered yes to any of these queries—it could be infected.

NO ↓

CONTINUED ⇨

YOUR VET MAY NEED TO:

Sedate or anesthetize your horse, and/or numb the tissues, in order to fully determine the depth and extent of the injury and help facilitate the best possible treatment.

ACTION PLAN (CONTINUED):

Will your horse allow you to treat the wound? **YES** → Apply **Home Treatment,** below.

NO ↓

Call your veterinarian *NOW*. The sooner the wound gets proper treatment, the better the odds of quick, uncomplicated healing.

HOME TREATMENT:

*(See **Action Plan** on previous page to determine whether home treatment is appropriate for your horse's abrasion. If at any time during home treatment, your answers on the action plan change for the worse, call your veterinarian.)*

Step 1. *Ice the wound.* This will numb painful nerve endings and limit swelling. Wet a clean cloth, slip an ice pack (see page 262) between its layers, and lay it over the wound, overlapping the wound's margins. Hold the pack in place, either manually or with a wrap, for 5 minutes.

Step 2. *Clean the wound.* Irrigate the wound with cold hose water or a trigger-type spray bottle filled with homemade saline solution (see page 242). Hose or spray for 1 full minute or until the wound appears visibly clean, whichever takes longer.

Step 3. *Dress the wound.* Apply a thin layer of non-antibiotic first-aid cream, such as povidone iodine ointment (see page 238) to keep exposed tissues moist and to act as a barrier to outside contaminants. If flies are a problem, apply an outer layer of Swat®, a fly repellant labelled for use on open wounds.

Step 4. *Review/renew tetanus immunization.* (See page 211.)

Step 5. *Exercise daily.* Daily light exercise, at the walk and jog, is advised to encourage circulation to the injured area and to speed healing. If your tack contacts the abraded area, don't use it: ride bareback, or exercise in hand.

Step 6. *Keep it up.* Repeat Steps 2 and 3 once or twice daily, depending on how gooey/dirty/crusty the wound becomes. Begin by cleaning it twice daily to assess the wound; reduce to once daily if the area is only slightly crusted or soiled. Continue until the wound remains clean and uncrusted between cleanings (about 2 to 3 weeks).

Avoid using antibiotic powders, sprays, or ointments without consulting your veterinarian. Indiscriminate use of antibiotics in any form can favor the growth of tougher, antibiotic-resistant bacteria.

1 - C

BURNS:

Thermal, chemical, electrical burns, and/or sunburn

What you see: Your horse's haircoat may be singed or gone; his skin's appearance will fit roughly into 1 of the following 3 levels:

1. Exposed skin is fiery red, moist, smooth (no blisters), and very sensitive to the touch. If you press on it lightly with your fingers, it blanches (turns white). This describes most first-degree burns.

2. Same as above, but with blisters. This describes most second-degree burns.

3. The skin can vary in color, from white to red to black. It's generally dry, with either a pliable or leathery texture. It seems non-painful, and when you press on it with your fingers, it doesn't blanch. This describes most third-degree burns.

What this might mean: A burn can be serious, depending on its depth (degree) and on how broad an area is involved. As a rule of thumb, the higher the degree of the burn and the broader the skin damage, the greater the potential for dehydration and infection.

ACTION PLAN:

Does the burn involve more than 15 percent of your horse's skin (roughly enough to cover one entire side of his rump)? Does it contain blisters, and/or is it discolored (white, blackened, bright red) or split?

YES → Call your veterinarian *NOW* if you answered yes to any of these queries—risk of infection and/or dehydration[G] is high.

NO ↓

Does the burn involve your horse's face, ears, or lower legs?

YES → Call your veterinarian *NOW*—treatment might be required to prevent scarring and loss of function.

NO ↓

Is it possible your horse inhaled smoke?

YES → Call your veterinarian *NOW*—lung damage from smoke inhalation might not immediately be evident. Without proper treatment it can be debilitating or fatal.

NO ↓

Is this a sunburn on white-haired or hairless areas? Does it seem excessive compared to other horses with the same coloration and level of sun exposure? Are the whites of your horse's eyes and/or his gums yellow-tinged?

YES → Call your veterinarian *NOW* if you answered yes to any of these queries—it could be an underlying condition that's made your horse overly sensitive to sunlight (photosensitivity[G]).

NO ↓

CONTINUED ⇨

YOUR VET MAY NEED TO:

Sedate or anesthetize your horse, and numb tissues, in order to treat a burn, which can be exquisitely painful if it's of first or second degree severity.

ACTION PLAN (CONTINUED):

Will your horse allow you to treat the wound? **YES** → Apply **Home Treatment**, below.

NO ↓

Call your veterinarian *TODAY*.

HOME TREATMENT:

(See ***Action Plan*** *on previous page to determine whether home treatment is appropriate for your horse's burn. If at any time during home treatment, your answers on the action plan change for the worse, call your veterinarian.)*

Step 1. *Remove source of burn.* If whatever has burned your horse is still in contact with his skin, remove it as quickly as possible. For instance, if he was scalded by hot water, quickly irrigate the area with cold water, using a gentle flood to avoid pressure damage to already injured tissues. If he was burned by a chemical agent, dilute/neutralize that agent. If he's sunburned, move him indoors.

DON'T apply butter or ointments, which contain a greasy/oily base that can hold in heat. Use only water-based creams or gels.

Step 2. *Ice the burn.* Wet a clean cloth, slip an ice pack (see page 262) between its layers, and lay it over the burn, overlapping the burn's margins. Hold the pack in place, either manually or with a wrap, for 5 minutes, to numb painful nerve endings and reduce skin damage from stored heat in tissues. Let tissues rest 15 minutes. Repeat cycle (ice on: 5 minutes, ice off: 15 minutes) for a total of 1 hour.

Step 3. *Clean the burn.* Irrigate the burn with cold water, clean gently with soap and water, and remove any debris. Allow to air dry.

Step 4. *Dress the burn.* Apply a thin layer of oil-free, soothing dressing such as 100 percent aloe vera gel mixed 50-50 with Betadine® cream (not ointment) or Silvadene cream. (The latter is a prescription item you'll have to get from your veterinarian.) This will keep tissues pliable and prevent cracking, and will disinfect the wound.

Step 5. *Protect against further burning.* Remove/repair whatever caused the burn in the first place. To protect against additional sunburn, keep your horse indoors in a cool, shaded stall. Cover the burned area loosely with a sun-blocking fabric (e.g., a fly mask), or coat with a non-chemical sunblock such as zinc oxide cream or titanium dioxide.

Step 6. *Keep it up.* Repeat Steps 3 and 4 once or twice daily, depending on how gooey, dirty, or crusty the burned area becomes. Begin with a twice daily schedule to assess the burn; reduce to once daily if the burn becomes only slightly moist. Continue until it remains clean and uncrusted between cleanings (about 2 to 3 weeks). Be sure to remove all residual dressings before reapplying.

The Nitty Gritty

Here are some possible causes of photosensitivity

- Ingestion of goatweed (Klamath weed, St. Johns-wort)
- Ingestion of buckwheat
- Ingestion of Senecio weeds (Groundsel and Hound's Tongue)
- Liver disease

1-D

PUNCTURE WOUNDS

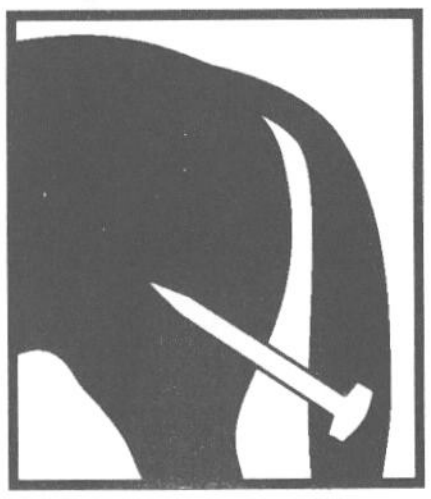

What you see: A flesh wound with one or more holes that penetrate into your horse's tissues. The area around the hole(s) may be swollen, and there may or may not be a discharge or foul-smelling odor.

What this might mean: A puncture wound is potentially serious, depending on its location and depth. Puncture wounds can cause direct damage to internal structures, and can introduce bacteria deep into tissues where infection can be devastating. Tetanus is of particular concern because the bacteria that cause it—*Clostridium tetani*—thrive in a puncture wound's deep, dark, airless recesses. Puncture wounds might also be the result of a snake bite[G], which is dangerous if the snake produces toxic venom. Holes that look like puncture wounds also can result from an internal problem rather than an external injury. For instance, the puncture might be a drainage hole that formed from the inside to release pressure and debris from an internal infection, or it might be a breathing/escape hole for a migrating cattle grub[G].

ACTION PLAN:

Is the wound bleeding profusely (about 1/4 cup or more per minute)? **YES** → Call your veterinarian *NOW*—stitches might be required to stop the bleeding. Go to ***While You Wait,*** next page.

NO ↓

Is there external evidence of tissue damage, such as tearing, missing tissue, tissue flaps, scorching of tissue at the hole's margins, or entry-exit holes? **YES** → Call your veterinarian *NOW*—the more tissue is traumatized, whether by gunshot or other cause, the greater the risk of infection and disability.

NO ↓

Are tissues near the wound drooping, or is the involved leg (if applicable) buckling (page 106), or severely lame (page 87)? **YES** → Call your veterinarian *NOW*—nerves or supporting structures (bone, tendon, ligament) may be damaged.

NO ↓

Is the wound on or near a joint? **YES** → Call your veterinarian *NOW*—the joint and/or tendon sheath may have been penetrated.

NO ↓

Is the wound on the underside of his neck/throat region? **YES** → Call your veterinarian *NOW*—vital structures in that area may be damaged or at risk for contamination and infection.

NO ↓

Is the wound in your horse's foot? **YES** → Go to **page 118.**

NO ↓

CONTINUED ⇨

YOUR VET MAY NEED TO:

Probe and/or X-ray the wound site to determine cause, depth, and direction of penetration, and to assess damage to internal structures.

ACTION PLAN (CONTINUED):

Are there 2 small holes visible, 1/2- to 3/4-inch apart?

YES → Call your veterinarian *NOW*—it could be a snakebite[G]. If venomous, and if located on your horse's muzzle, the resultant swelling could interfere with breathing.

NO ↓

Is there a foreign object visible?

YES → Call your veterinarian *NOW*—if possible, leave the object in place so your vet can determine depth, direction, and vital structures in its path, and can remove it with minimal additional damage.

NO ↓

Is the wound on your horse's face, near his cheekbones, or under his lower jaw? Is a white or yellow, foul-smelling liquid draining from it?

YES → Go to **page 74.**

NO ↓

Is the wound hot, swollen, and/or sensitive to the touch? Is it draining whitish or yellowish fluid?

YES → Go to **page 24.**

NO ↓

Is the hole on the side of your horse's neck, near his withers, along his back, or over his rump? Is it surprisingly benign looking, with little or no blood or swelling?

YES → Call your veterinarian for advice and/or an appointment—it could be a grub worm's breathing hole. See "Grubworm Prevention," opposite page.

NO ↓

Apply **Home Treatment,** opposite page.

WHILE YOU WAIT:

Unless directed to do so by your vet, NEVER administer a sedative or tranquilizer to a horse that's excited or frightened, or that's been exercising during the past half hour. Doing so could depress his heart and/or respiratory systems and cause fainting. If your horse requires chemical restraint, leave the decision to your vet.

1. *Calm your horse.* If he's excited, his heart will pump harder and his blood will run faster. If possible, have a helper hold and soothe him as you work.

2. *Apply direct pressure.* Forget about whether the blood's coming from an artery or a vein, the treatment's the same: Apply pressure over the bleeding site with a clean pad of sufficient size to cover the wound and its margins. A folded cloth, disposable diaper, or a 1-inch stack of gauze sponges will make a suitable pad. If an ice pack is immediately available, sandwich it between the pad's layers to further stem bleeding. (For how hard to press, see "How Much Pressure," page 16.) Resist the temptation to lift the pad again to check the bleeding—you'll only disturb tentative clots formed, undoing the good you've done. If your pad becomes saturated with blood, don't replace it. Keep pressing for a minimum of 5 minutes without moving it.

If there's so much blood you can't tell where it's coming from, press hard for 5 seconds to blanch the site, then briefly lift the pad to find the source. Center your pressure there.

Avoid pressure-spraying water, hydrogen peroxide, saline solution, or any other material directly into a puncture wound. Rather than cleaning it, this might force contaminants deeper, where they can cause infection.

3. *Apply a pressure bandage.* After 5 to 10 minutes of pressure, and if the bleeding is coming from a location that lends itself to bandaging, apply a pressure bandage. (See page 279.) Otherwise, just keep pressing in 5-minute shifts. If a bandage becomes saturated with blood, simply add a layer on top of it.

Avoid using antibiotic powders, sprays, or ointments without consulting your veterinarian. Indiscriminate use of antibiotics in any form can favor the growth of tougher, antibiotic-resistant bacteria.

4. *Confine your horse.* Keep him still to prevent a rise in blood pressure, and to restrict movement that might disturb tentative clots.

GRUBWORM PREVENTION

First estimate your horse's weight (see page 224). Administer the standard dose of ivermectin or moxidectin paste orally to kill grubworm larvae before they grow large enough to cause skin lesions. Separate your horse from cattle, which are the natural hosts for grub worms. Practice intensive fly control.

HOME TREATMENT

(See ***Action Plan*** *to determine whether home treatment is appropriate for your horse's puncture wound. If at any time during home treatment, your answers on the action plan change for the worse, call your vet.)*

Step 1. *Ice the wound.* Select an ice pack (see page 262) large enough to extend at least 2 inches beyond the wound's margins. Slip it between layers of a clean cloth, center it over the wound, and press gently to minimize swelling. Ice on: 5 minutes. Ice off: 15 minutes. Repeat the cycle 3 more times, for a total of 1 hour.

Step 2. *Clean the wound.* Irrigate the site with a gentle flow of cold hose water for 1 full minute or until the wound appears to be visibly clean, whichever takes longer.

Step 3. *Dress the wound.* Apply a thin layer of a non-antibiotic dressing such as povidone iodine ointment to lubricate and disinfect exposed tissues, being careful not to plug the wound's opening (which could prevent drainage). If flies are a problem, apply an outer layer of Swat®, a fly-repellant labeled for use on open wounds.

Step 4. *Review/renew tetanus immunization.* (See page 211.)

Step 5. *Keep it up.* Repeat Steps 2 and 3 once or twice daily, depending on how gooey, dirty, or crusty the wound becomes. Start twice daily to assess the wound; reduce to once daily if the wound becomes only slightly moist. Continue until it remains clean and uncrusted between cleanings (about a week). Call your veterinarian if you see an increase in swelling, discharge, pain, or lameness—these signs can be an indication of infection.

What you see: A minor flesh wound that's become swollen and warm. Your horse may resent it when you touch it, and there may be a discharge.

1-E

Hot, swollen, tender &/or draining WOUND

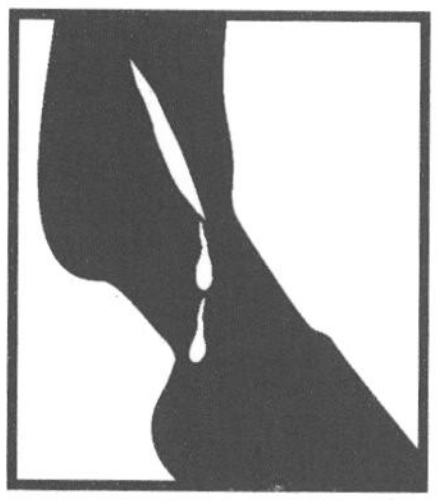

What this might mean: These signs can mean the wound's infected, but not necessarily. Heat, swelling, pain, and discharge can be normal components of uncomplicated inflammation, a necessary step in the healing process—it depends on their duration, and on the character and source of the discharge. They also can signal the development of infection, which can delay healing, increase the risk of scarring, and possibly spread to other locations in your horse's body.

ACTION PLAN:

Is your horse off feed, dull, or feverish?
YES → Call your veterinarian *NOW*—infection may have spread into the blood (septicemia[G]).
NO ↓

Is your horse lame? Is the wound on or near a joint?
YES → Call your veterinarian *NOW* if you answered yes to either query—his muscle, joint, and/or tendon sheath may be involved, injured, or infected.
NO ↓

Are heat, pain, and swelling still escalating the third day after the injury? Is the wound draining a thickened, pus-like, white, yellow, or green substance?
YES → Call your veterinarian *TODAY* if you answered yes to either query—the wound could be infected, and it may require surgery and/or flushing for complete drainage.
NO ↓

Are there tissue flaps? Are portions of the wound cold, hard, or mushy feeling?
YES → Call your veterinarian *TODAY*—dead or dying tissue will have to be removed for healing to proceed.
NO ↓

Is the wound located over a bony area with little soft tissue cushion, such as on the lower legs or skull?
YES → Call your veterinarian *TODAY*—there may be a bone chip interfering with healing (sequestrum[G]).
NO ↓

Is it possible there's a splinter, sliver, gravel, or other foreign material in the wound?
YES → Call your veterinarian *TODAY*—the wound won't heal as long as foreign matter is trapped inside.
NO ↓

ACTION PLAN (CONTINUED):

Is the wound located on or near your horse's withers? (See "Stop!" below.) **YES** → Call your veterinarian *TODAY*—it might be fistulous withers[G].

NO ↓

Will your horse allow you to treat the wound? **YES** → Apply **Home Treatment**, below.

NO ↓

Call your veterinarian today for an appointment.

YOUR VET MAY NEED TO:

Clarify the cause and/or extent of the wound with x-rays and/or exploratory surgery.

HOME TREATMENT:

(See ***Action Plan*** *to determine whether home treatment is appropriate for your horse's wound. If at any time during home treatment, your answers on the action plan change for the worse, call your veterinarian.)*

Step 1. *Clean the wound.* (For in-depth how-to information, see page 257.) Gently irrigate (don't pulverize) the wound with cold hose water or a trigger-type spray bottle filled with homemade saline solution. (See page 242). Spray for 1 full minute or until exposed tissues appear visibly clean, whichever takes longer.

Fistulous withers can be caused by bacteria that can infect you. Avoid getting drainage on skin/clothing/ house pets; disinfect all areas that become contaminated. (See page 232.)

Step 2. *Apply a stimulating hotpack.* To encourage your horse's local immune system, prepare a hot (but tolerable on your hand) solution of Epsom salts. (See page 242.) Grab a clean cloth large enough to extend 2 inches beyond the wound's edges when folded into fourths. Fold the cloth, dunk it into the Epsom salt solution to saturate, and lay it over the wound. Hold it there for 15 minutes, re-wetting as needed to keep it warm.

Step 3. *Poultice the wound.* Apply a safe, non-irritating poultice (see page 242) to the wound site, extending 2 inches beyond the wound's margins.

Step 4. *Review/renew tetanus immunization.* (See page 211.)

Step 5. *Keep it up.* Repeat Steps 1 through 3, three times daily until the wound drainage changes from pus to clear, amber-colored fluid. Then manage according to "Home Treatment," page 16.

1 - F

Pink, bubbly-looking GROWTH

What you see: What looks like pink cauliflower growing out of the center of a flesh wound. It seems to be getting bigger every day, and it's spreading the edges of the skin. It bleeds at the slightest touch and is ugly and angry-looking.

What this might mean: It's too soon to say if this is serious. There are several things it could be—some rather dangerous, others relatively harmless if you handle them right—and they all can look very similar.

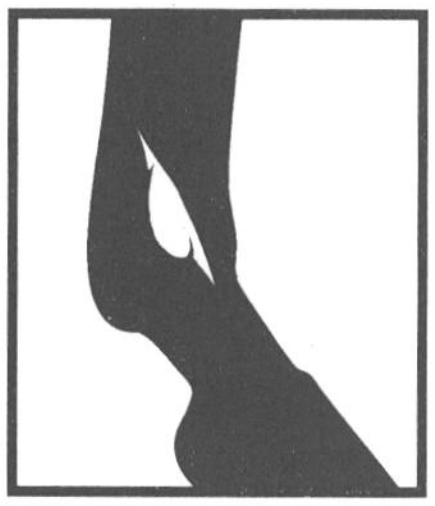

ACTION PLAN:

Do you see one or more similar-looking lesions elsewhere on the body?

YES → Call your veterinarian *TODAY*—it could be sarcoid[G] or other type of tumor.

NO ↓

Is the climate in your area semi-tropical? Does your horse have access to standing surface water or a swampy area? Is the growth visibly larger every day?

YES → Call your veterinarian *TODAY* if you answered yes to any of these queries—it could be swamp cancer[G].

NO ↓

Is there a thick, white or yellow discharge coming from the vicinity of the growth?

YES → Call your veterinarian *TODAY*—it could be a reaction to local infection.

NO ↓

Is the growth located in a flesh wound on a lower limb? Is the growth's diameter larger than the length of the wound? Is it protruding more than 1/2-inch beyond the leg's normal contour at the lesion's thickest point?

YES → Call your veterinarian *TODAY* if you answered yes to any of these questions—it sounds like proud flesh. Due to its size, surgery might be needed.

NO ↓

Is the growth located somewhere other than a lower limb?

YES → Call your veterinarian *TODAY*—this is atypical for proud flesh, so could be something more serious.

NO ↓

Is it on a lower leg, but smaller than the growth's dimensions described above?

NO → Call your veterinarian *TODAY.*

YES ↓

Apply **Home Treatment**, opposite page.

YOUR VET MAY NEED TO:

- **X-ray, biopsy, or culture the wound site to confirm the tentative diagnosis.**
- **Prescribe surgery to remove or reduce the size of the lesion first, then prescribe home-care procedures to resolve it further.**

HOME TREATMENT:

*(See **Action Plan** to determine whether home treatment is appropriate for your horse's lesion. If at any time during home treatment, your answers on the action plan change for the worse, call your vet.)*

Step 1. *Clean the wound.* (For in-depth how-to instructions, see page 258.) Because proud flesh is due in part to an irritation in the wound, you must keep the wound scrupulously clean, but without further irritating it. Irrigate the site with cold hose water or a trigger-type spray bottle filled with homemade saline solution (see page 242). Do so for 1 full minute or until the wound appears visibly clean, whichever takes longer.

Step 2. *Dress the wound.* Apply a thin film of soothing aloe vera gel to the proud flesh, using a folded sterile gauze pad or a rubber-gloved finger.

Products known as proud flesh digestants are used in selected cases to reduce the size of a lesion. However, their safe use requires veterinary supervision because they can damage normal tissue, expand the margins of a wound, and delay healing. If you think your horse's proud flesh lesion might benefit from the use of a digestant, consult your veterinarian.

Step 3. *Bandage the wound.* Apply a pressure bandage appropriate for the wound's location on the leg. (See page 267.)

Step 4. *Keep it up.* Repeat Steps 1 through 3 once or twice daily, depending on how gooey or dirty the wound and bandage become. Begin by changing the bandage twice daily to assess the wound; reduce to once daily if the wound and bandage are only slightly moist. Continue until the proud flesh is a smooth mound extending no more than 1/8 inch beyond the leg's surface at the lesion's edge. At this point, eliminate Step 2 and continue Steps 1 and 3 until new skin has grown in from the edges to cover it completely. This may take 2 to 4 weeks.

Swamp Cancer Alert...

In its early stages, swamp cancer (Pythiosis) can be mistaken for proud flesh. It differs in that it's intensely itchy and, as it progresses, is crisscrossed with pus-filled tracts and knobs of yellowish-gray tissue. Untreated lesions can spread to bones and joints, so if your horse's "proud flesh" lesion isn't resolving, have your veterinarian out for another look, to rule out swamp cancer. A biopsy might be required.

NOTES

CHAPTER 2

Problems of THE MOUTH

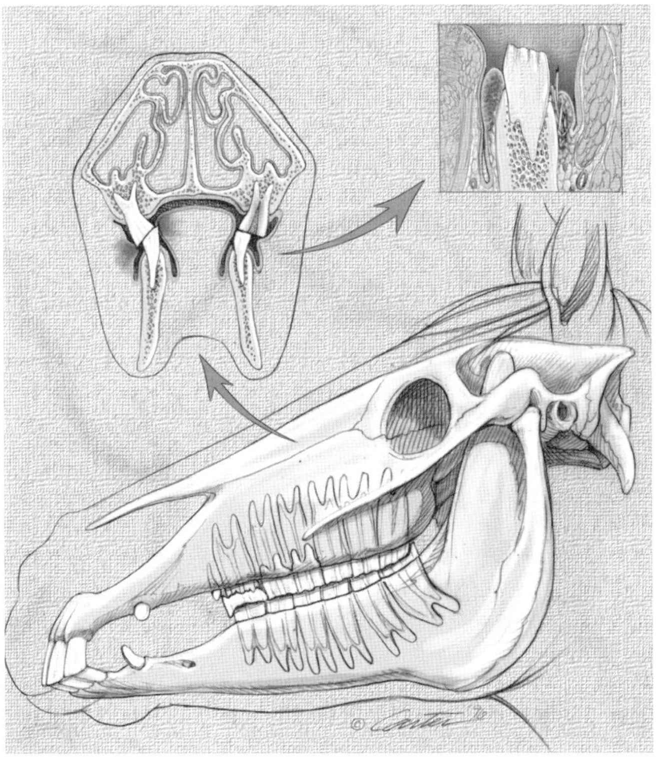

2-A

What you see: Your horse's gums are a noticeably abnormal color, such as yellow, very pale, or darker than usual.

Abnormal GUM COLOR

What this might mean: It could be normal, or it could indicate a serious underlying illness.

ACTION PLAN:

Are his gums a very deep or bright pink, like raspberry sherbet? Is your horse breathing rapidly or acting as though he's having trouble breathing? Is he acting anxious or weak?

YES → Call your veterinarian *NOW* if you answered yes to any of these queries—unless your horse has just finished a workout, intensely pink gums can be a sign of shock[G] or poisoning[G].

NO ↓

Are his gums a dark maroon or muddy color? Is his drinking water source reddish or infested with algae?

YES → Call your veterinarian *NOW* if you answered yes to either query—it could be blood poisoning (endotoxemia[G]).

NO ↓

Is there a blue line on his gums, just around the rims of his teeth? Does your horse seem weak? Does he knuckle over at the fetlocks? Does he make a roaring noise when breathing? Does food spill out his nostrils?

YES → Call your veterinarian *NOW* if you answered yes to any of these queries—it could be lead poisoning[G].

NO ↓

Are his gums white, or so pale that they're just barely pink?

YES → Call your veterinarian *TODAY*—it could be anemia[G].

NO ↓

Are his gums yellowish?

YES → Yellowish gums are usually accompanied by yellow whites of the eyes. Go to **page 54**.

NO ↓

Call your veterinarian for an appointment.

The Nitty Gritty

Here are some toxic plants and weeds that can cause bright or deep pink gums

- Arrowgrass
- Beets
- Corn stalks (in certain soils)
- Leaves and twigs of fruit trees
- Leaves, berries, flowers, and roots of Elderberry
- Pigweed
- Sorghum (sudan grass, johnson grass)

(For more information on toxic plants, see page 312.)

What you smell: A strong, unpleasant odor, reminiscent of rotting flesh or moth balls.

2-B

What this might mean: Bad breath. It could be serious, because bad odor can indicate the presence of decaying tissue. It could be a dental problem, or the decay could be located elsewhere.

BAD BREATH

ACTION PLAN:

Is your horse working his mouth even when not eating, and/or holding his head to one side when he chews?

YES → Call your veterinarian *TODAY*—it could be a lodged foreign body or an injury inside your horse's mouth.

NO ↓

Is your horse off his feed, dull, or feverish?

YES → Call your veterinarian *TODAY*—it could be pain and/or infection that may or may not have anything to do with his mouth.

NO ↓

Has your horse lost weight?

YES → Call your veterinarian *TODAY*—it could be disease and/or decay in the upper digestive tract.

NO ↓

Is your horse tossing his head in response to bit pressure? Is he quidding[G]? Does he pull back abruptly when drinking cold water? Is he drooling or slobbering?

YES → Call your veterinarian *TODAY* if you answered yes to any of these queries—it could be a dental problem.

NO ↓

Is there a swelling on your horse's face? Does his face seem asymmetrical? Is there a crusted or draining sore on his face? Is there a foul-smelling nasal discharge?

YES → Call your veterinarian *TODAY* if you answered yes to any of these queries—it could be an abscessed tooth root and/or a sinus infection[G].

NO ↓

Call your veterinarian for appointment. It could be early periodontal disease[G].

YOUR VET MAY NEED TO:

- **Sedate your horse in order to facilitate a thorough and safe examination of the horse's teeth and mouth.**
- **X-ray your horse's head if a fractured tooth root, abscess, or sinus problem is suspected.**

What you see: A pool of saliva accumulated in your horse's grain bucket, or strings of saliva hanging from his mouth.

2-C

DROOLING

Or slobbering

What this might mean: Drooling can indicate either an overproduction of saliva, or the inability to swallow. It can be a sign of a serious underlying problem, and it can cause significant losses of electrolytes within a day or two, particularly if your horse is feeling sick and not eating to replace those losses. Although it's rare, drooling also can be a sign of rabies[G].

ACTION PLAN:

Is your horse feverish? Has his behavior been unusually dull, or overly excitable? Is his gait abnormal? Does he seem weak, or drunk?

- **YES** → Call your veterinarian *NOW*—it could be an injury or disease of your horse's nervous system (including rabies[G]; see **Caution**, below).
- **NO** ↓

Is your horse off his feed?

- **YES** → Call your veterinarian *NOW*—it could be pain in your horse's mouth, jaw, or throat; or poisoning or disease of his nervous system.
- **NO** ↓

Is there a nasal discharge containing bits of feed? Is your horse stretching out his neck, working his jaw, and/or retching?

- **YES** → Call your veterinarian *NOW* if you answered yes to either query—it could be choke[G].
- **NO** ↓

Does your horse have foul-smelling breath?

- **YES** → Call your veterinarian *TODAY*—it could be a dental problem or a lodged foreign body in the mouth.
- **NO** ↓

Does your horse's hay and/or pasture contain legumes such as clover or alfalfa? Are your horse's eyes runny, but not reddened or squinted?

- **YES** → Call your veterinarian *TODAY*—it could be poisoning by a toxin sometimes present in some forages (slaframine[G]).
- **NO** ↓

Call your veterinarian for an appointment.

CAUTION

Among the possible causes of drooling, an inability to swallow, mental changes, and/or gait abnormalities is a rare but notorious one: Rabies. If rabies is a consideration in your horse's case, don't take chances—take precautions.

1. **Don't handle your horse unless it's absolutely necessary.**
2. **If you must handle him, wash your hands thoroughly, then don intact water-repellant gloves (such as exam gloves or household rubber gloves) and protect all other body parts from contact with his saliva.**
3. **Be alert for unexpected behavior (rabies can cause aggression and/or a lack of coordination), and stay out of harm's way.**

What you see: Your horse acts hungry. He's interested in eating, but shortly after lowering his muzzle to feed, he turns away.

2-D

INABILITY TO EAT

What this might mean: An inability to pick up, chew, and/or swallow feed could be a sign of a serious problem. Your horse literally can starve if someone fails to notice his problem soon enough. Certain neurological problems that affect the nerves of his lips and tongue also can affect other nerves, and can threaten your horse's career—even his life.

ACTION PLAN:

Is a food-tinged discharge coming from your horse's nostril(s)?

YES → Call your veterinarian *NOW*—it could be choke[G] or nerve damage that's preventing normal swallowing.

NO ↓

Does your horse nicker, watch intently, and/or otherwise act interested when you bring feed?

NO → Call your veterinarian *NOW*—loss of appetite can mean general illness.

YES ↓

Is your horse's gait abnormal? Does he seem drunk, weak, or dizzy? Does he have access to toxic weeds? (See page 312.)

YES → Call your veterinarian *NOW* if you answered yes to any of these queries—it could be poisoning or a disease of the central nervous system. (See **Caution**, page 34.)

NO ↓

Does one or more features of your horse's face droop or sag? Does his tongue loll outside his mouth? Was he under general anesthesia in the past week? Does he wear a halter all the time?

YES → Call your veterinarian *NOW* if you answered yes to any of these queries—it could be damage to the nerve(s) of your horse's head from injury or disease.

NO ↓

Is your horse quidding[G]? Does he pull back abruptly from a water source when drinking? Does he tilt his head to one side when eating?

YES → Call your veterinarian *TODAY* if you answered yes to any of these queries—it could be a painful dental or jaw problem.

NO ↓

Call your veterinarian for an appointment.

YOUR VET MAY NEED TO:

X-ray your horse's head if fractured or infected tooth roots, skull, or jaw are suspected.

2-E

Dropping or SPITTING OUT FEED (Quidding)

What you see: Wads of partially chewed feed on the ground or in your horse's feed container.

What this might mean: One of two things—difficulty chewing, or difficulty swallowing, either of which could be a sign of a serious underlying problem.

ACTION PLAN:

Is your horse's appetite depressed? Does he have a fever? Is he showing any abnormal behavior, such as circling, pressing his head against surfaces, dullness, or aggression?

YES → Call your veterinarian *NOW* if you answered yes to any of these queries—it could be illness of the central nervous system. (See **Caution**, below.)

NO ↓

Is either of his ears or eyes drooping? Is his muzzle pulled to one side? Is he drooling? Is there a thick discharge, consistently or occasionally, from one or both nostrils?

YES → Call your veterinarian *TODAY* if you answered yes to any of these queries—it could be infection in a guttural pouch[G], and/or damage to one or more facial nerves.

NO ↓

Does your horse have bad breath?

YES → Go to **page 31**.

NO ↓

Has your horse lost weight?

YES → Call your veterinarian *TODAY*—it could be a severe dental problem.

NO ↓

Call your veterinarian *TODAY* for an appointment—it could be a dental problem.

CAUTION

Among the possible causes of drooling, an inability to swallow, mental changes, and/or gait abnormalities is a rare but notorious one: Rabies. If rabies is a consideration in your horse's case, don't take chances—take precautions.

1. **Don't handle your horse unless it's absolutely necessary.**
2. **If you must handle him, wash your hands thoroughly, then don intact water-repellant gloves (such as exam gloves or household rubber gloves) and protect all other body parts from contact with his saliva.**
3. **Be alert for unexpected behavior (rabies can cause aggression and/or a lack of coordination), and stay out of harm's way.**

What you see: Your horse's tongue is protruding from his mouth.

What this might mean: It could be a type of nervous behavior. For some horses, tongue lolling and/or tongue "chewing" is akin to thumb sucking or fingernail biting in humans and indicates a need for adjustments in management (more pasture time, more exercise, less confinement and idle time). It could mean the tongue's main nerve is damaged, which may or may not be permanent. Without normal tongue function, your horse can't eat properly and his condition can deteriorate quickly.

2-F

TONGUE LOLLING

ACTION PLAN:

Is your horse showing any abnormal behavior, such as dullness, staggering, head-pressing, or unprovoked excitement?

YES → Call your veterinarian *NOW* if you answered yes to any of these queries—it could be illness or injury to your horse's central nervous system, such as rabies[G]. (See **Caution,** opposite page.)

NO ↓

Is your horse acting weak? Does he shuffle his feet as he walks? Are his legs knuckling over at the joints?

YES → Call your veterinarian *NOW* if you answered yes to any of these queries—it could be poisoning by lead[G], botulism[G], or ergot[G].

NO ↓

Is your horse's mouth hanging open? Does he tilt his head and work his jaw as if he has something stuck in his throat? Do the muscles of his lips and jaw seem wooden or rigid?

YES → Call your veterinarian *NOW* if you answered yes to any of these queries—it could be brain damage from poisoning with yellow star thistle[G] or Russian knapweed[G], or he could have something stuck in his mouth.

NO ↓

Is his tongue lolling consistent, rather than linked to anxiety or nervousness?

YES → Call your veterinarian *NOW*—it could be a disease of the brain, including rabies, or injury to the brain or nerves of the head.

NO ↓

Call your veterinarian *TODAY* for an appointment.

2-G

RESENTS BIT

What you see: Your horse resists being bitted, pins his ears angrily after bitting, or mouths the bit constantly.

What this might mean: It could be a sign of a poorly-fitted bit, or mouth discomfort due to an underlying problem that'll worsen if not treated properly.

ACTION PLAN:

When you look at your horse from the front, do you see anything about his face that's not symmetrical? Is his muzzle or nostril pulled to one side? Is one eye drooping? Does he react the same way when bridled without a bit?

YES → Call your veterinarian *TODAY* if you answered yes to any of these queries—it could be an injury or irritation of one or more facial nerves, causing tingling or pain when touched by the bridle, or an injury to the facial bones.

NO ↓

Does your horse have bad breath? Is he dropping feed? Does he hold his head tilted when chewing? Does he pull away abruptly when drinking cold water?

YES → Call your veterinarian *TODAY*—it could be emerging wolf teeth[G], or it could be an injury or disease in the mouth.

NO ↓

Does your horse flinch or pull away when you stroke the underside of his chin or jaw? Is there heat, drainage, or swelling there?

YES → Call your veterinarian *TODAY*—it could be a problem in the lower tooth roots, jawbone, or soft tissues beneath the chin, aggravated by a curb strap.

NO ↓

Does the problem discontinue when you switch to a milder bit and different bridle?

YES → Consult a training/tack expert—it could be due to a poor-fitting bridle and/or a poor-fitting or too severe bit.

NO ↓

Call your veterinarian for an appointment.

Jerks back from DRINKING WATER

What you see: Your horse acts thirsty but shies from his water source as though afraid of it.

What this might mean: It suggests that drinking is somehow painful or frightening to your horse. He quickly could become dehydrated.

ACTION PLAN:

Is your horse's water source electrified on purpose (with a water heater, etc.) or by accident (faulty wiring or grounding of nearby appliance)?

YES → Call an electrician *NOW* if you have the slightest doubt. Block all access to the source and provide safe water in the meantime.

NO → Call your veterinarian *TODAY*—it could be a dental condition that causes sensitivity to cold. Offer body-temperature (98.5-100.5° F) water in the meantime, alongside your horse's usual source of room-temperature water.

Did You Know...

The average, 1,000-pound horse drinks 10 to 15 gallons of water in an idle day. On days when he sweats, from high ambient temperature or exercise, his water intake might double or even triple.

2-1

TILTS HEAD

When chewing

What you see: When he chews, your horse tilts his head, usually to one side more often than the other.

What this might mean: It's a sign of discomfort associated with chewing.

ACTION PLAN:

Is your horse failing to clean up his feed?

YES → Call your veterinarian *TODAY*—it could be cuts, sores, and/or a foreign body in your horse's mouth, a dental problem, or something wrong with his jaw.

NO → Call your veterinarian for an appointment.

YOUR VET MAY NEED TO:

- **Sedate your horse in order to facilitate a thorough and safe examination and/or treatment of his teeth and mouth.**
- **X-ray your horse's head if he/she suspects fractured tooth roots, abscesses, or jaw problems.**

Tooth-Care Trivia...

It's a common mistake to think that if your horse is young, he shouldn't need to have his teeth checked. But in a 1994 study, severe cheek lacerations from sharp grinder teeth, painful enough to interfere with normal chewing, were identified most often in horses between the ages of birth and 7 years. Periodontal disease, which can cause bad breath and lead to premature tooth loss, was common in youngsters at the time their permanent teeth appeared.

2-J

COUGH

What you see: Your horse has developed a cough.

What this might mean: In most cases, a cough in an adult horse is a sign of irritation of the windpipe (trachea) due to a mild viral infection, usually the flu (equine influenza[G]), or rhino (equine viral rhinopneumonitis or equine Herpesvirus-1[G]). If treated promptly and properly, the cough should resolve within 3 to 4 weeks. But coughing also can be a sign of an allergy or a viral and/or bacterial infection in the lungs. The latter two causes can be extremely serious—even fatal.

ACTION PLAN:

Does your horse have a fever? Do his chest and/or nostrils obviously move when he breathes?

YES → Call your veterinarian *NOW* if you answered yes to either query—Fever indicates infectious disease and carries increased risk of dehydration[G]. Chest and/or nostril excursion at rest indicates labored breathing, a sign of possible lung involvement. Go to ***While You Wait,*** next page.

NO ↓

Is your horse stretching out his neck, working his jaw, and/or retching? Is feed or water coming from one or both nostrils?

YES → Call veterinarian *NOW*—it could be choke[G].

NO ↓

Does your horse make a roaring or snoring sound when he breathes heavily? Does he drool or slobber when eating? Does he have a thick nasal discharge?

YES → Call your veterinarian *NOW* if you answered yes to any of these queries—your horse could have nerve damage in his throat region. Possible causes include botulism[G], trauma, and guttural pouch infection[G].

NO ↓

Did the cough start within a few days of your horse being medicated by stomach tube, oral drench, or balling gun[G]? Has he recently suffered from choke[G]?

YES → Call your veterinarian *NOW* if you answered yes to any of these queries—your horse could have a throat injury, or aspiration pneumonia[G].

NO ↓

Is your horse having coughing fits (coughing over and over)?

YES → Call your veterinarian *NOW*—it could bronchitis[G], or foreign material stuck in your horse's airways.

NO ↓

CONTINUED ⇨

ACTION PLAN (CONTINUED):

Does your horse get this cough every summer? Every winter? Has this current cough lasted more than 2 weeks? Does he cough mainly when eating? Has he ever commingled with donkeys or mules?

YES → Call your veterinarian *TODAY* if you answered yes to any of these queries—it could be heaves[G], allergy[G], or lungworms[G].

NO ↓

It's probably a minor cold, such as a mild rhino virus[G] infection. **Apply Home Treatment,** below.

YOUR VET MAY NEED TO:

- **Move your horse to a quiet place so he can better hear his lung sounds when listening with a stethoscope.**
- **Take laboratory samples such as fluid from the throat (via transtracheal wash[G] or bronchoalveolar lavage[G]) or blood.**
- **X-ray and/or perform a sonogram on your horse's chest.**

WHILE YOU WAIT

1. *Isolate your horse* from other horses in case it's contagious. To prevent spread of possible infectious disease, confine your horse to an open-air paddock or stall with a separate water supply, apart from other horses by at least 20 feet. Wash your hands and disinfect your boots (see page 232) after handling your horse and before handling other horses.

EARLY infection with Equine Viral Arteritis (EVA)[G] can cause vague respiratory signs such as coughing and fever, and the disease can be spread via sexual contact. If you're planning to breed your horse, postpone breeding until your veterinarian can rule out EVA as the possible cause, or you'll risk infecting your horse's sexual partner. Pregnant mares should be kept isolated from possible carriers unless they've been vaccinated or have recovered from previous infection—EVA can cause abortion.

HOME TREATMENT

(See Action Plan to determine whether home treatment is appropriate for your horse's cough. If at any time during home treatment, your answers on the action plan change for the worse, call your veterinarian.)

Step 1. *Minimize irritants in his environment.* Avoid dusty trails. Replace dusty bedding (hay, straw, sawdust, shavings) with clean, less dusty bedding, such as shredded paper. Replace dusty hay with hay of better quality, or dampen it with water just before feeding so dust won't be inhaled.

Step 2. *Minimize irritating activities.* Tone down your horse's daily exercise program to avoid heavy breathing, which is irritating to his respiratory tract. For example, if he coughs after loping, don't lope. Instead, work at a slower, less strenuous gait that doesn't induce immediate or delayed coughing.

Step 3. *Help him stay hydrated.* Encourage water intake so discharges in his respiratory tract won't get thick, sticky, and difficult to clear out. Clean his water source daily and add new water sources. (Sometimes a new bucket in a new location is tempting.) Provide free-choice, loose, plain salt. If it's cold outside, offer an extra bucket of water that's been warmed to 120° F. (For more information on getting a horse to drink, see page 228.)

Step 4. *Minimize stress.* Postpone stressful activities such as vaccinations, breeding, trailer trips, long rides, or competitions, until your horse has been cough-free for at least 3 weeks. Stress during illness has been suggested to increase risk of secondary infections.

Step 5. *Be ready to call for help.* If a fever develops, if appetite wanes, if any of your responses on the **Action Plan** change for the worse, or if your horse simply fails to improve within 3 days on home treatment, call your veterinarian.

THE SUPER-SENSITIVE RESPIRATORY TRACT

Don't be in a hurry to return your horse to full work. While infected with an upper respiratory infection such as the flu or rhino, and for 3 to 6 weeks after recovery, your horse's respiratory tract will be super-sensitive to irritation. Any irritation that occurs during this time will prolong the period of super-sensitivity, which in turn prolongs the cough and decreases performance by narrowing breathing passages. It also takes several weeks for your horse's ciliary apparatus[G] to recover and return to duty.

If my horse has a cough, and my vet says it's probably rhino or the flu, should I give a rhino or flu vaccination now?

No, for 3 reasons. First, if your horse is in the throes of an infection, you shouldn't stress him with a vaccination of any sort. Second, the vaccination is unlikely to do any good at this time—your horse's heightened immune system, which is busy fighting off his current infection, will quickly inactivate it. And third, there's concern among the veterinary research community that vaccinating for rhino (EHV-1[G]) in the face of a rhino infection increases the risk that your horse will develop paralytic rhino[G], a rare, dangerous form of the disease that attacks the nervous system.

Should I give my horse a cough suppressant or expectorant?

No, unless your veterinarian tells you to do so. Here's why: The cough is a useful reflex that helps clear out pus and debris from your horse's respiratory tract. If you were to suppress it, you might contribute to a minor infection becoming a major one. The decision to suppress a cough should be made by your vet, after he or she listens closely to your horse's respiratory tract and finds no evidence of material that needs to be cleared out.

As for expectorants, current studies indicate that drinking plenty of water is the best way to keep respiratory secretions thin and flowing freely. Furthermore, expectorants are irritating to your horse's stomach. A horse with an irritated stomach is less likely to eat and drink adequately—two things he must do in order to recover from his illness.

NOTES

CHAPTER 3

Problems of
THE NOSE AND THROAT

What you see: Your horse has a runny nose. The discharge is watery, snotty, maybe blood-tinged, and/or it contains bits of feed.

3-A

NASAL DISCHARGE

What this might mean: It could signal the beginning of a viral or bacterial infection in his respiratory tract, possibly including the lungs. Or it could be a sign of something wrong in the nose itself—a growth, trauma, or a lodged foreign body such as a twig. It also can indicate that there's a problem in a sinus, tooth root, guttural pouch[G], or his throat.

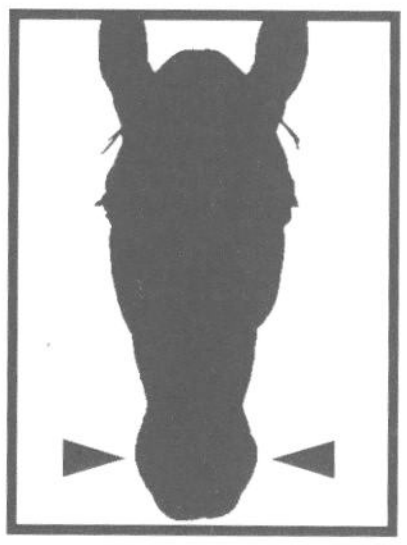

ACTION PLAN:

	YES
Does the discharge contain feed?	Call your veterinarian *NOW*—it could be choke[G].
NO ↓	
Does your horse have a fever? Weepy eyes? Swollen legs? Swollen glands under his jaw? Are other horses in your barn or pasture showing any of these signs?	Call your veterinarian *NOW* if you answered yes to any of these queries—it could be a viral infection such as EVA[G], the flu[G], or rhino[G], or a bacterial infection such as strangles[G]. Go to ***While You Wait,*** opposite page.
NO ↓	
Does your horse roar or snore when breathing heavily? Is one eyelid drooping? Are his lips or nostrils pulled to one side?	Call your veterinarian *NOW* if you answered yes to any of these queries—it could be an infection in his guttural pouches[G].
NO ↓	
Does the discharge look like undiluted blood?	Go to **page 46.**
NO ↓	
Is the discharge blood-tinged? Foul-smelling?	Call your veterinarian *TODAY* if you answered yes to either query—it could be a growth or a foreign body in the nasal cavity, or a sinus or tooth infection.
NO ↓	
Is your horse on pasture? Are his nostrils dusted with yellowish powder and/or spotted with grass seeds?	It's probably a minor nasal irritation from pollens/seeds. It should resolve itself.
NO ↓	
Call your veterinarian for an appointment.	

YOUR VET MAY NEED TO:

Sedate your horse in order to facilitate a thorough and safe examination of his teeth and mouth, and/or to relax his muscles in order to more safely pass a stomach tube or endoscope[G].

WHILE YOU WAIT

If your horse has nasal discharge, and your vet says it's probably rhino or the flu, should you give a rhino or flu vaccination now? **See page 41.**

1. *Isolate your horse from other horses in case it's contagious.* To prevent spread of possible infectious disease, confine your horse to an open-air paddock or stall with a separate water supply, apart from other horses by at least 20 feet. Wash your hands and disinfect your boots (see page 232) after handling your horse and before handling other horses.

2. *Postpone breeding dates.* If your horse is scheduled for breeding any time soon, postpone it until a viral respiratory infection is ruled out or resolved. Both rhino and EVA have been known to cause abortions, and EVA can be spread through sexual contact.

Did You Know...

Most life-threatening bacterial respiratory infections, such as pleuropneumonia or "shipping fever," are caused by bacteria that live normally in your horse's mouth. What caused them to move into the respiratory tract and wreak havoc? An impaired immune system, say most researchers, often the result of stress.

3-B

BLOODY NOSE

What you see: Dried blood in your horse's nostril, watery-looking blood dripping from one or both nostrils, or bright red blood flowing out at an alarming rate.

What this might mean: It can be a sign of a serious underlying problem, one that can cause major blood loss.

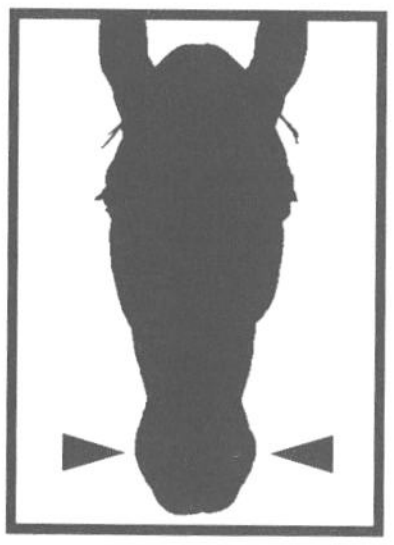

YOUR VET MAY NEED TO:

- **Move your horse to a quiet place so he/she can better hear his lung sounds when listening with a stethoscope.**
- **Examine your horse's throat and/or lungs with x-rays, ultrasound, or endoscopy[G], any of which may require sedation for safety and to facilitate a more thorough exam.**

ACTION PLAN:

Is the blood flowing profusely (1/4 cup or more per minute)?

YES → Call your veterinarian *NOW*—it could be due to trauma to the head. Go to **While You Wait,** opposite page.

NO ↓

Does your horse intermittently have a snotty or runny nose? Does he have a droopy eyelid or lips and/or nostrils pulled to one side? Does he make a roaring or snoring sound when breathing heavily?

YES → Call your veterinarian *NOW* if you answered yes to any of these queries—the nosebleed could be due to a condition that can cause fatal hemorrhage: guttural pouch mycosis[G].

NO ↓

When he gets a minor cut or scratch, does your horse seem to bleed more easily, more often, or for a longer time than you think is normal? Does he have access to sweet clover in his pasture or feed, or to rodent bait such as D-Con®?

YES → Call veterinarian *NOW* if you answered yes to any of these queries—it could be a form of hemophilia, or poisoning with a blood thinner present in some fields of sweet clover and in rodent poisons.

NO ↓

Did your horse have a cold, runny nose, or strangles[G] in recent months? Does the nosebleed occur only during, or within 2 hours after, a workout?

YES → Call your veterinarian *TODAY* if you answered yes to any of these queries—it could be lung abscesses[G] or EIPH[G].

NO ↓

Does your horse have poor exercise stamina? Does it take him longer than usual to recover from a workout?

YES → Call your veterinarian *TODAY* if you answered yes to either of these queries—it might be a heart problem.

NO ↓

Call your veterinarian for an appointment—the blood could be due to trauma, or an abnormality inside the nostril(s).

WHILE YOU WAIT:

1. *Calm your horse.* If he's excited, his heart will pump harder and his blood will run faster.

Unless instructed to do so by your vet, NEVER administer a sedative or tranquilizer to a horse that's excited or frightened, or that's been exercising during the past half hour. Doing so could depress his heart and/or respiratory systems and cause fainting. If your horse requires chemical restraint, leave the decision to your vet.

2. *Apply ice.* Select a flexible ice pack (see page 262) such as a bag of frozen peas, and lay it over the top of your horse's face, below his eyes. Hold it there without applying pressure. Ice on: 5 minutes. Ice off: 15 minutes. This will help slow the bleeding, if it's originating within the nasal cavity, without risk of displacing possible facial bone fracture fragments. Be sure to avoid covering your horse's nostrils with the ice pack. This would inadvertently impair his ability to breathe, causing him to panic and fight your efforts.

Timing is Everything...

How much blood loss is fatal? If your horse is bleeding slowly, he can lose up to 66 percent of his total blood volume over a period of 3 days and survive. For a 1,000-pound horse, that's about 6 gallons of lost blood. But if he loses about 3 gallons in a 24-hour period (about 33 percent of his total volume), he could die.

What you hear: An abnormal noise when your horse breathes during exercise, at rest, or all the time.

3-C

RESPIRATORY NOISE

(Roaring or snoring)

What this might mean: Something is partially obstructing his nasal cavity. Or it could signify nerve damage on one side of his throat, causing a stiff curtain of tissue to partially close the opening through which your horse breathes. (This tissue flutters, thus making the roaring sound, as air rushes past the half-closed curtain.) Some of the underlying causes of such nerve damage can be serious.

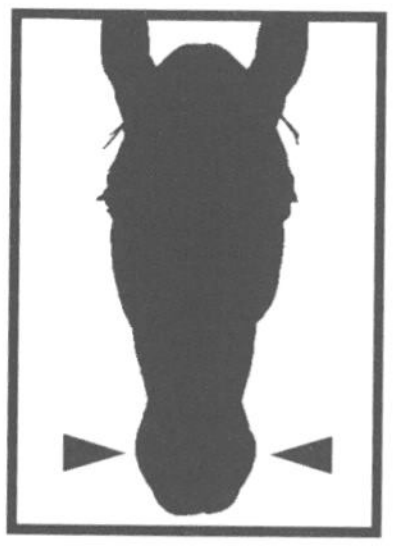

ACTION PLAN:

Does your horse drool, drop food from his mouth, or have food coming out his nostrils? Does his tongue loll out the front or sides of his mouth? Does his eyelid droop? Are his lips, muzzle, or nostrils pulled to one side? Does he have a decreased appetite or a dulled attitude?

YES → Call your veterinarian *NOW* if you answered yes to any of these queries—it could be brain damage due to injury, poison, or disease, causing paralysis of throat tissues. (See **The Nitty Gritty,** opposite page.)

NO ↓

Is your horse making respiratory noises whether he's exercising or not? Is this new?

YES → Call your veterinarian *TODAY* if you answered yes to either query—it could be an obstruction of your horse's nasal passages or throat by growths or thickened tissues.

NO ↓

Does your horse have a nasal discharge and/or foul-smelling breath?

YES → Call your veterinarian *TODAY* if you answered yes to either of these queries—it could be a growth or infection in the back of the nasal passages.

NO ↓

Does your horse make respiratory noise mainly during strenuous exercise? Does his performance suffer when this happens?

YES → Call your veterinarian *THIS WEEK*—it might be an exercise-related displacement of soft-tissue structures in the back of the throat.

NO ↓

Call your veterinarian for an appointment.

YOUR VET MAY NEED TO:

Examine the tissues deep within your horse's nasal passages and throat, using x-ray, ultrasound[G], and/or endoscopy[G]. Any of these may require sedation for safety and to facilitate a thorough exam.

The Nitty Gritty

Here are some general conditions that can cause abnormal repiratory noise in your horse

- Alar fold, excessive
- Botulism poisoning
- DDSP
- EEE
- Encephalitis
- Entrapped epiglottis
- EPM
- Laryngeal hemiplegia
- Lead poisoning
- Pharyngeal cyst
- Rabies
- Russian knapweed poisoning
- VEE
- WEE
- Yellow star thistle poisoning

(See Glossary for detailed descriptions.)

What you see: The upper edges of your horse's nostrils are elevated and pulled forward, enlarging the nostrils and giving his muzzle a squared-off appearance from the side.

What this might mean: That your horse needs air. It's normal if it occurs in association with a workout (and is accompanied by an elevated pulse and respiratory rate), followed by quick recovery and a return of the nostrils to normal. If not exercise-related, flared nostrils could mean a problem in your horse's respiratory tract, a problem in his blood, or heart trouble—anything that interferes with his ability to get oxygen successfully from the air, through his lungs, into his blood, and to the cells of his body.

3-D

FLARING NOSTRILS

(Elevated respiratory rate)

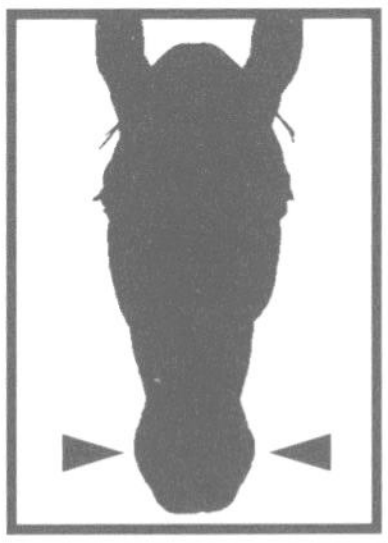

ACTION PLAN:

Has your horse recently spent half a day or longer traveling in a horse trailer? Does he flinch as though it's painful when you press firmly on his ribcage? Does he have a fever? Is he off his feed? Depressed?

YES → Call your veterinarian *NOW* if you answered yes to any of these queries—it could be an infection in the lungs (pneumonia[G]) and/or the surrounding tissues (pleuritis[G]).

NO ↓

Was your horse treated with an antibiotic, vitamin, vaccination, or tranquilizer/sedative within the past 2 hours?

YES → Call your veterinarian *NOW*—it could be a severe allergic reaction to medication.

NO ↓

Did this come on suddenly? Is your horse's breathing rapid? Is recent trauma possible (a kick, collision, or fall)?

YES → Call your veterinarian *NOW* if you answered yes to any of these queries—it could be a ruptured diaphragm[G], pneumothorax[G], shock[G], internal hemorrhage, or a metabolic imbalance.

NO ↓

In recent weeks, has your horse gradually become less energetic, short of breath, or depressed?

YES → Call your veterinarian *TODAY*—it might be severe anemia[G] or congestive heart failure[G].

NO ↓

Does your horse have a nasal discharge? Foul-smelling breath? Was he recently treated via stomach tube? Did he recently suffer a bout of choke[G]?

YES → Call your veterinarian *TODAY* if you answered yes to any of these queries—it could be an injury or infection in the throat, guttural pouch[G], and/or nasal passages.

NO ↓

ACTION PLAN (CONTINUED):

Is he sweating normally?

NO → It could be anhidrosis[G]. Go to **page 149**.

YES ↓

Does your horse have a cough?

YES → Call your veterinarian *TODAY*—it could be advanced heaves[G], allergy, or hypersensitive respiratory tract due to a recent infection.

NO ↓

Call your veterinarian for an appointment.

CAUTION

Your horse can develop a severe allergy to any medication, even if it's a treatment he's received before. In fact, previous exposure to that medication is usually a prerequisite for the severe allergic reaction: A horse must first become "sensitized" to the substance in order to have a "hypersensitive" reaction in the future.

Did You Know...

Fat, in the form of corn or vegetable oil, may be beneficial for horses with respiratory problems, such as heaves. When added to grain or a pelleted ration, it reduces the feed's dustiness, and has a stabilizing effect on respiratory cells. (For how to safely add oil to your horse's ration, see page 206.)

NOTES

CHAPTER 4

Problems of
THE EYE

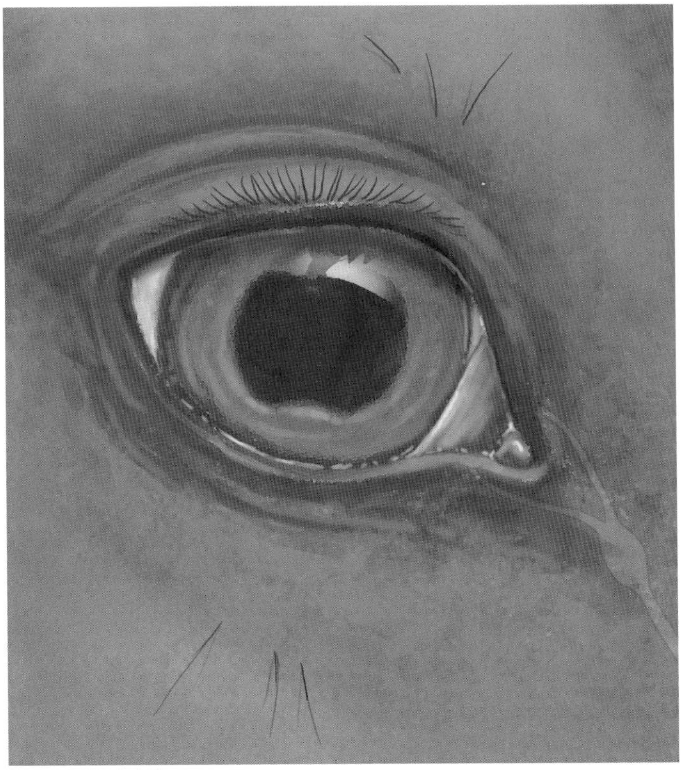

4-A

The whites of EYES ARE YELLOW

What you see: The whites of your horse's eyes are yellow-tinged, a condition called icterus[G] or jaundice[G]. You also may notice a yellowish cast to his gums.

What this might mean: Best-case scenario: your horse is hungry. Worst-case scenario: a blood disorder or liver disease.

ACTION PLAN:

Is your horse off his feed, depressed, or feverish?

YES → Call your veterinarian *NOW*. Jaundice plus any of these signs could indicate acute[G] liver disease. **Go to While You Wait,** opposite page.

NO ↓

Have you noticed your horse passing dark-colored urine?

YES → Call your veterinarian *NOW*—it could be a blood disorder called hemolytic anemia[G]. See **The Nitty Gritty,** opposite page.

NO ↓

Is your horse displaying abnormal behavior? Is he acting as though he can't see? Refusing to move? Fearful for no apparent reason?

YES → Call your veterinarian *NOW* if you answered yes to any of these queries—it could a condition affecting his central nervous system, such as poisoning, or toxins from liver disease (hepatic encephalopathy[G]).

NO ↓

Is your horse's appetite normal, but you're purposely withholding his feed?

YES → Call your veterinarian *TODAY*. Jaundice is a normal sign in a horse that's fasting, so depending on your reason for withholding feed, your horse might be okay. Check with your vet.

NO ↓

Does your horse act like he wants food, but then turns away after a tiny nibble?

YES → Call your veterinarian *TODAY*—it could be a sore jaw or a dental problem preventing feed intake.

NO ↓

Call your veterinarian *TODAY* for an appointment.

WHILE YOU WAIT:

1. *Isolate your horse from other horses in case it's contagious.* To prevent spread of possible infectious disease, confine your horse to an open-air paddock or stall with a separate water supply, apart from other horses by at least 20 feet. Wash your hands and disinfect your boots (see page 232) after handling your horse and before handling other horses.

TIP: Regardless of the cause of your horse's jaundice, the yellow pigment in his skin can make him super-sensitive to ultraviolet rays of the sun, particularly if he's a light-colored horse with white or pink skin anywhere on his body or face. As long as your horse's jaundice persists, protect him from the sun by keeping him indoors during the day, applying a UV-blocking face mask over susceptible skin of his face, and/or applying non-chemical sunblock to exposed, light-colored, hairless skin.

The Nitty Gritty

Here are some factors that can cause hemolytic anemia in your horse

- Bee sting
- Equine infectious anemia (EIA)
- Ingestion of onions or garlic
- Ingestion of phenothiazine-class oral dewormers
- Ingestion of phenothiazine-class oral tranquilizers (such as acepromazine)
- Ingestion of wilted or dried red maple tree leaves
- Snakebite

(See Glossary for detailed descriptions.)

What you see: Your horse is holding an eye partially or completely closed.

4-B

SQUINTING

What this might mean: His eye hurts. Depending on the cause of pain, the eye itself might be in jeopardy. Even if it's a minor eye problem, the discomfort your horse is displaying will tempt him to rub or scratch his eye, which could result in permanent damage.

ACTION PLAN:

Do you see any redness in or around your horse's eye and/or in his tears? Are the eyelids or skin around his eye swollen and/or abraded?

YES → Call your veterinarian *NOW* if you answered yes to either query—it could be injury, infection, or a foreign body in contact with your horse's eye, inflammation and/or infection of the tissues around the eye, or an eye condition called uveitis[G].

NO ↓

Is his eye weeping?

NO → Call your veterinarian *NOW*—eye pain without tearing could indicate irritation from dry eye[G].

YES ↓

Will your horse allow you to open the eyelid and treat his eye?

YES → Apply **Home Treatment**, below.

NO ↓

Call your veterinarian *NOW*—prompt treatment might be needed to prevent further eye injury.

YOUR VET MAY NEED TO:

Sedate your horse, and/or perform nerve blocks[G] to numb and immobilize the eye, in order to safely and thoroughly examine and treat it.

HOME TREATMENT:

*(See **Action Plan** to determine whether home treatment is appropriate for your horse's squinting eye. If at any time during home treatment, your answers on the action plan change for the worse, call your vet.)*

Step 1. *Ice the eye.* Slip an ice pack (see page 262) between layers of a soft, clean, folded cloth. Using the technique outlined on page 79, chill the inflamed tissues around your horse's eye to reduce inflammation, discomfort, and swelling, and to relax the muscles around it. Hold the ice pack on for 5 minutes.

Step 2. *Wash the eye.* Warm a bottle of sterile saline irrigating eye wash (see page 236) by immersing it in a bowl of tepid water until the saline is warm enough to feel barely perceptible when drizzled onto your wrist (about 98° F). Using the eye-rinsing technique outlined on page 293, irrigate your horse's eye.

Step 3. *Lubricate the eye.* Using the technique for applying ophthalmic ointment outlined on page 295, apply a thin film of boric acid or Lacri-lube™ ophthalmic ointment to soothe and lubricate your horse's eye.

Step 4. *Re-evaluate.* Five minutes after completing treatment, look at your horse's eye without approaching or touching his face. (If you were to do so, you might cause him to squint in anticipation.) Is the eye wide open, in its normal position? If so, the problem may have been due to irritation from dust or other loose debris, which you've washed out. If not, call your veterinarian NOW.

What you see: Instead of a normal, clear appearance, your horse's eye looks cloudy—either there's a white spot, or the whole eye looks foggy.

4-C

What this might mean: A serious problem within or beside the eyeball that threatens to impair your horse's vision.

CLOUDY EYE

ACTION PLAN:

Is your horse's eye reddened or squinting?

YES → Call your veterinarian *NOW*—redness or squinting can indicate eye pain, which in conjunction with cloudiness suggests a serious eye condition (e.g., corneal ulcer[G], corneal abscess[G], uveitis[G], or trauma).

NO ↓

Do you see red vein-like structures extending onto the eyeball from its outer margins?

YES → Call your veterinarian *TODAY*—the cloudiness could be due to edema or scar tissue from a well-established inflammatory eye condition.

NO ↓

Has your horse's eye been squinting within the past 2 weeks?

YES → Call your veterinarian *TODAY*—the cloudiness could indicate that a cataract[G], dislocated lens[G], or edema or scar tissue have occurred in response to previous eye injury or disease. The cloudiness can be permanent and can interfere with your horse's vision.

NO ↓

Is your horse over 15 years old? Is he in poor overall health (rough hair coat, thin, weak)? Does he drink more water than usual? Is his appetite poor?

YES → Call your veterinarian *TODAY* if you answered yes to any of these queries—general illness and/or advanced age can increase risk of degenerative eye conditions.

NO ↓

Call your veterinarian for an appointment.

What you see: Your horse appears to be having difficulty seeing. He's stepping on things he'd usually avoid, colliding with obstacles, lifting his legs higher than usual, or stepping extra cautiously, his ears constantly on the move as though straining to hear what he cannot see. (Note: The **Action Plan** that follows might mislead you if what you think is vision impairment turns out to be something else, such as dizziness or a mental disorder. If possible, confirm your suspicions with the **Quick Vision Test** that follows on the next page. If your horse's vision is not impaired, turn to the chapter that better describes his symptoms.)

4-D

IMPAIRED VISION

What this could mean: Brain injury or illness, or injury or illness within the eye itself. It also means your horse is more likely than usual to spook at noises or unexpected touches. Be alert, and give your horse plenty of warning when you approach.

ACTION PLAN:

Is the affected eye weeping, squinting, or cloudy looking?

YES → Go to **pages 61, 56, and 57,** respectively.

NO ↓

Did your horse suffer a blow to the head recently? (See **The Nitty Gritty,** opposite.)

YES → Call your veterinarian *NOW*—it could be an injury to your horse's brain and/or optic nerve.

NO ↓

Has your horse been dull, off his feed, feverish, or diagnosed with an illness within the past week?

YES → Call your veterinarian *NOW*—several diseases can cause blindness. Prompt treatment might restore your horse's vision.

NO ↓

Does your horse have Appaloosa in his pedigree? Does he seem blind only at night?

YES → Call your veterinarian for an appointment if you answered yes to either query—it could be night blindness[G], a problem that occurs more often in horses with Appaloosa breeding.

NO ↓

Call your veterinarian for an appointment.

Quick Vision Test

Use this test to help you decide whether your horse is truly vision-impaired, and whether the problem has affected one or both eyes.

1. Blindfold one eye by laying a thick pad, such as a disposable diaper folded in half, across the eye (absorbent side against his skin). Tape it to your horse's halter.

2. Wear clothing that doesn't "swish." In a well-lit area with minimal distractions, have a helper loosely hold your horse. Stand 3 feet away, to the side of the uncovered eye, and lob 3 cotton balls toward him, one after the other, so they bounce gently off the side of his face between his eye and muzzle. Did he flinch when the first one approached, before it touched him? Did he try to avoid the second? Did he watch the third one? If your answers are no, no, and no, he probably can't see. Repeat with the other eye.

3. If you're still unsure, in a well-lit area and with one of his eyes covered, lead your horse on a loose lead rope toward a bale of hay set 15 feet ahead. Walk purposefully—don't go so slowly that he has time to lower his head and smell it. Does he try to avoid hitting the bale? If not, he probably can't see it. Cover the other eye, and repeat.

The Nitty Gritty

Here are some accidents that can result in blindness in your horse

- Your horse reared up and fell over backward. Common scenario: He was roped, tied, or being halter broke, and fell over while fighting restraint. Or, a medication was accidentally given into his carotid artery (instead of the jugular vein), and he reacted by flipping over.

- Your horse reared up and struck his head on a ceiling beam, stall doorway, or the ceiling of your horse trailer. Common scenario: He was fine when loaded into trailer, but was vision-impaired within 3 days afterward.

➤

More Nitty Gritty

Here are things that may cause blindness in your horse

THE CAUSE	THE SOURCE
Poisoning	• Locoweed • Moldy corn (leucoencephalomalacia) • Selenium
Infectious encephalitis	• EEE • WEE • VEE • EPM • Neurologic EHV-1
General illness	• Strangles • Leptospirosis • Potomac horse fever • Influenza • Liver disease • EVA • Septicemia • EHV-1 • EHV-4 • EIA • Brucellosis
Cancer	• Malignant lymphoma • Multiple myeloma • Tumors of brain or eye
Eye conditions	• Uveitis • Moon blindness • Cataracts • Corneal degeneration • Retinal degeneration • Retinal detachment
Parasites	• Strongyles • Toxoplasmosis • Onchocerca cervicalis

(See Glossary for detailed descriptions.)

Did You Know...

Although up-close focusing ability is relatively poor in horses, they excel in long-distance and night vision. That's because as prey animals, horses are genetically "hard wired" to seek out wide-open spaces, where they can watch the horizon line for—and flee from—predators.

What you see: Your horse's eye is weeping. Watery tears, possibly mixed with a thicker discharge, run onto his face, where a crust is accumulating.

4-E

WEEPING EYE

What this might mean: Eye pain, due either to an internal eye problem or to external irritation (such as dust in the eye). Even if it's a minor external problem, the discomfort might tempt him to rub or scratch the eye, which could result in serious damage.

ACTION PLAN:

Do you see:
- Blood near the eye or in its tears?
- A foggy or cloudy spot on the eyeball?
- Foreign material on the eyeball or protruding from beneath an upper or lower lid?
- Injury to the face or tissues near the eyeball?

YES → Call your veterinarian *NOW* if you answered yes to any of these queries—it could be eye trauma or internal eye disease. Fast action might be required to minimize damage. Go to **While You Wait,** below.

NO ↓

Is the eye squinting or closed, even when you're making no motions to approach it?

YES → Call your veterinarian *NOW*—unprovoked squinting is a sign that the eye pain is severe, making self-trauma likely and treatment difficult. Go to **While You Wait.**

NO ↓

Do you see reddened and/or swollen tissues around the eyeball?

YES → Call your veterinarian *NOW*—the eye itself might be okay, but at risk from self-trauma. Go to **While You Wait.**

NO ↓

Are insects troubling the eye? Will your horse allow you to open the eyelid and treat his eye?

YES → Apply **Home Treatment** (next page) if you answered yes to both queries—it could be irritation from flies.

NO ↓

Call your veterinarian for an appointment. It could be a blocked tear duct.

YOUR VET MAY NEED TO:

Sedate your horse, and/or perform nerve blocks to numb and immobilize the eye, in order to facilitate a thorough and safe exam and treatment.

WHILE YOU WAIT:

1. *Ice the eye.* Slip an ice pack (see page 262) between layers of a soft, clean, folded cloth. Using the technique outlined on page 79, chill the inflamed tissues around your horse's eye to reduce inflammation, discomfort, and swelling, and to relax the muscles around it.

2. *Bandage the eye.* If your horse has been squinting and/or attempting to rub his eye, apply a padded eye bandage using the technique on page 284. This will help keep his eyelid closed. (When closed, the eyelid provides warmth, moisture, and form-fitting support to his eyeball; when open, its frequent blinking and squinting can add more irritation to an already irritated eye.) The bandage also will protect the eye from self trauma.

AVOID PULLING FOREIGN BODIES!
If you pull foreign matter (such as long hairs or grass stems) that are protruding from beneath your horse's eyelids, they could slice the cornea[G]. Instead, bandage the eye and call your veterinarian, who can sedate your horse if necessary, block his blink reflex if necessary, and safely lift any foreign matter off the cornea.

3. *Bring your horse indoors; stop him if he rubs.* If the eye is not bandaged, confine your horse to a dark stall or otherwise protect him from wind, dust, and bright light that can further irritate his eye. Place feed below eye-level so dust and chaff don't drift into his eye. Assign someone to watch and stop him if he rubs.

HOME TREATMENT:

*See **Action Plan** to determine whether home treatment is appropriate for your horse's weeping eye. If at any time during home treatment, your answers on the action plan change for the worse, call your vet.)*

Step 1. *Clean dried discharge from around eye.* Wet a clean gauze sponge with room-temperature saline solution (see page 242) until saturated but not dripping. Lay the gauze over the trail of discharge. Hold for several seconds or as needed to soften, then wipe clean. This will prevent skin irritation from developing beneath the crust, and eliminate the risk of it attracting face flies, which can further irritate the eyes.

Step 2. *Soothe and protect the eye and surrounding tissues.* Using the technique for applying ophthalmic ointment outlined on page 295, apply a thin film of boric acid or Lacri-lube™ ophthalmic ointment to soothe and lubricate your horse's eye.

Step 3. *Re-evaluate.* Five minutes after completing treatment, look at the eye: Is it still weeping? If so, call your vet NOW.

AVOID FORCING AN EYE OPEN!
Some eye injuries are so severe that the eyeball is at risk of rupturing, either because of direct damage from the injury or because the injured eye's layers are weakened from infection. Your horse's defense against further eye injury—his blink reflex—is too powerful to overwhelm if it's fully activated. If you were to persist, your efforts could cause a fragile eye to rupture.

TIP:

To get an unenhanced look at your horse's uncomfortable eye without touching it or otherwise activating his blink reflex, stand 3 feet away, just to the bad eye's side. Make a sound that'll arouse his interest (whistle, cluck, or rustle oats in a bucket). Unless the eye pain is extreme, he'll widen his eye to see what you've got.

HOW TO LOCK FLIES OUT!

Use one or more of these methods to keep flies away from your horse's eyes

- Apply a fly face mask.
- Make an artificial forelock. Attach knotted strips of low-lint, close-weave fabric to the poll strap on your horse's halter.
- Apply chemical insect repellants. Away from your horse, spray a horse-safe fly repellant (such as permethrin) onto the artificial forelock, let dry completely, then affix to your horse's halter. *Note:* Be careful when spraying, wiping, or dabbing repellants directly onto your horse's face. Most contain chemicals that can irritate his eyes. Thick, water- and sweat-proof ointments such as Swat® are less likely to drip into your horse's eyes and would be a safer choice of repellant for around them than thin solutions.

EYE GROWTHS

Or sores

4-F

What you see: Growths and/or ulcerated sores around your horse's eye, which are smooth, rough, and skin-covered, or raw and angry-looking. They can involve only the tissues around his eye, or they can invade the eyeball itself.

What this might mean: The presence of an invasive local condition, such as sarcoid or some other form of tumor, which could grow aggressively and impair your horse's vision and/or threaten his appearance. Some types of eye cancer can spread to other parts of the body.

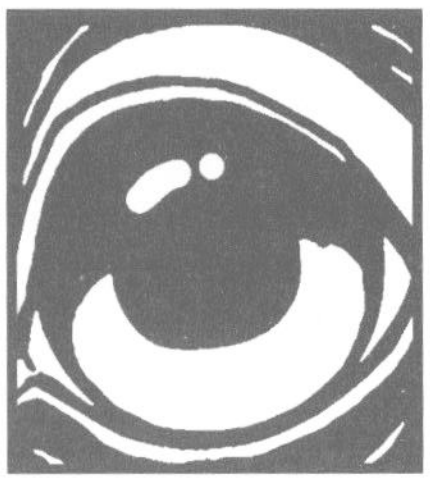

ACTION PLAN:

Is the growth a red, ulcerated lesion on white or pink skin around your horse's eye?

YES → Call your veterinarian *TODAY*—it could be an erosive skin condition such as photosensitization[G] or squamous cell carcinoma[G]. Go to **While You Wait**, below.

NO ↓

Is the growth red, raised, and lumpy looking, located in a corner where upper and lower lids meet?

YES → Call your veterinarian *TODAY*—it might be a sarcoid[G], squamous cell carcinoma, or a parasitic skin condition called Habronema[G].

NO ↓

Does the growth extend to or into the eyeball itself?

YES → Call your veterinarian *TODAY*—it could be sarcoid[G] or cancer.

NO ↓

Is your horse younger than 3 years old? Is there one or more pink, wart-like growths on his eyelids and possibly elsewhere on his face?

YES → Call your veterinarian *TODAY* if you answered yes to either of these queries, to confirm tentative diagnosis of juvenile warts[G].

NO ↓

Is the involved eye squinting, weeping, or cloudy?

YES → Go to **pages 56, 61, and 57,** respectively.

NO ↓

Is the growth an oval, pea-sized, smooth lump attached to the iris (the colored part inside his eye), just above the pupil, and the same color as the iris?

YES → Relax, it's a normal structure called the corpus nigrum[G]. (Notice that both eyes have one.)

NO ↓

Call your veterinarian for an appointment.

YOUR VET MAY NEED TO:

Obtain a sample of the growth to send to a laboratory for identification. This might require sedation, nerve blocks, or anesthesia.

WHILE YOU WAIT:

Protect against UV exposure. Until a veterinary exam rules out sun-sensitive lesions such as photosensitization[G] or certain kinds of skin cancer[G], bring your horse indoors, if possible. Otherwise, apply a UV-blocking fly mask.

4-G

DROOPING EYELID

What you see: On one side, your horse's upper eyelid seems to droop, draping across his eye and giving him a sad look.

What this might mean: A problem in part of the nerve supply to his head. It's the underlying problem, rather than the eyelid droop itself, that poses a threat.

ACTION PLAN:

Is your horse showing signs of loss of appetite, fever, dullness, weight loss, weakness, or dizziness?

YES → Call your veterinarian *NOW*—it could be a general illness affecting your horse's nervous system, including rabies[G]. (See **Caution**, below.)

NO ↓

Is his ear drooping on the same side as the droopy eyelid? Are his lips and/or muzzle drawn over to one side?

YES → Call your veterinarian *TODAY* if you answered yes to either query—it could be a paralyzed facial nerve (see **The Nitty Gritty,** next page). Go to **While You Wait,** below.

NO ↓

Are there patches of sweat at the base of his ear(s), on the side(s) of his neck, and/or the side(s) of his face? Is there a pale pink "curtain" (the third eyelid[G]) drawn up over the inner corner of his eyeball(s)?

YES → Call your veterinarian *TODAY* if you answered yes to either query—it could be damage to a specialized nerve supply to the head called the sympathetic nervous system[G].

NO ↓

Call your veterinarian for an appointment.

YOUR VET MAY NEED TO:

X-ray your horse's head and/or neck if injury in either area is suspected to have damaged the nerves there.

WHILE YOU WAIT:

1. *Protect the affected eye.* Facial nerve injury can cause decreased tear production and make it difficult for your horse to close his eyelids completely. This leaves the eyeball at risk of drying. Using the technique for applying ophthalmic ointment outlined on page 295, apply a thin film of boric acid or Lacri-lube® ophthalmic ointment to keep your horse's eye moist.

CAUTION

Among the possible causes of nervous system disease causing nerve dysfunction is a rare but notorious one: Rabies. Don't take chances—take precautions. See page 34.

The Nitty Gritty

Here are some possible causes of facial nerve paralysis in your horse

- *Blunt trauma to the side of your horse's face.* Sample scenario: He was cast in his stall, and banged his face repeatedly during his attempts to get up.
- *Prolonged recumbency.* Sample scenario: Your horse underwent a long surgical procedure under general anesthesia. The pressure on his facial nerve caused damage that may or may not be permanent.
- *Hardware pressure.* Sample scenario: Your horse slept, flat out on his side, on uneven pasture ground while wearing a halter. Pressure from the metal hardware caused facial nerve damage.
- *Guttural pouch infection*[G]. Branches of the facial nerve normally pass through the guttural pouches, and can be damaged by infection there.
- *Infection in the brain or spinal cord.*

More Nitty Gritty

Here are some possible causes of damage to nerve supply to your horse's head

- *Injury to his neck.*
- *IV injection.* Sample scenario: Injected medication leaked outside the vein and into adjacent tissues that house nerve fibers.
- *Poorly placed or infected IM injection in the side of his neck.*
- *Choke*[G]. This can cause bulging, inflammation, and/or infection around the obstruction, which can press against adjacent nerves in the neck.
- *Injury, abscess, or tumor in the brain, spinal cord, or chest.*

4-H

THIRD EYELID

Is evident

What you see: A pink curtainlike membrane is covering the inner corner of your horse's eyeball, as much as one-third of it. It extends across the eyeball at an angle.

What this might mean: What you're seeing is a normal structure called the third eyelid. Usually it's hidden, tucked into the inner corner of your horse's eye where the upper and lower lids meet. A variety of problems can make the third eyelid come out of hiding: Some are mild and temporary, such as superficial pain from dust; others can be severe and permanent, such as brain damage.

ACTION PLAN:

Are the third eyelids protruding in both eyes? Does your horse show signs of dizziness, lack of appetite, dullness, or fever? Does he have a stiff gait?

YES → Call your veterinarian *NOW* if you answered yes to any of these queries—it could be an illness or injury within the nervous system, or it could be tetanus[G]. Go to **While You Wait #1,** below.

NO ↓

Is your horse's ear on the same side drooping? Is his muzzle drawn to one side?

YES → Call your veterinarian *NOW* if you answered yes to either query—it could be facial nerve paralysis[G]. Go to **While You Wait #2,** below.

NO ↓

Is the affected eye squinting?

YES → Go to **page 56.**

NO ↓

Call your veterinarian for an appointment.

YOUR VET MAY NEED TO:

X-ray your horse's head and/or neck if injury in either area is suspected to have damaged the nerves there.

WHILE YOU WAIT #1:

1. *Isolate your horse from other horses in case it's contagious.* To prevent spread of possible infectious disease, confine your horse to an open-air paddock or stall with a separate water supply, apart from other horses by at least 20 feet. Wash your hands and disinfect your boots (see page 232) after handling your horse and before handling other horses.

2. *Protect yourself.* A horse with tetanus increasingly has trouble controlling his muscles and might move in spastic or unexpected ways. Be alert, and avoid putting yourself in harm's way.

3. *Keep him quiet.* Protect your horse against noises and excitement. It's common for tetanus victims to overreact to outside stimuli by falling, convulsing, or becoming rigid with muscle spasms.

WHILE YOU WAIT #2:

1. *Protect the affected eye.* Facial nerve injury can cause decreased tear production and make it difficult for your horse to close his eyelids completely. This leaves the eyeballs at risk of drying. Using the technique for applying ophthalmic ointment outlined on page 295, apply a thin film of boric acid or Lacri-lube™ ophthalmic ointment.

CHAPTER 5

Problems of

THE HEAD AND EARS

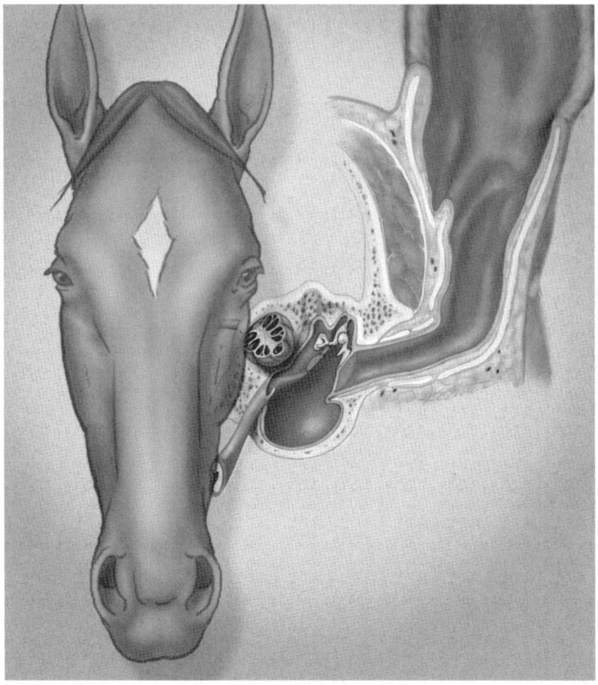

5-A

HEAD SHAKING

What you see: While being ridden, your horse suddenly and almost violently starts tossing and nodding his head. No obvious cause, such as an insect swarm, is apparent.

What this might mean: Head-shaking can be a sign of a medical problem—it isn't necessarily something your horse is doing in order to avoid being bitted and worked.

ACTION PLAN:

Does your horse appear dizzy? Does he walk with an abnormal gait? Does his face seem to droop or grimace? Does his head tilt? Is his tail pulled to one side?

YES → Call your veterinarian *NOW* if you answered yes to any of these queries—it could be encephalitis[G].

NO ↓

Is one or both ears held in an abnormal position?

YES → Call your veterinarian *TODAY*. It could be an inner ear infection[G] or an ear mite infestation[G].

NO ↓

Has your horse recently recovered from a respiratory infection or other generalized illness? Does his head shaking seem to start when you bring him out of the barn and into the sunlight?

YES → Call your veterinarian *TODAY* if you answered yes to either query—it could be a post-viral inflammatory condition (neuritis[G] or vasomotor rhinitis[G].) Go to **While You Wait**, below.

NO ↓

Does the head shaking occur only when your horse is wearing a bit? Does he behave normally when you work him with a different bit, or with no bit?

YES → Call your veterinarian *THIS WEEK*. It could be a dental problem.

NO ↓

Call your veterinarian for an appointment.

WHILE YOU WAIT:

1. *Avoid triggers.* If you've identified a possible trigger for the head-shaking (such as sunlight), help your horse avoid it until a veterinarian sees him.

2. *Minimize stress.* If your horse is showing any other signs of abnormal nerve function (abnormal gait, head tilt, dizziness, staggering, circling, body or tail bent to one side), minimize his stress and isolate him. This is both for his protection and to limit spread of a possible contagious condition. Wash your hands and disinfect your boots (see page 232) after handling your horse and before handling other horses.

DROOPY FACE

(Deviated muzzle, sagging eye, slanted ear)

What you see: Your horse's face is drooping, due to one or more of the following: One eyelid is sagging; an ear is drooping; there's a wad of feed bulging inside his cheek; his muzzle is pulled over to one side.

What this might mean: At the very least, it means a facial nerve is paralyzed, and there's no way of knowing right now whether it's permanent. What's more important is what caused the paralysis, and whether any other nerves, and/or the brain itself, are involved.

ACTION PLAN:

Is your horse off his feed, depressed, and/or feverish?

YES → Call your veterinarian *NOW*—it could be a disease involving the brain, including rabies[G]. See **Caution**, and go to **While You Wait,** next page.

NO ↓

Does one or more leg buckle when your horse walks? Does he make a roaring or snoring sound when he breathes? Is his tongue sticking out?

YES → Call your veterinarian *NOW* if you answered yes to any of these queries—it could be botulism[G] or lead poisoning[G].

NO ↓

Is your horse's head tilted? Does he stagger, or appear dizzy?

YES → Call your veterinarian *NOW*—it could be a problem in his brain, (including rabies[G]), or a middle or inner ear infection.

NO ↓

Does your horse have any discharge coming out of one or both nostrils?

YES → Call your veterinarian *TODAY*—it could be a guttural pouch infection[G].

NO ↓

Is your horse rubbing his tail? Does he flinch when you touch his rump or his face?

YES → Call your veterinarian *TODAY*—it could be a nerve disorder called polyneuritis[G].

NO ↓

Is his droopy face the only symptom?

YES → Call your veterinarian *TODAY*—it could be a facial nerve injury.

NO ↓

Call your veterinarian *NOW*.

➤

WHILE YOU WAIT:

CAUTION

Among the possible causes of nervous system disease causing nerve dysfunction is a rare but notorious one: Rabies. Don't take chances—take precautions. See page 34.

1. *Isolate your horse from other horses in case it's contagious.* To prevent spread of possible infectious disease, confine your horse to an open-air paddock or stall with a separate water supply, apart from other horses by at least 20 feet. Wash your hands and disinfect your boots (see page 232) after handling your horse and before handling other horses.

2. *Protect his affected eyes, if necessary.* Facial nerve injury can cause decreased tear production and make it difficult for your horse to close his eyelids completely. This leaves the eyeball at risk of drying. Using the technique for applying ophthalmic ointment outlined on page 295, apply a thin film of boric acid or Lacri-lube™ ophthalmic ointment to keep your horse's eye(s) moist.

A Bit About Botulism...

Though no scientific proof has been offered, the use of 400-pound and larger hay bales (as in the large, round or square bales used primarily to feed cattle) has been associated with an increased incidence of botulism poisoning in horses. Veterinarians surmise that when hay is in contact with wet ground and begins to decompose, it's invaded by the bacteria *Clostridium botulinum*, which reside in the soil of certain geographic regions. Horses that consume hay tainted with the botulism toxin are at risk of botulism poisoning.

If botulism poisoning has been reported in your area, it's a safe bet the organism is present in your soil. Avoid feeding large bales, and consider having your horse vaccinated against botulism poisoning. (Consult your veterinarian about the vaccine.)

What you see: Your horse is holding an ear angled to the side.

What this might mean: A mild, simple problem such as irritation of the upright portion of his ear, or a severe problem such as brain injury.

5-C

EAR HELD TO ONE SIDE

ACTION PLAN:

Is your horse off his feed, depressed, and/or feverish?

YES → Call your veterinarian *NOW*—it could be encephalitis[G]. Go to **While You Wait,** next page.

NO ↓

Does your horse stagger or act drunk when walking? Is his head held at a tilt?

YES → Call your veterinarian *NOW* if you answered yes to either of these queries—it could be a brain injury, encephalitis[G], or a deep infection in the inner ear[G].

NO ↓

Has he been shaking his head?

YES → Go to **page 68**.

NO ↓

Does your horse have a droopy eyelid? Is feed packed in one cheek? Is his muzzle pulled over to one side?

YES → Go to **page 64** and **page 69**, respectively.

NO ↓

Is there a brownish wax on the inside of the upright portion of his ear?

YES → Call your veterinarian *TODAY*—it could be ear mites[G].

NO ↓

Is the upright portion of his ear crusty on the inside (carefully explore it with your thumb)? Does the crust melt into a dark brown liquid when moistened? Will your horse allow you to treat his ear?

YES → If you answered yes to these queries, apply **Home Treatment,** next page. It could be inflammation from gnat bites.

NO ↓

Call your veterinarian for an appointment.

➤

WHILE YOU WAIT:

1. *Isolate your horse from other horses in case it's contagious.* To prevent the spread of possible infectious disease, confine your horse to an open-air paddock or stall with a separate water supply, apart from other horses by at least 20 feet. Wash your hands and disinfect your boots (see page 232) after handling your horse and before handling other horses.

2. *Protect your horse from further injury.* Remove protruding objects from his stall or paddock, and keep noise to a minimum to avoid startling him.

HOME TREATMENT

(See ***Action Plan*** *to determine whether home treatment is appropriate for your horse's case of ear drooping. If at any time during home treatment, your answers on the action plan change for the worse, call your veterinarian.)*

Step 1. *Clean the crust from his ear.* Dampen a clean washcloth with saline solution (see page 242) that's been warmed to 98º F. It should be just warm enough to be palpable on the inside surface of your wrist. Fold the cloth into eighths to make a neat bundle, fit it against the inner surface of the upright portion of your horse's ear, and hold it there for 1 minute to melt the crust. Remove the cloth, and wipe gently. Repeat as necessary until the ear surface is clean and smooth.

Step 2. *Protect your horse from further bites.* To prevent black flies or gnats from further irritating your horse's ear, apply a thin layer of petroleum jelly or Swat® to the area. Apply a fly mask with ear covers for complete protection.

Step 3. *Keep it up.* Repeat Step 1 daily until the ear no longer becomes encrusted. Continue Step 2 until fly season ends.

SWOLLEN EARS

What you see: The upright portion of your horse's ear is puffy, like a pillow.

What this might mean: This condition is called aural hematoma[G], and is the result of trauma to his ear flap. As it heals, it's common for your horse's ear flap to become misshapen from shrinkage of damaged cartilage.

ACTION PLAN:

Are both ears swollen?

YES → Call your veterinarian *TODAY*—it's probably due to trauma, as can occur when your horse tries to retrieve his head from between fence boards.

NO ↓

Is the swollen ear warm? Is your horse shaking his head often? Does he resent having the ear touched?

YES → Call your veterinarian *TODAY*—it might be ear mites[G] or infection in the middle ear[G] with self-trauma to the ear as a result.

NO ↓

Is the entrance to the ear canal swollen?

YES → Call your veterinarian *TODAY*—the ear canal should be cleaned out to prevent or treat infection.

NO ↓

Call your veterinarian for an appointment.

Keep Bugs at Bay...

To keep flying insects from pestering your horse's ears without using chemical insecticides, try these tips:

- Outfit him in commercial ear covers, designed to be used with a fly mask, or a fly mask equipped with ear covers. Check your local tack store or equine supply catalogs.
- Or, apply a thin coat of petroleum jelly on the inner surface of the upright portion of his ear, which will discourage bugs from landing.

5-E

DRAINING WOUND
On the face

What you see: There's a draining hole, called a fistula, on your horse's face, which you discovered after cleaning off a scab or wad of crust.

What this might mean: It could be a sign of a contagious disease, or the result of a deep wound that's gotten infected. Whatever the cause, your horse could suffer permanent damage without proper treatment.

ACTION PLAN:

Is the drainage coming from under your horse's lower jaw?

YES → Call your veterinarian *TODAY*—it might be strangles[G], injury, or an abscessed lower tooth. Go to **While You Wait,** below.

NO ↓

Is the opening behind his cheek, about 6 inches directly below his ear? Is the drainage brownish in color?

YES → Call your veterinarian *TODAY* if you answered yes to both queries—it might be an injury to one of the ducts that carries saliva to your horse's mouth.

NO ↓

Is the opening on or near the center of the bony ridge that forms the front of your horse's face? Is there a swelling, or a dent, in or near that location?

YES → Call your veterinarian *TODAY*—it might be a previous injury, possibly a facial bone fracture.

NO ↓

Is the opening below his eye? Does he have foul-smelling breath, or a foul-smelling nasal discharge (like rotting garbage, or mothballs)?

YES → Call your veterinarian *TODAY* if you answered yes to any of these queries—it could be a sinus infection (sinusitis[G]) or an infection in the root of one of your horse's upper cheek teeth.

NO ↓

Is the opening located on or beside your horse's ear?

YES → Call your veterinarian *TODAY*—it could be a benign growth called a dentigerous cyst[G], or an infection in the ear canal.

NO ↓

Call your veterinarian for an appointment.

YOUR VET MAY NEED TO:

Sedate your horse in order to facilitate a thorough and safe examination and/or treatment of the horse's teeth and mouth, if a dental problem is suspected.

TIP: If your horse has an infected tooth removed, the tooth's lower or upper partner should be examined and possibly filed every 2 to 3 months. (If your veterinarian uses a motorized dental file or dremel tool, a longer interval between exams may be allowed.) This is to keep the partner tooth from growing abnormally long, which causes its crown (food-grinding surface) to protrude into the soft tissue space where the extracted tooth had resided.

WHILE YOU WAIT:

1. *Isolate your horse from other horses in case it's contagious.* To prevent spread of possible infectious disease, confine your horse to an open-air paddock or stall with a separate water supply, apart from other horses by at least 20 feet. Wash your hands and disinfect your boots (see page 232) after handling your horse and before handling other horses.

FLESH WOUND
On the ear

What You See: The upright portion of your horse's ear has been cut, mangled, or the tip's missing.

What this might mean: The ear could become permanently misshapen.

ACTION PLAN:

Has the ear been lacerated?

YES → Call your veterinarian *NOW*—it might need stitches to prevent or minimize curling or puckering.

NO ↓

Has the ear been mangled or bitten?

YES → Call your veterinarian *NOW*—it might need surgical reconstruction for a cosmetically improved result.

NO ↓

Has the ear tip become blunted after a sub-zero cold spell?

YES → Call your veterinarian *TODAY*—it's probably frostbite. Frostbitten ears can be re-shaped surgically to look more normal.

NO ↓

Call your veterinarian *TODAY* for an appointment.

Ear Flap Fact...

Your horse's ear flap injury needs immediate veterinary attention in order to obtain the best possible cosmetic result. Here's why: The ear flap is built like a sandwich, with one layer of cartilage nestled between two layers of skin. When injured, the space between cartilage and skin can fill with blood, which can distort the normal tissue arrangement and lead to a puckered result. With expert help, this can generally be minimized—or even eliminated.

5 - G

What You See: Your horse holds his head cocked to one side.

HEAD TILT

What this might mean: It could mean there's been an injury or an irritating condition in his inner ear or brain.

ACTION PLAN:

Is your horse off his feed, depressed or feverish?

YES → Call your veterinarian *NOW* if you answered yes to any of these queries—it could be a brain disease, including rabies[G]. See **Caution** below, and go to **While You Wait,** below.

NO ↓

Call your veterinarian *TODAY* for diagnosis and treatment of underlying cause. Go to **While You Wait,** below.

WHILE YOU WAIT:

CAUTION

Among the possible causes of nervous system disease causing nerve dysfunction is a rare but notorious one: Rabies. Don't take chances—take precautions. See page 34.

1. *Isolate your horse from other horses in case it's contagious.* To prevent spread of possible infectious disease, confine your horse to an open-air paddock or stall with a separate water supply, apart from other horses by at least 20 feet. Wash your hands and disinfect your boots (see page 232) after handling your horse and before handling other horses.

2. *Protect your horse from accidents.* If your horse is having trouble with his equilibrium, remove protruding objects from his stall or paddock, keep your pets away and keep noises to a minimum, to avoid startling him.

What you see: Your horse's face or head has changed shape, and/or a swelling is evident. When you feel the misshapen area, it's either hard (as though it's part of his bone structure), or like swollen soft tissue.

What this might mean: Several potentially serious problems can cause facial distortion, ranging from severe nutritional imbalance to snakebite.

5-H

SWOLLEN
Or misshapen
FACE OR HEAD

ACTION PLAN:

Is the swelling in your horse's muzzle area? Do you see two small puncture wounds and/or a purplish discoloration of normally hairless areas?

YES → Call your veterinarian *NOW* if you answered yes to either query—it could be snakebite[G], or bee-, wasp-, or ant-stings (insect sting[G]). Go to **While You Wait,** next page.

NO ↓

Is the swelling in a bony area? Is it painful? Is there a crackly feeling when you touch the area? Is it abnormally warm?

YES → Call your veterinarian *NOW* if you answered yes to any of these queries—it could be a fractured facial bone.

NO ↓

Is your horse off his feed, depressed, or feverish?

YES → Call your veterinarian *NOW*—it could be infection or an abnormal growth in the deeper tissues of your horse's head.

NO ↓

Does your horse's head look enlarged on both sides? Do his cheekbones stick out more than usual? Does his nose look more "Roman" (humped) than usual? Has he been lame intermittently, not always on the same leg?

YES → Call your veterinarian *TODAY* if you answered yes to any of these queries—it could be bighead disease[G].

NO ↓

Is there a draining wound on or near the misshapen area? Is there a foul-smelling nasal discharge?

YES → Call your veterinarian *TODAY* if you answered yes to either query—it could be an infection in a tooth root or a sinus (sinusitis[G]).

NO ↓

CONTINUED ⇨

YOUR VET MAY NEED TO:

Sedate your horse in order to facilitate a thorough and safe examination of his teeth and mouth, if a dental problem is suspected.

ACTION PLAN (CONTINUED):

Is the swelling hard, not associated with any nasal discharge, not painful, and located on one side of his face, closer to the nose?

YES → Call your veterinarian *TODAY*—it could be a salivary duct stone[G] or a tumor of the jawbone (ossifying fibroma[G]).

NO ↓

Call your veterinarian for an appointment.

WHILE YOU WAIT:

1. *Cool—but don't ice—swollen soft tissues.* Seal a single ice cube and 3 cups of cold tap water in a 1-quart plastic bag. Place the bag over the swollen area, conforming it to the area's contours and being careful not to cover your horse's nostrils. In this way, you'll slow inflammation and tissue destruction possibly associated with venomous bites or stings, without risking frostbite-type damage to tissues made extra-fragile by the presence of toxins.

Tooth-Care Trivia...

It's a common mistake to think that if your horse is young, he shouldn't need to have his teeth checked. But in a 1994 study, severe cheek lacerations from sharp grinder teeth, painful enough to interfere with normal chewing, were identified most often in horses between the ages of birth and 7 years. Periodontal disease, which can cause bad breath and lead to premature tooth loss, was common in youngsters at the time their permanent teeth appeared.

What you see: A cut on your horse's upper or lower eyelid.

What this might mean: If not properly repaired, it could leave the eyeball unprotected and/or allow it to heal out of position (and cause trauma to your horse's eye).

5-I

CUT EYELID

ACTION PLAN:

Is the eyelid out of position? Is there a flap of eyelid tissue? Are the wound edges gaping?

YES → Call your veterinarian *NOW* if you answered yes to any of these queries—it sounds like a full-thickness laceration, which will require sutures for the best chance of an undistorted eyelid with its full complement of lashes. Go to **While You Wait,** below.

NO ↓

Is the eye squinting or watering, or does the eyeball appear damaged?

YES → Call your veterinarian *NOW*—the eye itself could have been injured.

NO ↓

It sounds like a superficial abrasion. Will your horse allow you to treat it?

YES → Apply **Home Treatment**, below.

NO ↓

Call your veterinarian *TODAY*.

YOUR VET MAY NEED TO:

Sedate your horse, and/or perform nerve blocks to numb and immobilize the eye, in order to facilitate a thorough and safe exam and treatment.

WHILE YOU WAIT:

1. *Ice the eye.* To reduce inflammation, discomfort, and swelling, and to relax the muscles around the eye, slip an ice pack (see page 262) between layers of a soft, clean, folded cloth. Lay the covered pack over your horse's eye, making sure there are no large clumps in the bag that might cause discomfort. Place a sanitary napkin or other thick, soft pad over the ice pack and tape the whole apparatus to his halter to keep his eyelid pressed gently closed. (For detailed instructions, see page 284.)

HOME TREATMENT

*(See **Action Plan** to determine whether home treatment is appropriate for your horse's eyelid laceration. If at any time during home treatment, your answers on the action plan change for the worse, call your veterinarian.)*

Step 1. *Ice the wound.* Slip an ice pack (see page 262) between layers of clean cloth. Lay the covered pack over the wound, making sure there are no large clumps in the bag that might cause discomfort. Hold it in place for 5 minutes.

Step 2. *Clean the wound.* Wet a stack of gauze sponges or a clean, folded washcloth in homemade saline solution (see page 242). Dab it gently over the wound until it appears visibly clean, replacing the gauze or cloth when it becomes soiled. ➤

Step 3. *Dress the wound.* Apply a thin layer of an emollient such as Lacri-Lube™ (see page 295) to keep the wound edges moist and to act as a barrier to dust and insects.

Step 4. *Review/renew tetanus immunization.* (See page 211.)

Step 5. *Keep it up.* Repeat Steps 2 and 3 once or twice daily, depending on how gooey, dirty, and/or crusty the wound becomes. Begin by cleaning it twice daily; reduce to once daily if it becomes only slightly crusty. Continue until the wound remains clean and uncrusted between cleanings (about 3 to 4 days).

Wound Watch...

That eyelid laceration may look nasty, but don't despair. Thanks to an exuberant blood supply to the lid, such wounds typically heal well. The key is for you to keep any flaps of tissue moist while you're waiting for your veterinarian.

CHAPTER 6

Problems of THE LEGS

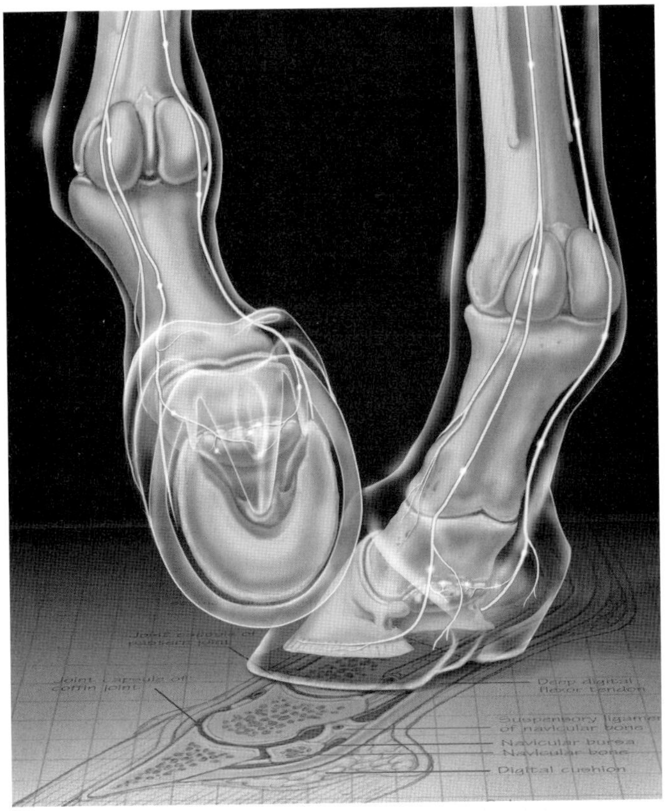

What you see: One or more of your horse's legs is swollen—areas that normally are concave or flat now are filled or puffy-looking. When you press on the swelling it feels spongey or springy. The swollen area may or may not feel abnormally warm, and your horse may or may not be lame. If the swelling you see primarily involves a *joint*, go to page 85.

6-A

LEG SWELLING

What this might mean: It could be the result of poor circulation from lack of exercise, or it could be a sign of a serious underlying problem, such as injury to structures within your horse's leg, or bodywide illness.

ACTION PLAN:

Is your horse off his feed, depressed, or feverish? Has he recently had a cold or other respiratory infection?

YES → Call your veterinarian *NOW* if you answered yes to either query—it could be a microbial-induced abnormality of the blood vessels (vasculitis[G], or purpura[G]), which can precede or follow a bodywide illness. (See **The Nitty Gritty,** page 84.) Go to **While You Wait #1,** page 84.

NO ↓

Are all 4 legs involved, all the way from the coronary band up to the knees (front legs) and hocks (rear legs)?

YES → Call your veterinarian *NOW*—it could be the early stages of a bodywide disease, too early for general signs of illness to be obvious. It also could be a sign of heart trouble. Go to **While You Wait #1.**

NO ↓

Is your horse stiff or reluctant to move? Is he bedded on shavings or sawdust that could possibly contain black walnut[G]?

YES → Call your veterinarian *NOW* if you answered yes to either query—it could be a toxic reaction to exposure to black walnut[G] shavings or sawdust. Go to **While You Wait #2,** page 84.

NO ↓

Is your horse showing heavy, labored breathing, even when at rest?

YES → Call your veterinarian *NOW*—it could be a heart problem.

NO ↓

Is your horse lame?

YES → Go to **pages 87 and 93.**

NO ↓

ACTION PLAN (CONTINUED):

Are there any flesh wounds on the swollen leg?

YES → Go to **page 13**.

NO ↓

Has an injection been given, or a wound occurred, near the swollen leg within past 72 hours?

YES → Call your veterinarian *NOW*—it could be malignant edema[G].

NO ↓

Has your horse been losing weight and/or muscle lately? Has he been acting weak or tired?

YES → Call your veterinarian *TODAY* if you answered yes to either query—it could be a severe protein deficiency[G].

NO ↓

Are/were there bumps, blisters, or sores on your horse's face, legs, or coronary bands, either now or in the recent past?

YES → Call your veterinarian *TODAY*—it could be a bodywide disease (pemphigus[G] or VS[G]).

NO ↓

Is the swelling limited to one or both hind limbs? Does your horse resent it when you touch it?

YES → Call your veterinarian *TODAY*—it could be lymphangitis[G], or a ligament disorder called degenerative suspensory ligament desmitis (DSLD[G]).

NO ↓

Is the swelling worse after exercise, or following a hard workout and a night of stall confinement?

YES → Call your veterinarian *TODAY*—it could be abnormal stress on your horse's tendons, due to poor conformation, improper farriery, or overwork. Go to **While You Wait #3**, next page.

NO ↓

Does the swelling go away after exercise?

YES → Sounds like your horse "stocks up," meaning his legs fill with fluid due to poor circulation from lack of exercise. Apply **Home Treatment,** next page.

NO ↓

Call your veterinarian for an appointment.

➤

WHILE YOU WAIT #1:

Isolate your horse from other horses in case it's contagious. To prevent spread of possible infectious disease, confine your horse to an open-air paddock or stall with a separate water supply, apart from other horses by at least 20 feet. Wash your hands and disinfect your boots (see page 232) after handling your horse and before handling other horses.

WHILE YOU WAIT #2:

Remove suspect bedding. Strip out bedding, saving 1 gallon for inspection by your veterinarian, forest service personnel, college extension official, or any other expert in wood identification. Replace it with a known safe substitute such as straw, certified pine shavings, or shredded paper.

WHILE YOU WAIT #3:

Minimize stress on vulnerable supportive structures. Lighten potential stress on supportive tendons and ligaments within the swollen leg(s) until angulation problems are either ruled out or corrected: Switch to groundwork (rather than under-saddle work) on flat, level ground, and limit gaits to the walk and trot.

HOME TREATMENT:

(See **Action Plan** *to determine whether home treatment is appropriate for your horse's leg swelling. If at any time during home treatment, your answers on the action plan change for the worse, call your vet.)*

Step 1. *Implement a daily light exercise program.* Stocking-up is believed to be the result of sluggish lymph circulation in the legs due to inadequate muscle activity. A session of 15 to 20 minutes of light exercise (at the walk and jog, plus a 5-minute warmup and cool-down) should resolve leg puffiness immediately. If swelling remains or worsens despite daily, light exercise, it's not a simple case of stocking-up. Call your veterinarian for an appointment.

The Nitty Gritty

Here are some bodywide conditions that can cause leg swelling

- Cardiac Disease
- Equine viral arteritis (EVA)
- Endotoxemia
- Hypoproteinemia
- Lymphosarcoma
- Pemphigus foliaceus
- Vasculitis, such as Purpura hemorrhagica (PH)
- Vesicular stomatitis (VS)

(See Glossary for detailed descriptions.)

What you see: One (or more) of your horse's joints is swollen. It might be subtle and barely noticeable, or so severe that anybody would notice it. He may or may not be lame.

6-B

SWOLLEN JOINT(S)

What this might mean: It's a warning of inflammation inside the joint, due to a mild to severe injury or infection, which, without proper care, can escalate to degenerative joint disease (DJD[G]). This can cause permanent damage to joint cartilage.

ACTION PLAN:

Are there any flesh wounds over the swollen joint? Is there a yellowish, syrupy or watery discharge? Are there white streaks dried on the hair below your horse's joint?

YES → Call your veterinarian *NOW* if you answered yes to any of these queries—the joint may have been penetrated, and if so, treatment is needed to prevent infection.

NO ↓

Is the leg lame? Does he flinch or pull away when you press on the joint? Is the joint warm to the touch (compared to the same joint on the opposite leg)?

YES → Call your veterinarian *NOW* if you answered yes to any of these queries—it could be capsulitis[G], which can occur by itself or after serious injury to ligament, bone, or cartilage. Go to **While You Wait**, next page.

NO ↓

Is your horse off his feed, depressed, feverish? Is he showing a lameness that seems to switch legs? Does he have a stiff neck or back?

YES → Call your veterinarian *TODAY* if you answered yes to any of these queries—it could be Lyme Disease[G] or a condition that mimics it. (See **The Nitty Gritty**, next page.)

NO ↓

Is the same joint swollen on both the right and left legs?

YES → Call your veterinarian *TODAY*—it could be a wear-and-tear injury that can lead to degenerative joint disease[G].

NO ↓

It appears to be uncomplicated joint swelling due to inflammation of the joint's lining (synovitis[G]). Apply **Home Treatment**, next page.

➤

CAUTION

Resist the urge to give your horse anti-inflammatory medication unless advised to do so by your vet. Giving medication to relieve swelling and pain without taking measures to correct the underlying problem can temporarily make you forget there is one and free you to resume your horse's regular work load. However, continued work could do serious, possibly permanent, damage.

WHILE YOU WAIT:

1. *Ice the joint.* Select an ice pack (see page 262) large enough to extend at least 2 inches beyond the joint's margins. Slip it between layers of a clean cloth, center it over the joint, and hold it there. Ice on: 5 minutes. Ice off: 15 minutes. Repeat this cycle 3 more times or until your vet arrives, whichever happens first.

2. *Wrap the joint.* If it's a joint that lends itself to wrapping (hock, knee, fetlock or pastern), apply a light pressure bandage (see page 279). Confine your horse to keep the bandage from loosening.

HOME TREATMENT:

*(See **Action Plan** to determine whether home treatment is appropriate for your horse's swollen joint. If at any time during home treatment, your answers on the action plan change for the worse, call your vet.)*

1. *Ice the joint.* Slow the spread of inflammation within the joint by chilling it. If weather permits, run cold hose water over the swollen joint for 10 minutes. (If it's cold outside, you can skip this step.) Then apply a loose ice pack. (Go to **While You Wait**, Step 1, at left. Repeat the cycle 4 times.)

2. *Exercise, then re-ice.* Walk your horse in-hand or under saddle for 15 minutes. Repeat 4 times over next 24 hours, with at least 4 hours (but no more than 8 hours) between walks. This will keep joint fluid circulating. Walk on flat ground, with level footing, making wide turns, to avoid stressing joints. After each walk, re-ice the joint, then confine your horse to a stall or small paddock.

3. *Re-assess.* 24 hours after you first noticed and treated the swelling, inspect the joint for visible and/or palpable puffiness. (When in doubt, compare it to the same joint on the opposite leg). If swelling is still present or is accompanied by heat, pain, and/or lameness, call your vet. If the swelling is gone, gradually return your horse to his regular exercise schedule over a period of 2 days. If swelling recurs, call your veterinarian.

The Nitty Gritty

Here are some conditions that can cause joint swelling or other signs that mimic Lyme Disease.

- Cauda equina syndrome (aka polyneuritis)
- EPM
- Neurologic rhino (EHV-1 myelitis)
- Traumatic injury
- Vertebral body osteomyelitis

(See Glossary for detailed descriptions.)

What you see: No question about it, your horse is lame. On a scale of 0 (sound) to 5 (unable to bear weight on the leg), you'd grade his lameness as a 3 to 5. At the very least, he's got a consistent limp at the trot (see "Lameness Grade and Location," page 298). At worst, he won't even put his foot on the ground.

What this might mean: An internal structure in his foot or leg is injured or diseased. It could be a simple stone bruise that'll resolve with conservative treatment, or a fracture that'll require surgery. The degree of lameness can be the same for either extreme.

6-C

Moderate to severe LAMENESS

ACTION PLAN:

Do you see a bone fragment protruding through the skin?

YES → Call your veterinarian *NOW*—it's a compound fracture, which is the most difficult kind to repair successfully. Aggressive treatment will be required to save your horse, or euthanasia may be considered to abbreviate suffering.

NO ↓

Is your horse's leg misshapen, or sticking out at a weird angle? Is there a hard swelling above the knee or hock? Is your horse refusing to move, or moving with an exaggerated limp?

YES → Call your veterinarian *NOW* if you answered yes to any of these queries—it could be a fracture, a dislocation, or a serious illness or injury to the muscle, requiring immobilization and/or treatment to prevent infection and shock. Go to **While You Wait,** next page.

NO ↓

Is there an open wound on the lame leg (without any evidence of protruding bone)?

YES → Call your veterinarian *NOW*—it's possible a vital structure has been injured. While you wait, go to the appropriate chapter on wounds.

NO ↓

Is there abnormal heat, swelling, and/or pain along the tendon at the back of your horse's cannon bone on the lame leg? Does the leg buckle or bend the wrong way when bearing weight?

YES → Call your veterinarian *NOW* if you answered yes to either query—a tendon or ligament may have been injured. Go to **While You Wait.**

NO ↓

CONTINUED ⇨

ACTION PLAN (CONTINUED):

Is your horse standing with his forelegs stretched out in front of his shoulders? Do both fore hoof walls feel warmer than the hind hoof walls? Do you feel a strong digital pulse in both front feet compared to the hind feet, or compared to other horses on the premises?

YES → Call your veterinarian *NOW* if you answered yes to any of these queries—it could be laminitis[G]. Go to **While You Wait**, below.

NO ↓

Does the lame leg's hoof wall feel warmer than the other three? Is the digital pulse stronger in that hoof? Were your horse's feet trimmed and/or shod within the past week?

YES → Call your veterinarian *TODAY* if you answered yes to any of these queries—it could be a sole abscess, a close nail, a shoe problem, or a fractured coffin bone. Go to **While You Wait.**

NO ↓

Call your veterinarian today.

WHILE YOU WAIT:

1. *Keep your horse still.* Further movement could worsen whatever's causing his lameness. Get him out of harm's way as best you can, then confine him. Provide a companion if necessary to discourage fretful movement.

2. *Ice the leg.* If you can easily determine where the pain is (see page 299), chill the area to limit pain and swelling. Select an ice pack (see page 262) large enough to overlap the injured area by at least 2 inches all around its margins. Slip it between layers of a clean cloth, center it over the injury, and hold it manually or secure with a wrap. Ice on: 5 minutes. Ice off: 15 minutes. Repeat this cycle 3 more times or until your vet arrives, which ever happens first.

3. *Apply a support wrap.* Again, if you're reasonably sure where the problem is, apply a support wrap appropriate to the area being bandaged, adding an extra layer of padding and being especially careful to apply the elastic layer evenly and firmly enough to prevent slippage. (For detailed how-to instructions, see page 271.)

4. *Avoid feeding him.* Give no feed—only water—until your vet arrives and can confirm or dismiss laminitis as a cause of the lameness, and/or determine that immediate surgery won't be necessary.

> **CAUTION**
>
> **Don't apply a splint without your vet's advice and without hands-on experience in applying such a device. Even though a splint can help to minimize further injury by helping to immobilize an unstable leg, in some cases it makes things much worse. If you know how to apply one skillfully, and your vet recommends it after you've described, in detail, your horse's specific injury, then it's your call.**

What You See: A subtle lameness in one leg—a mild head-bob, hip-hike, or shortening of stride that's difficult to observe and not necessarily consistent at the walk, trot, and/or when circling or moving over inclines (see page 299). Or, perhaps you haven't noticed a lameness when your horse is moving, but at rest he stands with the toe of one leg consistently pointed, or he frequently shifts weight off that leg.

What this might mean: It could be a minor problem that'll resolve itself, or the beginning of something major.

6-D

MILD LAMENESS

Single leg

ACTION PLAN:

Does your horse:
- Bear weight normally, but shift his weight off the leg more than once every couple of minutes when at rest?
- Show more prominent lameness when worked on soft footing?
- Have abnormal heat or swelling over the soft tissue area at the back of his cannon bone?
- Show signs of pain when you squeeze the tissues on the back of his cannon bone?

YES → Call your veterinarian *NOW* if you answered yes to any of these queries—it could be a bowed tendon[G], which could get more serious if proper treatment is delayed. Go to **While You Wait,** next page.

NO ↓

Did your horse receive any injections in or near the lame leg within the past 72 hours? Is the injection site swollen, painful, and/or abnormally hot?

YES → Call your veterinarian *NOW* if you answered yes to either query—it could be an infection in the muscle (Clostridial myositis[G]).

NO ↓

Do you see any open flesh wounds on the leg?

YES → Call your veterinarian *TODAY*—there could be an injury to vital support structures. While you wait, go to the appropriate section on wounds.

NO ↓

Does any swelling in the leg include a joint?

YES → Go to **page 85.**

NO ↓

CONTINUED ⇨

ACTION PLAN (CONTINUED):

Does the hoof wall feel abnormally warm when compared to the other hooves? Is the coronary band swollen (does the hair in that area stand on end)? Does your horse stumble at the trot? Was he trimmed and/or shod within the past week?

YES → Call your veterinarian *TODAY* if you answered yes to any of these queries—it could be a problem within the foot, such as a close nail, a shoe problem, navicular disease[G], ringbone[G], a sole abscess[G], or buttress foot.

NO ↓

Has the lameness come on gradually, over 3 weeks or longer? Has it failed to improve with rest?

YES → Call your veterinarian *TODAY* if you answered yes to both queries—it could be a degenerative problem that might become chronic[G] if not diagnosed and treated early.

NO ↓

Is your horse younger than 5 years of age, in training, and showing a mild forelimb lameness? Is there a mildly painful swelling on the front of the lame leg's cannon bone?

YES → If you answered yes to both queries, it could be a mild case of bucked shins[G]. Apply **Home Treatment**, below.

NO ↓

Call your veterinarian for an appointment.

WHILE YOU WAIT:

1. *Confine your horse.* Movement might make things worse. Confine him to a box stall or paddock and provide a companion if necessary to discourage fretful movement.

2. *Cool the foot, tendon, or joint suspected of being the problem.* Select an ice pack (see page 262) large enough to extend at least 2 inches beyond the affected area's margins. Slip it between layers of a clean cloth, center it over the area, and hold it there. Ice on: 5 minutes. Ice off: 15 minutes. Repeat this cycle 3 more times or until your vet arrives, whichever happens first.

3. *Apply a support wrap.* If you're reasonably sure where the problem is, apply a support wrap appropriate to the area being bandaged, adding an extra layer of padding and being especially careful to apply the elastic layer evenly and firmly enough to prevent slippage. (For detailed how-to instructions, see page 271.)

4. *If you suspect laminitis, don't feed him.* Give no feed—only water—until your vet arrives and can confirm or dismiss laminitis as a cause of the lameness.

HOME TREATMENT:

*(See **Action Plan** to determine whether home treatment is appropriate for your horse's mild, single-leg lameness. If lameness, heat, and/or swelling are still present*

after 3 days of home treatment, or if your answers on the action plan change for the worse at any time, call your vet.)

Step 1. *Ice the shin.* See **While You Wait**, Step 2. Repeat the ice on/off cycle 4 more times. Continue these sessions twice daily for 3 days, or until heat and swelling are no longer evident, whichever takes less time.

Step 2. *Wrap the shin.* Wrap the area with a standing bandage (see page 271). Change daily and continue for up to 3 days or until heat and swelling are no longer evident. If, after 3 days, heat/swelling are still evident, call your vet.

Step 3. *Rest your horse.* Confine him to a box stall or paddock for a minimum of 4 weeks. Hand-walk him twice daily during that time, for 15 minutes each session, to maintain good circulation and prevent stiffness. Then begin a gradual return to training, with his training program adjusted to prevent recurrence. Incorporate shorter work sessions, with less leg stress and concussion. If the lameness recurs, call your veterinarian.

Budget Bandaging Tip...

Recycle your worn-out tube socks by cutting off the feet and using the calf portion as a soft, conforming, security layer for your horse's lower leg bandages. Roll one up, slip it over your horse's hoof and leave it at the pastern while you apply your bandage padding. Then unroll the sock over the padding. Apply the compression layer as indicated. (See page 265 for bandaging guidelines.)

What you see: A stiffness, shortening of stride, and/or frequent shifting of weight when at rest, as though your horse can't get comfortable. (For help in identifying a lameness, see page 299.) You may not see the typical head-bob or hip-hike if paired legs (left and right) are equally lame—such signs appear only if one leg is more painful than the other.

6-E

MILD LAMENESS

Two or more legs

What this might mean: It could be a minor problem that'll resolve itself, or it could be a sign of something major, such as a bodywide illness.

ACTION PLAN:

Is your horse off his feed, depressed, or feverish? Does his lameness seem to switch from one leg to another?

YES → Call your veterinarian *NOW* if you answered yes to either query—it could be a bodywide illness such as Lyme Disease[G]. Go to **While You Wait #1**, opposite page.

NO ↓

Is there any swelling or abnormal heat over his rump, croup, and/or back muscles? Does he resent it when you probe any of these areas with your fingertips?

YES → Call your veterinarian *NOW* if you answered yes to either query—it could be tying-up syndrome[G]. Go to **While You Wait #2**, opposite page.

NO ↓

Do both front hooves feel warm compared to the hind ones? Or, do all 4 hooves feel abnormally warm? Does your horse resist picking up any of his feet? Does he stand with his forefeet farther forward than usual? Is the lameness/reluctance to move worse when he's on a hard surface? Does he have a strong digital pulse at the forefeet, compared to the hind feet or compared to other horses on the premises?

YES → Call your veterinarian *NOW* if you answered yes to any of these queries—it could be early laminitis[G]. Odds of successful treatment decrease with passing time. Go to **While You Wait #2 and #3.**

NO ↓

Do you see any swelling in one or more joints of the lame legs?

YES → Go to **page 85.**

NO ↓

ACTION PLAN (CONTINUED):

Does your horse seem to have a stiff neck or back, making turns without bending (like a weathervane), or having a hard time reaching feed or water that's low to the ground?

YES → Go to **page 191**.

NO ↓

Does your horse stumble at the walk or trot?

YES → Call your veterinarian *TODAY*—it could be a problem in his feet, such as navicular disease[G] or ringbone[G]. Go to **While You Wait #2 and #3.**

NO ↓

Has your horse's last farriery appointment been within the past week?

YES → Call your veterinarian *TODAY*—it could be a problem with the way your horse has been trimmed and/or shod.

NO ↓

Has the lameness come on gradually, over 3 weeks or longer? Has it failed to improve with rest?

YES → Call your veterinarian *TODAY*—it could be a degenerative problem that might become chronic[G] if not diagnosed and treated early.

NO ↓

Is your horse younger than 5 years of age? Is he in training? Is there a mildly painful swelling on the front of both forelimb cannon bones?

YES → If you answered yes to all these queries, it could be a mild case of bucked shins[G]. Apply **Home Treatment**, on page 90.

NO ↓

Call your veterinarian for an appointment.

WHILE YOU WAIT #1:

Isolate your horse from other horses in case it's contagious. To prevent spread of possible infectious disease, confine your horse to an open-air paddock or stall with a separate water supply, apart from other horses by at least 20 feet. Wash your hands and disinfect your boots (see page 232) after handling your horse and before handling other horses.

WHILE YOU WAIT #2:

Confine your horse. Movement might make things worse. Until proven otherwise, confine him to a box stall or small paddock and provide a companion if necessary to discourage fretful movement.

WHILE YOU WAIT #3:

1. *Chill the foot.* Select a flexible ice pack (see page 262) large enough to wrap around the entire hoof wall (this might take two packs). Apply the pack(s) and secure with a wrap. Leave on for 5 minutes. Repeat every half hour, or until your vet arrives, whichever happens first.

2. *Avoid feeding him.* Give no feed—only water—until your vet arrives and can confirm or dismiss laminitis as a cause of lameness.

What you see: The farrier trimmed and/or shod your horse within the past week. Now your horse seems tender-footed. He's reluctant to step out with his normal stride, possibly ouchy on stones or rocks, and maybe even downright lame.

6-F

LAME
After farrier visit

What this might mean: There are a number of problems that can develop in a horse's feet and/or legs after farriery. Don't be too quick to blame your farrier. The list of problems that can occur as a result of shoeing is dominated by conditions that don't suggest incompetence or malpractice on his/her part. Furthermore, don't let coincidence mislead you: What you're seeing might not be related to farriery at all.

ACTION PLAN:

Do you detect excess warmth on the walls of the affected foot or feet? Do you feel a strong digital pulse on that foot, compared to his other feet, or compared to that of other horses on the premises? Does your horse flinch when you press firmly on the toe area of the affected foot or feet? Is your horse lame?

YES → Call your veterinarian *NOW* if you answered yes to any of these queries—there could be inflammation within the foot, from a condition such as laminitis[G], navicular disease[G], thrush[G], a close nail, or a sole abscess[G].

NO ↓

Does your horse react to hoof testers in the toe area of the affected foot or feet?

YES → Call your veterinarian *NOW*—laminitis is among the possibles, along with thrush, navicular disease, or a sole abscess.

NO ↓

Is your horse showing an obvious head-bobbing or hip-hiking lameness?

YES → Go to **page 87.**

NO ↓

Do you detect puffiness or filling of the tendon sheaths above and below the fetlock joint(s) of your horse's affected legs?

YES → Call your veterinarian *TODAY*—it could be tendinitis[G].

NO ↓

Does your horse react to hoof testers pressed over fresh nailholes?

YES → Call your veterinarian *TODAY*—a misplaced nail might have "quicked" your horse (gone too deeply and nicked sensitive tissues).

NO ↓

YOUR VET MAY NEED TO:

Review/renew your horse's tetanus immunization.

ACTION PLAN (CONTINUED):

Does the sole of your horse's affected feet yield easily to finger pressure? Does your horse flinch when you do this?

YES → Call your veterinarian *TODAY*—it could be an infection within the foot, or a too-thin sole from overtrimming, underdevelopment, or overwear.

NO ↓

Inform your farrier of the situation, and keep him/her advised of your horse's progress. Review this decision chart every day for 3 days. If your responses change, and/or if tenderfootedness fails to resolve, call your veterinarian. If your vet feels it would be helpful, arrange to have your farrier attend.

Sole-ful Insights...

If your horse is typically (but temporarily) tender-footed after a farrier visit, particularly when walking on rocks, he may have thin soles. Ask your farrier to evaluate your horse's soles to see if they're too thin (or if there's some other, more sinister reason for his ouchiness). Consider having the horse shod with pads to protect against stone bruises.

6-G

LUMPS & BUMPS

On hock

What you see: A lump, bump, or some other kind of deformity on your horse's hock. Perhaps it's sore to the touch, or maybe it's affecting his gait. Even if it's not causing him any discomfort, it's definitely abnormal.

What this might mean: It might be nothing more than a blemish. It might be a warning sign of stresses within the joint that could lead to injury. Or, it might be a sign of a serious bone, muscle, tendon, ligament, or joint problem. Even if it's not a serious condition, its location might interfere with normal movement.

ACTION PLAN:

Is your horse showing any sign of lameness on the affected leg? Is there a doughy thickening along the broad tendon that runs over the point of his hock?

YES → Call your veterinarian *NOW* if you answered yes to either query—it could be an injury to supportive structures. Go to **While You Wait,** page 88.

NO ↓

Is there a flesh wound associated with the lump?

YES → Go to the **Action Plan** appropriate for that wound type.

NO ↓

Is there a firm swelling (the consistency of a tennis ball) on his inner leg where the hock joins the cannon bone? Does his toe show abnormal wear from dragging on the ground as he advances his foot?

YES → Call your veterinarian *TODAY* if you answered yes to either query—it could be a bone (Jack) spavin[G]. Go to **While You Wait,** opposite page.

NO ↓

Is there a squishy swelling (feels like a water balloon) protruding from both sides of the hock?

YES → Call your veterinarian *TODAY*—it could be a bog spavin[G]. Go to **While You Wait,** opposite page.

NO ↓

Is there a doughy swelling just below the hock, on the outer and/or rear surface of your horse's leg?

YES → Call your veterinarian *TODAY*—it could be a curb[G]. Go to **While You Wait,** opposite page.

NO ↓

Is there a floppy, golf-ball-sized swelling over the point of his hock, with no abnormal heat or discomfort evident?

YES → Call your veterinarian *TODAY*—it's probably a capped hock, which could become a permanent blemish. Go to **While You Wait,** opposite page.

NO ↓

Call your veterinarian for advice.

WHILE YOU WAIT :

1. *Apply alternating cold/heat.* Prepare a hot (tolerable to your hand, like a hot bath) solution of Epsom salts (see page 242). Soak a disposable diaper or terrycloth hand towel in the solution, fold it in half and place it over the capped hock. Hold it there for 2 minutes. Remove the cloth and run cold hose water (no pressure nozzle) over the hock for 5 minutes, or apply an ice pack. (See page 262.) Repeat heat/cold cycle 3 more times, for a total of 4 cycles. Do this 4-cycle session 3 times a day until your veterinary appointment.

2. *Apply a poultice.* After each heat/cold session, apply a thin layer of a commercial poultice. (Don't use a product that's supposed to generate heat or cause blistering.) Cover the poultice loosely with plastic wrap and secure with a track bandage applied in a figure-eight configuration. Be careful to angle the wrap around the point of the hock so as not to rub and irritate it further. Let the poultice sweat for 1 hour, then remove all wrappings.

3. *Prevent recurrence.* If your horse is causing repeated trauma to his hocks, no treatment will resolve the resultant cap. If he's a stall-kicker, move him to a paddock, or to a stall away from possibly objectionable neighbors. If he kicks in the horse trailer, consider removing the center divider or switching to a slant-load or open stock trailer. If he's abrading his hocks while struggling to rise on slippery footing, consider switching bedding, installing floor mats, or moving him to pasture.

Did You Know...

When DMSO (dimethylsulfoxide) is mixed with water (or applied to wet skin), the resultant emulsion undergoes a chemical reaction and releases an impressive amount of heat. This could irritate your horse's skin, particularly if he's sensitive.

6-H

LUMPS & BUMPS

On knee

What you see: A lump or bump or some other kind of deformity on your horse's knee. Perhaps it's sore to the touch, or maybe it's affecting his gait. Perhaps it's not causing him any discomfort at all, but it's definitely abnormal.

What this might mean: It might be nothing more than a blemish. It might be a warning sign of stresses within the joint that could lead to injury. Or, it might be a sign of a serious problem in your horse's bone, muscle, tendon, ligament, or joint. Even if it's not a serious problem, its location might interfere with normal movement.

ACTION PLAN:

Is your horse showing any sign of lameness on the affected leg?

YES → Call your veterinarian *NOW*—it could could be an injury to the knee joint or its supportive structures. Go to **While You Wait #1,** opposite page.

NO ↓

Does the involved leg knuckle over at the fetlock?

YES → Call your veterinarian *NOW*—it could be an injury to the tendon that straightens the knee and advances the leg (common digital extensor tendon). Go to **While You Wait #2**, opposite page.

NO ↓

Is there a flesh wound associated with the lump?

YES → Go to **page 13** for the Action Plan appropriate for that wound type.

NO ↓

Is the joint uniformly swollen?

YES → Call your veterinarian *TODAY*—it could be a hygroma[G] or synovitis[G]. Go to **While You Wait #1.**

NO ↓

Call your veterinarian *TODAY*—it could be a hygroma[G], or injury to the soft tissues outside the joint, due to trauma. Go to **While You Wait #1.**

CAUTION

Resist the urge to give your horse anti-inflammatory medication unless advised to do so by your vet. Giving medication to relieve swelling and pain without taking measures to correct the underlying problem can temporarily make you forget there is one and free you to resume your horse's regular work load. However, continued work could do serious, possibly permanent, damage.

WHILE YOU WAIT #1:

1. *Ice the knee.* Select an ice pack (see page 262) large enough to extend at least 2 inches beyond the joint's margins. Slip it between layers of a clean cloth, center it over the joint, and hold it there. Ice on: 5 minutes. Ice off: 15 minutes. Repeat this cycle 3 more times or until your vet arrives, whichever happens first.

2. *Wrap the knee.* Apply a light pressure bandage (see page 276). Confine your horse to keep the bandage from loosening.

WHILE YOU WAIT #2:

1. *Confine your horse.* Movement might make things worse. Confine him to a box stall or paddock and provide a companion if necessary to discourage fretful movement.

2. *Cool the knee.* Select an ice pack (see page 262) large enough to extend at least 2 inches beyond the affected area's margins. Slip it between layers of a clean cloth, center it over the area, and hold it there. Ice on: 5 minutes. Ice off: 15 minutes. Repeat this cycle 3 more times or until your vet arrives, whichever happens first.

3. *Apply a support wrap.* Use a standing wrap to support the buckling fetlock. Add an extra layer of padding and be especially careful to apply the elastic layer evenly and firmly enough to prevent slippage. (For detailed how-to instructions, see page 271.)

Did You Know...

Horses can get their own version of "carpal tunnel syndrome," the bane of computer hackers and musicians in the human world. In horses it's called carpal canal syndrome, and it affects tissues at the back of the knee in the fore leg (comparable to the underside of your wrist). Symptoms can include lameness (subtle to very severe), heat and puffiness in the joint (particularly on the rearward side), and reluctance to bend the knee, due to pain.

6-1

LUMPS & BUMPS
On lower leg

What you see: A lump, bump, or other kind of deformity on your horse's leg, between his coronary band and hock (hindlimb) or knee (forelimb). Perhaps it's sore to the touch, and maybe it's affecting his gait. Even if it's not causing him any discomfort, it definitely looks abnormal.

What this might mean: It might be nothing more than a blemish, or it could be a sign of a serious bone, muscle, tendon, ligament, or joint problem. Even if it's not a serious problem, the location might interfere with normal movement.

ACTION PLAN:

Is your horse showing any sign of lameness on the affected leg?

YES → Call your veterinarian *NOW*—it could be an injury to supporting structures. Go to **While You Wait,** opposite page.

NO ↓

Is there a mounded, firm thickening in the tendons along the back of your horse's cannon bone? Is it abnormally warm, and painful to the touch, even though you haven't noticed any lameness?

YES → Call your veterinarian *NOW* if you answered yes to both queries—it could be an early injury or infection in a flexor tendon (bowed tendon[G]) or its sheath.

NO ↓

Is there a flesh wound associated with the lump?

YES → Go to the **Action Plan** appropriate for that wound type.

NO ↓

Is there a mounded, firm thickening in the tendons along the back of the cannon bone, with no abnormal warmth, and no evidence of pain when you squeeze or press on it firmly while the leg is in a non-weight-bearing position?

YES → Apply **Home Treatment #1,** opposite page. It sounds like scar tissue from an old tendon bow[G].

NO ↓

Are the grooves on either side of your horse's cannon bone, just above his fetlock, filled with a firm, springy swelling?

YES → Call your veterinarian *TODAY*—it could be windpuffs[G], due to inflammation of the sheath that surrounds the tendon there. If the fetlock itself is swollen, go to **page 85.**

NO ↓

ACTION PLAN (CONTINUED):

Is there a firm knob, thumb-sized or smaller, on the inner and/or outer surface of the cannon bone below the knee or hock? Is it tender and abnormally warm?

YES → Call your veterinarian *TODAY* if you answered yes to both queries—it could be a splint bone injury.

NO ↓

Is there a firm knob, appearing just as described above, but it's painless and cool?

YES → Sounds like an old, resolved, "cold" splint[G]. Apply **Home Treatment #2,** next page.

NO ↓

Is there a firm swelling (looks like a smooth mound, with the consistency of a tennis ball) on the front of the mid-cannon bone(s), that's tender and feels abnormally warm?

YES → It sounds like bucked shins[G]. Apply **Home Treatment**, page 90.

NO ↓

Call your veterinarian for an appointment.

WHILE YOU WAIT:

1. *Confine your horse.* Assume that whatever's causing the abnormal lump and lameness could get worse with movement. Confine your horse to a stall or small paddock, with a companion if necessary to limit fretful movement.

2. *Ice the leg.* If you detect abnormal heat and/or swelling associated with the lump or bump, select an ice pack (see page 262) large enough to extend at least 2 inches beyond its margins. Slip it between layers of a clean cloth, center it over the affected area, and hold it there. Ice on: 5 minutes. Ice off: 15 minutes. Repeat this cycle 3 more times or until your vet arrives, whichever happens first.

HOME TREATMENT #1:

*(See **Action Plan** to determine whether home treatment is appropriate for your horse's "old bow." If at any time during home treatment his tendon shows signs of heat, renewed swelling, tenderness when you squeeze or press on it while the leg's in a non-weight-bearing position, or lameness, call your veterinarian.)*

Step 1. *Apply alternating heat/cold.* Prepare a hot but tolerable on your hand solution of Epsom salts (see pages 242). Soak a disposable diaper or terrycloth hand towel in the solution, fold it in half and place it over the tendon. Hold it there for 5 minutes, re-wetting as needed to keep it warm. Remove the cloth and run a moderate stream (pressure nozzle on medium) of cold hose water over the area for 5 minutes. Then ice the site. (See **While You Wait**, Step 2, for icing instructions.) Hold the ice pack over the bow for 5 minutes. Repeat the cycle of heat, cold hose, then ice once more, ending with heat. Frequency: Twice daily for 2 weeks. ➤

Step 2. *Apply physical therapy.* These 3 steps are to be applied after each heat/cold session.

A. Immediately after the final heat treatment, rub liniment into the tendon with the balls of your fingers (no long fingernails, please), running the length of the tendon fibers in a 5-minute session of deep massage. Envision your fingers "combing" the fibers, separating and straightening them. Be as firm as you can, without causing discomfort.

B. Repeat the 5-minute massage, this time with your horse's toe elevated on the edge of a 1-inch board. (This helps to isolate and stretch the tendons.) If he objects (lifts his leg or snatches it away), start with a 1/2-inch board and shorter sessions, and work up to the 1-inch board and 5 minute sessions as his comfort level permits.

C. Hand-walk him for 15 minutes on a flat, level, hard surface.

Step 3. *Apply a poultice.* After walking, apply a thin layer of a commercial or homemade poultice (see page 242) to the tendon. Cover loosely with plastic wrap, and follow with roll cotton and a track bandage. (For how-to bandage instructions, see page 271.) Let the poultice sweat for 2 to 4 hours, then remove all wrappings and wash the poultice off thoroughly with soap and warm water. Rinse and pat dry. Apply a standing wrap (see page 271) for light support until the next treatment.

Step 4. *Re-assess in 2 weeks.* Whether or not the bow diminishes will depend on the severity of the initial injury, how old it is, and how much scar tissue it has. Don't expect to see a significant improvement right away—this requires reorganization of chaotically arranged tendon fibers, which can take several weeks. But within the first 2 weeks, you'll know you're making progress if the thickened tendon feels more pliable and your horse's tolerance of the massage-with-toe-elevated treatment in Step 2 improves.

If so, continue Steps 1 through 3 for additional 2-week intervals. If there's no evidence of improvement, the bow may not improve with further home treatment. (Other options include surgery, to break down excessive scar tissue and help direct the orientation of new tendon fibers, or injection of the tendon with various medications. Aftercare is similar to what's outlined in Steps 1 through 3.)

Caveat: Even if the appearance improves, healed tendon contains tissue that's weaker and less elastic than the pre-injury original, which means it's more susceptible to future injury. If your horse is an athlete, consider switching him to a less strenuous career.

HOME TREATMENT #2 :

*(See **Action Plan** to determine whether home treatment is appropriate for your horse's cold splints. If lameness, abnormal heat, or tenderness appears at any time during treatment, call your veterinarian—the splint bone might be fractured.)*

Note: "Cold" splints rarely cause lameness or mechanical interference with normal leg function. The primary reason they're treated at all is because they're considered an undesirable blemish. If your veterinarian feels your horse's cold splint is not a problem, and you don't mind the looks of it, one option is to leave it alone. If you want to try and reduce its size and prominence, try the following regimen.

Step 1. *Apply alternating heat/cold.* Follow Step 1 of Home Treatment #1 (page 101), applying the treatment to the splint area(s). Frequency: Twice a day, for 2 weeks.

Step 2. *Apply a poultice.* Follow Step 3 of Home Treatment #1, but this time apply the treatment to the splint area(s).

Step 3. Re-assess in 2 weeks. Check the splint(s) for signs of diminished size. If you think you're making progress, continue treatment for another 2 weeks and re-assess. If not, it may not improve with further home treatment. But don't despair: Over several months, many lumpy splints become smoother and less prominent on their own.

Other treatment options include surgery, or injection of the splint with a medication that'll incite an inflammatory response, followed by aftercare that's similar to what's outlined above.

How to Sweat a Leg...

You can use a sweat in lieu of a poultice, to help reduce lower-leg swelling in a benign condition such as stocking up, or when your veterinarian directs you to "sweat" an injury. Here's how to do it:

- Apply the leg-sweat preparation according to label or veterinary instructions (or make your own—see recipe on page 242).
- Cover the area loosely with plastic kitchen wrap (such as Saran®), smoothly conforming the plastic to your horse's leg.
- Apply a standing bandage over the site. (For how to apply a standing bandage, see page 271.)
- As a rule of thumb (unless directed to do otherwise by label instructions or your vet), leave the sweat on for 12 hours. Then unwrap and rinse the leg(s), allow it to "rest" for 12 hours, then re-apply a sweat for another 12 hours. Repeat as needed or directed.

6-J

LUMPS & BUMPS

On upper leg

What you see: A lump, bump, or other kind of deformity on your horse's leg, above his hock (hindlimb) or knee (forelimb). Perhaps it's sore to the touch, and maybe it's affecting his gait. Even if it's not causing him any discomfort, it looks abnormal.

What this might mean: It might be nothing more than a blemish. It might be a tumor. It could be an external sign of a serious problem in bone, muscle, tendon, ligament, or joint. Even if it's not a serious problem, its location might interfere with normal gaits.

ACTION PLAN:

Is your horse showing any sign of lameness on the affected leg?
YES → Go to **pages 87 to 90**.

NO ↓

Is it a swelling on his elbow or stifle joint?
YES → Go to **page 85**.

NO ↓

Is there a flesh wound or broken skin over the lump?
YES → Go to the **Action Plan** appropriate for that type of wound.

NO ↓

Does your horse resent having the affected leg flexed?
YES → Call your veterinarian *TODAY*—it could be an injury to the bone or supportive structures in or near a joint.

NO ↓

Is the lump associated with a thickening and/or hairless area over the elbow joint?
YES → Call your veterinarian *TODAY*—it could be a shoe boil.

NO ↓

Is there a hard, painless knob under the skin on the outside of the leg, just beneath the stifle?
YES → Call your veterinarian *TODAY*—it could be a tumor-like growth called calcinosis circumscripta[G].

NO ↓

Does the lump/bump move when you move your horse's skin?
YES → Go to **page 142** and **page 151**.

NO ↓

ACTION PLAN (CONTINUED):

Is the lump a soft-to-firm swelling (like a water balloon or tennis ball) over a heavily muscled area like your horse's rump, thigh, brisket, or shoulder, with no abnormal heat or pain?

YES → Sounds like a hematoma[G] or a seroma[G]. If it feels like a water balloon and is larger than a hockey puck, call your veterinarian today—he/she may be able to drain it, which could bring faster results. Otherwise, apply **Home Treatment,** below.

NO → Call your veterinarian for an appointment.

HOME TREATMENT:

(See **Action Plan** *to determine whether home treatment is appropriate for the lump/bump on your horse's upper leg. If at any time during home treatment, your answers on the action plan change for the worse, call your veterinarian.)*

Step 1. *Apply ice and pressure to stop the bleeding under the skin.* Select an ice pack large enough to overlap the hematoma's margins (see page 262). Place it directly on the skin and press almost hard enough to push your horse off-balance. (Ask a helper to press on the opposite side, to steady him). Ice on: 20 minutes; off: 5 minutes. Repeat twice more, with fresh packs.

Avoid using chemical cold packs for this icing procedure—they can get much colder than ice packs and when applied this long can actually cause frostbite.

Step 2. *Confine your horse, to protect blood clots that have formed to stop the bleeding.* For the next 12 hours, confine your horse to a box stall or paddock, with fresh grass or hay and a companion, if necessary, to prevent fretful movement.

Step 3. *Stimulate the area to encourage uptake of accumulated blood/serum.* The following day:

- Place a hot water bottle filled with hot (but tolerable on your hand) water over the swelling; hold it there for 5 minutes.
- Follow immediately with an ice pack for 5 minutes.
- Follow with 2 minutes of brisk stimulation with a rubber curry to soften tissues and increase circulation.
- Repeat the cycle twice more, for a total of 3 cycles per session.
- Frequency: Twice a day.

Step 4. *3 or more days after the injury, consider exercise to improve circulation and discourage scarring.* Immediately following Step 3, exercise your horse. For an idle horse, walk for 5 minutes, intersperse walking and jogging for 15 minutes, then walk 10 minutes for a cool-down. For a horse on a regular exercise program, perform a 50 percent easier version of his usual daily routine.

Step 5. *Keep it up.* Repeat Steps 1 through 4 until the architecture of the area has returned to normal. This might take as long as 6 weeks, depending on the severity and age of the hematoma/seroma when you started treatment. (The older it is, the longer it'll take to resolve.)

6-K

BUCKLING Or knuckling OVER

What you see: One or more of your horse's legs seems to be buckling or knuckling over, as though it's very weak or not working right.

What this might mean:
Unless your horse has just been given a strong sedative known to make horses act drunk, it can mean there's a problem in his nervous system, or in the support structures (muscles, tendons, ligaments, bone) of the involved leg(s).

ACTION PLAN:

Is it happening in more than one leg? Do you see a drooping ear, eyelid, or muzzle? Is his third eyelid evident?

YES → Call your veterinarian *NOW* if you answered yes to any of these queries—it could be a neurological disease or overall weakness. (See **The Nitty Gritty**, opposite page.) See **Caution**, below, and go to **While You Wait,** below.

NO ↓

Is it happening in only one leg?

YES → Call your veterinarian *NOW*—it might be an injury to supportive structures and/or the leg's nerve supply. Go to **While You Wait.**

WHILE YOU WAIT:

1. *Protect yourself.* With this kind of gait anomaly, your horse is likely to move in unexpected ways. Be alert, and don't put yourself in a position where you could be stepped on, knocked over, or conked on the head.

2. *Protect your horse.* Your horse can do serious damage to himself if he feels compelled to move. If it can be done safely, halter and hold him where he is while you wait for your vet. Or, if possible, have a helper hold him while you set up portable corral panels around the horse, to protect him from other horses.

> CAUTION
>
> **Among the possible causes of nervous system disease causing nerve dysfunction is a rare but notorious one: Rabies. Take precautions. See page 34.**

The Nitty Gritty

Here are some possible causes of buckling/knuckling

INFECTIOUS DISEASES	NONINFECTIOUS DISEASES	INJURIES & STRUCTURAL ABNORMALITIES
• Encephalomyelitis	• Botulism	• Excessively upright conformation
• Equine Herpesvirus-1 (EHV-1)	• Electrolyte disturbances	• Fracture
• Equine infectious anemia (EIA)	• Heart disease	• Head trauma
• Equine protozoal myeloencephalitis (EPM)	• Hyperkalemic periodic paralysis (HYPP)	• Nerve damage
• Rabies	• Lead poisoning	• Physeal dysplasia (epiphysitis)
	• Stroke	• Ruptured ligament
	• Tumor	• Ruptured tendon
		• Spinal cord trauma
		• Tendon contracture
(See Glossary for detailed descriptions.)		• Torn muscle

6 - L

HIND LEG CATCHING

Or locking

What you see: If you're astride at the time, it's hard to tell what's happened. Your horse is walking or trotting normally, then suddenly his hip drops on one side, or the stride in his hind limb "catches." If you're on the ground, you can see very clearly what's happened: Your horse's hind limb reaches forward normally, bears weight, and propels him forward, then extends behind him, momentarily locking there in the fully extended position.

What this might mean: Either an enlarged or displaced ligament near the kneecap (on the stifle area of your horse's hind leg), or lack of muscle strength in your horse's upper hind leg.

ACTION PLAN:

Is your horse relatively unfit (such as in the early phases of training?) Is this the first time this has happened?

YES → It sounds like a condition called upward patellar fixation[G]. Apply **Home Treatment,** below.

NO → Call your veterinarian for an appointment—treatment might be needed to correct inflammation and/or abnormal size or position of a ligament that steadies the kneecap. Go to **While You Wait,** below.

WHILE YOU WAIT:

Limit exercise. Because it's not good for your horse's leg to lock up repeatedly, avoid any movement that results in leg catching or locking until your veterinarian can advise you. If this means confining your horse to a small paddock or a stall, do so.

HOME TREATMENT

*(See **Action Plan** to determine whether home treatment is appropriate for your horse's stifle-lock. If at any time during home treatment your answers on the action plan change for the worse, call your vet.)*

Step 1. *Review your horse's management and conditioning program.*

- If your horse is less than 3 years of age, turn him out to pasture and let him grow up some more before you ride him. Lack of maturity might be the main cause of his lack of muscle strength.
- Ask your veterinarian or an equine nutritionist to review your horse's diet and make adjustments if it's deficient in any area.
- If your horse is 3 years of age or older, impose a 2-day rest period and consult your veterinarian for advice on whether your

horse should be given a brief course of anti-inflammatory medication such as bute. Both measures will help if the culprit ligament is inflamed and swollen from repeatedly locking. (A swollen ligament is more likely to continue locking despite improvement in muscle strength.)

- Consult a trainer to help you design a regular, controlled exercise program to improve your horse's overall condition, particularly to build strength in the muscles of his upper hind limb. Hill work (both uphill and down) is especially effective for building hind limb muscles. If you feel unsafe astride your horse, pony him or work from the ground. (If his leg locks while longeing, switch to line-driving.)
- If, after 1 week of muscle-building, your horse's patella continues to lock, cease your program. Call your veterinarian to evaluate your horse's shoeing and fitness level, and to determine whether corrective shoes, injections around the ligament, or surgery will be warranted.

Question...

What causes some of your horse's (and your) joints to make a popping noise?

Answer...

There are a number of theories, but here's the most popular one: About 15 percent of joint fluid consists of dissolved gas, mostly carbon dioxide. When a joint moves or is manipulated, the pressure within it suddenly decreases. A portion of this dissolved gas comes out of solution, coalesces into a single bubble, and pops. It's not painful, and most researchers say it doesn't create any problems in the joint.

6-M

What you see: Your horse is moving stiffly, taking slow, short steps.

STIFF MOVEMENTS

What this might mean: If it's just muscle stiffness the day after a vigorous workout, it could be perfectly normal. Otherwise, it could be a sign of pain, muscle disease, or general illness.

ACTION PLAN:

Is your horse off his feed, depressed, or feverish?

YES → Call your veterinarian *NOW*—it could be a general illness with muscle stiffness/soreness as an early symptom. (See **The Nitty Gritty**.) Go to **While You Wait,** below.

NO ↓

Is he showing any signs of lameness? Any abnormal swellings? Any areas on his body that are painful to finger pressure? Are any muscles tight and hard? Is he sweating?

YES → Call veterinarian *NOW* if you answered yes to any of these queries—it could be a spinal injury/disease, a muscle disorder, or a lameness affecting both sides. Go to **While You Wait.**

NO ↓

Did your horse undergo strenuous exercise or a greater than 4-hour trailer ride within the past 24 hours? Is his appetite normal? Is his drinking water volume normal? Is he passing a normal volume of manure? Is his attitude normal?

YES → Apply **Home Treatment,** opposite page, if you answered yes to all of these queries—it sounds like simple muscle fatigue.

NO ↓

Call your veterinarian *NOW* if you answered no to any of these queries—it could be early signs of a general or muscle disease.

WHILE YOU WAIT:

1. *Isolate your horse from other horses in case it's contagious.* To prevent spread of possible infectious disease, confine your horse to an open-air paddock or stall with a separate water supply, apart from other horses by at least 20 feet. Wash your hands and disinfect your boots (see page 232) after handling your horse and before handling other horses.

2. *Restrict movement.* Until a definitive diagnosis can be made, assume your horse has a disorder that can be worsened by movement. Don't move him unless absolutely necessary.

HOME TREATMENT :

*(See **Action Plan** to determine whether home treatment is appropriate for your horse's muscle stiffness. If at any time during home treatment, your answers on the action plan change for the worse, call your veterinarian.)*

Step 1. *Walk your horse.* Give him a light day, but don't give him the day off. A warm bath, brisk rubdown with a rubber curry, and an hour of easy walking twice a day will loosen up and lubricate cramped muscles, improve circulation, and brighten his outlook.

The Nitty Gritty

Here are possible causes of stiff movement

- Back pain
- DSLD
- Hyperkalemic periodic paralysis (HYPP)
- Laminitis
- Lyme disease
- Navicular disease
- Post-exertion muscle stiffness
- Tetanus
- Tying-up syndrome
- Viral illness

(See Glossary for detailed descriptions.)

Maturity Matters...

As your horse enters the realm of senior citizenship, he'll be more prone to injury and illness, due to a decrease in flexibility and a gradual decline in immune system competence. And, he may lose status within his social circle. When age starts encroaching on well-being, a horse's social niche can erode, and lower herd members sense it. This sets the stage for conflict (and injury) as younger horses increasingly issue challenges in an attempt to improve their social status. If you see your horse becoming involved in such conflicts, separate him from any top-dog wannabes before somebody gets hurt.

What you see: Your horse is carrying his foot or leg lower than normal as he brings it forward, so that he's actually scuffing it across the ground.

6-N

DRAGGING A TOE

What this might mean: It could be a sign of a nervous system problem, either centrally (brain or spinal cord) or in the nerves of the leg itself. Or it could mean there's pain in the leg; your horse has found the pain is lessened if he carries it lower than usual.

ACTION PLAN:

Is your horse off his feed, depressed, or feverish? Is an ear, eyelid, or muzzle drooping? Is his third eyelid[G] evident?

YES → Call your veterinarian *NOW* if you answered yes to any of these queries—it could be illness or injury in the brain, spinal cord, or nerves. Go to **While You Wait,** below.

NO ↓

Are there any signs of trauma?

YES → Call your veterinarian *NOW*—it could be an injury to vital structure(s) within your horse's leg, spinal cord, or head. Go to **While You Wait.**

NO ↓

Are there any areas of swelling, heat, and/or pain upon finger pressure?

YES → Call your veterinarian *TODAY*—it could be an injury or disease to supportive structures in your horse's leg or foot.

NO ↓

Call your veterinarian *TODAY*, for an appointment.

WHILE YOU WAIT:

1. *Isolate your horse from other horses in case it's contagious.* To prevent spread of possible infectious disease, confine your horse to an open-air paddock or stall with a separate water supply, apart from other horses by at least 20 feet. Wash your hands and disinfect your boots (see page 232) after handling your horse and before handling other horses.

2. *Restrict his movement.* Until a definitive diagnosis can be made, assume your horse has a disorder that can be worsened by movement. Don't move him unless absolutely necessary.

6-0

STOMPING HIND FOOT

When walking

What you see: While walking, your horse seems to be slamming his hind foot/feet into the ground harder than he normally does, making a slapping sound on impact. When viewed from the side, he appears to be lifting the leg higher than usual before slamming it down.

What this might mean: A disorder of the muscles, or the nervous system controlling them.

ACTION PLAN:

Has your horse lost a lot of weight lately? Does he paddle his rear feet inward when he walks, often interfering with the opposite fetlock? Does he have sores on his inner fetlocks?

YES → Call your veterinarian *TODAY* if you answered yes to any of these queries—it could be a nervous system disease called EDM[G].

NO ↓

Is your horse a kicker? Is he involved in an athletic activity that puts excessive strain on his hind limbs, such as cutting, reining, or endurance racing on rough, hilly terrain?

YES → Call your veterinarian *TODAY* if you answered yes to either query—it could be an injury to muscles at the back of your horse's thigh (fibrotic myopathy[G]), or a condition called stringhalt[G].

NO ↓

Did this gait abnormality appear before he was 2 years of age? Does he have Morgan Horse blood in his pedigree?

YES → Call your veterinarian *THIS WEEK* if you answered yes to either query—it could be an inherited nerve disorder called NAD[G].

NO ↓

Call your veterinarian for an appointment.

NOTES

CHAPTER 7

Problems of THE FEET

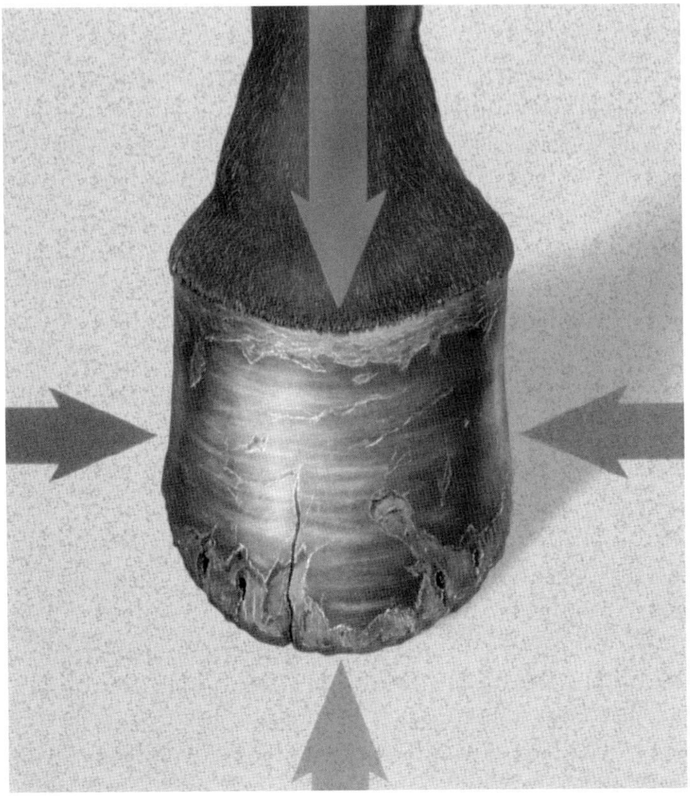

What you see: There's a crack in the wall of your horse's hoof. It might appear to originate at the coronary band, working its way downward; or start at the ground, working its way up. Or, it could be roughly parallel to the ground surface, or running at an angle across the hoof. It may be narrow, or wide enough that there's a chunk of hoof wall missing.

7-A

HOOF WALL CRACK

What this might mean: It could be insignificant, the result of a collision between hoof and rock; the next time your horse's hoof is trimmed the crack will be rasped right off. Or it could be serious, depending on the depth of the crack, whether it extends into live tissue that could become contaminated (and thus infected), and on whether the crack makes your horse's hoof wall unstable (and thereby likely to separate further).

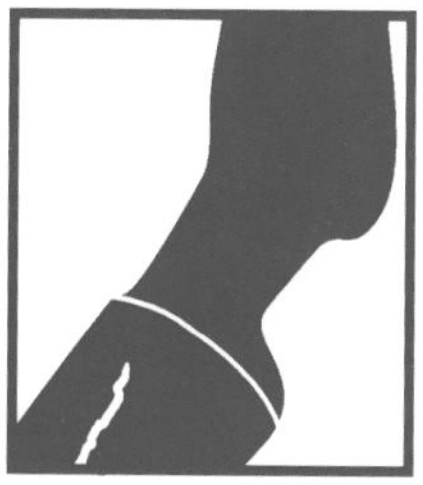

ACTION PLAN:

Is your horse lame on that foot? Does he flinch when you press firmly on the wall near the crack? Do you feel a strong digital pulse on that foot, compared to his other feet, or compared to other horses on the premises?

YES → Call your veterinarian *TODAY* if you answered yes to any of these queries—they're a sign that the crack is deep, unstable, and/or infected. Go to **While You Wait,** opposite page.

NO ↓

Is the coronary band involved?

YES → Call your veterinarian *TODAY*—the crack might need repair to prevent future hoof deformities. Go to **While You Wait.**

NO ↓

Are your horse's hooves dry and brittle, always seeming to chip and crack? If he's shod, does he often lose his shoes, as though his hoof walls can't hold a nail? Does his mane and tail hair seem dry and brittle, always breaking off?

YES → Call your veterinarian *TODAY* if you answered yes to any of these queries—your horse's diet could be deficient in nutrients essential for healthy hoof growth, or he could be ingesting a toxin that's affecting the growth of his hair and hooves.

NO ↓

Call your farrier *TODAY*—your horse's hooves need trimming, balancing and, if he's not shod, possibly shoes.

YOUR VET MAY NEED TO:

Review/renew your horse's tetanus immunization.

WHILE YOU WAIT :

1. *Clean the hoof.* With your horse on a solid, clean surface such as concrete or wood (clean, mowed grass and clean snow are acceptable alternatives), clean his hoof using a hoof pick, followed by a stiff-bristled (but not wire) brush, being careful to sweep away from the crack.

2. *Apply a hoof boot.* Enclose the hoof in a clean rubber or plastic hoof boot, or make a temporary one using bandage materials. (See page 267.)

3. *Confine your horse.* To help keep the hoof clean, confine him to a clean, dry area without loose bedding or debris, which can become trapped in crevices. A small, mowed paddock is ideal.

Brush Up on Safety...

If you're using a wire brush to clean the bottom of your horse's foot, you might want to reconsider. Those stiff bristles easily could puncture and damage the soft tissues of his frog. A plastic-bristled vegetable brush, available in most supermarkets, makes an equally effective (and much safer) alternative.

7-B

HOOF HOLE, BRUISE

Or black spot

What you see: While cleaning the sole and frog area of your horse's foot, you find a hole. It may be a nail hole, a bruised area (purple discoloration or blood staining just beneath surface), or a black spot.

What this might mean: It depends on the underlying cause and on how deep, and in what direction, the lesion extends.

YOUR VET MAY NEED TO:

- **Administer local or general anesthesia, if deep penetration of the foot is suspected, to facilitate thorough inspection and cleaning of the lesion. (This could involve surgical debridement[G] to remove all contaminated tissue.)**
- **Review/renew your horse's tetanus immunization, if a penetrating wound or infection is suspected.**

ACTION PLAN:

Is the hole in frog tissue, or in the crevice alongside the frog?
YES → Call your veterinarian *NOW*—a wound in this region threatens vital structures.

NO ↓

Is blood, pus, or amber-colored serum draining from the lesion?
YES → Call your veterinarian *NOW*—it could be a deep puncture wound, threatening vital structures within the foot Go to **While You Wait #1,** opposite page.

NO ↓

Is your horse lame on that foot? Does he flinch when pressure is applied near the lesion? Does any area on the foot feel warmer, and/or have a strong digital pulse, compared to his other feet, or compared to that of other horses on the premises? Does the hair near the coronary band stick out abnormally (a sign of swelling)?
YES → Call your veterinarian *NOW* if you answered yes to any of these queries—they can signify inflammation and/or infection within the foot, possibly involving vital structures.

NO ↓

Is the heel of his shoe positioned such that it's causing pressure on the sole, rather than the wall, of that hoof?
YES → Call your farrier *TODAY*—it could be an early corn[G]. Go to **While You Wait #2,** opposite page.

NO ↓

Apply **Home Treatment,** opposite page.

WHILE YOU WAIT #1 :

1. *Poultice the foot.* Apply a poultice (see page 129) to draw out infection and soften the hoof while you await your vet's arrival.

2. *Apply a hoof boot.* Apply a rubber or plastic hoof boot, or a hoof bandage. Confine him to a clean stall or paddock to help keep the slipper clean and secure.

WHILE YOU WAIT #2 :

1. *Pull the shoe.* If you have the proper tools and know how to pull a shoe (see page 306) and your farrier will be delayed, pull the shoe to relieve pressure on the developing corn[G].

2. *Apply a hoof boot.* Apply a rubber or plastic hoof boot, or a temporary hoof bandage (see page 267) to protect untrimmed hoof edges from chipping. Confine your horse to a clean stall or paddock to help keep the boot clean and secure.

HOME TREATMENT :

*(See **Action Plan** to determine whether home treatment is appropriate for your horse's hoof wound. If at any time during home treatment, your answers on the action plan change for the worse, call your vet.)*

Step 1. *Clean the foot.* Move your horse to a clean work area with level, solid footing, such as a concrete wash rack. Pick out the hoof, then pare away a paper-thin layer of sole around the lesion: Use a clean, sharp hoof knife to remove tiny curls of old, soiled, stained tissue, leaving fresh, clean tissue. Clean the floor surface repeatedly as necessary to keep working area free of loose debris.

Step 2. *Pare the lesion.* Clean the hoof knife by dipping it in a disinfectant solution (see page 234), then wipe it dry with a clean gauze pad. Taking no more than paper-thin curls with each stroke, and going no deeper than three strokes in any one area, pare the lesion away, just as you'd pare away a dark spot while peeling a potato. If, after three strokes the lesion is still present, stop there—your veterinarian should be the one to go deeper. Call TODAY for an appointment to explore a possible penetrating hoof wound. Go to **While You Wait #1,** at left.

TIP:

Take away no more sole tissue than a vegetable peeler takes in a single swipe across a carrot.

What you see: Your horse's shoe has come loose: It wiggles, or you hear a clinking or slapping sound when that foot hits the ground. Maybe the shoe hasn't only loosened but actually has been wrenched out of position.

7-C

LOOSE SHOE

What this might mean: If it pulls off on its own, the shoe can take a substantial amount of your horse's hoof wall with it, possibly leaving him with insufficient hoof to re-shoe. This not only could spoil your plans to ride, show, or perform with him, but also could make him lame. If the shoe is still attached but has pulled askew, protruding edges or nails could injure your horse's other legs, or could cause a sole puncture on the foot of the affected limb.

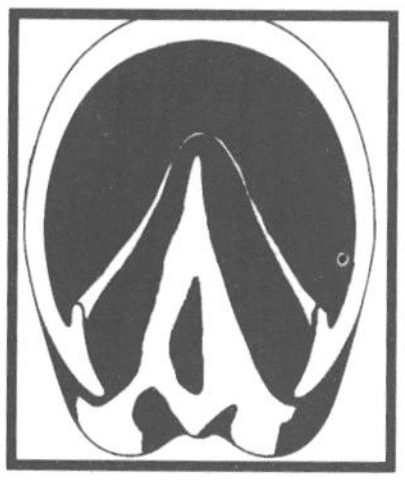

ACTION PLAN:

Is your horse lame on that foot?

YES → Call your veterinarian *NOW*—your horse may have injured the foot and/or joints by misstepping. Go to **While You Wait,** below.

NO ↓

Has the shoe pulled away from its normal placement on his hoof?

YES → Call your farrier *NOW*—if the shoe is misaligned, it can damage the hoof and other legs. Go to **While You Wait**.

NO ↓

Is the shoe still in place on your horse's hoof?

YES → Call your farrier *TODAY*—even if it's not necessary to re-set the shoe, at least it'll require a tightening of clinches. Go to **While You Wait**.

WHILE YOU WAIT:

1. *If the shoe's askew, pull it.* To avoid or minimize damage to that hoof and your horse's other legs, cut the clinches and pull the shoe, following the proper steps to prevent further damage to the hoof. (See page 306.)

2. *Protect the bare foot.* Protect the hoof's edges with a rubber or plastic hoof boot or a hoof boot made of duct tape. (See page 267.)

3. *Confine your horse.* Move your horse to an enclosure with soft footing that restricts his movement and won't cause chipping, such as a small grassy paddock with no rocks, or a well-bedded stall.

CAUTION

Excess moisture can accumulate in plastic hoof boots after as little as 2 hours. This can weaken hoof walls and increase the chance of nail failure when your horse is re-shod. If his hoof becomes stinky and spongey, take the boot off and clean it with soapy water and a rinse of rubbing alcohol. Allow the boot and your horse's hoof to air-dry before re-applying. Repeat as necessary until help arrives.

HEAT IN FEET

What you feel: The walls of your horse's feet are warmer to the touch than normal.

What this might mean: It's one of the cardinal signs of laminitis[G] and can indicate other internal foot problems.

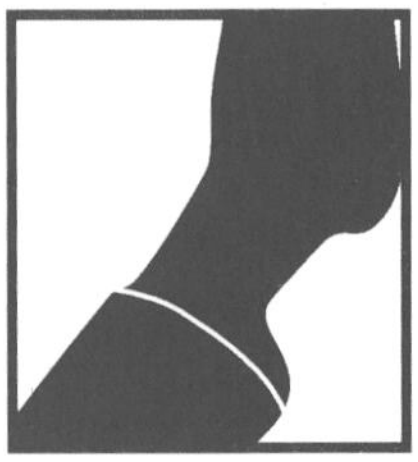

ACTION PLAN:

Is your horse moving stiffly, as if walking on glass? Is he reluctant to move at all? Rocking back on his hind feet when moving forward? Holding his forefeet forward of his shoulders when at rest?

YES → Call your veterinarian *NOW* if you answered yes to any of these queries—it could be laminitis[G]. Go to **While You Wait,** next page.

NO ↓

Has your horse been off his feed, depressed, or feverish?

YES → Call your veterinarian *NOW*—it could be the early stages of laminitis[G]. Go to **While You Wait**.

NO ↓

Was your horse's ration changed, and/or did he eat more than usual within the past 3 days?

YES → Call your veterinarian *NOW*—it could be the early stages of laminitis[G]. Go to **While You Wait**.

NO ↓

Are both front feet or all four feet warm? Do you feel a strong digital pulse on the affected feet, compared to his other feet, or compared to that of other horses on the premises?

YES → Call your veterinarian *NOW* if you answered yes to any of these queries—it could be the early stages of laminitis[G]. Go to **While You Wait**.

NO ↓

Is only one hoof excessively warm?

YES → Call your veterinarian *TODAY*—it could be infection, injury, or disease within the affected foot.

NO ↓

Has your horse been exercised within the past hour? Is he standing in hot sun? Are your hands cold?

YES → Re-evaluate your responses to this Action Plan in 1 hour.

NO ↓

Call your veterinarian *TODAY*.

➤

WHILE YOU WAIT:

1. *Confine your horse.* Confine your horse to a small (12 x 12) stall or paddock with soft footing. If he moves stiffly, is reluctant to move, rocks back on his hind legs, or has an exaggerated digital pulse, don't move him. Rather, confine him where he stands, using portable corral panels or a makeshift enclosure. Or, simply stay with him until your vet arrives.

To avoid possibly starving stricken tissues of needed blood and oxygen, do not exceed the 5 minute ice-on period or shorten the 30-minute interval between icings. And, don't increase chilling intensity by, for example, plunging the foot in a bucket of ice water.

2. *Don't feed him.* Offer water only. Your horse should have no feed of any kind until your vet's ruled out laminitis, which might be the result of, or be worsened by, certain kinds of feeds.

3. *Chill his feet.* Draw out excess heat in the affected feet by applying flexible ice packs (see page 262) to his hoof walls for 5 minutes every half hour.

The Patient is...In

If your horse has a condition that requires him to be confined and separated from herdmates, try these tips to make the ordeal as non-stressful as possible for all concerned:

- Erect a barrier between your horse and the sights and sounds of his buddies. (For example, make a wall of out-of-reach stacked hay or straw.) An isolated horse generally gets over his separation anxiety faster if he can't see or hear his buddies.
- Reduce or eliminate the concentrate portion of your horse's ration while he's confined. (Check with your veterinarian for guidelines.) The extra energy not only will contribute to added weight, but also added exuberance, making the confinement harder on him—and you.
- Supply the bulk of his dietary needs with good quality roughage, such as grass hay. This will meet most, if not all, of his needs, while filling his idle hours with plenty of chew-time.
- To help ensure adequate water intake, provide a salt block or free-choice, loose salt, and make sure that fresh water is available at all times.

Persistent SKIN SORES ON HEELS

What you see: The skin on and around the bulbs of your horse's heels and/or the backs of his pasterns (on one or more feet) is red, cracked, swollen, raw, oozing, and/or scabby. It may be sore to the touch.

What this might mean: It can be the early sign of a tumor-like skin condition that requires surgery, or an aggressive infection that can become chronic if not treated promptly.

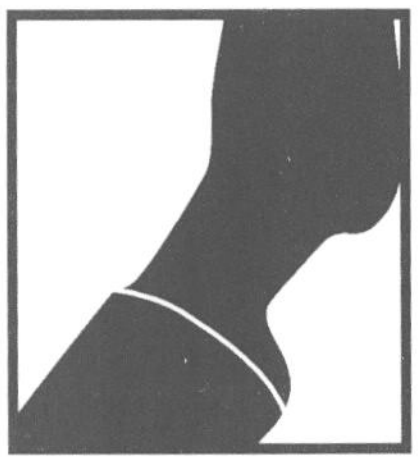

ACTION PLAN:

Is your horse lame?

YES → Call your veterinarian *TODAY*—this skin problem might involve deeper tissues, or it might be an abrasion due to a fall or misstep.

NO ↓

Is the coronary band swollen (the hair around the band is standing on end)?

YES → Call your veterinarian *TODAY*—a permanent deformity to future hoof growth might result if there's an infection in the coronary band.

NO ↓

Have you noticed any portion of the sore(s) growing rapidly over the past couple of days in a tumor-like manner, protruding from the skin surface?

YES → Call your veterinarian *TODAY*—it could be a skin disease such as Pythiosis[G] or greasy heel[G], which can require surgery to remove the bulbous growth.

NO ↓

It's probably scratches[G] or bacterial folliculitis[G]. Will your horse allow you to treat the affected area?

YES → Apply **Home Treatment,** below.

NO ↓

Call your veterinarian *TODAY.*

YOUR VET MAY NEED TO:

- **Sedate your horse and/or administer nerve blocks to facilitate examination and initial treatment, if the condition is painful.**
- **Submit a tissue sample of the lesion(s) to a laboratory for definitive diagnosis.**

HOME TREATMENT:

(See ***Action Plan*** *to determine whether home treatment is appropriate for your horse's heel sores. If at any time during home treatment, your answers on the action plan change for the worse, call your vet.)*

Step 1. *Soften and clean the thickened skin, crust, and scabs.* Apply an emollient dressing or poultice (see page 238 and 242), leaving it on overnight. Then wash the area thoroughly with a foaming human acne cleanser ➤

containing 10 percent benzoyl peroxide. Leave the lather in contact with affected skin for 10 minutes before rinsing thoroughly. Towel dry, then allow to air dry completely before moving to Step 2.

Step 2. *Clip the site.* Clip hair from the affected area and 1/2-inch beyond it using electric clippers and a sharp, clean, No. 40 blade. Be careful not to nick the skin or allow the blade to become too hot.

Step 3. *Dress the site.* Coat all affected surfaces with a thin layer of povidone iodine ointment (see page 238). Don't bandage unless absolutely necessary to keep tissues clean. The condition will respond better if left open to air.

Step 4. *Confine your horse.* For the next 2 to 3 weeks, keep your horse in an area that's clean and dry. A mowed, grassy paddock is ideal in dry weather; a scrupulously cleaned rubber-floored stall with no bedding, or bedded with shredded office paper (not newspaper, which contains ink) is ideal if indoor confinement is necessary. Stay away from wood shavings, sawdust, and straw or hay, which contain bacteria, and can poke and adhere to sensitive skin.

Step 5. *Keep it up.* Repeat Steps 1 and 3 once or twice daily (depending on how crusty, oozy, and/or scabby the area gets between cleanings). Expect to see an improvement within 3 days. Healing should be complete within 2 to 4 weeks, or longer in severe cases.

Step 6. *Re-evaluate every 3 days.* If the skin isn't improving steadily, the inflammation and/or infection might be too deep to reach with external treatments. Call your veterinarian for confirmation of your diagnosis and to help in treatment, possibly with a systemic (bodywide) medication.

Ugly, tumor-like GROWTH on front or back of PASTERN

What you see: An angry, cauliflower-like growth in your horse's pastern area. It could be pink, gray, greenish, black, or a combination. It's oozing, and it's mounding up like proud flesh[G]. You may notice a foul odor, like rotting flesh. Two or more feet could be affected.

What this might mean: A destructive, aggressive organism has invaded your horse's skin.

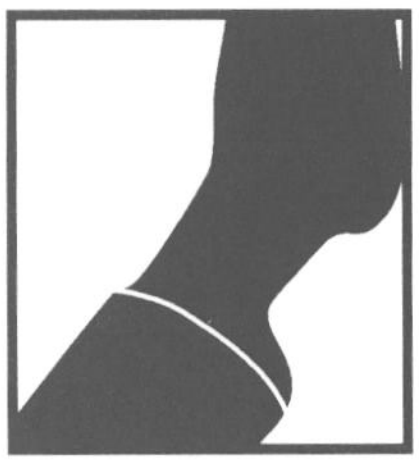

ACTION PLAN:

Is the growth on the back of your horse's pasterns?

YES → Call your veterinarian *TODAY*—it could be greasy heel[G] or Pythiosis[G], both of which can require surgery.

NO ↓

Is the growth on the front or sides of the pasterns, or involving the coronary band? Is your horse trying to scratch it?

YES → Call your veterinarian *TODAY* if you answered yes to either query—it could be Pythiosis[G] or a deep fungal or bacterial infection.

NO ↓

Call your veterinarian *TODAY* for an appointment.

YOUR VET MAY NEED TO:

Submit a sample of the abnormal tissue to a laboratory for definitive diagnosis.

Swamp Cancer Alert...

In its early stages, swamp cancer (Pythiosis) can be mistaken for proud flesh. It differs in that it's intensely itchy and, as it progresses, is crisscrossed with pus-filled tracts and knobs of yellowish-gray tissue. Untreated lesions can spread to bones and joints, so if your horse's "proud flesh" lesion isn't resolving, have your veterinarian out for another look, to rule out swamp cancer. A biopsy might be required.

7-G

Bottom of foot THRUSHY/ MUSHY

What you see/smell: As you're picking out your horse's feet, you notice the rubbery tissue of his frog and the deep crevices alongside it are mushy and smell foul. He may or may not be tenderfooted or obviously lame.

What this might mean: The soft tissues of your horse's sole, possibly compromised by prolonged wet weather, mud, and/or filth in his environment, have become infected.

ACTION PLAN:

Is the frog smaller in the affected feet than in normal feet? Is the gunky stuff grayish-black in color? Does your horse seem to object to having the crevices along the frog cleaned out?

YES → It sounds like thrush[G]. If your horse resents having affected tissues touched, or if you're queasy about this, call your veterinarian *TODAY*. Otherwise apply **Home Treatment,** below.

NO ↓

Is the frog larger in the affected feet than normal feet, with extra lumps and folds, as though it's actually growing? Does the gunky stuff resemble gray cottage cheese?

YES → It sounds like canker[G]. If your horse resents having affected tissues touched, or if you're queasy about this, call your veterinarian *TODAY*. Otherwise apply **Home Treatment**.

YOUR VET MAY NEED TO:

Sedate your horse and/or administer nerve blocks to facilitate a thorough initial cleaning of the infected area, because severe cases of thrush are deep and can be painful.

HOME TREATMENT:

(See ***Action Plan*** *to determine whether home treatment is appropriate for your horse's infection. If at any time during home treatment, your answers on the action plan change for the worse, call your vet.)*

Step 1. *Clean the hoof.* Scoop out easily removed diseased/dead tissue with a dull hoof knife, dipping the knife often in a disinfectant solution (see page 234). Then scrub the affected area and adjacent sole with a nylon-bristle vegetable or pot-scrubber brush, using two disinfectants one after the other: ∂-phenylphenol (Lysol disinfectant solution, mixed 2 tablespoons per gallon of water), and Betadine® solution diluted with water to the color of weak tea. Rinse well between each application of disinfectant. Repeat until the hoof looks (and smells) clean.

Step 2. *Disinfect the hoof.* Pour Kopertox® or Betadine® solution as in Step 1 onto the freshly cleaned tissues. Hold the leg flexed, sole up, while the disinfectant soaks in. Once it has, repeat with 1/4 cup of the Lysol solution used in Step 1.

Step 3. *Request an appointment with your farrier.* Call your farrier and request trimming, balancing, and shoeing if your horse isn't shod. (Shoes will raise his diseased foot higher off the ground, which will aid in drying.)

Step 4. *Adjust your horse's living situation.* To help keep his feet dry, house your horse in a clean, mowed, grassy paddock, clean drylot, or large, well drained box stall with straw or shredded paper bedding kept scrupulously clean.

Step 5. *Be diligent, and re-assess regularly.* Repeat Steps 1 and 2 twice daily and gauge your horse's progress: Is normal-looking tissue visible? Is the smell dissipating? Is the foot less sensitive? If you don't see definite improvement after 1 week, call your veterinarian. Your horse might need more aggressive trimming under sedation or anesthesia, and he might need systemic antibiotics. If improvement is evident, keep it up: It could take 4 to 6 weeks for complete healing.

The Great Pretender...

Equine canker is often misdiagnosed as thrush, which is a milder condition requiring a different treatment approach. If treated as thrush, canker is unlikely to resolve and, in some cases, will flourish. If your horse has been diagnosed with thrush, but the soft tissues of his affected foot are not improving with treatment, call your veterinarian for a second look.

What you see: Swelling at the coronary band of one or more of your horse's feet, which causes the hair to stick out rather than lie flat down. Perhaps there's also some moisture there, or an obvious drainage of foul-smelling liquid.

7-H

Swelling and/or drainage of the CORONARY BAND

What this might mean: Usually it means there's an infection (abscess[G]) within the foot, which is in the process of creating a drainage route through the coronary band. If more than one foot is involved, it could suggest the presence of a general, bodywide disease.

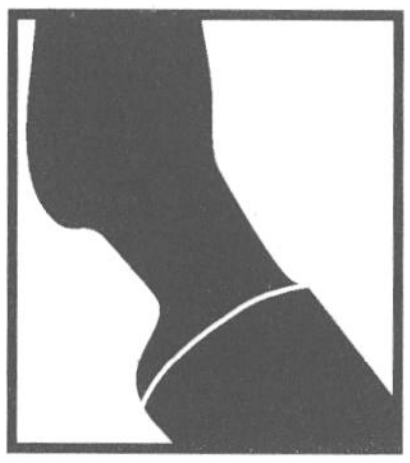

ACTION PLAN:

Do you see the coronary band swelling on more than one foot? Are there sores and/or blisters inside your horse's lips, gums, and/or tongue?

YES → Call your veterinarian *NOW*—it could be vesicular stomatitis[G]. Go to **While You Wait #1,** below.

NO ↓

Is swelling present only on white legs? Is white or pink skin adjacent to the coronary band also swollen, thickened, and/or crusty?

YES → Call your veterinarian *NOW*—it could be photoactivated vasculitis[G]. Go to **While You Wait #2,** below.

NO ↓

Is your horse lame?

YES → Call your veterinarian *TODAY*—it could be a sole abscess[G].

NO ↓

Is there moisture or an opening or other evidence of drainage from the coronary band?

YES → Apply **Home Treatment,** opposite page.

WHILE YOU WAIT #1:

1. *Isolate your horse.* If more than one foot is affected and your horse has blisters or sores in his mouth—even if he has no other signs of illness—there's an outside chance he has the contagious disease vesicular stomatitis or VS[G]. To prevent spread of the disease, confine your horse to an open-air paddock or stall with a separate water supply, apart from other horses by at least 20 feet. Wash your hands and disinfect your boots (see page 232) after handling your horse and before handling other horses.

WHILE YOU WAIT #2:

1. *Bring your horse indoors.* Photoactivated vasculitis is triggered by sunlight on light-colored skin. To protect your horse from further discomfort bring him into a stall or shed.

HOME TREATMENT:

*(See **Action Plan** to determine whether home treatment is appropriate for your horse's coronary band lesion. If at any time during home treatment, your answers on the action plan change for the worse, call your vet.)*

Step 1. *Clean the affected skin.* To prevent infection of swollen/weakened skin around the coronary band, irrigate the area with cool hose water or saline solution in a trigger-spray bottle (see page 242) until clean and free of crust and/or scab. Towel dry.

Step 2. *Clean the bottom of his foot.* Clean out the sole, white line area, frog, and crevices alongside the frog, then brush free of debris.

Step 3. *Apply a poultice.* Holding the cleaned foot between your legs, apply a poultice (see page 242) to the sole, frog, crevices alongside the frog, and coronary band. (Use about as thick a layer as you'd put peanut butter on bread). Wrap the entire foot up to the fetlock with a foot bandage (see page 267).

Step 4. *Control your horse's exercise.* To improve circulation within the foot, while protecting the bandage from wear-through, hand-walk your horse for 10 minutes, 3 to 4 times a day on soft footing (such as mowed grass), then confine him to a well-bedded stall.

Step 5. *Keep it up.* Repeat Steps 1 through 4 every day until there's no further drainage from the coronary band, and no crust on the skin adjacent to the coronary band—usually about 1 week. If drainage continues for longer than 1 week, or if at any time the hoof begins to feel hot or your horse shows signs of lameness, call your veterinarian. Vital structures might be involved in the infection, and your horse might need more aggressive exploration of the abscess, including surgery, with sedation and local and/or general anesthesia, and systemic antibiotics.

What you see: Your horse's hooves chip and crack when barefoot, so you shoe him. But his dry, brittle hooves can't seem to hold the nails securely, and it seems he's always throwing a shoe—and pulling more of his hoof off with it.

7-1

DRY, BRITTLE HOOVES

What this might mean: It can mean your horse's nutritional status is deficient. Or it can mean he's ingested a toxin that affects hoof growth. Dry, brittle hooves also can mean there's a low-grade infection within the hoof wall.

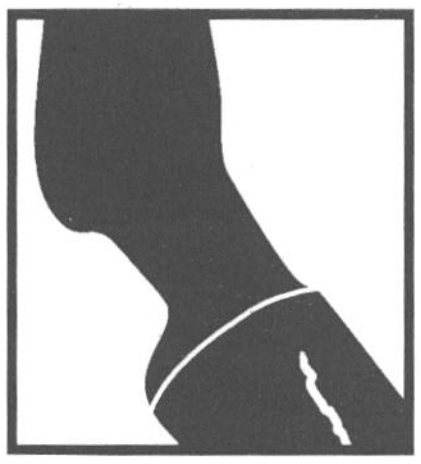

ACTION PLAN:

Is your horse in poor condition overall: thin, lacking muscle and/or stamina, unthrifty looking?

YES → Call your veterinarian *TODAY*—it could be nutritional deficiency from poor quality/quantity diet or due to an internal problem affecting his ability to digest and/or absorb nutrients.

NO ↓

Is your horse's haircoat dry and dull? Is his mane broken off? Is his tail thin and ratty?

YES → Call your veterinarian *TODAY*—it could be selenium poisoning[G].

NO ↓

Is your horse's hoof crumbly or powdery? Do his feet have a foul odor? Do his white lines appear mottled? Do his hooves feel spongey?

YES → Call your veterinarian *TODAY* if you answered yes to any of these queries—it could be an infection within the hoof wall.

NO ↓

When viewed from the bottom, is your horse's hoof wall (the portion outside the white line) thinner than the wall on a same-sized horse with healthy hooves?

YES → Apply **Home Treatment,** below.

NO ↓

Call your veterinarian for an appointment.

HOME TREATMENT:

*(See **Action Plan** to determine whether home treatment is appropriate for your horse's dry, brittle hooves. If at any time during home treatment, your answers on the action plan change for the worse, call your vet.)*

Step 1. *Evaluate your horse's diet.* Have an equine nutrition expert evaluate your horse's overall diet, paying particularly close attention to trace minerals, quantity and quality of protein, and essential amino acids. If your horse is obese, ask your veterinarian and/or equine nutrition expert for advice on a weight reducing ration, which will reduce the burden on weak hooves while improving overall nutrition.

Step 2. *Evaluate and, if necessary, change your horse's living situation.* If your horse's current environment is unhealthy for his hooves—lots of rocks, or low-lying and wet—move him to an enclosed location that's smooth, dry, and soft. A clean, mowed, grassy paddock would be ideal. Limit strenuous exercise that can stress feet; rather, keep your horse limbered up and his circulation flowing with daily controlled walks on good footing.

Step 3. *Seek expert, and frequent, farriery.* Have your horse's hooves tended to as often as every three weeks by a competent farrier who can trim, balance, and, if necessary, shoe your horse in a manner that helps hold his hooves together.

Step 4. *Supplement your horse's balanced diet.* Having adjusted your horse's diet as necessary to ensure good balance, add the following amino acids in the form of a commercial supplement formulated specifically for horses with unhealthy hoof horn: lysine, biotin, and dL-methionine. (An example of a good commercial product: Farrier's Formula®, also known as Nutritone®. Life Data Laboratories: 800-624-1873.)

Did You Know...

If you're considering giving your horse a nutritional biotin supplement to strengthen his hooves, select one that includes the amino acids dL-methionine and lysine, for optimal effectiveness. When in doubt, read the label.

NOTES

CHAPTER 8

Problems of THE SKIN AND HAIRCOAT

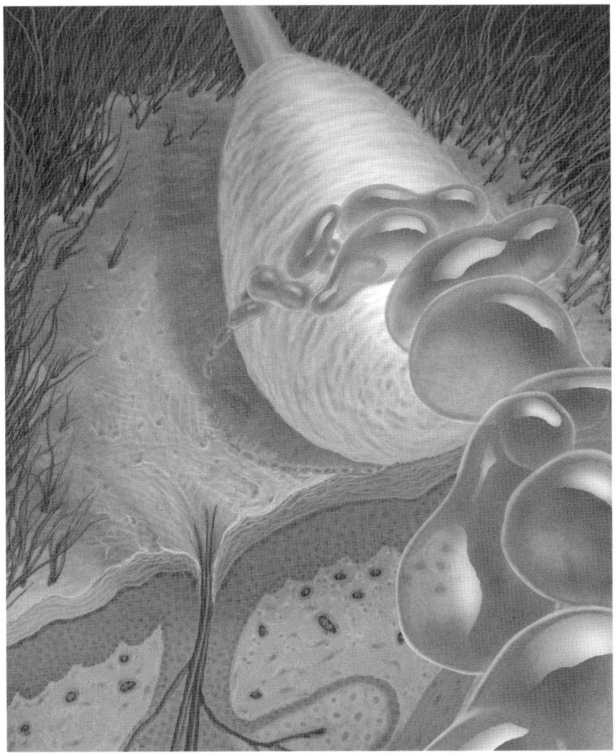

8-A

Dull, shaggy, or non-shedding HAIRCOAT

What you see: Your horse's coat looks shaggy and dull, despite your grooming efforts.

What this might mean: It can be a signpost of a serious underlying problem.

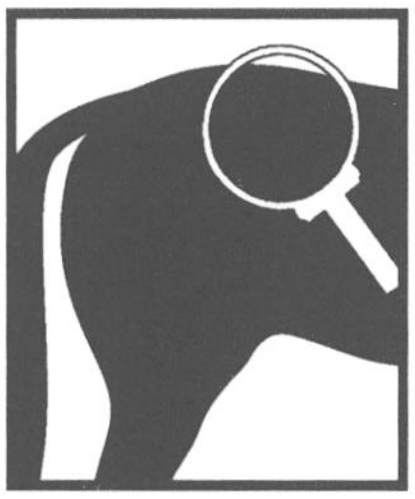

ACTION PLAN:

Is your horse's coat abnormally long? Are there long patches on his legs, withers, chest, and/or croup area? Is he swaybacked? Overweight?

YES → Call your veterinarian *TODAY* if you answered yes to any of these queries—it could be a thyroid or pituitary gland[G] problem.

NO ↓

Is your horse thin and hungry? Is his manure dotted with unchewed grain? Has it been more than 6 months since his manure was examined for worm eggs? Is he dewormed[G] infrequently or sporadically?

YES → Call your veterinarian *TODAY* if you answered yes to any of these queries—it could be malnutrition due to an unbalanced diet, dental problem, or parasite load.

NO ↓

Call your veterinarian for an appointment.

Fast Fat Fact...

If your horse has a dull haircoat, but is otherwise healthy, consider adding fat to his ration, to add luster to his coat. The essential fatty acids in fat are necessary for normal oil-gland function, making it a great tool for coat shine. But be sure to carefully monitor his body weight and condition, as fat will also fatten him up! (For how to safely add fat to your horse's ration, see page 206.)

What you see: Portions of your horse's formerly dark skin have begun to develop pink spots, which are most noticeable when he's wet.

8 - B

LOSS OF SKIN PIGMENT

(Also known as vitiligo)

What this might mean: Loss of pigmentation can follow deep injury to the skin, such as a wound, burn, or surgical procedure such as cryosurgery[G]. It's suspected to be congenital in some horses, but this hasn't been confirmed. It's also seen occasionally in association with general illnesses such as thyroid disease, anemia[G], diabetes, and pituitary tumor[G].

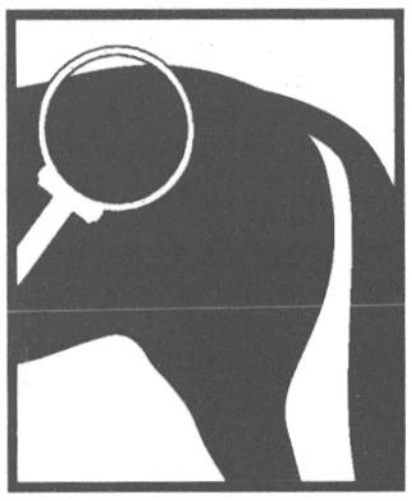

ACTION PLAN:

Is your horse off his feed, depressed, or feverish?
- **YES** → Call your veterinarian *TODAY*—it could be anemia[G], thyroid disease, or diabetes.
- **NO** ↓

Is your horse rubbing or scratching at the area?
- **YES** → Go to **page 140**.
- **NO** ↓

Is the skin in the depigmented area flaky, crusty, or scaly?
- **YES** → Go to **page 138**.
- **NO** ↓

Is your horse's haircoat dull, shaggy, or failing to shed normally?
- **YES** → Go to **page 134**.
- **NO** ↓

Call your veterinarian *THIS WEEK* for advice.

8-C

LOSS OF HAIR

What you see: Hair is missing from your horse's coat, in a single location, in broad patches, or in a moth-eaten pattern disseminated over his entire body. On closer inspection, individual hairs may or may not be broken off, and the skin in the hairless area may or may not appear irritated.

What this might mean: A cosmetic problem, at the least. It also can indicate a serious underlying problem.

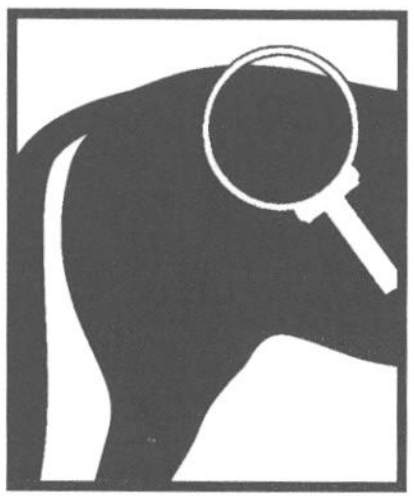

YOUR VET MAY NEED TO:

Submit skin scrapings or a biopsy to a laboratory for definitive diagnosis.

ACTION PLAN:

Is your horse rubbing or scratching at his skin?
YES → Go to **page 140**.

NO ↓

Is the hair loss in an area where his skin has been damaged previously, such as over a healed flesh wound?
YES → It's likely to be a permanent scar-related hair loss called cicatricial alopecia[G]. Call your veterinarian for advice.

NO ↓

Is the hair loss primarily at your horse's mane and tail?
YES → Call your veterinarian *TODAY*—it could be alkali disease[G].

NO ↓

Is the hairless area flaky or scaly?
YES → Go to **page 138**.

NO ↓

Is the hair loss primarily around your horse's head and neck? Does he sweat less than other horses on same work schedule and in same environment?
YES → Go to **page 149** if you answered yes to either query—it could be anhidrosis[G].

NO ↓

Does your horse shiver when the weather cools? Has he previously had bouts with tying-up syndrome[G] or laminitis[G]? Does he frequently have swollen lower legs?
YES → Call your veterinarian *TODAY* if you answered yes to any of these queries—they may seem unrelated, but each could be a sign of a thyroid problem[G].

NO ↓

Is his hair coming out in tufts, with a crust or scab at the base of each tuft? Is it coming out in circular spots of various sizes, in the saddle, girth, and/or halter region?
YES → Go to **page 138**.

NO ↓

ACTION PLAN (CONTINUED):

Is the hair loss arranged in lines along the neck and the sides of his body?

YES → Call your veterinarian *TODAY*—it could be a skin condition called linear alopecia[G].

NO ↓

Call your veterinarian *TODAY* for an appointment.

Be Careful About That Coverup...

Your horse's hair loss can affect his ability to stay warm and dry in the winter, and protected from the sun in the summer. If sunburn is a risk, keep him indoors during the day, and turn him out at night. If the weather's cool and you think your horse might be more comfortable with a sheet or blanket, first consult your veterinarian. Horse clothing can exacerbate some skin conditions.

8-D

Flaky, crusty, or SCALY SKIN

What you see: When you touch your horse's skin, you feel scabs and crust. When you curry his coat, dandruff emerges.

What this might mean: It can be a sign of a serious underlying problem.

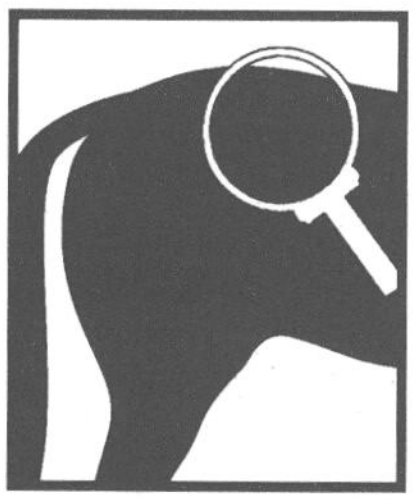

ACTION PLAN:

Does your horse scratch or rub the area?
YES → Go to **page 140**.

NO ↓

Is the problem limited to the fetlock, pastern, or heel region of his lower legs?
YES → Go to **page 123**—it could be scratches[G].

NO ↓

Is it limited to pink/hairless skin?
YES → Call your veterinarian *TODAY*—it could be light eruption[G].

NO ↓

Is your horse pure or part Appaloosa? Are there pimples and/or blisters at various sites on his body?
YES → Call your veterinarian *TODAY* if you answered yes to either query—it could be pemphigus[G].

NO ↓

Do tufts of hair pull out easily, leaving a raw spot?
YES → It sounds like rainrot[G]. Apply **Home Treatment,** below.

NO ↓

Is the saddle area affected?
YES → It sounds like ringworm[G]. Apply **Home Treatment** and take precautions to prevent the spread of this condition to you and other animals. If you're queasy about dealing with it, call your veterinarian *TODAY.*

YOUR VET MAY NEED TO:

Submit a skin biopsy for laboratory confirmation of pemphigus, or start a fungal culture (it generally takes about a week to confirm ringworm).

HOME TREATMENT:

*(See **Action Plan** to determine whether home treatment is appropriate for your horse's skin condition. If at any time during home treatment, your answers on the action plan change for the worse, call your vet.)*

Step 1. *Soften and loosen scabs.* Apply a medicated scab softener (see page 242) generously to affected skin areas. Leave on for 1 to 2 hours.

Step 2. *Apply a medicated bath.* Wet your horse. Lather him with a povidone iodine shampoo or scrub (not the surgical solution, which doesn't lather), or Nolvasan scrub (a prescription item you can obtain from your veterinarian). Let the lather stand for 10 minutes, then rinse thoroughly, gently removing as many of the scabs/loose tufts of hair as possible. (If it's too cold to bathe your horse, spot-treat affected areas.)

Step 3. *Dry, fresh air and sunshine.* Keep the skin as dry as conditions permit, avoid blanketing your horse, and maximize his exposure to fresh air and sunshine's ultraviolet rays. These measures can help control infectious organisms in the skin.

Step 4. *Keep it up, and re-evaluate.* Repeat Step 2 daily for 7 days, then continue twice a week until lesions are healed. If significant improvement is not seen in 3 days, call your veterinarian for an appointment.

Did You Know...

A horse cools when sweat evaporates from his body. When he sweats so heavily that it drips off rather than evaporates, or when the humidity is too high for easy evaporation, the fluid and electrolytes he loses in his sweat provide no cooling effect—they're simply wasted.

8-E

ITCHY SKIN

What you see: Your horse is repeatedly rubbing and scratching an itch.

What this might mean: It's not likely to signal a life-threatening problem. But the itch can be intense, and in an effort to relieve it your horse can damage his haircoat, skin, and structures near the itchy spots (eyes, for example, or joints). If the itchiness is a sign of a contagious skin problem, there's a danger the condition will spread to other horses.

ACTION PLAN:

Are there distinct, smooth bumps that look like hives or welts, with unbroken skin? Is your horse acting anxious, breathing rapidly, or wheezing?

YES → Call your veterinarian *NOW* if you answered yes to either query—it could be a severe allergic reaction called anaphylaxis[G].

NO ↓

Is the season too cool for biting insects? Do you see "moving dandruff" when you examine his skin with a magnifying glass?

YES → Call your veterinarian *TODAY*—it could be lice[G].

NO ↓

Does he have only a few, isolated, red/oozing sores?

YES → Call veterinarian *TODAY*—it could be Pythiosis[G].

NO ↓

Is your horse rubbing primarily at the base of his tail?

YES → It sounds like pinworms[G]. Apply **Home Treatment,** opposite page; Steps 3, 5, and 6.

NO ↓

Is he rubbing primarily at his lower legs?

YES → It sounds like leg mange[G]. Apply **Home Treatment;** Steps 4, 5, and 6.

NO ↓

Is the involved skin primarily on his underbelly?

YES → It sounds like Onchocerca[G]. Apply **Home Treatment;** Steps 3, 4, 5, and 6.

NO ↓

Is the itchy skin crusty, scaly, or flaky? Is it fly season?

YES → If you answered yes to both queries, it sounds like insect bites. Apply **Home Treatment;** Steps 1, 2, 5, and 6.

NO ↓

Call your veterinarian for an appointment.

YOUR VET MAY NEED TO:

Identify skin parasites under the microscope.

HOME TREATMENT:

*(See **Action Plan** to determine whether home treatment is appropriate for your horse's itchy skin. If at any time during home treatment, your answers on the action plan change for the worse, call your vet.)*

Step 1. *Minimize biting insects in your horse's environment.* If biting insects are a problem, choose one or more of the following:

- Compost manure and soiled/wet bedding at least 500 feet from your horses' living environment.
- Eliminate chronically moist areas where some insects breed.
- Use premises insecticides or pest predators to decrease pest insect population.
- Install fine screens in your barn to help keep insects out.
- Install fans to evaporate sweat and physically blow away weak-flying pests.

Step 2. *Minimize biting insects on your horse's body.*

- Apply horse-safe insecticides, following label instructions, daily for 3 days, then twice per week for 3 weeks to kill juvenile parasites as they mature (most insecticides kill only the adult skin parasites).
- Use horse-safe insect repellants on days between insecticide treatments.
- Scrape sweat and keep your horse clean (sweat and dirt attract pests).
- Outfit your horse in a fly mask and fly sheet.
- Bring him indoors during the day, and turn him out at night, when biting flies are less prevalent.

Step 3. *Eliminate external parasites that feed on blood.* Administer ivermectin or moxidectin dewormer according to your horse's body weight (see page 224) at the deworming dose indicated on the label.

Step 4. *Eliminate skin parasites from the affected area.* If mites are a problem (as in leg mange[G]), apply an equine insecticide directly to the affected area, following label instructions, daily for 3 days, then twice per week for 3 weeks to kill juvenile parasites as they mature. Use repellants on days between insecticide treatments.

Step 5. *Soothe irritated skin.* Bathe affected areas with a mild horse shampoo (such as Hylyt-efa®) to remove irritating scurf/bacteria and cool inflamed skin. After bathing, apply a topical anti-itch, anti-sting preparation, such as colloidal oatmeal (Aveeno®, 1 tablespoon per gallon of water), witch hazel (alone or in commercial preparations such as Allerderm®), calamine lotion, or zinc oxide paste. If your horse's skin is dry and flaky, top that layer with an emollient product such as a solution of Avon Skin-So-Soft® (diluted 1-to-3 in water, and spritzed from a spray bottle), Hylt-efa®, or Humilac®.

Step 6. *Remove scale and scurf.* For crusty, scaly, flaky skin conditions, clip hair from the affected areas, extending well into healthy skin around the lesion's perimeter. This will eliminate bacteria residing in the hair, and prevent the accumulation of serum or crust, which would attract more bacteria and insects.

8-F

LUMP, BUMP OR WART

On skin or ears

What you see: Your horse has one or more lumps in or under his skin. Each lump might be pea-sized, or as large as your hand.

What this might mean: At the least, it's a cosmetic problem. It could indicate an infection or previous injury in that location, or it could be a sign of a serious bodywide disorder.

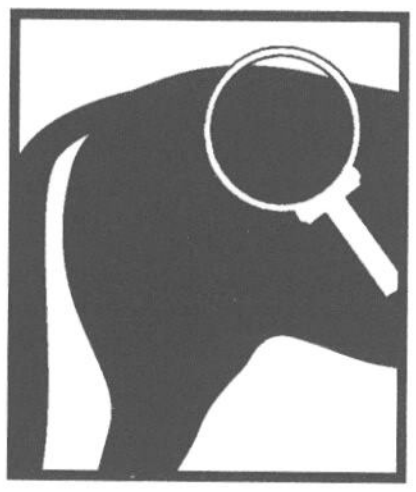

ACTION PLAN:

Are there several, distinct, smooth bumps that look like hives or welts, covered by unbroken skin? Is your horse acting anxious, breathing rapidly, or wheezing?

YES → Call your veterinarian *NOW* if you answered yes to either query—it could be hives or a severe, allergic-type reaction called anaphylaxis[G]. While you wait, go to **page 151**.

NO ↓

Is the lump where an injection was given within the past 3 days?

YES → Go to **page 144**.

NO ↓

Does the lump feel warmer than surrounding tissues? Does your horse flinch when you touch it?

YES → Call your veterinarian *TODAY*—it could be a deep bruise or abscess.

NO ↓

Is the area on a lower leg? Is it raw or ulcerated? Is it associated with a previous wound?

YES → Call your veterinarian *TODAY* if you answered yes to any of these queries—it could be proud flesh[G] or Pythiosis[G].

NO ↓

Has it been present for more than 2 weeks, with no sign of healing? Is it located at the base of his tail or around his anus, genitals, or eye? Have additional lumps appeared elsewhere?

YES → Call your veterinarian *TODAY* if you answered yes to 2 or more of these queries—it could be a tumor, sarcoid[G], cyst[G], or cattle grub[G].

NO ↓

Does the lump feel soft (like a water balloon), as though filled with fluid? Is it smaller than your open hand?

YES → It sounds like a small, superficial hematoma[G] or seroma[G]. Apply **Home Treatment,** page 105.

NO ↓

ACTION PLAN (CONTINUED):

Does the lump feel soft (like a water balloon), as though filled with fluid? Is it larger than your open hand?

YES → Call your veterinarian *TODAY*—it sounds like a large hematoma[G] or seroma[G], which might require drainage.

NO ↓

Are the lumps beige, pink, or brown, clustered around the muzzle of your young horse (less than 3 years old)?

YES → Call your veterinarian for appointment if you answered yes to either query—it sounds like warts[G].

NO ↓

Are the lumps chalky-white, flat, clustered in the ear flap of your adult horse?

YES → Sounds like aural plaques, suspected to be a viral condition carried by biting flies. They pose no health problem, and there's no treatment except prevention (use fly repellants).

NO ↓

Call your veterinarian for an appointment.

Keep Bugs at Bay...

To help control biting insects, try these tips:

• Bathe your horse every week or so, to remove sweat residue. (Sweat is a magnet for biting/stinging pests, and also contributes to overall skin itchiness.)
• Spritz him as needed with a mixture of 1 part Avon's Skin-So-Soft® bath oil to 3 parts water. (Spray him at least once a day—this mixture's not toxic.)
• Apply a fly sheet, and a fly mask equipped with ear covers.
• Provide a shady, breezy place for your horse to stand when flies are bad. (Many biting flies are active mainly where it's hot and sunny.)
• Keep him indoors during the day, and turn him out at night, when flies are less of a problem.

What you see: Your horse received an injection within the past 72 hours, and now the injection site is hot, swollen, and painful to the touch.

8-G

Hot swelling at SHOT SITE

What this might mean: It may be a minor inflammation, but it can be life-threatening if muscle tissue is infected with a particular family of bacteria, called *Clostridium*.

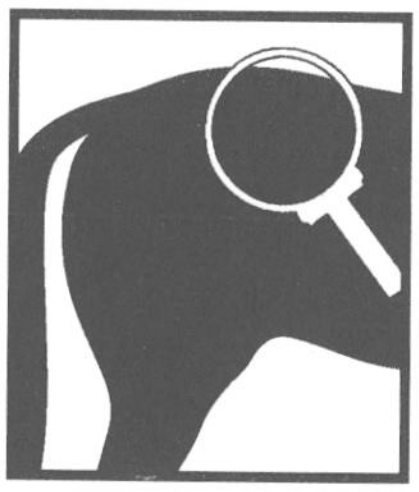

ACTION PLAN:

Has the swollen area increased in size in the past 12 hours? Is your horse off his feed and/or feverish?

YES → Call your veterinarian *NOW* if you answered yes to either query—it could be Clostridial myositis[G].

NO → It sounds like a local inflammatory reaction, rather than an infection. Apply **Home Treatment,** below.

HOME TREATMENT:

(See ***Action Plan*** *to determine whether home treatment is appropriate for your horse's hot swelling. If at any time during home treatment, your answers on the action plan change for the worse, call your vet.)*

Step 1. *Ice the area.* Select an ice pack (see page 262) large enough to extend at least 2 inches beyond the swelling's margins. Slip it between layers of a clean cloth, center it over the area, and hold it there for 5 minutes. Repeat every 15 minutes for a total of 6 treatments.

Step 2. *Massage; light exercise.* Massage the area gently with your fingertips, rubbing in the direction of the muscle fibers. Handwalk your horse to increase circulation.

Step 3. *Re-evaluate often.* At least every 4 hours, re-assess your horse's condition: Has the swelling increased in size, heat, or tenderness? Is he becoming generally ill—losing his appetite, becoming depressed, spiking a fever? If you observe any of these signs, call your veterinarian NOW.

SHOT SAVVY:

Clostridial myositis can happen anytime a drug is given via intramuscular injection. Clostridial bacteria are present everywhere in your horse's environment—in the soil, in dust, in his manure, and on his skin. If the needle carries bacteria into his tissues, an infection can result, causing tissue death, shock, and death. Treatment can be successful, but the key is recognizing the problem and treating it early, before shock sets in. By far the best recourse is to prevent Clostridial myositis by following a few simple steps when giving non-antibiotic injections to your horse.

1. If you vaccinate your own horses, don't use tank-dose vials (bottles that contain 10 doses of the vaccine).

Instead, use single-dose vials or pre-loaded, single-dose syringes, which will help minimize the risk of contamination.

2. Always use a brand-new, disposable needle and syringe for each horse and for each injection. Even if the same-horse is to receive more than 1 injection, don't re-use a needle or syringe.

3. Use a safe but effective disinfectant to swab the skin before inserting the needle. (For how to disinfect the area, see page 255.)

4. If the needle strikes a blood vessel (see page 255), pull it out before administering the dose. Using a fresh needle at a new site, try again. Loose blood within the tissues might serve as an energy source for bacteria that gain entry via the puncture.

A Word of Caution...

Injections are not the only means by which your horse can get Clostridial myositis. The causative *Clostridium* species of bacteria is known to thrive in deep, airless recesses. (The bug that causes tetanus is also a member of this family.) Puncture wounds into muscle, and contaminated incisions following castration, also can lead to Clostridial myositis. Early signs include swelling, pain and/or lameness; the first signs of advanced Clostridial myositis can include depression and loss of appetite.

8-H

CRUSTY SORES

On legs

What you see: The skin on one or more of your horse's legs is irritated, itchy, and crusted.

What this might mean: It might be an infection or parasite infestation of the skin. Or, it could be evidence of a serious internal problem.

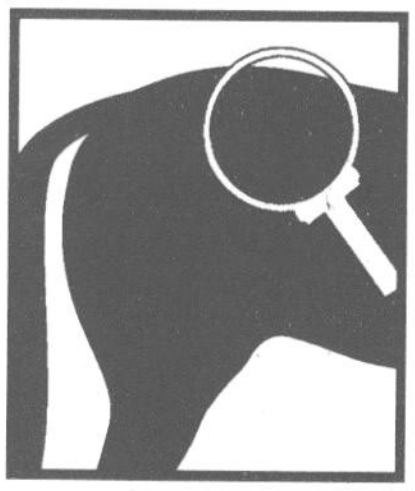

ACTION PLAN:

Are only his white legs involved?

YES → Call your veterinarian *TODAY*—it could be an internal problem called photoactivated vasculitis[G]. Go to **While You Wait,** opposite page.

NO ↓

Are the affected areas located exclusively on the fronts of your horse's hind cannon bones?

YES → Sounds like cannon keratosis[G]. Apply **Home Treatment #1,** below.

NO ↓

Does your horse stomp, rub, or chew the affected legs?

YES → It sounds like skin irritation from infection or parasite infestation, such as leg mange[G], folliculitis[G], rain rot[G], or greasy heel[G]. Apply **Home Treatment #2,** opposite page.

NO ↓

It could be ringworm[G], which can be contagious to you, your pets, and other horses. If you're queasy about dealing with this, call your veterinarian *TODAY*. Otherwise, Apply **Home Treatment #3,** opposite page.

YOUR VET MAY NEED TO:

Submit a small biopsy sample of skin to a laboratory for definitive diagnosis.

WHILE YOU WAIT:

Protect your horse's irritated skin from sunlight. Apply a moisturizing sunblock to affected areas, or bring your horse indoors.

HOME TREATMENT #1:

*(See **Action Plan** to determine whether home treatment is appropriate for your horse's hind-limb skin condition. If at any time during home treatment, your answers on the action plan change for the worse, call your vet.)*

Step 1. *Soak affected areas with medication to remove excess keratin.* Clean legs by hosing with cool water. Pat dry, then apply a human acne cream or gel containing 10 percent benzoyl peroxide (see page 237). Cover with a track wrap and confine your horse for 2 hours.

Step 2. *Wash affected areas with medicated shampoo.* Unwrap the legs, wet them, then lather affected areas with a povidone-iodine-based shampoo or surgical scrub such as Betadine®.

Step 3. *Soothe inflamed tissue.* Daub freshly

cleaned tissues with a witch hazel-soaked cotton pad.

Step 4. *Change your horse's living situation, if necessary.* Move your horse to an environment that doesn't irritate the skin of his legs, if necessary. For example, if your pasture grass is tall or infested with weeds, move him to a clean, mowed pasture.

Step 5. *Keep it up.* Repeat Steps 1 through 3 once or twice daily as needed to maintain crust-free legs. If this condition truly is cannon keratosis, the cause is unknown and affected skin tends to overreact to simple irritation, so you won't cure it—only manage it and minimize its effects.

HOME TREATMENT #2:

*(See **Action Plan** to determine whether home treatment is appropriate for your horse's infected/infested skin condition. If at any time during home treatment, your answers on the action plan change for the worse, call your vet.)*

Step 1. *Soften thickened skin, crust, and scabs.* Apply a medicated scab softener (see page 242) generously onto affected areas. Leave on for 1 to 2 hours.

Step 2. *Apply medicated bath.* Wet your horse. Lather him with a povidone-iodine shampoo or scrub (such a Betadine®) leaving the lather in contact with affected skin for 10 minutes. Rinse thoroughly. Towel dry, then allow to air dry completely before moving to Step 3. (If it's too cold to bathe your horse, spot-treat affected areas, then towel or blow-dry.)

Step 3. *Clip the area.* Clip hair from the affected area, overlapping 1/2-inch into unaffected perimeter using electric clippers and a sharp, clean, #40 blade. Be careful not to nick skin or allow the blade to become hot.

Step 4. *Eliminate external parasites.* Apply an equine insecticide labeled to be effective against the leg mange mite *Chorioptes equi.*

Step 5. *Dress the area.* Half an hour after applying insecticide, coat all affected surfaces with a diluted Betadine® solution, like weak tea, in a trigger spray bottle set for wide mist. Don't bandage unless it's absolutely necessary to keep tissues clean. The condition will respond better if left open to air.

Step 6. *Confine your horse.* For the next 2 to 3 weeks, keep your horse in an area that's clean and dry. A mowed, grassy paddock is ideal in dry weather; a cleaned rubber-floored stall with no bedding, or bedded with shredded office paper (preferable to newspaper, which contains ink) is ideal if indoor confinement is necessary. Avoid wood shavings, sawdust, and straw or hay, which contain bacteria and can poke and adhere to sensitive skin.

Step 7. *Keep it up.* Repeat Steps 1, 2, and 5 once or twice daily depending on how crusty, oozy, and/or scabby the area gets between cleanings. Re-apply insecticide according to label instructions. Expect to see improvement within 3 days; healing should occur in 2 to 4 weeks (longer in severe cases).

Step 8. *Re-evaluate every 3 days.* If heat, swelling, redness, pain, crusting, and scabbing aren't improving steadily, the list of tentative diagnoses might be missing your horse's specific condition, or your horse's inflammation and/or infection might be too deep to reach with external treatments. Call your veterinarian.

HOME TREATMENT #3:

Follow all steps as outlined in #2, omitting the insecticide.

8-1

YELLOW-TINTED SKIN

What you see: Your horse's light-colored, hairless, normally pink skin appears yellowish. Depending on his normal coloration, observable areas might include his muzzle, white legs and coronary bands, and his penis and sheath.

What this might mean: What you're seeing could be jaundice[G], which could indicate liver disease.

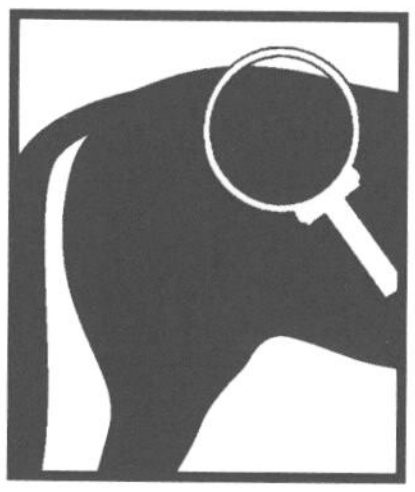

ACTION PLAN:

Is your horse off his feed, depressed, or feverish?
YES → Call your veterinarian *NOW*—it could be a serious problem such as liver disease, poisoning[G], anemia[G], or internal bleeding. Go to **While You Wait,** below.

NO ↓

Do the whites of his eyes and/or his gums appear yellow-tinged?
YES → Go to **page 54**.

NO ↓

Is the skin in the affected area oozing and/or crusty?
YES → Go to **page 138**.

NO ↓

If you wipe your horse's skin with a damp, white cloth, does the cloth turn yellow?
YES → It's pollen. You can stop worrying.

NO ↓

Call your veterinarian for an appointment.

WHILE YOU WAIT:

1. *Isolate your horse from other horses in case it's contagious.* To prevent spread of possible infectious disease, confine your horse to an open-air paddock or stall with a separate water supply, apart from other horses by at least 20 feet. Wash your hands and disinfect your boots (see page 232) after handling your horse and before handling other horses.

8 - J

Decreased amount of SWEAT

What you see: Your horse isn't sweating the way he normally does. Even when it's hot out, and even when he's working hard, the sweat doesn't seem to come, or it's scant and spotty. As a result, it takes him a long time to cool down.

What this might mean: Diminished ability to sweat is called anhidrosis[G]. It can cause your horse to become dangerously overheated, particularly if he lives and works in a hot, humid environment and/or has a physically demanding career.

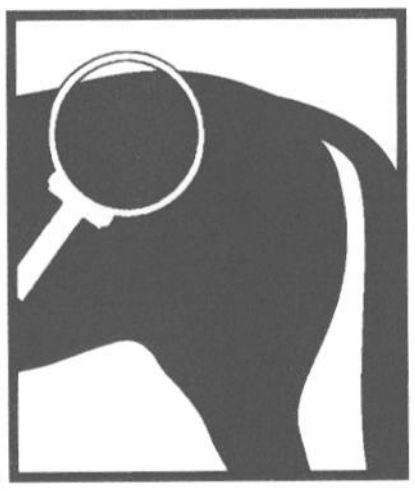

ACTION PLAN:

Is your horse in a physically demanding career?

YES → Call your veterinarian *TODAY* to have diagnosis of anhidrosis confirmed so you can plan accordingly. Go to **Home Treatment,** below.

NO → Call your veterinarian for an appointment to have diagnosis of anhidrosis confirmed. Go to **Home Treatment**.

YOUR VET MAY NEED TO:

Perform a skin testing procedure to confirm the diagnosis.

HOME TREATMENT:

*(See **Action Plan** to determine whether home treatment is appropriate for your horse's sweating problem. If at any time during home treatment, your answers on the action plan change for the worse, call your vet.)*

Step 1. *Choose activity times strategically.* Avoid strenuous activity when the sum of ambient temperature and relative humidity exceeds 120. (Example: 80 degrees F, 50 percent humidity; 80 + 50 = 130). For regular workouts in hot, humid climates, consider scheduling exercise at cooler times of the day, such as early morning or late evening.

Don't run ice-cold water over his rump and back with a hose. This could cause the blood vessels in those muscles to clench, thereby depriving those tissues of blood, which could slow the cool-down process and increase the risk of muscle cramping and/or myositis (tying-up).

Step 2. *Provide artificial sweat.* Help your horse cool down when he's warm (rectal temperature 102 degreees F or higher) by wetting him and providing air movement to facilitate evaporation: Swab him with a washcloth drenched in room-temperature or cool (not cold) water, concentrating on the areas behind and between his ears, on his forehead, the underside of his neck where the jugular vein is, in his armpits, and on his groin and underbelly. Place him in the shade where there's a natural breeze or an electric fan to encourage evaporation. Re-wet him every 5 minutes or sooner if he dries off. Continue until his temperature is below 101 degrees F.

Step 3. *Make sure his diet isn't making things worse.* Though untested in controlled scientific studies, some investigators believe that mineral deficiencies in the diet can increase your horse's risk of developing anhidrosis. And, certain feeds generate more heat than others. Have your horse's diet evaluated by an equine nutrition expert; adjust as indicated.

Step 4. *Consider a nutritional supplement.* Consider adding a commercial vitamin B supplement containing tyrosine, cobalt, and niacin. Though untested in controlled studies, limited clinical use has yielded reports of resumed sweating in confirmed anhidrotic horses after 1 week of supplementation.

Salt for Sweat...

Try this home treatment for your anhidrotic horse:

- Provide 4 tablespoons of Morton's Lite Salt® per day in his usual grain ration, divided into 2 doses. (Note: This product is a mixture of regular salt and potassium chloride, which is needed to stimulate sweating. Don't substitute with a product that's 100 percent potassium chloride.)

Watch for improvement in sweating ability within a few days to a week (the effect is cumulative). Avoid the temptation to rely on this treatment alone. Your horse still will require special management to protect him against overheating.

Keep 'Em Cool...

If your horse has anhidrosis, he may need cooling assistance even if he's idle. Check him often during warm and/or sunny conditions, for signs of elevated respiratory rate (one of the first clues of heat stress). If his breathing rate is up, bring him into the shade, wet him with cool water, and put him in front of a fan.

What you see: A forest of smooth, BB- to pea-sized bumps under your horse's skin. They usually start on the side of his neck, and in severe cases they soon appear on his face, chest, and upper front legs. As they spread, they can coalesce into large, doughy areas of swelling. Press on their centers, and your fingertip will leave a temporary depression.

What this might mean: Hives, a sign of an allergic reaction. It could be something he's eaten, something that's bitten him, something he's inhaled, or a medication you or your veterinarian gave him. Whether you realize it or not, it's something he's been exposed to before. What makes hives potentially dangerous is that they tell you your horse has become *sensitized* to the allergen, and at some point his body might react to further exposure by throwing a sort of allergic tantrum—an often fatal, body-wide reaction called anaphylaxis[G]. A horse having an anaphylactic reaction can die within hours.

8-K

HIVES

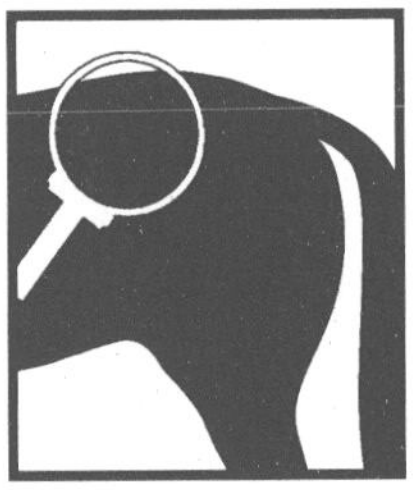

ACTION PLAN:

Is your horse wheezing, breathing rapidly, or flaring his nostrils?

YES → Call your veterinarian *NOW*—it could be an anaphylactic reaction. Go to **While You Wait,** next page.

NO ↓

Is your horse behaving anxiously, for no apparent reason?

YES → Call your veterinarian *NOW*—it could be an anaphylactic reaction. Go to **While You Wait**.

NO ↓

Does your horse have an especially noisy belly (see page 173)? Is his manure looser than normal? Is he showing any signs of colic?

YES → Call your veterinarian *NOW*—it could be an anaphylactic reaction. Go to **While You Wait**.

NO ↓

Would you like to figure out what it is he's reacting to? Is he scheduled to perform in an event that he might have to miss because of his hives?

YES → Call your veterinarian *TODAY*—skin tests and/or detective work might identify the allergen. A prescription (antihistamines and/or cortico-steroids) might hasten shrinkage of hives.

NO ↓

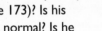

Try to minimize allergens in your horse's environment. Go to **Home Treatment,** next page.

➤

WHILE YOU WAIT:

1. *Protect yourself.* If your horse is displaying anxious behavior—pacing, whinnying, eyes open wide, nostrils flared—his judgment is impaired and he might inadvertently hurt you. Don't go near him unless you must, and if you must, be especially cautious.

2. *Improve ventilation.* If your horse is having difficulty breathing, make fresh air available. Much of the anxiety displayed in horses with anaphylaxis is the result of panic due to difficulty breathing.

Check performance schedule and drug testing rules for any events you'd planned to participate in with your horse. He might be disqualified because of medications used.

The use of corticosteroids in horses has been linked with an increased risk of laminitis[G]. The decision to administer corticosteroids to your horse should be made jointly, after you and your veterinarian have discussed potential benefits and risks.

Report all suspicions to your veterinarian.

3. *Recall all potential allergens.* Think back: can you think of anything that might have brought on this allergic response? A change in feed source? A change to different pasture? Any medications, dewormers, vaccinations, or vitamin products given? Any topical cosmetic or therapeutic substances applied to his skin? Any biting or stinging bugs noticed?

The Scoop on Protein

NRC Recommended Protein Intake:

Idle Mature Horse	8%
Growing Horse	
(weanling)	14.5%
(yearling)	12.6%
(2-year-old in training)	11.3%
Performance Horse	9.8-10.4%
Strenuous Athlete	11.4%

HOME TREATMENT:

*(See **Action Plan** to determine whether home treatment is appropriate for your horse's hives. If at any time during home treatment, your answers on the action plan change for the worse, call your veterinarian.)*

Step 1. *Reduce protein in your horse's ration to NRC recommendations (see "The Scoop on Protein").* If the roughage portion of his ration consists of alfalfa, switch to grass hay.

Step 2. Reduce potential allergens in your horse's environment. Examples:

- Switch from hay to a complete feed, to reduce dust. Or dampen hay just prior to feeding.
- Switch from shavings, sawdust, or straw bedding to shredded paper, to reduce dust.
- Switch from stall confinement and hay to pasture, to improve ventilation and reduce dust.
- Switch from arena work to outdoor exercise, to reduce dust.
- Clean your horse's indoor environment of spider webs, wasp/hornet nests, and other biting/stinging insects.
- Eliminate, minimize, or switch chemical exposure (insecticides, grooming sprays, etc.).

What you see: Your horse has a blister or sore in his armpit area, where the saddle cinch has rubbed.

8-L

GIRTH GALL/ CINCH SORE

What this might mean: A girth gall. It could be infected and/or require a minor surgical procedure to help drain out any accumulated serum, blood, or pus. Any plans to saddle your horse will have to be postponed until the sore has healed.

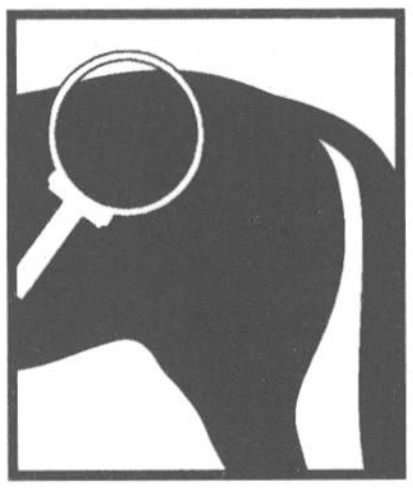

ACTION PLAN:

Can you see and feel a pocket of fluid beneath the skin, below the open sore, where it can't drain out? Does your horse refuse to let you touch it? Does it smell foul?

YES → Call your veterinarian *TODAY* if you answered yes to any of these queries—it might require surgical drainage and/or treatment for infection.

NO ↓

Apply **Home Treatment,** below.

YOUR VET MAY NEED TO:

Administer a sedative and/or pain medication to facilitate complete examination and treatment of the lesion.

HOME TREATMENT:

*(See **Action Plan** to determine whether home treatment is appropriate for your horse's girth gall. If at any time during home treatment, your answers on the action plan change for the worse, call your vet.)*

Step 1. *Ice the wound.* Select an ice pack (see page 262) large enough to extend about 2 inches beyond the wound's margins. Slip it between layers of a clean cloth, center it over the wound, and hold it there for 5 minutes.

Step 2. *Clip the wound.* After removing the ice pack, clip the hair from the sore's margins and 1 inch beyond, using a sharp, clean, #40 blade. Be careful not to nick the skin or allow the blade to become hot. If your horse's coat is long, clip any portions hanging into the wound area.

Step 3. *Clean the wound, then re-ice.* Using a garden hose, a clean, trigger-type spray bottle, or a 60-cc syringe with blunted 16-gauge needle (see page 258), irrigate the wound with clean, cool water or homemade saline solution (see page 242) for 1 full minute or until visibly clean, whichever takes longer. Repeat step 1.

Step 4. *Dress the wound.* To draw out swelling and accumulated blood/serum/pus, and to keep the wound dry and insect-free, apply a thin film of an astringent first-aid cream such as calamine lotion. If beads of serum "sweat" through the dressing, coat the skin below the wound with petroleum jelly. That way, the serum will slip off rather than accumulate, where it could attract bacteria and insects. ➤

Step 5. *Review/renew tetanus immunization.* (See page 211.)

Step 6. *Keep it up.* Repeat Steps 3 and 4 once or twice daily, depending on how dirty and/or crusty the wound gets between cleanings, until it remains dry and smooth.

Step 7. *Avoid putting tack over the area until the wound's completely healed.* Shift your horse's exercise program to bareback riding, longeing, ponying, treadmill, or swimming until new skin has covered the defect. This could take 2 to 4 weeks, depending on the sore's depth.

A Couple of Clip Tips...

Keep these safety precautions in mind when using electric clippers on your horse:

- Clip only dry hair. When clipping a wet area, the risk of electric shock to you and/or your horse is great. If you've already gotten the area wet, towel it off, and allow it to air-dry completely before clipping.
- Use a properly installed and grounded GFI (ground fault interrupt) outlet. That way, if a mishap occurs, the outlet's circuit will be interrupted and power to the clippers will be cut off.
- Stand on a dry surface while you're clipping, to reduce the risk of shock.

CHAPTER 9

Changes in your HORSE'S MANURE

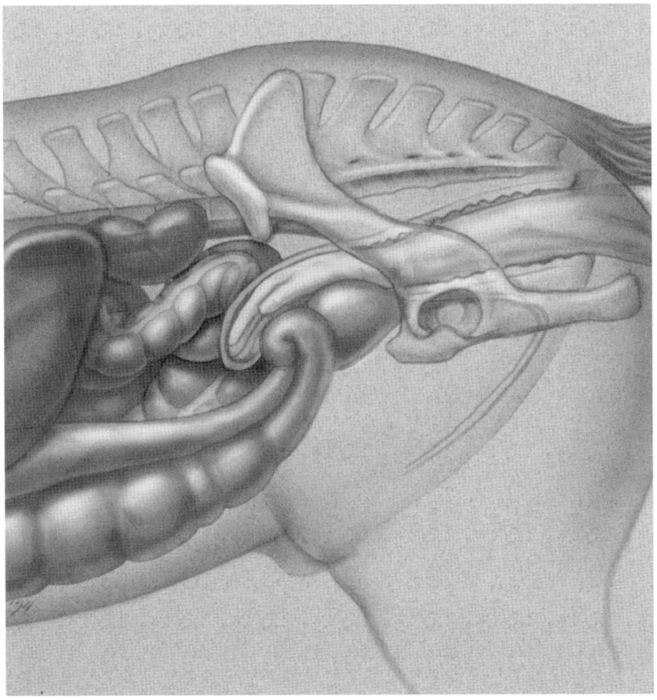

9-A

DIARRHEA

What you see: Strong-smelling, watery manure in shapeless puddles on the ground, splattered on walls, and/or dried on your horse's tail, buttocks, or hocks.

What this might mean: Massive losses of fluid, electrolytes, and protein can occur too rapidly for your horse to cope and adjust. The result: dehydration and electrolyte imbalance. Protein levels in your horse's blood can drop so low that his legs and/or lower belly wall swell with edema[G].

ACTION PLAN:

Is your horse breathing rapidly, and/or flaring his nostrils with each breath? Is he acting anxious, for no apparent reason? Do you see/feel multiple bumps under his skin?

YES → Call your veterinarian *NOW* if you answered yes to any of these queries—it could be an anaphylactic reaction[G], or a form of shock[G]. While you wait, go to **While You Wait,** opposite page.

NO ↓

Is your horse showing any signs of colic[G] (see page 176)?

YES → Call your veterinarian *NOW* for diagnosis and treatment of colic. While you wait, go to **page 178**.

NO ↓

Is your horse passing one or more watery stools per hour? Is his environment (walls, fences, etc.) splashed with watery stool? Is his manure black and/or bloody looking?

YES → Call your veterinarian *NOW* if you answered yes to any of these queries—your horse is at risk for dehydration, electrolyte depletion, and/or shock. Go to **While You Wait.**

NO ↓

Has he been passing cowpie-to-watery stool at a slightly increased frequency (up to 1-1/2 times more often than usual), or intermittently, for 3 days or more?

YES → Call your veterinarian *TODAY*—it sounds like chronic[G] diarrhea[G]. Go to **While You Wait.**

NO ↓

Does he pass abnormally wet stool only occasionally, while some scary, anxiety-producing activity or event is going on?

YES → It's probably just a case of temporary, nervous loose stool. No action is necessary unless it continues for more than an hour. (If it does repeat the Action Plan.)

NO ↓

Call your veterinarian for advice and/or an appointment.

Your horse's diarrhea might be contagious to you. Take the following precautions:

1. Wash your hands thoroughly with soap and hot water after handling your horse and/or any materials contaminated with manure (clothing, boots, gloves, stall bedding, etc.).

2. Keep your hands, gloves, and sleeves away from your face.

3. Isolate your horse from children less than 1 year of age, or from any adult with a compromised immune system.

4. Call your doctor if you or a family member shows any evidence of illness, even if it's not diarrhea.

5. Keep your pets locked up. Family members might be infected by contact with a pet that came into contact with infected manure.

WHILE YOU WAIT:

1. *Isolate your horse from other horses in case it's contagious.* To prevent spread of possible infectious disease, confine your horse to an open-air paddock or stall with a separate water supply, apart from other horses by at least 20 feet. Wash your hands and disinfect your boots (see page 232) after handling your horse and before handling other horses.

WARNING: Acute[G] diarrhea in the adult horse is often followed by an "aftershock"—laminitis[G], also known as founder. Even if your horse isn't showing any signs of laminitis now, you and your vet will have to make a judgment call about whether or not to give preventive treatment.

2. *Remove his feed.* To avoid worsening an already irritated intestinal tract, remove grain and hay from your horse's stall feeders; remove bedding if he eats it (it's not unusual for a horse with intestinal upset to eat straw or shavings).

3. *Give him the opportunity to replenish some of his fluid/electrolyte deficits voluntarily.* Provide three 5-gallon buckets of fresh, room-temperature water prepared as follows:

- One plain bucket of water.
- One mixed with a commercial electrolyte product made specifically for horses (follow label directions).
- One with 1/3 of a 1-pound box of baking soda mixed in.

9-B

Hard, small MANURE BALLS

What you see: Your horse's manure consists of manure balls that are smaller and harder than usual.

What this might mean: That his manure is too dry. The drier his manure, the greater is the chance that it'll impact within his intestines, leading to colic.

ACTION PLAN:

Is your horse showing any signs of colic[G] (see page 176)?

YES → Call your veterinarian *NOW* for diagnosis and treatment of colic. While you wait, go to **page 178**.

NO ↓

Does your horse have bloodshot eyes? Has he been losing weight lately? Does his manure have white, worm-like strands of mucus on it?

YES → Call veterinarian *TODAY*—it could be a chronic[G] intestinal and/or general illness.

NO ↓

Go to **Home Treatment,** below.

HOME TREATMENT:

(See ***Action Plan*** *to determine whether home treatment is appropriate for your horse's dry manure. If at any time during home treatment, your answers on the action plan change for the worse, call your vet.)*

Step 1. *Offer fresh drinking water, in a clean container.* If it's cold outside, or abruptly/significantly colder than it has been, offer a second bucket alongside the first, containing warm water (120 degrees F). Use a cook's thermometer to get the temperature just right.

Step 2. *Encourage your horse to drink.* (See page 228.)

Step 3. *Provide light exercise.* To stimulate gut motility and drinking, hand-walk your horse, take him for an easy walking trail ride, or provide turnout in a paddock with a companion for at least 20 minutes. Offer room-temperature water every 10 minutes during the workout.

Step 4. *Watch for signs of deterioration.* Inspect consistency and total volume of manure passed (see page 196). If there's no improvement within 8 to 12 hours, or if at any time you see new evidence of mucus, colic, or decreased manure output, call your veterinarian immediately.

WHAT CAUSES HARD, DRY MANURE?

1. Slow gut motility **2.** Dehydration[G] **3.** Partial obstruction in the intestine.

What you see: Stones, debris, baler's twine, nuts and bolts, pieces of glass, or other such foreign material in your horse's manure.

9-C

FOREIGN MATERIAL

In manure

What this might mean: If there's no foreign material still working its way through (or lodged within) your horse's intestines, then what you see in his manure is evidence that the problem is already solved. Otherwise, it's a signpost of potential trouble.

ACTION PLAN:

Is your horse showing any signs of colic[G] (see page 176)?

YES → Call your veterinarian *NOW* for diagnosis and treatment of colic. While you wait, go to **page 178**.

NO ↓

Does the object have one or more protrusions or sharp edges? Is it a linear object, such as string, twine, a stick, or a piece of wire? Does the object have red blood or a dark tarry residue on it?

YES → Call your veterinarian *NOW* if you answered yes to any of these queries—diagnosis and/or treatment for intestinal damage is needed.

NO ↓

Are you certain he's passed all of it? Are you certain it didn't originate inside his intestines, as an enterolith[G]?

NO → Call your veterinarian *TODAY*—diagnosis and/or treatment to encourage passage is warranted.

YES ↓

Call your veterinarian today for advice and/or an appointment.

The Nitty Gritty

Here are some common sources of foreign objects in your horse's manure

- **Non-food debris:** Your horse accidentally picked up a foreign object(s) when feeding on the ground; the material was accidentally incorporated into processed feed; or your horse ate it out of curiosity.

- **Stones (enteroliths[G]):** Formed by your horse's intestines around a piece of debris, these "equine pearls" are made of minerals, and can range in size from tiny pebbles to grapefruit-sized rocks.

NOTES

CHAPTER 10

UROGENITAL PROBLEMS

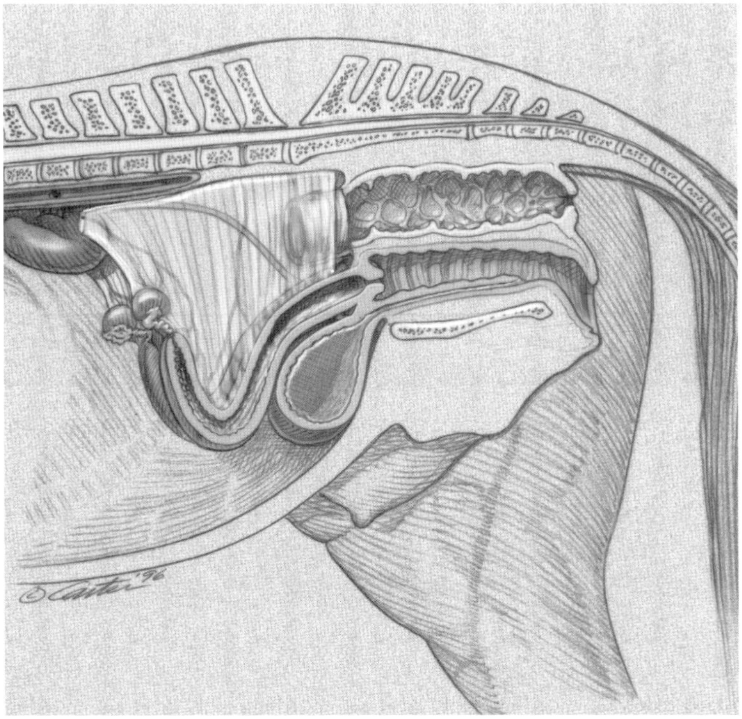

10-A

SORE OR LUMP On or near GENITALS

What you see: There's a lump of some kind—it might be covered with smooth, normal skin, or it might be raw—on or near your horse's genital area. You might not notice it until your gelding urinates, and there it is: a pink angry knob affixed to the end of his penis. Or you see it only when your maiden mare runs, when it appears between the lips of her vulva like a pink bubble, only to disappear when she stops.

What this might mean: It could be an abnormal growth, or a local inflammatory condition.

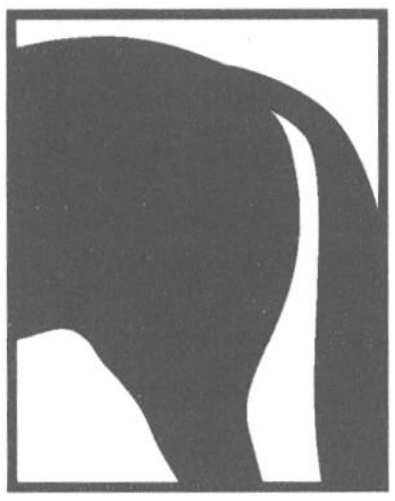

ACTION PLAN:

Is the bump located on your stallion's or gelding's penis and/or sheath? On the hairless pink skin around your horse's anus and vulva? Is it ulcerated and raw-looking?

YES → Call your veterinarian *TODAY* if you answered yes to any of these queries—it could be a cancerous growth, or a parasite infestation.

NO ↓

Is the lump(s) around your horse's anus and/or vulva, and/or on the underside of his tailhead? Is your horse white or gray?

YES → Call your veterinarian *THIS WEEK*—it could be melanoma[G].

NO ↓

Is the lump a bubble-gum pink color, appearing at your maiden mare's vulva when she runs, disappearing when she stops?

YES → Relax—that's her hymen. If you plan to have her bred, call your veterinarian for appointment to make sure it's separated before breeding.

NO ↓

Is the sore angry and raw-looking, located near your horse's anus and buttocks? Is the hair on your horse's tailhead frayed and broken?

YES → It could be pinworms[G], and to relieve his/her itchy anus your horse has rubbed raw spots. Apply **Home Treatment,** opposite page.

NO ↓

Call your veterinarian for an appointment.

HOME TREATMENT:

*(See **Action Plan** to determine whether home treatment is appropriate for your horse's lesion. If at any time during home treatment, your answers on the action plan change for the worse, call your vet.)*

1. *Administer dewormer.* Choose a dewormer with better than a 95 percent kill rate against pinworms (*Oxyuris equi*). Administer it according to your horse's weight (see page 224) and label instructions.

2. *Treat abrasions.* Inspect wounds for evidence of foreign bodies (such as splinters, from rubbing against wood) and/or blisters from chemical burns (from rubbing against treated wood). Treat wounds as detailed in appropriate chapters.

Tail Care Tip...

It takes about 2 years for your horse to grow full-length tail hairs, so any tail-rubbing he does can have long-term consequences on his appearance and fly-swatting ability. If your horse has broken the hairs at the base of his tail, try this grooming tip to improve the tail's cosmetic appearance. (And check with your veterinarian, to determine and resolve the underlying cause for your horse's tail-rubbing.)

- Wash the entire tail with a gentle shampoo to remove scurf and dirt.
- Rinse thoroughly. Add 1/4 cup white vinegar to a gallon of cool water for the final rinse, to neutralize any residual soap.
- Soak the tail base in witch hazel, to soothe irritated skin. Do not rinse out.
- Apply a tail conditioner, according to label instructions, working the product into the skin at the base of the tail hairs.
- Apply a tail wrap, smoothing all tail hairs to lie flat, tightly enough to be secure but loose enough to admit one finger at all locations. Leave in place until the hair has dried.
- Remove the wrap, and smooth the hairs in place with a wide-tooth comb or your fingers.

What you see: Your stallion's or gelding's penis has been out for longer than usual.

10-B

PROTRUDING PENIS

What this might mean: It can mean that your horse can't pull it back up into his sheath, which leaves the penis at risk of serious injury. It can mean that your horse is generally ill, and/or feeling weak. Or it can be a sign of a problem in the penis itself, or in the urinary tract.

ACTION PLAN:

Has your horse been given a sedative or tranquilizer within the past half hour?

YES → Re-evaluate in 1 hour. It's common for a horse's penis to protrude when he's relaxed or drugged.

NO ↓

Has your horse been given a sedative or tranquilizer within the past 3 days?

YES → Call your veterinarian *NOW*—it could be penile paralysis[G] due to drug reaction to certain kinds of tranquilizers. Go to **While You Wait #1,** opposite page.

NO ↓

Does your horse's penis look swollen? Does the opening of the sheath look tight around it, as though constricting it? Are there sores on it?

YES → Call your veterinarian *NOW* if you answered yes to any of these queries—it could be paraphimosis[G], which requires prompt attention to prevent serious damage. Go to **While You Wait.**

NO ↓

Is your horse off his feed, depressed, or feverish? Is he sweating, drooling, shuffling his feet, and/or trembling? Is urine dribbling from his penis? Is his anus gaping open?

YES → Call your veterinarian *NOW* if you answered yes to any of these queries—it could be botulism[G], colic[G], or a disease of the nervous system (such as polyneuritis[G]). Go to **While You Wait**.

NO ↓

Is your horse standing stretched-out, as though about to urinate? Does he fail to urinate, or urinate small amounts, more often than usual? Is there blood in his urine? Is there blood on the tip of his penis?

YES → Call your veterinarian *NOW* if you answered yes to any of these queries—it could be a blockage or infection in the urethra[G] or bladder[G], or it could be colic. While you wait, go to **page 178**.

NO ↓

Call your veterinarian *TODAY.*

WHILE YOU WAIT:

1. *Minimize the damage.* Unless your horse is showing signs of severe colic (see page 176, confine him to a shaded stall or shed, where there's less chance of irritation and trauma to the penis from insects, accidental kicking, contamination, and contact with abrasive materials. (If he wants to lie down and roll due to colic pain, confinement could increase risk of injury. Move him to an open area with soft ground, such as a small paddock.) If he's having trouble with his equilibrium, remove protruding objects from the area, and keep noises to a minimum, to avoid startling him.

2. *Isolate your horse from other horses in case it's contagious.* To prevent spread of possible infectious disease, be sure the paddock or stall has a separate water supply, and is apart from other horses by at least 20 feet. Wash your hands and disinfect your boots (see page 232) after handling your horse and before handling other horses.

Just Say Whoa...

Stallions are more susceptible to drug-related penile paralysis than geldings. This is believed to relate to the presence of the hormone testosterone. If your gelding is a cryptorchid (one testicle is retained in his abdomen), and the retained testicle has not been located and removed, the testosterone produced by that testicle increases his risk of penile paralysis related to phenothiazine drugs, such as acepromazine ("ace"). This would be an important fact to post prominently on his stall card, in case your horse should need treatment in your absence. Say simply, "No ace!"

What you see: Your horse's urine is an abnormal color, and/or his urinating behavior has changed (for example, he's assuming the position more often, and/or for longer periods of time, but passing a smaller volume than usual).

10-C

URINE/URINATING ABNORMALLY

What this might mean: That there's a problem in your horse's urinary tract, or elsewhere in his body that's creating signposts that mimic urinary tract discomfort.

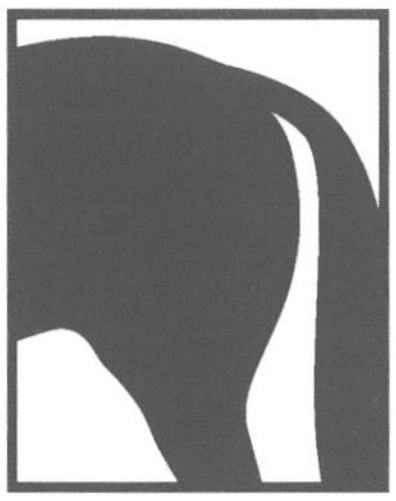

ACTION PLAN:

Is your horse straining to urinate (stretching out in the urinating stance) more often than usual, and sustaining it longer than usual, but only a meager stream of urine dribbles out?

YES → Call your veterinarian *NOW*—it could be colic[G], or a urinary tract blockage, which can be fatal if not treated promptly.

NO ↓

Is your horse assuming the typical urinating stance more often than usual? Is he passing a normal stream of urine each time (normal pressure, flowing freely), even though the total volume might be less than usual?

YES → Call your veterinarian *NOW* if you answered yes to both queries—it could be a urinary tract infection.

NO ↓

Is your horse dribbling urine even when he's not trying to urinate?

YES → Call your veterinarian *NOW*—it could be an injury or disease in his nervous system, such as spinal injury, encephalitis[G], cauda equina syndrome[G], rhino neuritis[G], or sorghum poisoning[G].

NO ↓

Is your horse's urine red-tinged or bloody? If your horse is a mare, is her tail blood-stained?

YES → Call your veterinarian *NOW* if you answered yes to either query—it could be an infection, stones, or a tumor within the kidneys or bladder, or varicose veins in the vagina.

NO ↓

ACTION PLAN (CONTINUED):

Is your horse's urine coffee-brown? Have you observed urine with that coloration coming out of your horse?

YES → Call your veterinarian *NOW* if you answered yes to both queries—your horse may have suffered muscle damage (either from an injury, or from a muscle disease such as tying-up[G]); he may have a type of anemia[G]; or he may have ingested a toxin.

NO ↓

Do you see red, orange, or brown urine spots in the snow, but you haven't actually observed abnormal-colored urine coming out of your horse?

YES → Continue this chart—unless you see other signs of abnormality, it could be a normal color change that's known to occur with equine urine on snow.

NO ↓

Is your horse producing more urine and/or drinking more water than usual? Is his coat dull, overlong, or failing to shed?

YES → Call your veterinarian *TODAY* if you answered yes to either query—it could be kidney disease, or a problem with the pituitary gland[G].

NO ↓

Is your horse's urine creamy-looking?

YES → Call your veterinarian *TODAY*. Horse urine often looks creamy, depending on its protein, calcium, and normal mucus content and (in mares) depending on heat cycles. But a kidney infection can cause pus in your horse's urine, so if this is the first time you've noticed the urine looking creamy, consult your veterinarian.

Did You Know...

One unique aspect of horses is the way their bodies handle excess dietary calcium: Whereas other animals excrete the excess in their feces, horses process it through their kidneys and excrete it in urine. This can set the stage for the formation of kidney and bladder stones and is one reason alfalfa (which is higher in calcium than other forages) is not the best choice for your horse's main roughage source.

NOTES

CHAPTER 11

A guide to MISCELLANEOUS SYMPTOMS

11-A

FEVER

What you see: You thought your horse felt excessively warm or seemed depressed, so you took his temperature and found that he's got a fever—it's higher than his normal range (see page 199, and "A Matter of Degrees," on opposite page).

What this might mean: It can be a sign of infectious disease, drug reaction, or heat exhaustion.

ACTION PLAN:

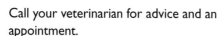

Take your horse's temperature again, using a different thermometer. Fever confirmed?

→ NO: Time for a new thermometer!

↓ YES

Has your horse been exercising, either free or controlled, within the past hour?

→ YES: Walk your horse for 30 minutes to cool him, then re-check his temperature. Still high? If so, continue this chart.

↓ NO

Is it hot outside? Is your horse in the sun? Are other horses sweating, while your horse is not? Is the sum of ambient temperature + relative humidity greater than 120?

→ YES: Call your veterinarian *NOW* if you answered yes to 2 or more of these queries—it could be heat exhaustion[G] and/or anhidrosis[G]. Go to **While You Wait,** opposite page.

↓ NO

Is your horse a mare that foaled within the past 72 hours? Or within the past 2 months?

→ YES: Call your veterinarian *NOW* if you answered yes to either query—it could be acute[G] endometritis[G] or lactation tetany[G], respectively.

↓ NO

Has your horse been vaccinated or treated with any medication within the past 24 hours?

→ YES: Call your veterinarian *NOW*—it could be a mild reaction to a live vaccine, or a dangerous reaction known as malignant hyperthermia[G].

↓ NO

Within the past 3 weeks, has your horse had contact with a sick horse?

→ YES: Call your veterinarian *TODAY*—your horse could be coming down with an infection.

↓ NO

Call your veterinarian for advice and an appointment.

WHILE YOU WAIT:

1. *Cool your horse.* If the ambient temperature is 80 degrees F or above, swab your horse with a washcloth drenched in room-temperature or cool (not cold) water, concentrating on the areas behind and between his ears, on his forehead, on the underside of his neck where the jugular vein is, in his armpits, and in his groin and underbelly. Don't run ice-cold water over his rump and back with a hose. This could cause the blood vessels in those muscles to clench, thereby depriving those tissues of blood, which could slow the cool-down process and increase the risk of muscle cramping and/or myositis (tying-up[G]). Place him in the shade where there's a natural breeze or position him in front of a fan to encourage evaporation. Re-wet him every 5 minutes or whenever he dries off.

A Matter of Degrees...

A fever occurs when your horse's hypothalamus, which regulates his body temperature, adjusts his "thermostat" such that he'll tolerate higher temperatures before cooling mechanisms kick in. This allows his body to battle invading organisms, by creating a hot, unfriendly environment for them—his body is literally trying to burn them out. His temperature also is a good indicator of his health. When you think something's wrong with your horse, one of the first questions your veterinarian is likely to ask is,"What's the horse's temperature?" Here's what those degrees can mean.

Temperature	Possible Causes
105 or higher	Serious viral infection; heat stroke
102 to 104.5	Post-exercise heat; at rest, pain, inflammation, or mild infection
99.5 to 101.5	Normal
97.5 to 99	Mild to moderate shock; hypothermia
97 or below	Severe shock

11-B

ROLLING

What you see: Your horse is rolling.

What this might mean: It could be that your horse is scratching his back, dusting himself for protection against insects, and generally letting his hair down. It also could be a sign of colic[G] pain.

ACTION PLAN:

Does your horse stand up after the roll? Does he shake off, like a wet dog, after he stands up? Does he resume grazing, if he's in pasture? Or, if in a drylot or stall, does he view his environment with interest (ears forward, eyes bright?)

YES → If you answered yes to two or more of these queries, relax—it was probably a normal back-scratching roll. Check him again in 10 minutes.

NO ↓

Call your veterinarian *NOW*—it could be colic. While you wait, go to **page 178**.

When Bugs are Bugging Him...

Frequent rolling in a horse that's not colicky could be a sign that the flies are driving him buggy. Rolling in dust or mud is an age-old method horses use to defend themselves against insect onslaught. To help your horse gain the upper hand without having to over use potentially toxic repellants or insecticides, try these tips:

• Bathe your horse every week or so, to remove sweat residue. (Sweat is a magnet for biting/stinging pests, and also contributes to overall skin itchiness.)
• Spritz him daily with a mixture of 1 part Avon's Skin-So-Soft® bath oil to 3 parts water. (Spray him at least once daily—the mixture's not toxic.)
• Apply a fly sheet, and a fly mask equipped with ear covers.
• Provide a shady, breezy place for him to stand when flies are bad. (Many biting flies are active mainly where it's hot and sunny.)
• Keep him indoors during the day, and turn him out at night, when flies are less of a problem.

What you hear: Your horse's belly is gurgling so loudly that you can hear it from several paces away. When you listen with a stethoscope (see page 201), the growling and gurgling are almost constant, no matter where on his abdomen you listen. He may or may not be passing more gas than usual.

What this might mean: It's possible for your horse to have a lot of gurgling and growling if he's just eaten and his gut is mixing and moving feed and liquids through the digestive system. However, loud gut noises can indicate that the amount of intestinal activity and/or fluid within his intestines is excessive, due to eating a too-large meal; eating something toxic, irritating, or too rich; or intestinal infection. And lots of gas can mean there's been a change in the bacterial population living in your horse's gut, either due to infection or because he got into the grain bin and over-ate.

11-C

EXCESSIVELY NOISY BELLY

and/or lots of gas

ACTION PLAN:

Is the manure your horse passed within the past hour abnormal in any way?
YES → Go to **page 156** and **page 158.**

NO ↓

Does your horse have a fever?
YES → Go to **page 170**.

NO ↓

Is your horse showing signs of colic[G] (see page 176)?
YES → Go to **page 178**.

NO ↓

Within the past 24 hours, has your horse had access to a creep feeder, grain room, poisons, unlimited alfalfa, a change in feed, cold drinking water after strenuous exercise, lush pasture, or toxic weeds?
YES → Call your veterinarian *NOW* if you answered yes to any of these queries—signs of discomfort might not show up until it's too late for treatment to be effective.

NO ↓

Has your horse received any medication within the past 2 days? Do you see/feel multiple bumps under his skin that you hadn't noticed before?
YES → Call your veterinarian *NOW* if you answered yes to either query—it could be an anaphylactic[G] reaction. Go to **While You Wait,** page 152.

NO ↓

CONTINUED ⇨

ACTION PLAN (CONTINUED):

Within the past 3 weeks, has your horse had contact with other horse(s) with a history of recent illness such as Potomac horse fever[G], Salmonellosis[G], or unspecified colitis[G]?

YES → Call your veterinarian *TODAY*—it could be the early stages of an intestinal infection.

NO ↓

Take your horse through this decision chart again in 1 hour. Still overly gurgly? Call your veterinarian for advice and/or an appointment.

Did You Know...

One of the most common causes of digestive upset and colic is a too-rapid change in your horse's diet. When making a change in the grain portion of his ration, introduce the new feed in small amounts. As a rule of thumb, add no more than 1/2 cup of the new feed on the first day, divided among your horse's two or three daily meals. Gradually increase the amount in small increments, taking three weeks or longer to complete the switch.

What you see: Your horse didn't eat all (or any) of his ration. Maybe he ate the hay, or part of it, but left the grain. Maybe he didn't touch a bite.

What this might mean: It could indicate a simple problem. It's not uncommon for a horse to defecate accidentally into his grain bucket, making his grain unappetizing. Or rodents or scavenger birds might have gotten into his dinner bucket while he was out to pasture, leaving unappetizing bits of feces in his grain. But true loss of appetite can be one of the first signs that he's not feeling well. It's a sign you should never ignore.

11-D

OFF FEED

ACTION PLAN:

Does your horse have a fever?

YES → Call your veterinarian *NOW*—it could be early stages of a viral or bacterial disease. Go to **While You Wait,** below.

NO ↓

Does your horse show interest in food—ears perked, eyes bright—then refuse to eat it, even though other horses will eat it (meaning there's nothing wrong with the feed itself)?

YES → Call your veterinarian *NOW*—it could be a problem that makes eating painful (an infected tooth, mouth sores, or a jaw injury). Or, it could be something that makes eating impossible, such as a neurological problem, or tetanus[G].

NO ↓

Call your veterinarian *NOW*—it could be colic[G]. (Go to **page 176**.)

WHILE YOU WAIT:

1. *Isolate your horse from other horses in case it's contagious.* To prevent spread of possible infectious disease, confine your horse to an open-air paddock or stall with a separate water supply, apart from other horses by at least 20 feet. Wash your hands and disinfect your boots (see page 232) after handling your horse and before handling other horses.

What you see: Any of the signs outlined on the Colic Symptom Checklist on the opposite page. (For Information on how to identify and interpret behavior and vital signs, see pages 196 and 198.)

What this might mean: "Colic" is not a diagnosis. It's merely a collection of signs that usually mean "belly ache." With few exceptions, colic pain means there's a problem in your horse's digestive system. The seriousness is not necessarily dictated by the level of pain you see at this moment. A horse showing Level 3 discomfort might be about to pass a harmless gas bubble and be fine, or he might be heading for higher levels of pain and endotoxic shock[G]. Right now you have no way of knowing which road he's going to take.

11-E

COLIC

ACTION PLAN:

Are your horse's current symptoms limited to Level 1? **YES** → Call your veterinarian *NOW*—it could be early stages of colic, or later stages involving the large intestine, which often causes milder signs (though it's not necessarily less serious). Go to **While You Wait,** page 178.

NO ↓

Are your horse's current symptoms no higher than Level 2? **YES** → Call your veterinarian *NOW*—fast treatment could halt absorption of endotoxins[G] through the lining of the affected intestines. Go to **While You Wait**.

NO ↓

Have your horse's current symptoms reached Level 3? **YES** → Call your veterinarian *NOW*—your horse is showing early signs of poisoning from absorption of endotoxins[G]. Go to **While You Wait**.

NO ↓

Have your horse's current symptoms reached Level 4? **YES** → Call your veterinarian *NOW*—signs could indicate circulatory shutdown[G] from endotoxic shock[G]. Go to **While You Wait**.

NO ↓

Have your horse's current symptoms reached Level 5? **YES** → Call your veterinarian *NOW*—it'll take fast, aggressive, intensive care to save your horse's life.

YOUR VET MAY NEED TO:

Perform a belly tap[G]. Fluid that's free within the belly is sampled by passing a needle through the lower belly wall; analysis of that fluid can help determine your horse's prognosis and whether he's a candidate for surgery.

Colic Symptom Checklist

What you see	Level 1 Colic Pain (mild)	Level 2 Colic Pain (moderate)	Level 3 Colic Pain (severe, early)	Level 4 Colic Pain (severe, advanced)	Level 5 Colic Pain (severe, grave)
Attitude	Sleepy; behaves almost normally if stimulated.	Preoccupied; pays attention if interrupted but slips back into preoccupied state if left alone.	Anxious, pays attention only briefly if interrupted.	Consumed with pain; oblivious to surroundings.	Stuporous; unresponsive.
Up or down?	Stands or lies down quietly.	Repeatedly lies down and gets up.	Occasionally lies down and rolls.	Crashes to the ground without warning.	Down; won't get up.
Possible signs of pain	May yawn frequently.	Swishes or wrings tail; stretches neck; turns to look at flanks; paws; stomps hind feet.	Sweats; kicks at belly; bites at flanks.	Violent thrashing.	No apparent pain connection; "beyond pain."
Heart rate	45 to 50 beats per minute.	50 to 55 beats per minute.	55 to 65 beats per minute.	65 to 100 beats per minute.	over 100 or irregular.
Gum color	Normal to slightly pale.	Normal to bright pink.	Reddish or bluish.	Muddy colored.	White to muddy.
Capillary refill time	Normal (1 to 1-1/2 seconds).	1-1/2 to 2 seconds.	2 to 3 seconds.	3 seconds or longer.	Over 3 seconds.
Gut sounds	Variable; gas "ping" sounds mean call your vet.	Variable; gas "ping" sounds mean call your vet.	Variable; gas "ping" sounds mean call your vet.	Usually quiet; short blurps and/or pings might be heard.	Usually quiet; short blurps and/or pings might be heard.

Note: There may be some overlap between signs shown at the various levels.

➤

The Big Fallacy:
Keep your colicking horse walking.

Fact: In a mild to moderate colic, walking your horse might help move bubbles of gas and/or jostle loops of bowel back into their correct positions. But if your horse is intent on lying down, you're not going to be helping the situation by slapping, whipping, kicking, or shouting at him to get up and keep moving. You'll only be adding stress on an already stressful situation, and forcing him to expend energy he'll need to get well. If walking seems to help your horse feel better, walk on. If it's a struggle to keep him on his feet, let him lie down. If he'll lie quietly, all the better. If he's intent on thrashing, no amount of physical abuse is going to stop him, and you might get yourself hurt trying. Instead, do what you can to protect him (without getting hurt yourself): Go to **While You Wait,** below.

WHILE YOU WAIT:

Level 1. *Remove all feed.* Remove grain and hay from stall feeders; remove bedding if your horse eats it (it's not unusual for a horse with mild intestinal upset to eat straw or shavings). Leave his water.

Levels 2 to 5. *If your horse wants to roll or thrash, protect him (and his human attendants).*

- To keep your horse from hurting himself, and to make it easier for human attendants to stay out of harm's way: Re-bed his stall with extra-deep bedding; line stall walls with 1 or 2 layers of hay or straw bales; and remove all movable protrusions (movable feeders, buckets).
- Or, remove him to an arena or grassy paddock with obstacles removed.
- Replace his standard halter with a padded one (such as a fleece-lined travel halter), so the halter's hardware won't damage facial nerves if he falls.
- Unless your horse is thrashing (which would make this too dangerous for you), apply padded shipping bandages to his legs, and a padded crash helmet[G] to his head, if he's accustomed to them.
- If it can be done safely, check and record baseline statistics every 5 minutes and provide the data to your veterinarian.
- If your horse is insured (mortality or major medical), call your insurance agent and report that he's colicking. Be sure to familiarize yourself with the policy before a crisis, so you know what's required to comply.

What you see: Perhaps your horse is moving more slowly than usual. Perhaps he's less interested than usual in activities around him. In pasture, his efforts to keep with the herd may seem halfhearted. He'll rise to an occasion, but is quick to slip back into neutral gear, uninterested in his environment and socially withdrawn. When left alone, he seems content to stand still, lower lip drooping and head hanging, eyelids at half-mast as though he's dead tired. This is where knowledge of your horse's baseline behavior is invaluable (see page 196).

11-F

Dull, depressed ATTITUDE

What this might mean: It can signify that your horse is experiencing mild to moderate physical pain and is distracted by it. Or, it might be exactly what it appears to be: mental dulling, due to a problem in the brain.

ACTION PLAN:

Does your horse have a fever?

YES → Call your veterinarian *NOW*—it could be an infectious illness. Go to **While You Wait #1,** next page.

NO ↓

Do you see evidence of trauma—wounds, swellings, lameness, or resentment to finger pressure? Does he refuse to move? Is his head tilted? Tail pulled to one side?

YES → Call your veterinarian *NOW* if you answered yes to any of these queries—it could be severe pain, mental confusion, or loss of balance due to injury or disease. Go to **While You Wait #2,** next page.

NO ↓

Does your horse have an abnormally noisy, or abnormally quiet, belly? Is his gum color and/or capillary refill time abnormal? Is his heart rate elevated? Appetite decreased? Is he sweating?

YES → Call your veterinarian *NOW* if you answered yes to any of these queries—it could be colic. While you wait, go to **page 178**.

NO ↓

Does he walk with a shuffling gait? Is he trembling? Is he staggering as though drunk?

YES → Call your veterinarian *NOW* if you answered yes to any of these queries—it could be weakness from injury or disease. Go to **While You Wait #2**.

NO ↓

CONTINUED

ACTION PLAN (CONTINUED):

Check your horse again in 15 minutes. Any improvement? Has he shown any encouraging signs, such as eating, drinking, passing manure, and/or flicking at flies?

YES → Re-evaluate once more. If all seems well, relax. It might have been nothing, or it might have resolved itself. Plan to check on him often over next few hours to be sure.

NO ↓

If you find anything abnormal, refer to the appropriate chapter, and call your veterinarian.

WHILE YOU WAIT #1:

1. *Isolate your horse from other horses in case it's contagious.* To prevent the spread of possible infectious disease, confine your horse to an open-air paddock or stall with a separate water supply, apart from other horses by at least 20 feet. Wash your hands and disinfect your boots (see page 232) after handling your horse and before handling other horses.

CAUTION

Among the possible causes of nervous system disease causing nerve dysfunction is a rare but notorious one: Rabies. Don't take chances—take precautions. (See page 34.)

WHILE YOU WAIT #2:

1. *Avoid moving your horse (unless your veterinarian instructs you to do so).* If he's weak, dizzy, or in pain, forced movement might do significant harm. If at all possible, provide confinement by erecting portable corral panels around him, or stay with him until the vet arrives. Bring fresh water to him, as he might not have been able to get to a water source on his own.

2. *Protect yourself.* A weak or dizzy horse can stagger or fall without warning. Stay alert and out of harm's way.

WEIGHT LOSS

What you see: Your horse is losing weight and/or body condition. (For how to assess your horse's body weight and condition, see page 224.)

What this might mean: It can mean one of a full spectrum of problems, ranging from something as simple as an inadequate quantity/quality diet for current needs, to cancer.

ACTION PLAN:

Are two or more of the following true?
- Your horse's ribs are visible.
- His spine is prominent.
- There's a prominent bony bump at the tailhead.
- His haircoat is unthrifty.
- He's been looking thinner for 4 weeks or more.

YES → It might be an unhealthy loss of weight. Continue this chart.

NO ↓

Does your horse mouth his feed without picking it up, as though he can't eat? Does his face droop or grimace? Does food fall out of his mouth, or out his nostrils?

YES → Call your veterinarian *NOW* if you answered yes to any of these queries—it could be a problem in his nervous system. See **Caution**, page 183.

NO ↓

Is your horse's appetite decreased? Is he acting depressed? Is he feverish?

YES → Call your veterinarian *TODAY* if you answered yes to any of these queries—it could be chronic[G] pain and/or illness.

NO ↓

Has your horse been given pain-killing medication during the past two months?

YES → Call your veterinarian *TODAY*—use of many pain-killing medications such as bute can cause inflammation and/or ulcers in your horse's intestinal tract.

NO ↓

Is your horse's manure abnormal?

YES → Go to **page 155**.

NO ↓

Does your horse eat more slowly than usual? Does he tilt his head while eating? Has he been quidding[G]? Is his manure peppered with unchewed grain?

YES → Call your veterinarian *TODAY* if you answered yes to any of these queries—it could be a dental or jaw problem. Go to **page 34**.

NO ↓

CONTINUED

ACTION PLAN (CONTINUED):

Can you agree to all these statements?
- Your horse's diet is the same as it was last year at this time, and his weight was fine then.
- His activity level is the same as it was last year at this time, and his weight was fine then.
- Other horses eating the same diet look fine.
- He has access to all the fresh water he wants.

YES → Have your horse's ration evaluated and adjusted by an equine nutrition expert, based on your horse's age, activity level, and condition. Continue this chart.

NO ↓

Is your horse fed/watered in a group?

YES → Observe at feeding time; if necessary feed/water your horse separately, free of competition and stress. Continue this chart.

NO ↓

Is any of the following true?
- It's been 6 months or longer since your horse's manure has been checked for worm eggs by a veterinarian.
- The pasture/paddock is, or was within the past 20 years, heavily grazed by horses, ponies, donkeys and/or mules.
- Your horse spent time within the past 3 months at another facility.

YES → Have a fresh manure sample examined today for parasite infestation.

NO ↓

Apply **Home Treatment,** below. If no improvement is seen within 6 weeks, call your veterinarian for an appointment.

HOME TREATMENT:

(See ***Action Plan*** *to determine whether home treatment is appropriate for your horse's weight loss. If at any time during home treatment, your answers on the action plan change for the worse, call your vet.)*

Step 1. *Eliminate internal parasites.* Administer a purge dewormer such as ivermectin or moxidectin according to your horse's estimated weight (see page 224) and the instructions on the label. Consider treatment with a daily dewormer product such as pyrantel tartrate (Strongid C®).

Step 2. *Increase calories without increasing carbohydrate intake.* Assuming you've gone through the decision chart and ruled out a physical problem and a dietary imbalance with your horse, it's possible he simply needs more calories. Provide free-choice grass hay of good quality. Add 1/4 cup of vegetable or corn oil to his regular ration twice daily for one week, and monitor his manure output: If no manure softening occurs during that week, increase the oil volume by 1 tablespoon every 2 days until oil volume equals 1/2 cup twice a day. If at any time your horse's manure becomes loose, decrease oil to previous level. Re-evaluate your horse's body condition after 6 weeks. If no improvement is seen, call your veterinarian for an appointment. (Notice that the grain ration remains unchanged—the goal is to increase calories without a disproportionate increase in carbohydrates, in order to avoid carbohydrate-associated diseases such as laminitis[G] and colic[G].)

Beware: Among the possible causes of nervous system disease causing nerve dysfunction is a rare but notorious one: Rabies. Don't take chances—take precautions. **(See page 34.)**

Maturity Matters...

As your horse enters the realm of senior citizenship, he'll be more prone to injury and illness, due to a decrease in flexibility and a gradual decline in immune system competence. And, he may lose status within his social circle. When age starts encroaching on well-being, a horse's social niche can erode, and lower herd members sense it. This sets the stage for conflict (and injury) as younger horses increasingly issue challenges in an attempt to improve their social status. If you see your horse becoming involved in such conflicts, separate him from any top-dog wannabes before somebody gets hurt.

NOTES

CHAPTER 12

Miscellaneous symptoms causing ABNORMAL MOVEMENT

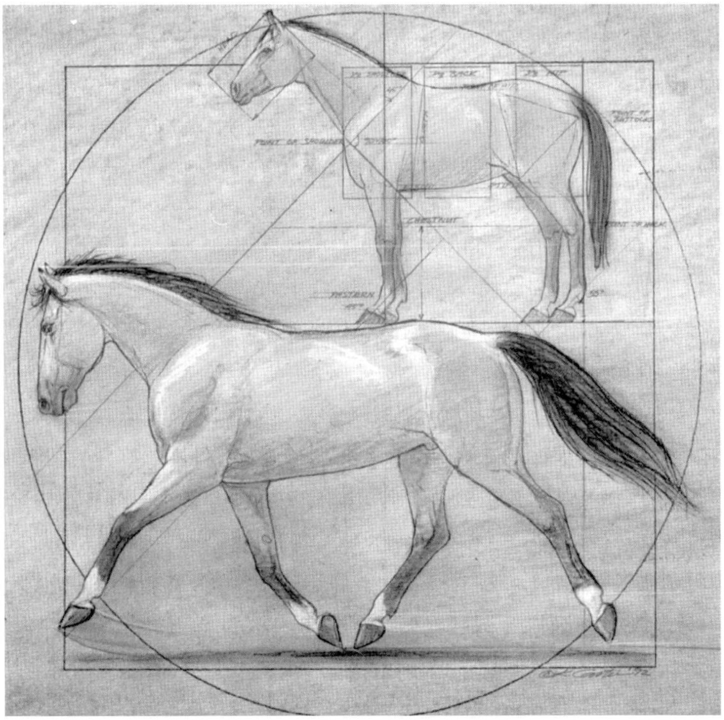

12-A

BIZARRE GAIT

What you see: Your horse is walking with a strange gait: He may stagger as though drunk, shuffle his feet as though weak, or move his legs in a spastic, jerky way, lifting them up too high, and slapping them down too hard.

What this might mean: The problem could be neurological or muscle-related. Or, it could be due to a genetic condition called HYPP[G], found in some Quarter Horses.

ACTION PLAN:

Does your horse seem mentally abnormal (demented, aimless, circling, excitable, or unresponsive)?

YES → Call your veterinarian *NOW*—it could be injury/swelling in the brain or poisoning. Go to **page 190**. See **Caution**, page 34.

NO ↓

Is your horse off his feed, depressed, or feverish?

YES → Call your veterinarian *NOW*—it could be an infectious disease. Go to **While You Wait #1,** opposite page.

NO ↓

Is your horse's gait consistently and/or progressively spastic/jerky or staggering/weak?

YES → Call your veterinarian *NOW*—it could be neurological, a muscle problem, or poisoning.

NO ↓

Is more than one leg affected?

YES → Call your veterinarian *NOW*—it could be a spinal cord problem.

NO ↓

Is only one leg involved?

YES → Call your veterinarian *NOW*—it could be injury or illness in a nerve.

NO ↓

Is your horse having distinct episodes of weakness, stumbling, and muscle trembling, but he's normal between these bouts? Does he trace to the AQHA sire Impressive in his pedigree?

YES → Call your veterinarian *NOW* if you answered yes to either query—it could be HYPP[G]. Go to **While You Wait #2,** opposite page.

NO ↓

Call your veterinarian *TODAY*.

WHILE YOU WAIT #1:

1. *Isolate your horse from other horses in case it's contagious.* To prevent spread of possible infectious disease, confine your horse to an open-air paddock or stall with a separate water supply, apart from other horses by at least 20 feet. Wash your hands and disinfect your boots (see page 232) after handling your horse and before handling other horses.

WHILE YOU WAIT #2:

Although most attacks of HYPP are transient, a severe attack can be fatal.

1. *Minimize stress.* Confine your horse to a quiet stall or paddock free of loose objects.

2. *Don't feed him.* Attacks can be triggered by feeds that aren't low in potassium. Assuming your veterinarian is coming within an hour or so, provide water, but no feed.

The Nitty Gritty

Here are some possible causes for your horse's gait abnormality

THE CAUSE	THE SOURCE
Injury	• Skull trauma • Spinal cord trauma • Peripheral nerve trauma • Vascular thrombosis • Spinal malformation • Fibrotic myopathy
Illness	• Liver disease • Equine protozoal myeloencephalopathy (EPM) • Equine Herpesvirus-1 (EHV-1) • Eastern equine encephalomyelitis (EEE) • Western equine encephalomyelitis (WEE) • Venezuelan equine encephalomyelitis (VEE) • Rabies • Brain abscess • Equine degenerative myeloencephalitis (EDM) • Polyneuritis • Shivers • Neuroaxonal dystrophy (NAD) • Stringhalt • Parasitic encephalopathy
Poisons	• Lead • Arsenic • Strychnine • Organophosphate • Yellow star thistle • Russian knapweed • Bracken fern • Horsetail • Locoweed • Milkweed • Botulism
Cancer	• Pituitary adenoma • Lymphosarcoma • Invasive tumor

(See Glossary and Chapter 19 for detailed descriptions.)

12-B

DOWN HORSE

What you see: Your horse is down, and for some reason he can't get back up on his own.

What this might mean: He might be cast (see opposite page). Or, he might be ill or injured, and unable to perform the complex and strenuous steps required for him to rise to his feet.

ACTION PLAN:

Does your horse seem mentally off—weak, or depressed[G], and apparently unconcerned about being down?

YES → Call your veterinarian *NOW*—it could be a severe injury or illness causing weakness or an altered mental state. Go to **While You Wait,** below, and see **Caution,** page 34.

NO ↓

Is there evidence of severe injury preventing your horse from getting up (external wounds, deviated or misshapen legs, joint swellings?

YES → Call your veterinarian *NOW*—whether the injury is the cause or effect of your horse being down, additional damage occurs with every failed attempt to rise. Go to **While You Wait.**

NO ↓

Is your horse free of the barrier that caused him to be cast, and there's no obvious injury preventing him from standing, yet his attempts still fail?

YES → Call your veterinarian *NOW*—it could be muscle and/or nerve injury from being down so long. Go to **While You Wait.**

NO ↓

Is your horse cast?

YES → Apply **Home Treatment,** opposite page.

NO ↓

Call your veterinarian *NOW*—the longer your horse is down, the more damage may occur.

WHILE YOU WAIT:

1. *Protect your horse from self-inflicted injury.* The most common injury resulting from being down is head/eye injury from swinging the head, and slamming it against the ground or a wall in repeated attempts to rise. If you have a crash helmet for your horse (see page 333), and can do so safely, put it on. Alternatively, pad the environment: Add thick, soft bedding and strategically placed bales of hay or straw around him.

2. *Keep him warm.* If your horse's mental state is depressed, he'll make little if any effort to rise and could become hypothermic, particularly if it's cold outside. Surround him with thick bedding, and cover him with a blanket.

HOME TREATMENT:

*(See **Action Plan** to determine whether home treatment is appropriate for your cast horse. If at any time during home treatment, your answers on the action plan change for the worse, call your vet.)*

Step 1. *Get help.* Enlist the aid of two or more strong helpers.

Step 2. *Test your strength.* If you and your helpers collectively are strong enough to do so without hurting your backs, grab handfuls of mane and tail and try to pull your horse away from the wall, then quickly get out of the way to avoid injury when he rises.

Step 3. *Get ropes.* If you can't find enough muscle power for Step 2, or if you've executed that step and your horse still can't get up (and you see no visible reason why), it could be that he's been cast so long that his down legs have "gone to sleep," and you'll have to turn him over. Get two strong, soft ropes that are each at least 20 feet long (tie non-clip ends of two soft lead ropes together to make one rope).

Step 4. *Position the ropes.* Stand behind your horse's spine, away from the danger of struggling legs. Lean over his torso and loop one rope under each of the two bottom legs, then work each rope up the leg until it's well above his hock (hind leg) and knee (fore leg).

Step 5. *Pull him over.* With one or two people at each rope, pull both legs simultaneously to turn him over. This will be difficult, but one strong person or two people with average strength can do it. Caution: Don't let his hooves hit you on their way over. To help avoid risk of injury, be alert and ready to move out of his way as he rises.

Definition: The Cast Horse

A horse is cast when he has the physical capability to rise, but there's external interference. Because of the way his weight is distributed, a horse must follow a routine in order to get to his feet:

Step 1: Position himself on his chest, with hind limbs drawn up beneath him.
Step 2: Extend his forelimbs in front of him.
Step 3: Swing his head and neck as ballast, while simultaneously pushing with his hindlimbs to raise his hindquarters, and bracing himself with his forefeet.

In the typical cast-horse scenario, the stall is freshly bedded, just begging your horse to roll. He lowers himself, rolls up onto his back for a brisk scratch...and rolls over onto his other side, his legs bunched up against the wall. He can't get positioned to stand up.

12-C

ABNORMAL MENTAL STATE

What you see: Your horse's mental state is abnormal. He may be depressed, unresponsive, stargazing (looking skyward), or wandering aimlessly. Or, he may be hyperexcitable, frenzied, wide-eyed, and fearful of invisible predators. He may be walking in circles, pressing his head against a wall, running into things, whinnying for no apparent reason, or charging at you.

What this might mean: There's a problem in his brain, which might not resolve even with prompt, proper treatment.

ACTION PLAN:

Does your horse have a fever?

YES → Call your veterinarian *NOW*—it could be an infectious disease. See **Caution,** below; go to **While You Wait,** below.

NO ↓

Is your horse spending more and more time lying down? Is his abnormal behavior intensifying over time?

YES → Call your veterinarian *NOW* if you answered yes to either query—it could be an expanding problem in your horse's brain, such as swelling from a recent injury. Go to **While You Wait**.

NO ↓

Does your horse have episodes during which he's normal one minute, then suddenly crumpled on the ground, apparently asleep, or displaying abnormal behavior without provocation?

YES → Call your veterinarian *NOW*—it could be narcolepsy[G] or a seizure disorder.

NO ↓

Does his abnormal behavior occur every time you deworm him?

YES → Call your veterinarian *NOW*—it could be a migrating parasite lost in his nervous system (parasitic encephalopathy).

NO ↓

Call your veterinarian *NOW*—it could be liver disease, electrolyte disturbance, poisoning, a heart problem, or trauma.

WHILE YOU WAIT:

1. *Isolate your horse from other horses in case it's contagious.* To prevent spread of possible infectious disease, confine your horse to a paddock or stall with a separate water supply, apart from other horses by at least 20 feet. Wash your hands and disinfect your boots (see page 232) after handling your horse and before handling other horses.

2. *Protect your horse.* Remove protruding objects from your horse's enclosure that could result in collisions or spills, and keep stress and noise to a minimum to avoid exciting him.

> **CAUTION**
>
> **Whenever a horse suddenly appears mentally "off", rabies must be considered. Don't take chances—take precautions. (See page 34.)**

What you see: Your horse is showing signs of decreased flexibility. Perhaps he's refusing to take leads, and/or his gaits are unusually choppy and short-strided. He may be reluctant to flex his neck and/or torso, instead turning his whole body stiffly, like a weathervane. He may refuse to lower his head to drink or eat from a low feeder. He may flinch, arch his back, move away, or pin his ears when you're saddling him or grooming his neck and/or back.

12-D

STIFF OR SORE NECK and/or Back

What this might mean: Pain and/or stiffness in the neck and/or back, from injury or disease of the bones, muscles, and/or nerves in or near the spine; or possibly from illness involving internal tissues (such as kidney disease).

ACTION PLAN:

Is your horse off his feed, depressed and/or feverish?

YES → Call your veterinarian *NOW*—it could be an internal illness. Go to **While You Wait #1,** next page.

NO ↓

Has your horse been treated with any injectable medication or vaccination within the past 3 days? Is the injection site abnormally warm, painful, swollen, and getting worse by the hour?

YES → Call your veterinarian *NOW* if you answered yes to both queries—it could be an infection at the injection site (Clostridial myositis[G]). While you wait, go to **page 144**.

NO ↓

Has your horse been treated with any injectable medication or vaccination within the past 3 days? Is the injection site abnormally warm, mildly painful, and swollen, but *not* worsening by the hour?

YES → This sounds like a common inflammatory reaction to a vaccine or medication. Call your veterinarian for advice, and go to **While You Wait #2,** opposite page.

NO ↓

Are your horse's third eyelids evident? Does he have any evidence of a recent flesh wound or infection? Is he having any difficulty picking up, chewing, and/or swallowing his food? Does he make abnormal noise when breathing heavily?

YES → Call your veterinarian *NOW* if you answered yes to any of these queries—it could be tetanus[G].

NO ↓

CONTINUED ⇨

ACTION PLAN (CONTINUED):

Is your horse's gait affected? Does he stagger, as though drunk? Do you live in an area known or suspected to have a soil selenium deficiency? Is he between 1 and 3 years of age?

YES → Call your veterinarian *NOW* if you answered yes to any of these queries—it could be an injury or disease to bone, muscles, or nerves in the neck, or a developmental error there (such as wobbler syndrome).

NO ↓

Do his symptoms seem to abate as he progresses through his exercise program?

YES → Call your veterinarian *TODAY*—it could be arthritis.

NO ↓

Does he resent finger pressure along or beside his backbone?

YES → Call your veterinarian *TODAY*—it could kissing spines[G].

NO ↓

Call your veterinarian for an appointment.

WHILE YOU WAIT #1:

1. *Isolate your horse from other horses in case it's contagious.* To prevent spread of possible infectious disease, confine your horse to an open-air paddock or stall with a separate water supply, apart from other horses by at least 20 feet. Wash your hands and disinfect your boots (see page 232) after handling your horse and before handling other horses.

WHILE YOU WAIT #2:

1. *Help him eat and drink.* Stiffness and soreness at a vaccination site can make it painful for your horse to lower his head to eat and drink. Elevate his feed and water so he can reach them without hurting himself. (Note: If, after doing this, you observe that your horse is uninterested in eating, go back to the beginning of the Action Plan and reassess your responses.)

SECTION I

HANDS-ON HORSEKEEPING SKILLS

CHAPTER 1

How to establish your horse's BASELINE BEHAVIOR

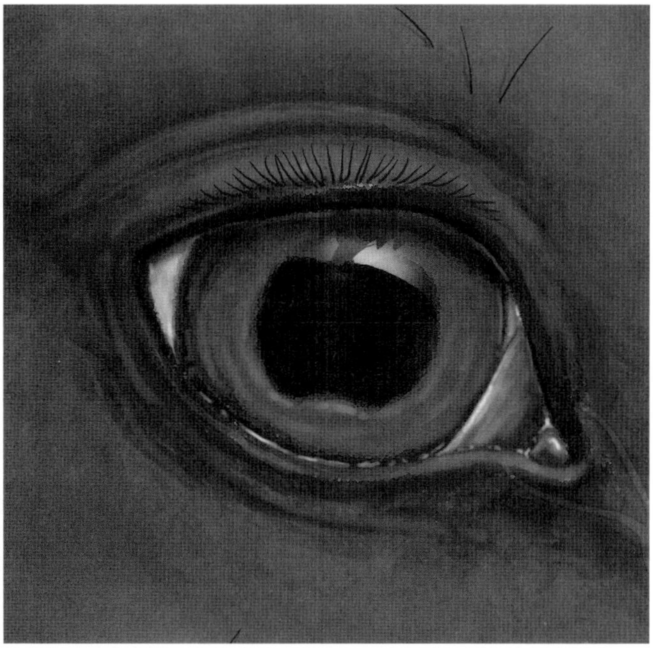

How to establish your horse's

BASELINE BEHAVIOR

Here's a chart of typical behaviors for the average horse—behaviors that can reveal how your horse feels. Fill in his personalized version of baseline behavior, then copy and post the chart in a prominent place. Take a mental inventory every time you see him. If you notice abnormal behavior, turn to "Baseline Vital Signs" (page 197). If your findings convince you there's a problem, refer to your horse's symptoms in Section 1.

BASELINE BEHAVIOR

Setting	Average Horse	Sample Entries	Your Horse
Pasture	Sticks with herd	*Stays on the fringes*	
Pasture	Grazes with herd	*Grazes when others do*	
Pasture	Naps at noon	*Naptime: 11:30 am*	
Stall, pasture, paddock	Lays down to nap	*Usually doesn't lie down*	
Stall or paddock	Cleans up all feed	*Cleans up grain and fine hay, shuns coarse stems*	
Stall or paddock	Watches activity over fence or through window	*Weaves at stall door or paces fence*	
Group feeding	Feeds according to social position	*Herd boss: first to eat*	
Water source	Usually drinks after eating	*Drinks after eating grain and after licking salt*	
Water source	Drinks 10-15 gal/day	*Drinks 12 gal/day*	
At liberty	Rolls 1-2 times/day; shakes off afterward	*Rolls when wet, bothered by flies, or after exercise; shakes off afterward*	
Stall or paddock	8-12 bowel movements per day	*5 piles at night; 5-6 during the daytime*	

CHAPTER 2

Baseline VITAL SIGNS

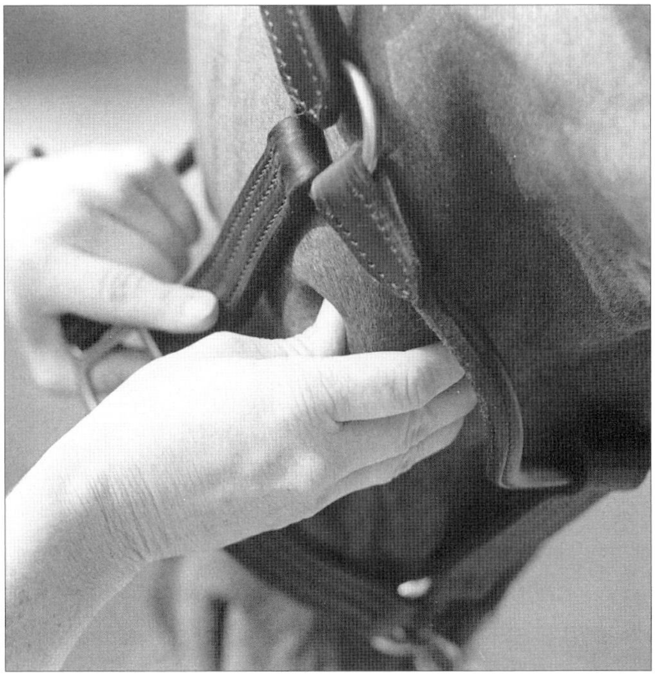

2 BASELINE VITAL SIGNS

Step-by-step instructions for how to take your horse's vital signs are provided in this section. Compare your findings to the chart on the opposite page. Be ready to relay abnormal readings if you call your veterinarian to report a suspected problem. Your knowledge of both current and baseline readings can help him or her determine how quickly he/she needs to see your horse.

What Kind of Thermometer?

- **Glass type: about $5 to $10 at tack/feed stores or through vet supply catalogs. A loop at one end is for string and a clip to help prevent loss.**
- **Electronic type: about $10 at variety/drug, tack/feed stores, or through vet supply catalogs. Get one that beeps when it's ready to read, and signals when its battery is low.**

HOW TO TAKE YOUR HORSE'S TEMPERATURE

Shake down a glass thermometer or activate an electronic one. Lubricate the tip with a dab of K-Y® or petroleum jelly. Lift your horse's tail and gently insert the thermometer into his anus, to a depth of 2 inches. With the heel of your hand resting against his buttock for stability, hold the thermometer in place. Release his tail if he fusses (shifts his weight, clamps or swishes his tail). Some horses will tolerate a thermometer better if their tails are free. It takes about 2 minutes for a glass thermometer to register; about 30 seconds for an electronic one (listen for the beep).

CAUTION

DON'T leave a rectal thermometer unattended, even if yours has a "safety" string and clip. If your horse should rub his hindquarters, he might break off the thermometer, injure his rectum, and/or spill poisonous mercury. It takes 2 minutes or less for the temperature to register. Stay with your horse, and hold the end of the thermometer constantly.

Tip 1: *Your horse's normal temperature will be lowest in early morning, and up to 2 degrees F higher in late afternoon. It's unaffected by weather unless he's shivering or sweating. To establish a baseline, record his morning, midday, and late afternoon temperatures daily for 1 week, then average the readings for each time of day.*

Tip 2: *Exercise causes a normal rise in your horse's temperature—to as high as 106 degrees F. It can take up to 2 hours to return to baseline. To determine whether an elevated temperature is due to illness or exercise, check at 15-minute intervals.*

Tip 3: *Keep an extra thermometer. If you get an abnormal reading, check again with the backup thermometer to confirm the reading and rule out technical error.*

Baseline Vital Signs

Vital Sign	Normal Range	Abnormals & Possible Cause	Your Horse
Temper-ature	99-101.5°F	*Below normal:* hypothermia; shock. *Above normal:* infection; heat exhaustion; exercise/ muscle exertion.	6 a.m.: Noon: 6 p.m.:
Heart rate	30-44 beats per minute	*Below normal:* good athletic condition; heart problem; poisoning; hypothermia; shock. *Above normal:* exercise; pain; fever; heat exhaustion; shock; heart problem; anxiety.	
Respiratory rate	10-15 breaths per minute	*Below normal:* athletic condition; hypothermia; shock; drug effect. *Above normal:* exercise; pain; fever; heat exhaustion; electrolyte imbalance; shock; respiratory infection.	
Gut sounds	Long, rolling rumbles interspersed with shorter gurgles; quiet periods no longer than 2 minutes	*Quieter than normal:* gut motility slowed or stopped, often associated with illness or colic. *Noisier than normal:* hunger; digestion of a meal; nervousness; or gut inflammation. *High-pitched pings interspersed with periods of quiet:* accumulated gas (often a sign of colic).	
Digital pulse	Subtle and difficult to feel	*No pulse:* could be normal, or it could indicate poor circulation. *An obvious or strong pulse:* could indicate a variety of foot problems, including laminitis[G] (founder) or an abscess[G].	
Gum color	Pale to bubble-gum pink	*Whitish gums:* could indicate anemia or shock. *Bright pink gums:* could indicate illness; poisoning; shock; or could be normal if the horse has just been exercising. *Brick-red, blue, or muddy-colored gums:* could indicate poisoning or shock[G].	
Capillary refill time (CRT)	CRT: 1-2 seconds	*Faster-than-usual CRT:* means your horse's blood pressure is elevated, probably due to recent exercise; excitement; or anxiety. *Slow CRT:* can indicate illness; poisoning; or shock.	

What Kind of Stethoscope?

- **Littman-type: about $10-$15 at tack/feed stores, medical supply stores, or vet supply catalogs. Usually comes with 2 bells, a wide one and a narrow one. Use the wide one. Tubing connecting the bell to the earpieces comes in a variety of lengths; for use in horses, the longer the better so you can position the bell deep in your horse's armpit without having to stick your head in there, too. The wide bell makes accurate placement less critical for listening to heart rate, breathing sounds, or gut sounds.**
- **Hewlett-Packard type: about $25-$50 at medical supply stores and through vet supply catalogs. The bell is narrower and deeper than in a Littman-type, for clearer sounds over a smaller area. Tubing connecting the bell to the earpieces generally is shorter than is convenient for listening to your horse's heart rate.**

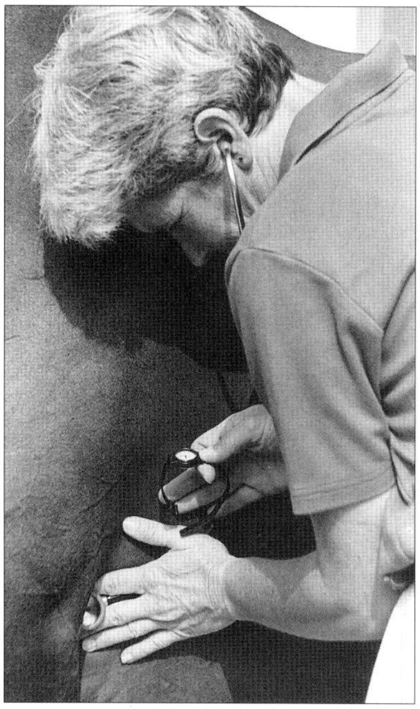

Checking heart rate with a stethoscope.

HOW TO TAKE YOUR HORSE'S HEART RATE

Grab a watch with a second hand or digital timer. Stand on your horse's left side, facing his left elbow, as shown (left). Place the bell of the stethoscope behind the point of his elbow and press it gently into his armpit. His heart beat should have both a lub and a dub component—count the two together as one beat. Count the number of beats in a 15-second period and multiply by 4 for beats-per-minute.

HOW TO CHECK YOUR HORSE'S HEART RATE DIGITALLY

While holding you horse's halter with one hand, place the fingertips of your other hand on the underside of the jawbone beneath his cheek, to locate the facial artery which crosses under the jaw (left). (Tip: The artery is firm and about half the diameter of a pencil. If you move your fingers forward and back along the jawbone, you'll feel the artery slip back and forth.) Once you've found it, gently feel for the nudge of your horse's pulse through the artery, and count the number of beats in 15 seconds. Multiply by 4 for beats-per-minute.

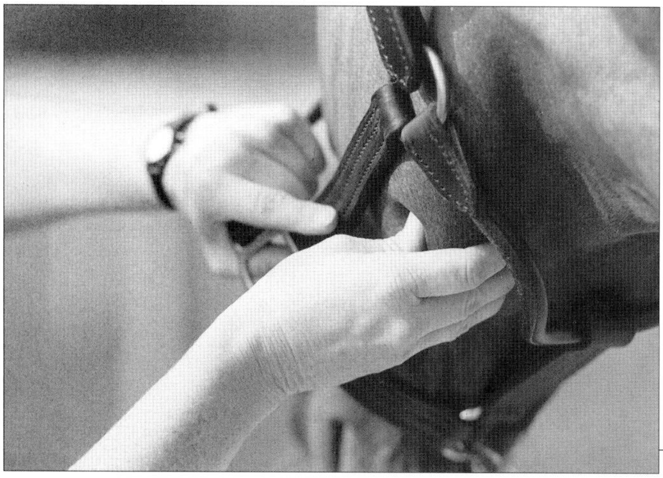

Checking heart rate digitally.

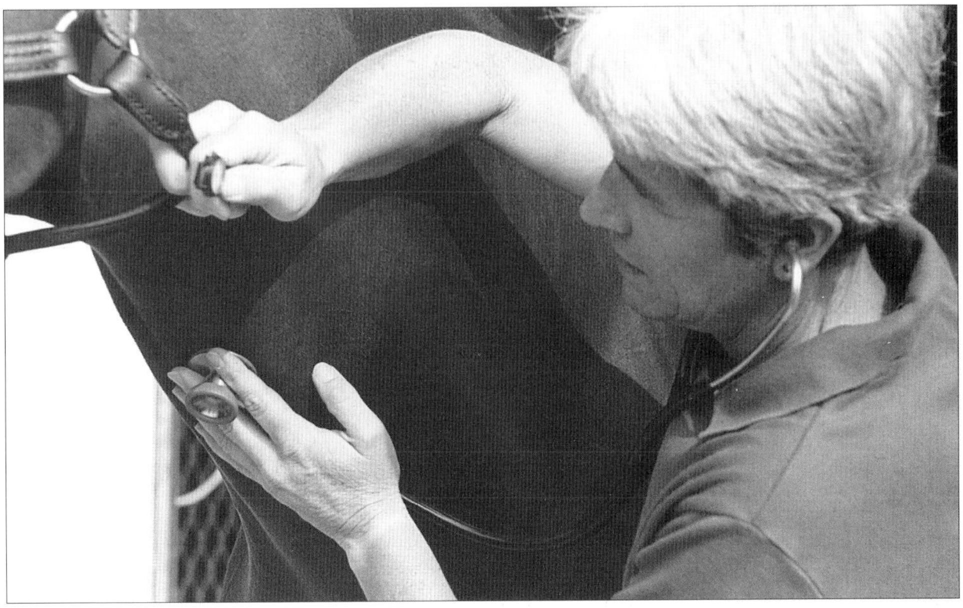

Checking respiratory rate using a stethoscope.

HOW TO TAKE YOUR HORSE'S RESPIRATORY RATE

Place the bell of the stethoscope in the center of your horse's throat, approximately 6 to 8 inches below his throatlatch (above). Listen to the air rush by as he inhales and exhales. Count the number of breaths taken in a 15-second period and multiply by 4 for breaths-per-minute.

> ***Tip:*** *If you don't have a stethoscope, you can take your horse's respiratory rate by:*
>
> • *Watching the rise and fall of his chest wall or flanks with each breath. In a healthy horse at rest, there should be little external movement with each breath.*
>
> • *Watching for nostril movement with each breath, or holding a mirror in front of his nostril and watching for fogging with each breath. In a healthy horse at rest, there should be little nostril flare. (Note: Your horse might sniff at the mirror and give a falsely elevated reading.)*

HOW TO LISTEN TO YOUR HORSE'S GUT SOUNDS

Divide each side of your horse's abdomen into five sections: high flank; low flank; high belly (between flank and ribs); low belly; and ventral midline (just to one side of the seam that divides his lower belly into left and ride sides). Press the stethoscope firmly into each section and listen for a minimum of 30 seconds, the longer the better. (It can be normal for there to be up to a 2-minute interval of quiet between prolonged rumbles. If you don't listen long enough, you might mistakenly think there are no sounds.) ➤

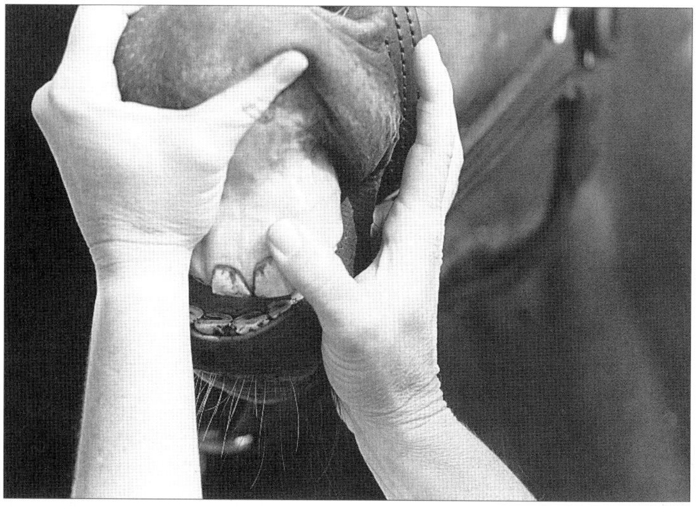

Capillary refill time: Press with a finger...

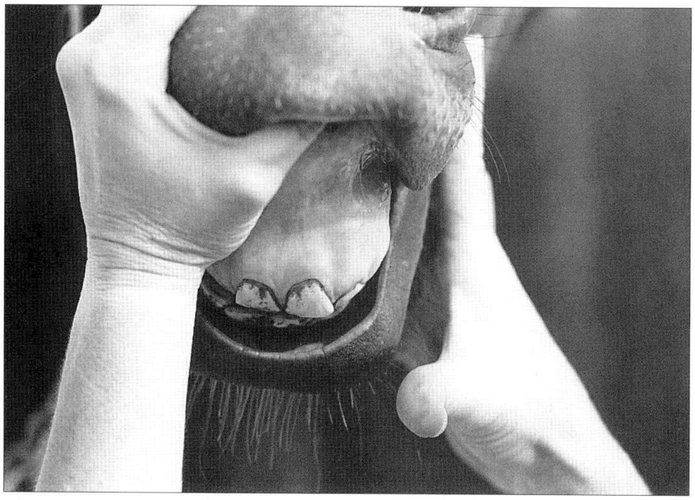

...then release.

HOW TO CHECK YOUR HORSE'S DIGITAL PULSE

Squat beside your horse's front leg, facing his rear. Place your fingertips along the outside of his pastern area (between his fetlock joint and coronary band). Feel for a pulse in the artery that resides there. A normal digital pulse should be subtle and hard to feel. You don't count beats per minute, but rather feel for increased intensity.

HOW TO CHECK YOUR HORSE'S MUCUS MEMBRANE COLOR AND CAPILLARY REFILL TIME

Lift your horse's upper lip and look at the color of his gums. To check capillary refill time, press on the gums with a finger to blanch out the color (above left), then count how many seconds it takes to resume its original color (left).

CHAPTER 3

The PREVENTION DIET

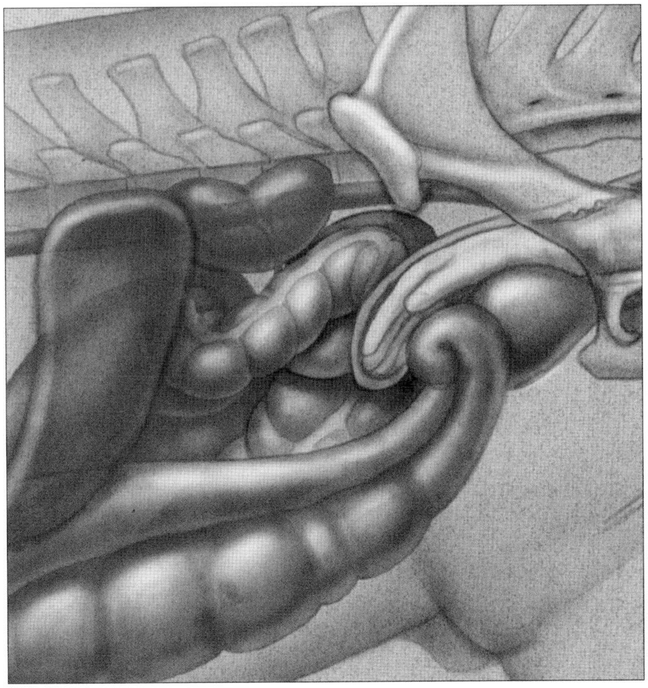

THE PREVENTION DIET

Let's start with a menu of three sample diets for an "average" adult horse. (Work with your vet to develop a ration for broodmares, young, or geriatric equines.) None of these diets will be perfect for your adult horse, because his activity level and physical needs will be unique, but all three are comprised of forages and grains that are commonly used to feed horses and are readily available most anywhere. The components of each diet have been adjusted so they're reasonably close to the dietary guidelines provided by the National Research Council (NRC) .

An unbalanced diet can lead to obesity, weight loss, colic, laminitis, poor hair coat and hoof condition, poor performance, unruly behavior, muscle disorders, and susceptibility to disease. Can the right diet prevent these nightmares?

Your best source for detailed guidance in this area is your veterinarian, who can help you develop a ration that meets your horse's unique needs, or refer you to an expert in equine nutrition.

THREE SAMPLE DIETS FOR THE AVERAGE ADULT HORSE

The horse: Casey, a 7-year-old Quarter Horse gelding in show shape (body condition score 6/10; see page 223).

Weight: 1,120 lbs.

Activity: Moderate work, consisting of pleasure and trail; shown 3 to 4 times per year in Western pleasure. Ridden 45 minutes to an hour, 4 days per week.

MENU #1 **(Daily total, divided into 2-3 meals)**	**Roughage (% of body weight)**	**Protein (kg)**	**Calcium (g)**	**Phosphorus (g)**
15 lbs. grass hay *(11.5% protein, .3% calcium, .3% phosphorous)*	1.3	0.78	13.6	13.6
6 lbs. whole oats *(13% protein, .1% calcium, .3% phosphorous)*	negligible	0.35	2.7	8.1
1 measure vitamin-mineral supplement formulated for region, for horses on grass hay or pasture, plus grain	negligible	negligible	15	5
TOTAL	1.3	1.13	31.3	26.7
NRC recommendations for an adult horse in moderate work	1-2	.98-1.16	30-36	21-25

MENU #2 **(Daily total, divided into 2-3 meals)**	**Roughage (% of body weight)**	**Protein (kg)**	**Calcium (g)**	**Phos. (g)**
7.5 lbs. second-cutting alfalfa hay (22% *protein, 1% calcium, .28% phosphorous)*	.7	.8	34.1	9.5
5 lbs. grass hay *(11.5% protein, .25% calcium, .2% phosphorous)*	.4	.3	5.7	4.5
1 measure vitamin-mineral supplement formulated for region, for horses on alfalfa forage without grain	negligible	negligible	0	10
TOTAL	1.1	1.1	39.8	24
NRC recommendations for an adult horse in moderate work	1-2	.98-1.16	30-36	21-25

MENU #3 **(Daily total, divided into 2-3 meals)**	**Roughage (% of body weight)**	**Protein (kg)**	**Calcium (g)**	**Phos. (g)**
15 lbs. grass-alfalfa mixed hay *(14% protein, .6% calcium, .25% phosphorous)*	1.3	.9	38.1	15.9
6 lbs. shelled corn *(9% protein, .02% calcium, .31% phosphorous)*	negligible	.2	.5	8.4
1 measure vitamin-mineral supplement formulated for horses on alfalfa forage plus grain	negligible	negligible	0	0
TOTAL	1.3	1.1	38.6	24.3
NRC recommendations for an adult horse in moderate work	1-2	.98-1.16	30-36	21-25

➤

Hay should have been harvested before the seed heads were fully opened so its nutrients are optimally digestible. It should be less than 1 year of age, as nutritional quality can deteriorate even when hay is stored in a weather-tight barn. It should be clean, free of mold and debris, and only minimally dusty. (All hay is dusty, but the dust shouldn't make obvious clouds when flakes are separated.)

So Your Adult Horse Is Healthy But Too Thin?

Here's how to increase his weight safely.

To increase your horse's weight, increase the fat in his diet without increasing his levels of protein (a liver and kidney burden) or carbohydrate (a laminitis, myositis, and colic risk factor). To do this, add corn oil or vegetable oil to his ration.

- Start by adding 2 tablespoons of oil, mixed in a small amount of grain, twice a day. Do this for 1 week.
- The second week, increase the oil to 3 tablespoons per twice-a-day feeding.
- Continue increasing the twice-daily amount of oil by 1 tablespoon per week, until your horse is getting up to 1 cup (16 tablespoons) per twice-a-day feeding, or 2 cups per day. If, at any time, you notice a softening or loosening in the consistency of his manure, back off the amount of oil to the previous level and leave it there.

When you're happy with your horse's weight and condition, decrease the amount of oil to a level that maintains them.

DID YOU KNOW...?

Of all the commonly available grains for horse feed (oats, barley, wheat, milo, and corn), oats are the least likely to cause digestive disturbances because of their high fiber content and the ease with which their starches are broken down and digested. Corn is the most difficult for the horse to digest.

7 SIMPLE RULES OF THUMB

1. Make good-quality forage—grass hay or pasture—the foundation of your horse's diet, and avoid feeding his total daily ration in one or two large, quickly eaten meals. Horses were designed as wandering herbivores, to munch and step, munch and step, their digestive systems busy around the clock, chewing and digesting high-fiber feed. Your horse will get too hungry, eat too fast, and risk choke[G], indigestion, and colic[G] if fed in one or two large meals. Provide 1 to 2 percent of his body weight per day in roughage (hay or pasture), for optimal function of his intestinal tract. For a 1,100-lb. horse, that'd be 11 to 22 lbs. of roughage.

2. Have your horse's hay or pasture analyzed at a reputable agricultural laboratory (ask your veterinarian for a reference). That way, you can choose grain concentrates and vitamin-mineral supplements that fill nutritional gaps left by the forage, without resulting in excesses.

3. Add grain concentrates only if you need to boost your horse's energy level and/or body weight. (See box above, for a weight-adding alternative.) Don't use grain products to balance his diet. Instead, provide a separate, balanced vitamin-mineral supplement formulated for horses on his particular type of forage, in your geographic area.

4. If you're feeding grain concentrates, never allow the weight of grain fed to exceed the weight of hay or forage. Doing so could increase your horse's risk of laminitis[G], colic[G], and other conditions linked to high-grain diets. And never give more than 5 pounds of grain in a single feeding—your horse's stomach is too small for more than that.

5. If your horse's ration includes grain, and he's not on pasture, feed him his hay first. This will take the edge off his hunger and discourage bolting of food. It'll also slow the passage of feed through his intestinal tract, thereby decreasing his risk for indigestion and colic.

6. If you're switching to a new feed, make the change gradually, over a 2-week period or longer. This will allow the digestive bacteria in your horse's intestines to adjust, which in turn will help prevent indigestion and colic.

7. Provide access to clean, fresh water at all times, for optimal function of your horse's intestinal tract.

How Much Does Your Pasture Horse Eat?

Generally speaking, when grazing an actively growing pasture, a horse can consume 2 pounds of forage per hour. It depends on weather, time of year, and social conditions. When it's extremely hot outside, horses tend to graze less. When pasture is actively growing, they get more grass per hour of grazing. In group situations, they tend to graze more hours in a day.

NOTES

CHAPTER 4

The right VACCINATION PROGRAM

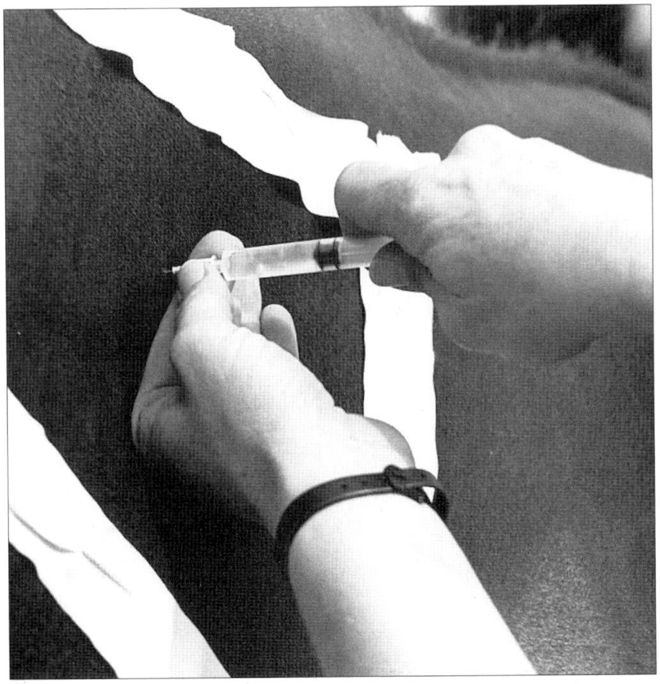

4

The Right
VACCINATION PROGRAM

Depending on where you and your horse live, and on your horse's lifestyle, your equine vaccination program is going to entail giving shots at least once, and maybe as often as four times, per year. Which shots does your horse need? To help you decide, read the following chart, checking the box in the right-hand column for the optional vaccines your horse should have. (We've checked the column for you, for must-have vaccinations.) Then mark your calendar and make sure proper shots are given at the proper time.

Disease	What it is	Frequency & time of year to vaccinate	Does your horse need it?	
Eastern equine encephalomyelitis and western equine encephalomyelitis (EEE/WEE; also known as sleeping sickness)	Potentially deadly viral diseases of the central nervous system. There is no treatment. Survivors often have residual brain damage.	In regions with cold winters, vaccinate 1x per year, in the spring, just before mosquitoes emerge. If winters are warm enough for year-round mosquitoes, vaccinate 2x a year, in spring & fall.	Yes.	✔
Venezuelan equine encephalomyelitis (VEE—the other sleeping sickness)	Similar to EEE/WEE, but more survivable. There is no treatment. Survivors often have residual brain damage.	Government restricts use to areas where the disease has been reported; usually near Mexico-USA border. Give 2x a year, in spring & fall.	If reported in your area, yes.	?

Disease	What it is	Frequency & time of year to vaccinate	Does your horse need it?	
Tetanus (Lockjaw)	Usually fatal disease caused by bacteria common in your horse environment. Risk is high in horses that aren't vaccinated.	*Tetanus toxoid:* 1x per year, in the spring or at the time of a broken-skin injury if it occurs 12 months or more after the last tetanus toxoid vaccination. *Tetanus antitoxin:* To be used only if a broken-skin injury occurs in a horse with no known history of tetanus toxoid vaccination.	Yes.	✔
Influenza (Flu)	A viral infection that leaves your horse's respiratory tract irritable and prone to cough for weeks after recovery.	1x per year, in the spring, if your horse lives alone and stays home, or if he lives in a closed herd of flu-vaccinated horses. Every 3 months if your horse travels or commingles with other horses of unknown vaccination history.	Yes.	✔
Equine viral rhinopneumonitis (equine Herpesvirus or rhino)	Same as for flu.	Due to short-lived protection from vaccine and questionable efficacy, consult your vet for recommendations for your horse.	Consult your vet.	? ➤

Disease	What it is	Frequency & time of year to vaccinate	Does your horse need it?	
Strangles	A bacterial respiratory disease that can make your horse a carrier for years afterward if the bacteria manage to conceal themselves in his guttural pouches[G].	Routine use of this vaccination has become controversial and is not generally recommended, due to the incidence of tissue reaction at the injection site and questionable effectiveness.	If strangles is endemic in your area, discuss the pros and cons with your veterinarian.	?
Rabies	Fatal viral disease spread by the bite or saliva of infected mammals; all other animals (including humans) that come into contact with an affected horse are at risk.	1x per year, in the spring, if your horse is exposed to domestic animals or wildlife. Must be given by licensed veterinarian.	Yes, if rabies has been reported in domestic or wild animals in your area in the past 10 years. Otherwise, optional.	?
Potomac horse fever (PHF)	Potentially deadly protozoal disease, believed to be transmitted by ticks, that can cause severe diarrhea and laminitis.	1 to 2x per year: In the spring,before disease-carrying ticks become active, and again in fall if PHF is endemic in your area.	If PHF is endemic in your area, discuss the pros and cons of this vaccine with your vet.	?

Disease	What it is	Frequency & time of year to vaccinate	Does your horse need it?	
Botulism	Often fatal paralysis caused by bacterial toxins present in contaminated feed or soil.	1x per year in the spring in endemic areas.	Yes, if botulism is endemic in your area. Otherwise, no.	?
Equine viral arteritis (EVA)	A viral disease, spread by sexual contact or by coughing or sneezing, that causes flu-like respiratory disease, leg swelling, and can cause abortion. Vaccine must be purchased and given by state-approved veterinarian. Exposed stallions not vaccinated prior to sexual maturity can become carriers.	One lifetime vaccination, given 1 month prior to breeding season.	Yes, if your mare has never been diagnosed with EVA and is booked to a stallion with unknown EVA history. Otherwise, no.	?

BE SHOT SMART

• *If your horse needs a tetanus shot because of an injury occurring 12 months or more after his last tetanus toxoid vaccination, but he has had a tetanus toxoid vaccination within the past 5 years, he should receive another toxoid shot, not a tetanus antitoxin shot. Tetanus antitoxin should be used only when it's been longer than 5 years since the last tetanus toxoid shot. The antitoxin provides only short-lived protection against tetanus and does not stimulate your horse's own immunity against the disease. (The immune response to tetanus toxoid, on the other hand, is quite strong in horses.) Also, antitoxin has been implicated as a possible cause* ➤

of serum sickness, an often fatal liver disease that can occur months later. Tetanus toxoid has not been associated with that increased risk.

• *Avoid use of tank-dose vaccinations (usually containing 10 doses per bottle). While you might save a few dollars per horse this way, there's a chance of contamination that increases every time you push a needle through the stopper to draw out the next dose. (Some researchers believe the potentially deadly infection Clostridial myositis*[G] *is more likely when using tank-dose vials of vaccinations.) Instead, have your horse vaccinated with products provided in single-dose, pre-loaded syringes, available through your veterinarian or from feed/tack stores and veterinary supply catalogs. This way, the vaccine is less likely to become contaminated.*

A Word of Caution...

Injections are not the only means by which your horse can get Clostridial myositis. The causative *Clostridium* species of bacteria is known to thrive in deep, airless recesses. (The bug that causes tetanus is also a member of this family.) Puncture wounds into muscle, and contaminated incisions following castration, also can lead to Clostridial myositis. Early signs include swelling, pain, and/or lameness; the first signs of advanced Clostridial myositis can include depression and loss of appetite.

CHAPTER 5

The right DEWORMING PROGRAM

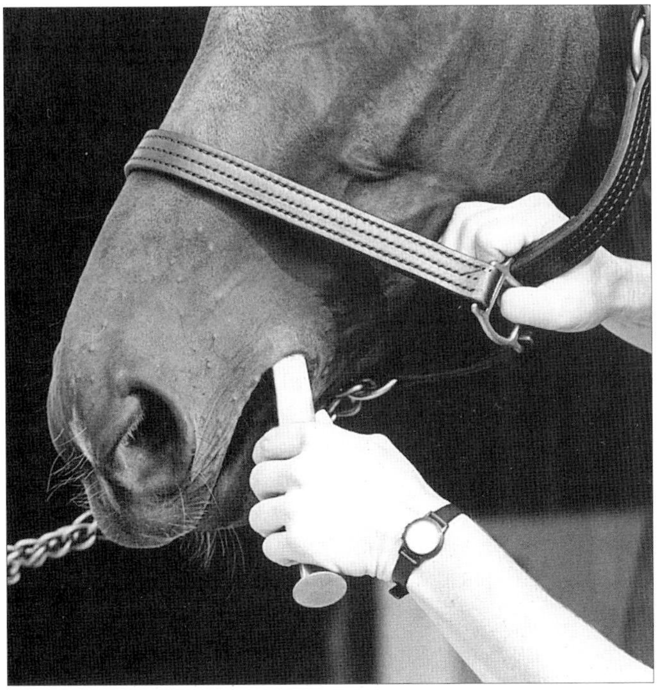

5

The Right

DEWORMING PROGRAM

There are two main methods for deworming your horse: purge deworming, and daily deworming. Each method has a different goal, so to decide which method to use for your horse, you must decide what your goal is. What follows is the information you'll need to make that decision, and guidelines for using either method.

Why should you deworm your horse...

...when horses lived in the wild for generations with nobody stuffing them full of worm-killing medicine? Because instead of nibbling and moving on to fresh meadows, your horse is confined, forced to eat where horses have, er... gone before. Under natural circumstances, he'd prefer not to feed where even the slightest hint of manure and parasite eggs/larvae remained. Under domestic circumstances, he has no choice. Diligent manure management can reduce parasite eggs and larvae in your horse's environment. But that won't be enough, so regular treatment with deworming medication is needed.

• **Purge deworming:** The goal of purge deworming is not to keep your horse worm-free, but rather to help keep the load of eggs and larvae in his environment to a minimum, so he won't pick up a heavy infestation with every nibble. When done every 4 to 8 weeks via oral paste or nasogastric tube, purge deworming kills the adult worms inside your horse before they start producing eggs. After treatment, your horse begins re-infesting himself with eggs and larvae, which mature as they migrate to his intestines. How fast and heavily he becomes re-infested depends on the population of parasites in his environment and on his own natural resistance to them.

• **Daily deworming:** The goal of daily deworming is to prevent the damage done by immature worms migrating through your horse's internal organs. With this method, a low dose of the dewormer pyrantel tartrate is given to your horse via a top-dressing every day, so he constantly has low levels of the chemical in his system—just enough to kill the parasite larvae before they begin their migratory phase. Because few worms survive to maturity, there will be few if any worm eggs in your horse's manure, which prevents further infestation of his environment.

DRAWBACKS OF PURGE DEWORMING

1. If your horse lives with other horses that are infested with egg-producing adult parasites, your efforts to reduce environmental infestation are wasted. And if your horse visits other horse facilities, he can pick up heavy egg loads there and bring them home.

2. Even if your horse never leaves home, and if he either lives alone or shares his environment with horses that are properly purge-dewormed, his environment still could be heavily seeded with parasite eggs from horses that lived there anytime during the past 30 years—some parasite eggs can live that long!

3. As immature intestinal parasites mature into egg-producing adults, they migrate through your horse's internal organs, blazing trails of damage as they go. Purge deworming does not prevent this damage—it kills the adult worms after the fact. Several studies have indicated that the damage from migrating parasites can cause colic.

4. The success of a purge deworming program depends on timing. Give the dewormer too late, and hundreds of thousands of eggs already will have passed in your horse's manure. Give it too early, and the treatment is wasted because the worms are still migrating, out of reach of many common dewormers.

5. Many purge dewormers do not kill bots. A boticide such as ivermectin or one of the organophosphate compounds must be given at the beginning and end of bot season (early spring, and one month after the first killing frost of autumn) for bot control. ➤

HOW DO YOU KNOW HOW MUCH DEWORMER TO GIVE?

Follow the manufacturer's instructions, based on your horse's body weight. For how to determine your horse's body weight, see page 224.

HOW TO GET A FECAL EGG COUNT

Seal two fresh (preferably still warm) manure "muffins" in a zip-lock plastic bag and submit within 1 hour to a laboratory-equipped veterinary facility for a fecal egg count.

Tip: Take the sample directly to the clinic, rather than handing it to your on-the-road veterinarian, who might not get back to the lab for several hours. The test likely will be run by a technician at the facility right away. Results will be given in "eggs per gram" (epg). On an effective purge program, your horse's count should be below 100 epg. On a daily program, his count should be 0 to 50.

Tip: For best accuracy, have your horse's fecal egg count done daily for 3 to 5 days and average the results.

Daily Dewormer: *Sample Program*	
March 1 (spring thaw)	Administer ivermectin or moxidectin paste or gel per manufacturers' instructions, or arrange for your vet to administer liquid dewormer and boticide via nasogastric tube, to kill bots in your horse's stomach as well as any adult (and some immature) stages of intestinal parasites.
March 2-May 31	Administer daily dewormer. Scrape bot eggs from your horse's legs daily.
June 1	If tapeworms are a problem in your area (ask your vet), administer a double dose of pyrantel pamoate paste (such as Strongid-P), or arrange for your vet to give a double dose of liquid pyrantel pamoate via nasogastric tube, to kill tapeworms as well as intestinal parasites that may have reached adulthood.
June 2 until 1 month after first killing frost	Administer daily dewormer. Scrape bot eggs from your horse's legs daily.
1 month after first killing frost	Have your vet lab perform a fecal egg count; there should be fewer than 50 epg. (If the sample contains more than 50 epg, consult your vet—your horse might have a heavy load of adult and/or encysted parasites.) Adult botflies should be dead, and your horse's legs should be free of eggs. Administer ivermectin or moxidectin to kill bots in the stomach, as well as any adult intestinal parasites.
From above treatment through beginning of spring thaw	Administer daily dewormer.
March 1 (or time of spring thaw)	Administer ivermectin or moxidectin paste or gel, per manufacturers' instructions, or arrange for your vet to give a liquid dewormer and boticide via nasogastric tube, to kill bots as well as any adult intestinal parasites.

DRAWBACKS OF DAILY DEWORMING

1. The active ingredient in a daily dewormer does not kill bots. A boticide such as ivermectin or moxidectin must be given at the beginning and end of bot season (early spring, and one month after the first killing frost of autumn) for bot control.

2. Some experts believe your horse should be allowed to have a light infestation of internal parasites so his immune system is stimulated to build natural resistance against them. If this is true, the daily deworming program might work too well for your horse's best interests—he might become heavily infested if suddenly taken off the program and exposed to parasite eggs, because he could be immunologically naive.

3. Giving your horse a potentially toxic chemical agent every day, day after day, can be an unattractive notion for those of us who wish to keep our horses' care more "natural." Although safety studies have not revealed significant toxic effects of daily pyrantel tartrate administration, sufficient time has not passed to determine if there are cumulative, long-term adverse effects on your horse's system.

PURGE DEWORMING, SAMPLE PROGRAM

Year #1

• Have your vet lab perform a fecal egg count. Record the results.
• Administer ivermectin paste, per manufacturer's instructions, or arrange for your vet to give ivermectin liquid via nasogastric tube, to kill adult and some stages of immature intestinal parasites, as well as bots in your horse's stomach.

Year #1, 4 weeks later

• Have your vet lab perform a fecal egg count. Record the results.
• If the count is less than 100 epg, repeat the test every 2 weeks until the count reaches or exceeds 100 epg. Note how long it took for the count to reach this level after the purge deworming from the previous month, and subtract 1 week: This will be your horse's deworming interval for the rest of the year. (For example, if it took 6 weeks for the egg count to reach 100 epg, administer a purge dewormer to your horse every 5 weeks; if it took 8 weeks, treat your horse every 7 weeks.)
• If the count exceeds 100 epg, administer ivermectin paste per manufacturer's instructions, or arrange for your vet to give ivermectin liquid via nasogastric tube, and repeat the test in another 4 weeks. Continue treating with ivermectin at 4-week intervals until the fecal egg count is less than 100 epg, then proceed as above. ➤

NOTE:

Standard dewormer regimens are ineffective against tapeworms. Studies have shown that giving twice the purge-dose of pyrantel pamoate will safely kill them. To figure a double-dose, check the label on a pyrantel pamoate paste dewormer. Calculate the standard dose according to your horse's body weight, then double it and give all at once. Or, ask your veterinarian to give a double-dose of the liquid form via nasogastric tube.

Year #1, remaining months

• Continue using ivermectin as your main dewormer for the year, at the interval determined on page 219. If tapeworms are a problem in your area (ask your veterinarian), substitute one ivermectin treatment with a double-dose of pyrantel pamoate paste, or arrange for your vet to administer a double-dose of pyrantel pamoate liquid via stomach tube, to kill tapeworms as well as the usual intestinal parasites.

Year #2

• Beginning at the interval determined the previous year, administer a benzimidazole paste product as your main dewormer, per manufacturer's instructions, or arrange to have your vet give a benzimidazole liquid product via nasogastric tube. For help in determining which benzimidazole product to use, consult your veterinarian: Some strongyle species in your area might be resistant to some products and susceptible to others.

• Have your vet lab perform a fecal egg count before every other treatment, and adjust the interval if necessary to maintain a count below 100 epg between treatments.

• In early spring, and one month after the first killing frost of autumn, substitute the regular treatment with ivermectin or moxidectin paste or gel, administered per manufacturers' instructions, or arrange for your vet to give a liquid dewormer and boticide via nasogastric tube, to kill intestinal parasites and bots.

• If tapeworms are a problem in your area, replace one benzimidazole treatment with a double-dose of pyrantel pamoate paste, or arrange for your vet to give a double-dose of liquid pyrantel pamoate via nasogastric tube, to kill tapeworms in addition to the usual intestinal parasites.

CAUTION

If your horse has not received any dewormer for more than a year, the massive kill-off of a heavy parasite load could make him sick or cause an intestinal blockage. Ask your vet to recommend a mild dewormer for his first treatment.

Year #3

• Beginning at the interval determined the previous year, administer pyrantel pamoate paste as your main dewormer, per manufacturer's instructions, or arrange to have your vet give liquid pyrantel pamoate via nasogastric tube.

• Have your vet lab perform a fecal egg count before every other treatment. Adjust your horse's deworming interval if necessary to maintain a count below 100 epg between treatments.

• In early spring, and one month after autumn's first killing frost, replace the regular treatment with ivermectin or moxidectin paste or gel, administered per manufacturers' instructions, or arrange for your vet to give a liquid dewormer and boticide via nasogastric tube, to kill intestinal parasites and bots.

• If tapeworms are a problem in your area, double the dose of one pyrantel pamoate treatment, or arrange for your vet to give a double-dose via nasogastric tube, to kill tapeworms in addition to the usual intestinal parasites.

Deworming Product Samples (Note: This chart is not meant to represent a complete listing of dewormer products available.)

Category	Active ingredient	Brand names	Comments
Avermectin	Ivermectin	• Eqvalan (Merial) • Zimecterin (Farnam) • Equimectrin (Horse Health) • Rotectin-1 (Farnam)	Highly effective against a broad spectrum of equine parasites, including bots, with a wide safety margin.
Milbemycin	Moxidectin	Quest (Fort Dodge)	Kills some of the encysted larval forms of small strongyles and has extended control over this specific parasite; its effectiveness against other parasites is similar to ivermectin.
Benzimidazole	Febantel	Cutter Paste (Bayer)	Effective against roundworms, large and small strongyles, and pinworms; not bots. Wide safety margin.
	Fenbendazole	• Panacur (Hoechst Roussel Vet) • Safe-Guard (Hoechst Roussel Vet)	Effective against roundworms, large and small strongyles, and pinworms; not bots. Wide safety margin.
	Oxfendazole	Benzelmin (Syntex)	Effective against roundworms, large and small strongyles, and pinworms; not bots. Wide safety margin.
	Oxibendazole	Anthelcide EQ (SmithKline Beecham)	Effective against roundworms, large and small strongyles, and pinworms; not bots. Wide safety margin.
Organophosphates	Dichlorvos	Cutter Dichlorvos Wormer (Bayer)	Effective against roundworms, large and small strongyles, pinworms, and bots. Narrow safety margin; to be used in adult horses only.

➤

Deworming Product Samples
(continued)

Category	Active ingredient	Brand names	Comments
Piperazine	Piperazine	Alfalfa Pellet Wormer (Farnam)	Mild dewormer, variably effective against roundworms, large and small strongyles, and pinworms; not bots. Wide safety margin. Good choice as a first dewormer for foals or any horse suspected of having a heavy worm infestation, when a massive kill-off of worms might be injurious to his health.
Pyrimidines	Pyrantel pamoate	• Strongid Paste (Pfizer) • Strongid Liquid (Pfizer) • Rotectin-2 (Farnam)	Effective against roundworms, large and small strongyles, and pinworms; not bots. Wide safety margin. Not to be used with piperazine (antagonistic). When purge-dose is doubled, effective against equine tapeworms.
	Pyrantel tartrate	• Strongid C (Pfizer) • Strongid C2x (Pfizer) • Equine Wormer Pellets (Kaeco) • Foal & Horse Pelleted Wormer (Manna Pro)	When given as a daily dewormer (Strongid C and C2x), effective against larval forms of parasites picked up in the environment; not bots. When given as a purge-dewormer (Equine Wormer and Foal & Horse Pelleted Dewormer), effectiveness equivalent to pyrantel pamoate. Wide safety margin.

CHAPTER 6

How to estimate your horse's BODY WEIGHT AND CONDITION

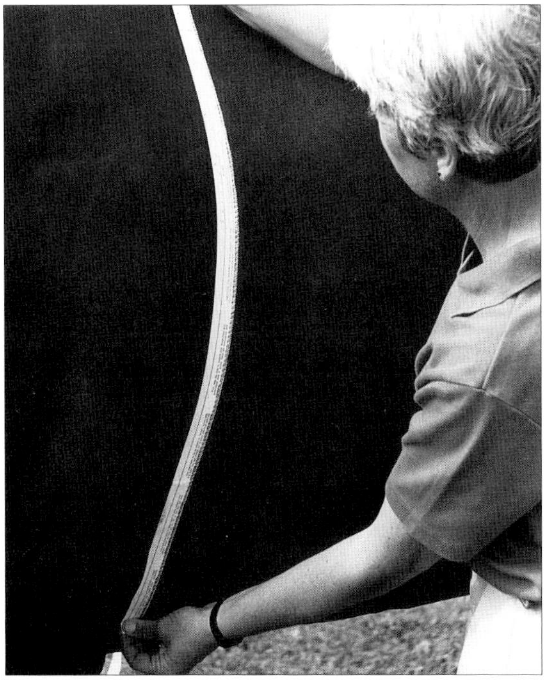

How to estimate your horse's

BODY WEIGHT AND CONDITION

Following are step-by-step guidelines for estimating your horse's body weight and condition. You'll need to know his current weight to calculate the proper dose of medications such as dewormers, and to provide a baseline for future reference as you monitor his condition throughout life. And you'll need an objective assessment of your horse's condition–what one horse owner sees as being in "show shape," for example, might be considered obese by veterinary standards. (Obesity can be a significant risk factor for serious, even life-threatening diseases such as laminitis[G].)

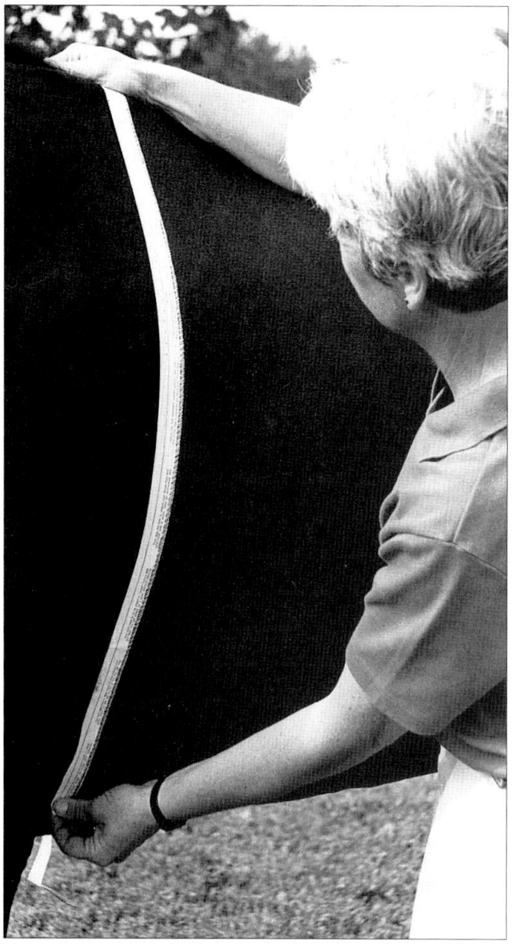

Step 1.

HOW TO ESTIMATE YOUR HORSE'S BODY WEIGHT

Use this method for an estimate that's usually more accurate than what you'll get from a standard commercial weight tape.

Step 1: Using a flexible (but not stretchy) tailor's measuring tape, measure the circumference of your horse's girth, in inches, running the tape just behind the elbow on both sides and straight over his withers. (See photo at left.) Write this number down.

Step 2: Using a rigid carpenter's measuring tape or a 6-foot folding ruler, measure the length of your horse's torso on one side, in inches, from the point of his shoulder to the point of his hip. Write this number down.

Step 3: Apply your measurements to the following formula:

$$\frac{[(\text{Girth})^2 \times \text{Length}]}{330} = \text{Body weight}$$

Example: Say your horse has a girth of 66 inches and a body length of 62 inches. His body weight would be:

$$\frac{66^2 \times 62}{330} = 818.4 \text{ pounds}$$

HOW TO ESTIMATE YOUR HORSE'S BODY CONDITION

Now that you've got a good estimate of current body weight, determine your horse's body condition by assessing six body-condition checkpoints. For each checkpoint, choose the description that most closely matches your horse's body. Then add up the points and divide the total by 3 to calculate his body condition score, on a scale of 1 to 10 (see below). If your horse scores from 1 to 3, or 8 or above, consult your veterinarian for a safe ration adjustment to address the too-thin or too-fat condition.

THE CHECKPOINTS:

1. Ribs

- **a.** You have to dig to find them . . . . 5 points
- **b.** They're not visible, but easily felt with your fingers . . . . 3 points
- **c.** You can see them . . . . 1 point

2. Shoulders

- **a.** A thick "loaf" of fat behind the shoulders blends them flush with your horse's ribcage . . . . 5 points
- **b.** His shoulders are rounded and blend smoothly into his body. . . . 3 points
- **c.** Bone structure of shoulders is easily seen with no fatty covering . . 1 point

3. Back

- **a.** There's a prominent crease along his back . . . . 5 points
- **b.** His back is level, with no crease or ridge . . . . 3 points
- **c.** There's a ridge along his back . . . . 1 point

4. Tailhead

- **a.** His tailhead is surrounded by bulging fat . . . . 5 points
- **b.** Fat can be felt around his tailhead, but isn't visible as a bulge . . . . 3 points
- **c.** The tailhead bone is prominent . . . . 1 point

5. Withers

- **a.** There's a sofa-like cushion of fat on both sides of his withers . . . 5 points
- **b.** His withers are slightly rounded, not buried in fat . . . . 3 points
- **c.** The bone structure of his withers is prominent . . . . 1 point

6. Neck

- **a.** There's a doughy loaf of fat along the crest of his neck . . . . 5 points
- **b.** His neck is smooth . . . . 3 points
- **c.** The bone structure of the neck is visible . . . . 1 point

THE SCALE

1 = Poor condition
2 = Very thin
3 = Thin
4 = Lean
5 = Neither fat nor thin
6 = Show shape
7 = Plump
8 = Fat
9 = Very fat
10 = Dangerously obese

NOTES

CHAPTER 7

How to STIMULATE THIRST

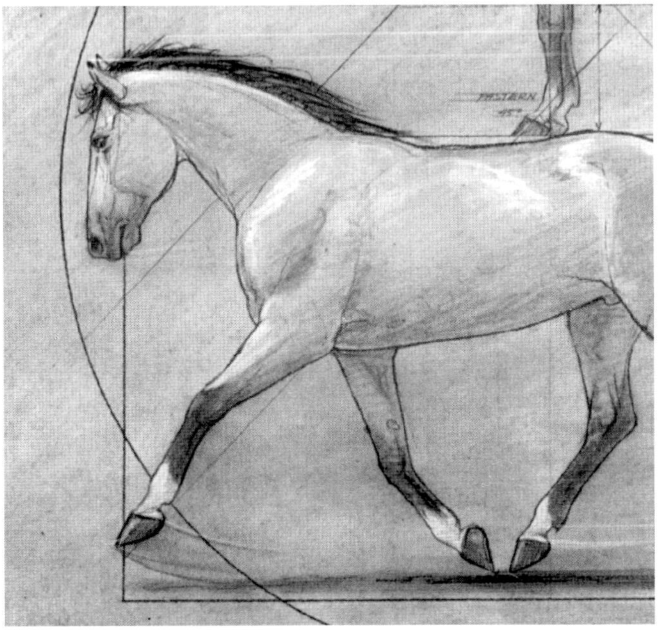

HOW TO STIMULATE THIRST

You've heard the old saying, "You can lead a horse to water, but...". Well, there may come a time when it's in your horse's best interest to drink, even if he seems disinterested. Perhaps your vet has determined that your horse's hydration is borderline, your horse has a slight fever from a viral infection and doesn't feel like eating or drinking, or maybe the weather's turned suddenly cold and his water intake has plunged. It'll fall upon you to try and get him to take in some water in order to avoid the stress, expense, and discomfort of having fluids administered in some other way (such as by stomach tube or intravenously). Is it possible to make your horse drink? No. But there are ways of triggering the thirst sensation. Try these tricks.

HOW TO STIMULATE THIRST

1. Mix 1 teaspoon of table salt with 2 tablespoons of applesauce and squirt it on the back of your horse's tongue, using a cleaned-out paste-deworming syringe. (Tip: Ivermectin and moxidectin syringes are too small; use a different kind.) While your horse works the applesauce around in his mouth, remove his water bucket, clean and rinse it thoroughly, and return it to the stall filled with fresh water. If the salt's going to work, your horse will drink within 5 minutes. No luck? Don't repeat this until he drinks at least 1 gallon of plain water. Try the next step.

2. Squirt 5 cc (1 teaspoon) of light corn syrup on the roof of your horse's mouth, using a clean dosing syringe. While your horse works his tongue over the super-sweetness, add a second bucket of fresh water to his stall, placing it in a novel location so he'll be compelled to investigate. Give this ploy 5 minutes. No luck? Don't repeat this step until he drinks at least 1 gallon of plain water. Move to Step 3.

3. Remove the extra bucket, dump half the water out, and top it off with hot water. Adjust the temperature until it reads 120° F on an instant-read thermometer. Some horses will drink deeply when offered warm water, especially (but not necessarily) when the weather has turned abruptly chilly. Be sure to have a bucket of the room temperature water available also, so your horse has a choice. Still no luck? No problem, we've got a few more tricks up our sleeve....

4. Leave the warm-water bucket in your horse's stall, and add a third bucket of room-temperature water mixed with a commercial electrolyte product labeled for equine use. (Follow the mixing directions for that particular product.) Wait 20 minutes. Still no luck? Keep going....

5. If your horse's condition doesn't forbid solid foods (ask your veterinarian, if you have any doubts), offer a bran mash (see page 244) laced with molasses, apple slices, and lots of warm water. Not interested? (Report this lack of appetite to your veterinarian, if he/she isn't already aware of it.) You've got one more shot....

6. If your horse's condition doesn't preclude a little exercise, halter him and take him for a brisk 15-minute walk for some fresh air, a fresh outlook, and (if his condition and the season permit), a few mouthfuls of fresh grass. The boost to his circulation should brighten his eye and his outlook, and sharpen the sensation of thirst that you've augmented with Steps 1 and 2. When he returns to his stall, he'll likely investigate his smorgasbord of buckets and drink. If not, consult your veterinarian.

If your horse does drink, keep track of the volume he takes in and the time passed. Your veterinarian will tell you how much water your horse needs to take in over a 24-hour period. Renew your efforts every few hours to keep the water moving.

Water Works...

A plastic kitchen strainer makes a nifty sieve to lift out leaves, hay, and other floating debris from an otherwise clean tubfull of water. If you use the kind that has a handle, you'll keep your hands dry and warm in winter weather.

NOTES

CHAPTER 8

How to DISINFECT YOUR HORSE'S ENVIRONMENT

8 HOW TO DISINFECT YOUR HORSE'S ENVIRONMENT

HOW TO DISINFECT A STALL

To help prevent the spread of contagious disease, you might have to disinfect a stall that was inhabited by a sick horse. Here's how.

1. Remove all bedding.

2. Remove all removable objects, such as buckets and feeders. Using a mixture of hot water and dish detergent, scrub them free of residue. Rinse thoroughly, then scrub again with a solution of 1 part laundry-type chlorine bleach to 10 parts water. Allow them to air-dry without rinsing. Scrub one more time with hot water and dish detergent. Rinse thoroughly to remove any bleach or detergent residue.

3. Sweep cobwebs, dust, hay, etc. from the stall floor, walls, ledges, and door.

4. Wash walls and other solid surfaces using a pressure washer (or garden hose), a stiff scrub brush, and dish-washing detergent.

5. Mix Lysol® Disinfectant Concentrate (2-1/2 tablespoons per gallon of water) in a garden-type spray tank. Wear protective clothing, including long sleeves, long pants, gloves, goggles and head gear. Spray a soaking mist of disinfectant onto all surfaces and allow to air-dry. Repeat.

6. Return clean buckets and feeder to your horse's stall. Bed with clean bedding.

HOW TO DISINFECT YOURSELF

Use these tips to help prevent carrying a contagious disease on your skin or clothing after handling a sick horse.

1. When entering the horse's stall or paddock: Wear rubber boots and close-weave fabric coveralls with long sleeves. Confine your hair in a hat. Use disposable latex or rubber examination gloves whenever working with/around the sick horse. Leave these garments at the stall door or paddock gate, where they can be donned before entering and taken off when you leave.

2. Upon leaving the horse's stall or paddock: Discard the used disposable gloves in a closed receptacle outside the enclosure. Disinfect your boots with a plastic scrub brush and Lysol® Disinfectant Concentrate (2-1/2 tablespoons per gallon of water) in a dishpan or bucket. Leave boots outside the enclosure to dry. Cover or discard the Lysol® solution for safety. (It's toxic if swallowed.)

3. When tending to more than one horse, take care of the sick one last.

HOW TO DISINFECT GROOMING TOOLS

Clean your brushes and grooming tools at least once a month to help prevent skin problems from developing and spreading, particularly if grooming tools are shared among several horses.

1. Remove all hair.

2. Soak and scrub your brushes and tools in hot water and dish detergent to loosen and remove all oils, dander, scabs, and other residue.

3. Prepare Lysol® disinfectant solution (2-1/2 tablespoons per gallon of water); soak all grooming tools for 30 minutes. Discard solution, allow tools to air-dry, preferably in the sun. (Note: Wooden-handled tools might be damaged by soaking. Use tools that are made of materials that can be soaked safely, such as plastic or metal.)

HOW TO DISINFECT SADDLE PADS AND BLANKETS

Clean blankets and pads weekly or monthly, depending on how frequently they're used. Doing so will help prevent skin problems from developing and spreading, particularly if these items are shared among several horses.

1. Remove hair with a plastic brush and/or vacuum cleaner. Discard vacuum cleaner bag.

2. If machine-washable, run pads through the wash cycle with Lysol®. (Use 1 cup in a standard top-loader.) Spin dry, and run through a second wash cycle with Ivory soap flakes. Add vinegar to the rinse water to help remove soap residue. (Use 1 cup in a standard top-loader. Some horses have a skin sensitivity to detergent residues in saddle pads and blankets.) Tip: If your washing machine is too small to wash saddle pads, inquire at local laundromats for permission to use their machines. Most will allow this but will require that you run the machines once more, empty, after you're finished, to remove hair and other residue.

3. Allow to air-dry, preferably in the sun. ➤

Commonly Used Disinfectants

Category	Example	Uses	Comments
Iodophors 10%	Undiluted Betadine® solution	Skin	Will kill most equine pathogens, even in the presence of organic matter. May stain surfaces permanently.
O-phenylphenol	Lysol® Disinfectant Concentrate, prepared 2-1/2 T per gallon water	Objects, premises	Will kill most equine pathogens, even in the presence of organic matter. Should not be used on broken skin. Toxic to cats, horses, and humans if ingested or absorbed through open wounds. In a recent study, this category of disinfectant was deemed best for horse facilities.
Chlorhexidine	Nolvasan®, Virusan	Skin, objects, premises	Effective against most equine pathogens; ineffective against Rotavirus; inactivated in the presence of organic matter.
Hypochlorites	Bleach	Objects, premises	Effective against many equine pathogens; ineffective against Rotavirus; inactivated in the presence of organic matter.
Pine oil	Pine Sol®	Objects, premises	Ineffective against most equine pathogens.

WHAT'S ORGANIC MATTER?

Anything that is, was, or came from living cells. This includes pollens, molds, cobwebs, fly "tracks," feed, saliva, manure, urine, sweat, dirt, hay, straw, sawdust, hair, blood, scabs, pus....

CHAPTER 9

The well-stocked EQUINE FIRST-AID KIT

The well-stocked

EQUINE FIRST-AID KIT

Talk to your veterinarian about items appropriate for your home first-aid kit. These will be used for care of your horse's minor illnesses or injuries, or to use on your veterinarian's advice while you wait for his/her arrival in more serious cases. Here's a list of medications and devices to consider. Each list has a column marked "E" for items you might want to include in your quick-grab emergency kit. Unless stated otherwise on their labels, perishable items should be replaced every 3 years. Over time, medications can lose their potency or become contaminated.

CAUTION

The "COMMENTS" column, in which common uses are described, is meant to help you decide what items, if any, to stock in your home pharmacy. It is not meant to substitute for the careful, step-wise, conditional advice given in the Action Plan flow charts in Section I.

Do not administer any treatment, topically or internally, to your horse without consulting your veterinarian and the flow chart for your horse's specific symptom(s).

MEDICATIONS

PRODUCT	USE	E	COMMENTS
Electrolyte powder, paste *Available at tack/feed stores, and from veterinarians and veterinary supply catalogs.*	To restore lost electrolytes, stimulate thirst.	✔	Use only those products made specifically for horses.
Ivermectin or moxidectin dewormer *Available from tack/feed stores, and from veterinarians and veterinary supply catalogs.*	For purge deworming and parasitic skin conditions.		Can cause temporary increase in inflammation as parasites die.

EYE PRODUCTS

PRODUCT	USE	E	COMMENTS
Eye-wash solution *Available at human pharmacies, tack/feed stores, and from veterinarians and veterinary supply catalogs.*	For irrigation of irritated eyes.	✔	If opened, replace within 3 weeks.
Boric acid or Lacri-Lube® eye ointment *Available at human pharmacies.*	For protection of dry and/or irritated eyes.	✔	If opened, replace within 3 weeks.

**"Homemade" substances are designated with an asterisk (*); recipes follow.*

Cleansing and/or Debriding Agents			
PRODUCT	**USE**	**E**	**COMMENTS**
Saline solution* (homemade or use commercial saline for contact lens rinse)	For irrigating wounds.	✔	Can be used warm or cold.
Double-strength saline solution*	For wet dressings when drawing is desired.		Can be used warm or cold.
10% benzoyl peroxide acne cleanser *Available in acne section at most human health and beauty aisles.*	For removing scurf from thickened or scaly skin.		Also available as leave-on gel, for use when rinsing is difficult (e.g., inclement weather).
Medicated scab softener*	For painless removal of scabs due to infectious skin conditions.		Will keep up to 1 week; store loosely covered.
Drawing Agents			
Commercial poultice *Available at tack/feed stores, and from veterinary supply catalogs.*	For drawing out swellings and festered wounds.	✔	Can be used hot, cold, or dry.
Homemade poultice*	For drawing out swellings and festered wounds.		
Commercial or homemade sweat*	For drawing out swelling.		If using a product containing DMSO, apply to clean leg that doesn't harbor toxic residues that could be absorbed. ➤

Disinfectants			
PRODUCT	**USE**	**E**	**COMMENTS**
Betadine® (povidone iodine) or Nolvasan® solution *Available at human pharmacies, or from veterinarians and veterinary supply catalogs.*	To clean certain open wounds.	✔	Water-based; can be daubed, sprayed, or poured on.
Betadine® ointment *Available at human pharmacies, from veterinarians, tack/feed stores, and veterinary supply catalogs.*	To treat certain open wounds.	✔	The petrolatum base makes it an effective protectant.
Betadine® scrub *Available at human pharmacies, from veterinarians, tack/feed stores, and veterinary supply catalogs.*	For certain infectious skin conditions.		The lathering base makes it a good cleanser/debrider.
Lysol® Concentrate *Available in grocery stores.*	For disinfection of premises and certain contaminated foot conditions.		For dilution at 2-1/2 T per gallon or 2 drops per cup of water.
Emollient, Anti-Inflammatory, Anti-Itch, &/or Protectant Agents			
Non-antibiotic first-aid cream, such as zinc oxide, Bactine®, Corona Ointment®, A & D Ointment®, and 100% aloe vera gel *Available at human pharmacies, grocery stores and from veterinary supply catalogs.*	For soothing and protecting certain open wounds or burns.		On burns, use water-based creams rather than petrolatum-based ointments.
DMSO gel *Available from veterinarians, tack/feed stores, and veterinary supply catalogs.*	A topical anti-inflammatory and a vehicle for other topicals.		Do not mix with toxic substances. Wear latex or rubber gloves when handling. Do not apply to fresh (less than 3 days old) or open wounds.

Emollient, Anti-Inflammatory, Anti-Itch, &/or Protectant Agents (continued)

PRODUCT	USE	E	COMMENTS
Cortisone ointment *Available at human pharmacies.*	Human product, used as a topical anti-inflammatory.	✔	Absorption/strength increased if used under waterproof bandage.
Fly repellant labelled for use on open wounds, such as Swat® *Available from tack/feed stores and veterinary supply catalogs.*	For superficial wounds or over dressings.	✔	Do not use under bandages or waterproof dressings (which would increase absorption of insecticide).
Zinc oxide or titanium dioxide cream *Available at human pharmacies and grocery stores.*	For use as a sunblock.		
Witch hazel *Available at human pharmacies and grocery stores.*	Topical anti-itch for certain skin conditions; anti-itch agent.		More effective/longer-lasting if used after bathing.
Calamine lotion *Available at human pharmacies and grocery stores.*	To dry, soothe, & protect certain skin conditions.		A good anti-itch agent.
Petroleum jelly *Available at human pharmacies and grocery stores.*	To moisturize and protect tissues.	✔	Also aids in applying hoof boots.

Useful Devices and Gadgets to Have on Hand

ITEM	USE	E	COMMENTS
Instant-read cook's thermometer *Available at kitchen shops and grocery stores for about $10.*	For adjusting temperature of medicated solutions such as eye washes and drinking water.		Registers in about 20 seconds. ➤

Useful Devices and Gadgets to Have on Hand (continued)

ITEM	USE	E	COMMENTS
Stethoscope *Available from medical supply stores, tack/feed stores, and veterinary supply catalogs for about $10-$50.*	For accurately taking heart and respiratory rate counts, and to listen to gut sounds.	✔	Choose Littman-type with about a 20-inch center tube.
Rectal thermometer *Available at grocery stores, human pharmacies, and from veterinary supply catalogs for $5-$10.*	For taking rectal temperature.	✔	Choose electronic-type with memory and beeper or standard glass type. Have a spare.
Chemical cold pack *Available at human pharmacies, medical supply stores, and from veterinary supply catalogs, for about $15.*	For chilling wounds when ice is not available.	✔	Follow directions. Can cause frostbite if direct skin contact is prolonged.
Electric clippers, #40 blade *Available from tack/feed stores and veterinary supply catalogs for about $100 (clippers) and about $20 for a #40 blade.*	For clipping hair from around wounds and skin conditions.		Clean blade after each use. Have professionally sharpened after every 6 uses.
Plastic-bristled pot-scrubber brush *Available at grocery and variety stores for about $3.*	For cleaning hoof before soaking, poulticing, or bandaging; for applying disinfectant to infected hoof conditions.		
Latex or rubber examination gloves *Available at human pharmacies and from medical supply stores or veterinary supply catalogs for about $10 per box of 100 gloves.*	For safe handling of infected body fluids; for use when applying medications and/or DMSO.	✔	Choose rubber if you're allergic to latex.

Useful Devices and Gadgets to Have on Hand (continued)			
ITEM	**USE**	**E**	**COMMENTS**
Hoof pick *Available from tack/feed stores and veterinary supply catalogs for $5.*	For routine foot care.	✔	
Hoof knife *Available from tack/feed stores and veterinary supply catalogs for about $5.*	For investigating possible foot problems.		If you're left-handed, get a hoof knife that's made for south paws.
Shoe pullers *Available from tack/feed stores for about $50, or farrier supply catalogs (ask your farrier).*	For cutting clinches and pulling loose or improperly seated shoe.	✔	
Hoof boots *Available from tack/feed stores and veterinary supply catalogs for about $35 each.*	For hoof protection or medication.	✔	Buy two if different size is required for fore vs. hind hoof.
Combination pocket knife/tool kit *Available at camping supply stores and from outdoorsman-type catalogs for about $35-$100.*	For cutting rope/wire; pulling nails; impromptu repairs.	✔	Choose tool that includes straight knife, serrated blade, leather punch/awl, pliers, and wire cutters.
Trigger-type spray bottle *Available at grocery and variety stores for about $2 each.*	For pressurized irrigation of wounds with saline solution.		Alternative: 30-60 cc syringe with blunted 18-gauge needle.

➤

USEFUL DEVICES AND GADGETS TO HAVE ON HAND (CONTINUED)			
ITEM	USE/QUANTITY	E	APPROXIMATE PRICES
Bandaging materials *Available at human pharmacies, grocery stores, and from veterinary supply catalogs and tack/feed stores.*	(4) 1-lb rolls fluffy cotton	✔	$6 each
	(6) thick sanitary napkins	✔	$7/box of 30
	(6) disposable diapers	✔	$5/box of 40
	(1) package 4 x 4 gauze sponges	✔	$5 per package of 200
	(12) 4-inch rolls stretch gauze	✔	$1.50 each
	(12) 4-inch rolls Vetrap	✔	$2 each
	(12) 4-inch rolls Elastikon	✔	$3 each
	(6) 4-inch rolls Expandover	✔	$3 each
	(1) roll 2-inch duct tape	✔	$3 each
	(1) bandage scissors	✔	$6 each

RECIPES

Saline solution

- 1 tsp. table salt
- 1 quart water

Mix in clean container until salt is completely dissolved.

Double-strength saline solution

- 2 tsp. table salt
- 1 quart water

Mix in clean container until salt is completely dissolved.

Scab softener

- 1-16 oz. bottle mineral oil (baby oil is okay)
- 1-16 oz. bottle 3% USP hydrogen peroxide
- 1 1/2 oz. bottle tincture of iodine

Combine all in large container. Do not close tightly. Mixture will bubble slowly and expand, and can cause a messy explosion.

Epsom salt soaking solution

- 1/2 cup Epsom salts
- 1 gallon warm water (like a hot bath)

Mix until salts are dissolved. Soak affected body part by immersing in a container (such as for a hoof), or by applying a wet dressing.

Poultices (All are non-irritating)

1. Mix Epsom salts with enough warm water to make a paste.

2. Mix 1/2 cup Epsom salts + 4 cups miller's bran; mix with enough warm water to make a paste.

3. Kaopectate® mixed with enough flour or miller's bran to make a paste.

4. Sodium bicarbonate (baking soda) mixed with enough witch hazel to make a paste.

5. "Sugardine:" Table sugar mixed with enough Betadine® solution to make a paste.

RECIPE BONUS

LEG SWEAT
Mix Furacin® liquid or ointment with an equal amount of medical-grade DMSO. (See page 103 for how-to sweat a leg.)

CHAPTER 10

How to make a WHEAT BRAN MASH

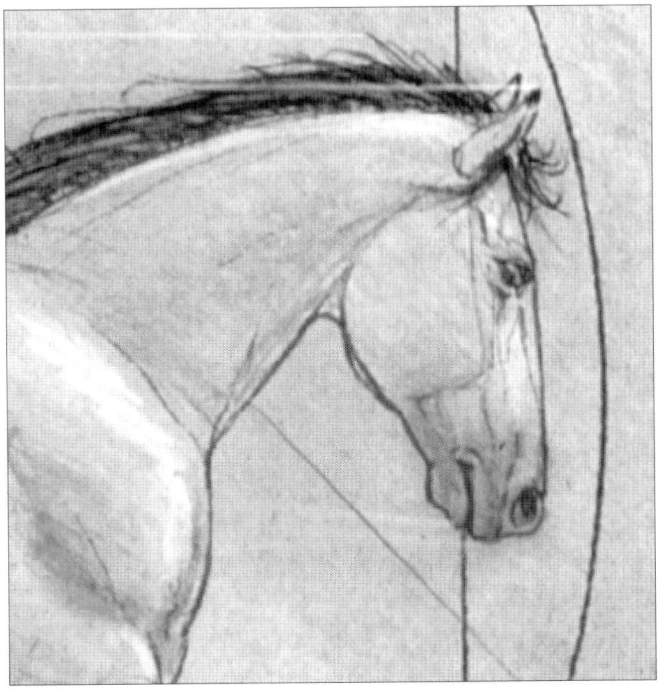

10

How to make a

WHEAT BRAN MASH

A wheat bran mash can serve several purposes. It's comfort food, as fulfilling to prepare as it is for your horse to eat. But it's also an effective way to get your horse to eat and drink what might otherwise elicit an upturned nose—vegetable oil, mineral oil, medicines, and a good dose of water. Here's how to make a lip-smacking mash for your horse.

CAUTION

Because of its high phosphorus content, don't give your adult horse a bran mash more often than twice a week, and wait until your youngsters are over 3 years of age before giving them one. Excessive phosphorus in the daily diet can cause bone development problems and has been linked with the formation of enteroliths[G].

BRAN MASH

3-lb coffee can of wheat bran
1/4 cup dark molasses
1 grated carrot
3-4 cups hot tap water

Mix first 3 ingredients in a clean bucket. Add water slowly, stirring constantly, until mash is uniformly damp and "weeps" some of its moisture out in a gravy when you allow it to sit for a moment. Be sure to allow it to cool before feeding.

Variations: Substitute apple sauce for the molasses; substitute a diced or grated apple for the carrot; or add 1 cup of your horse's regular grain (subtract that amount of grain from his regular daily ration, so you're not increasing his total grain intake).

Note: Contrary to popular belief, wheat bran does not have laxative or stool-softening effects in your horse, because horses can digest it. Therefore, feeding bran is not an effective means of removing sand or dry manure impactions.

CHAPTER 11

How to give ORAL MEDICATION

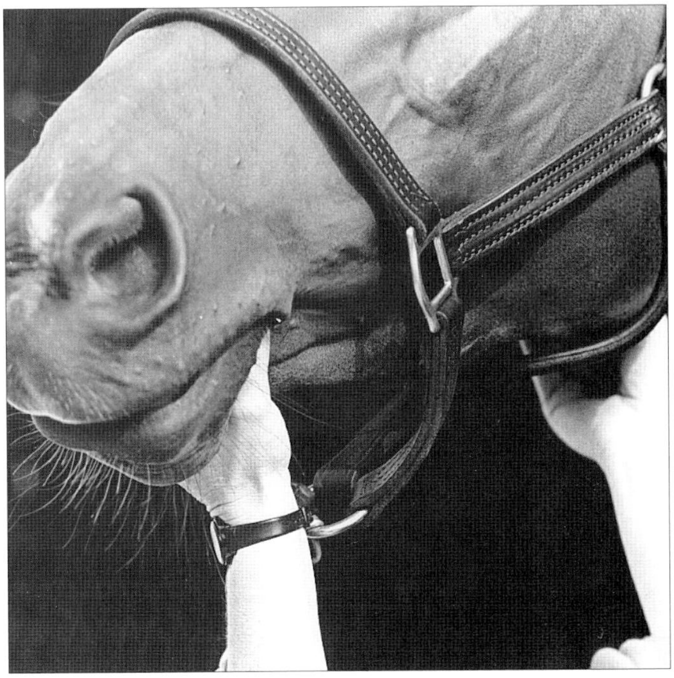

11

How to give
ORAL MEDICATION

Whether it's your horse's regular paste-dewormer or a medication prescribed by your veterinarian to treat an illness or injury, from time to time you'll be expected to administer oral medication. Following are guidelines for getting the job done without a fight, and without winding up with a glob of medication on the stall floor.

HOW TO CALCULATE A PROPER DOSE

Make sure the dose you're giving is based on an estimate of your horse's weight that's as accurate as possible. (See page 224.) Report your horse's weight to your veterinarian so prescribed medications are dosed properly.

USE FINESSE, NOT FORCE

• Whenever possible, choose a paste medication that's been flavored for palatability. Many common horse medications are profoundly bitter. (Bute is probably the worst in this regard, but there's an apple-flavored product that's less awful.) An unpleasant taste will stick in your horse's mind, making your next dose more difficult to deliver. (Tip: For several days in a row, administer a dose of molasses or applesauce. This will condition your horse to believe that whenever a plastic nozzle is inserted between his lips, what's coming will taste good.)

• Horses that are distrustful of any sort of mouth manipulation may have had an unpleasant past experience—a rough tongue grab, for example, or a painful dental procedure—and will require patience and intelligence on your part to replace fear with cooperation. Rather than try and out-muscle your horse (a competition you're sure to lose), bridle him with his usual bit so you have easy mouth access with confirmed control.

BASIC TECHNIQUE FOR ADMINISTERING PASTE MEDICATION

Step 1. Make sure your horse's mouth is empty. If he's got a wad of partially chewed feed in there, he'll spit it—and the expensive medication—out as soon as you've medicated him. If he's eating, halter or bridle him. Move him away from his food, and wait until he's finished chewing and swallowing. (Tip: While you wait, groom him, so he'll be relaxed and will finish what's in his mouth. Some horses will stop chewing and hold a wad of feed in their mouths if they anticipate something unpleasant.

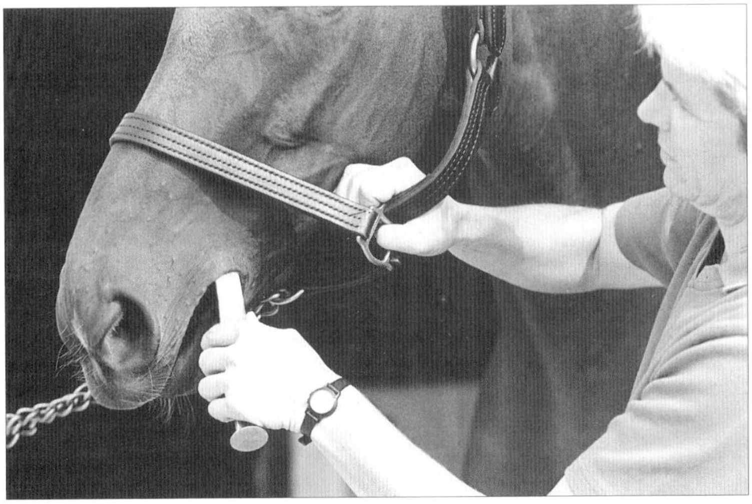

Step 3.

Step 2. If your horse is cross-tied, unsnap the ties and move him to an area where there's a solid wall behind him. Stand to one side, out of striking distance. Hold the halter with one hand while you rub the side of the syringe along the side of his face with the other hand. Your goal is to get him relaxed and aware of the syringe's presence near his mouth, not to ambush him. That would work only once or twice, after which he'd be suspicious of your every move.

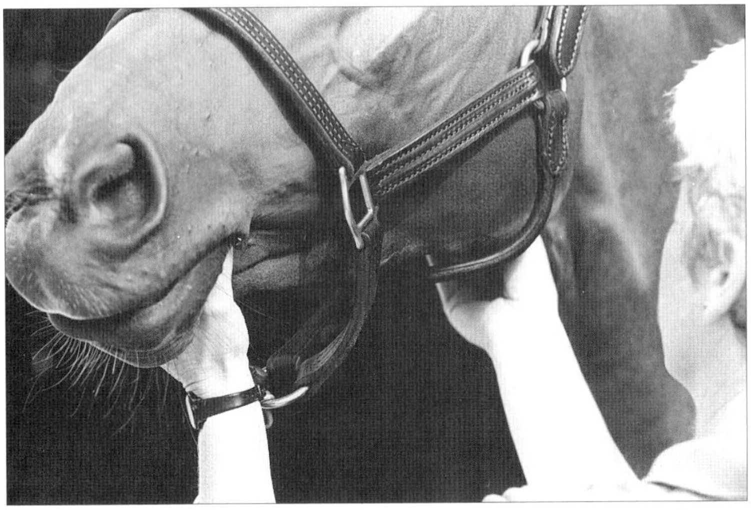

Step 4.

Step 3. As soon as your horse is relaxed (head lowered, slow blinking, heavy sigh emitted), slip the tip of the syringe into his mouth at the bars, where the bit would rest. Direct it back and upward toward the roof of his mouth, advancing it until your knuckles touch his chin. In a single, smooth motion, push the plunger and pull out the syringe.

Step 4. Place one hand under your horse's chin and lift slightly, to raise his head a bit and to encourage his mouth to stay closed while the wad of medication spreads out and adheres to his mouth and tongue. With your other hand, massage his throatlatch area to stimulate swallowing.

Step 5. To make dosing a pleasant experience, immediately follow with a dose syringe of molasses or apple sauce.

NOTES

CHAPTER 12

How to give an INTRAMUSCULAR INJECTION

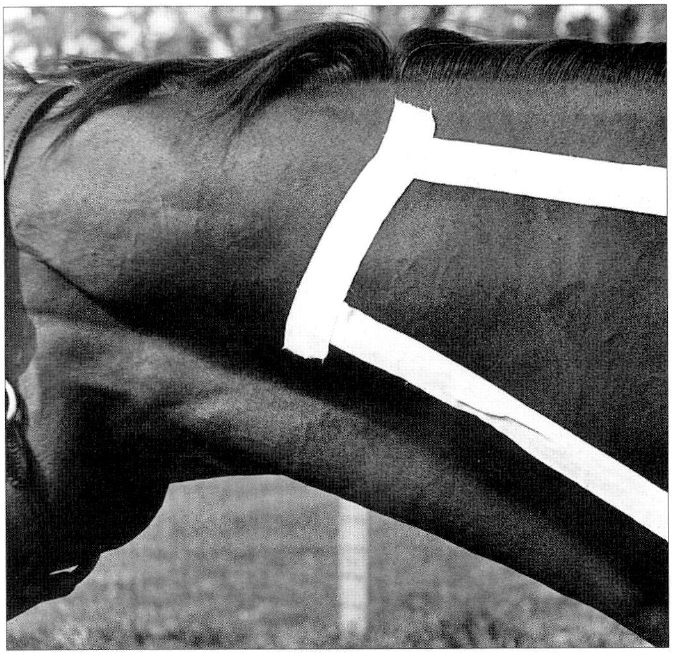

12

How to give an
INTRAMUSCULAR INJECTION

If you and your veterinarian feel it's appropriate for you to give intramuscular (IM) injections to your horse, request a hands-on training session first. This not only will boost your confidence, it'll also help make your technique more comfortable—and therefore safer and more positive—for you and your horse. In addition, it'll give your veterinarian the opportunity to watch your technique and satisfy himself/herself that you understand the important do's and don'ts of safely administering IM injections. After you've passed this hands-on lesson, use the following roadmap when you need a refresher course. Be sure to review the signposts that warn of potential pitfalls.

CAUTION

It's true that non-veterinarians give IM injections to their own horses all the time. It's also true that many of them are taking unnecessary risks in doing so—risks to their own health and safety and that of their horses. It's not a particularly difficult procedure to follow, but there definitely is a right way to give an IM shot, in order to minimize those risks. If you intend to give IM injections to your horse, there are two things you must do first:

1. Understand that even when done properly, there is still a risk of mishaps, including allergic-type medication reactions, accidental injection into a blood vessel (particularly if your horse twitches or moves while you administer the medication), infection at the injection site, and the ever-present danger that you'll be stepped on, bitten, shoved, or kicked while you're giving the shot. Decide whether you accept these risks before proceeding.

2. Learn the proper technique. This will require your veterinarian's cooperation as well as your commitment to refresh your memory before each injection.

STEP 1: GETTING SET UP

• Use only new, sterile, individually wrapped, disposable needles and syringes.

• *Needle size:* For most medications given to an adult horse, choose an 18- or 19-gauge needle, 1-1/2 inches long, so the medication will be deposited deep in the muscle where inflammatory reactions will be less likely to occur. (Accidental placement of the needle in a blood vessel will be easier to detect with this size needle than if you use a smaller gauge. Blood will be more likely to appear in the hub of the larger needle, warning you that it's trespassed into forbidden territory.) For foals, minis, and ponies, choose 19- or 20-gauge needles that are 1-inch long.

• *Syringe size:* Choose a syringe that's at least 30 percent larger than needed to for the dose. (Example: For 15 cc's of medication, use a 20-cc syringe.) This way, the plunger will be fully seated and it'll be easy to manipulate with one hand.

• Use only fresh, properly stored medications that aren't outdated. (Check the expiration date on the label.)

• When drawing medications from a multiple-dose bottle, disinfect the stopper of the bottle with alcohol and let it air-dry before drawing up the dose.

• If giving vaccinations, avoid multiple-dose vials. Every time a dose is retrieved, what's left in the vial is at risk of contamination, which can cause serious infection.

• With the needle facing upward, tap any bubbles out of the medication into the space at the base of the needle, and press the plunger carefully to bring bubble-free medication to the needle's hub.

STEP 2: CHOOSING AN INJECTION SITE

Locations marked with a star (*) are the preferred injection sites of the American Association of Equine Practitioners (AAEP). Each site has advantages and disadvantages: ➤

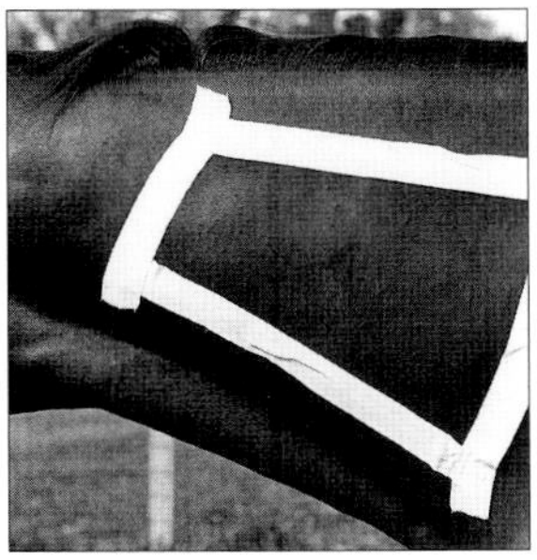

Neck

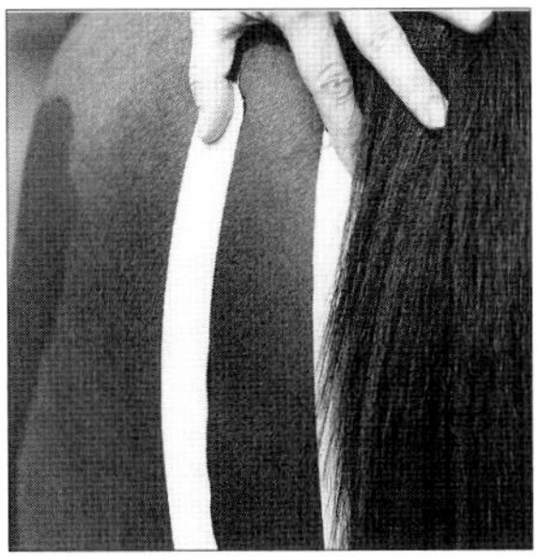

Thigh

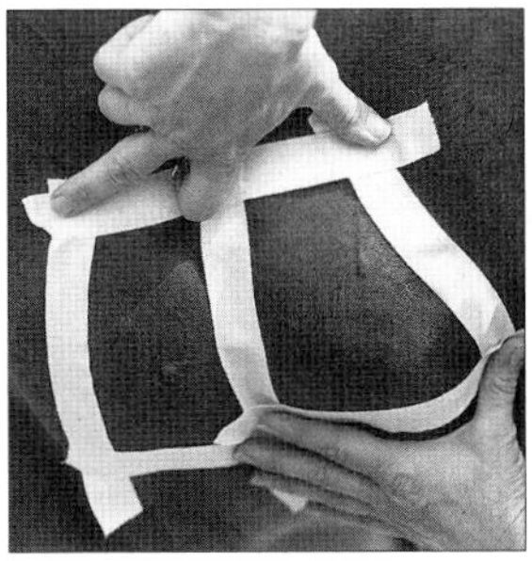

Brisket

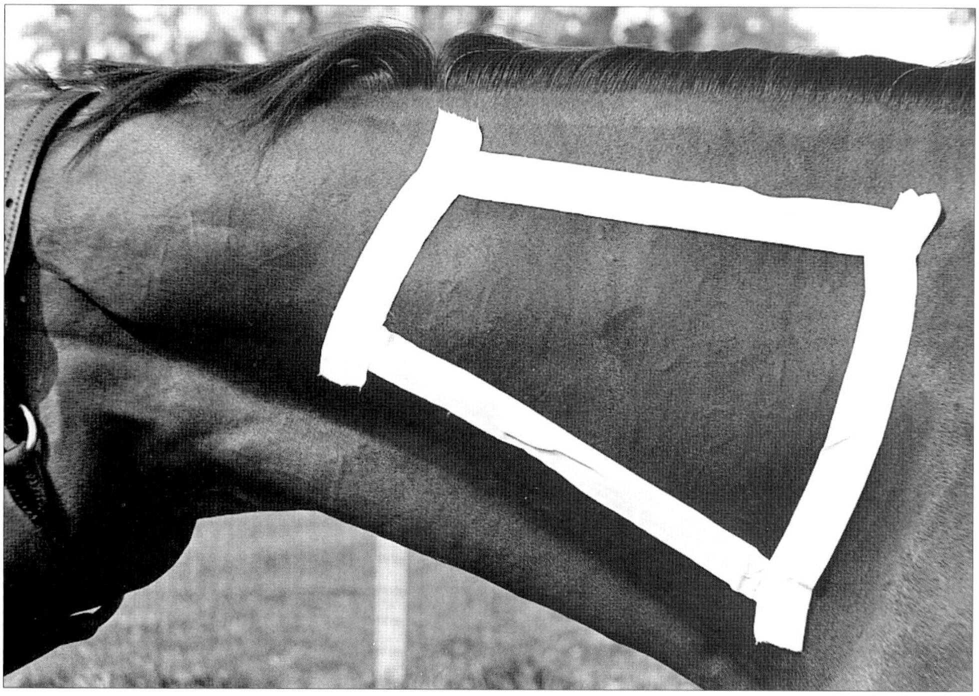

The neck site.

NECK INJECTION*

Advantages: Well tolerated; easy to restrain horse and give injection without a helper. Vertical position means good dissipation of medication—it doesn't sit in a pool, which can lead to inflammatory reaction and abscess formation.

Disadvantages: Inflammatory reaction means stiff neck, making it painful for your horse to eat or drink, and interfering with training. Nearby vital structures make misplaced injection dangerous.

Good site for:

• As a general rule, doses of 15 cc or less. (For larger volumes, split the dose into several injections.)

• Thin preparations, such as vaccines. (Note: With such watery substances, you can give up to a 30 cc dose in a single neck injection to a 1,000-pound adult horse in good condition.)

• Transparent or translucent medications, such as vitamins and certain antibiotics. (See "Note" above.)

• Thick, opaque medications such as penicillin, in 15 cc doses, or less. (Such medications require a large mass of muscle tissue to dissipate effectively, hence the "15 cc" rule.)

** Denotes AAEP preferred site.*

THIGH INJECTION*

Advantages: Active muscles and vertical position encourage dissipation of medication. This means less risk of pooling, inflammatory reaction, and abscess formation.

Disadvantages: Highest risk of being kicked; not well tolerated in adult horses; requires an assistant to hold/restrain horse; misplaced needle risks injury to sciatic nerve; some horses aren't well-muscled enough to accommodate a 1-1/2 inch needle here.

Good site for: Small volume injections, of 15 cc or less. (Same guidelines as those for neck; see opposite page.)

The thigh site.

RUMP INJECTION

Advantages: A popular site for injection among non-veterinarians. Lots of thick muscle to receive medication.

Disadvantages: Some horses more likely to kick or jump; horizontal position increases risk that medication will "pool" rather than disperse, increasing risk of inflammatory reaction and abscess formation. To lessen that risk, this site should be considered only in horses with a sloping croup.

Good site for:

- Doses of 15 to 30 cc, consisting of viscous antibiotics, such as penicillin, or other medications.
- If the dose exceeds 30 cc, divide it into several injections.

Note: Not approved by the AAEP. Check with your veterinarian before administering a rump injection. Many veterinarians frown on the use of this site. However, others advocate and use the site, with no more reports of problems than with injections given at other sites.

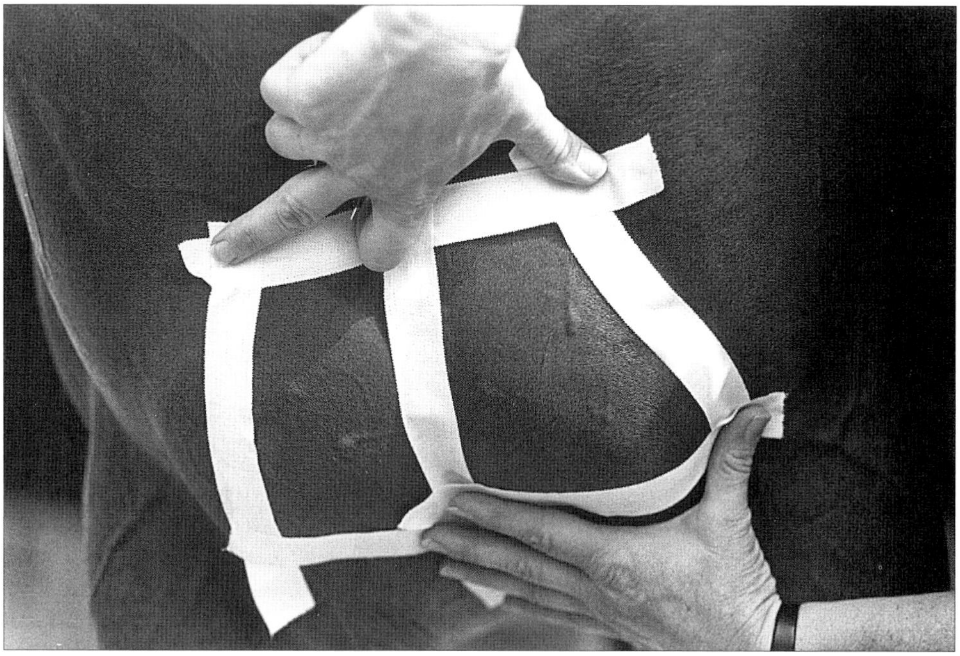

The brisket site.

BRISKET INJECTION

(Muscle mass in front, between legs, as shown above.)

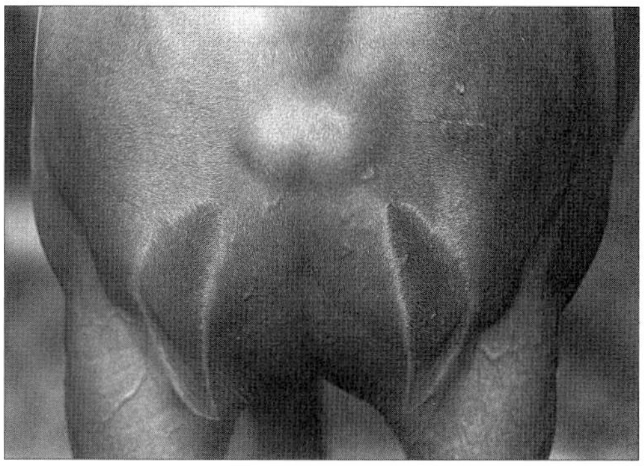

An example of a well-muscled brisket.

Advantages: Usually well tolerated. Use only on well-muscled horses, such as the one shown at right.

Disadvantages: Not appropriate for narrow-chested horses that aren't well-endowed with muscle in this location; limited to small-volume injections; naturally lends itself to gravity "pooling" which can lead to inflammatory reaction and abscess formation.

Good site for:

- Thin, watery medications in doses of 10 cc or less. (See Caution, at left.)
- Thin-skinned or shot-weary horses. With few exceptions, horses show little or no discomfort with an injection here.
- Giving a shot when you're by yourself, since you can do so without requiring a helper to hold your horse.

Note: Many veterinarians frown upon the use of this site, because of the potential for pooling of medications and a high associated risk for abscess formation. Check with your veterinarian before giving an injection here.

CAUTION

Due to the brisket's small muscle mass and the tendency of medications to pool rather than dissipate here, never exceed the 10 cc rule. And, no substances that are potentially irritating (such as vaccinations), viscous, and/or opaque should be given here.

STEP 3: PREPARING THE SITE

• Clean the injection site: Curry and/or bathe the site if it's visibly dirty. Use a clean brush to remove dirt/dust.

• Studies have shown that the risk of causing an infection when a horse is given an injection through undisinfected skin is small. Therefore, unless your horse's skin and/or haircoat is visibly dirty, there's likely no need to disinfect his skin before administering an injection. However, if it is dirty, here's an easy, effective way to disinfect the site.

1. Prepare a small, sealable bottle of disinfectant and label it: "Shot Swab." (Choose from one of the following two.)

- Tamed iodine solution: 1 teaspoon Betadine® solution plus enough water to make it look like a weak tea.
- Chlorhexidine solution: 1 teaspoon Nolvasan® solution in 3/4 cup of water.

2. Dampen a clean cotton ball with your disinfectant solution, select your injection site, and swab the site. Repeat, using a fresh cotton ball for every swipe, until the cotton ball comes off clean. (It's important that the cotton ball be damp, but not soaked—you don't want the skin so wet it drips, or it'll take too long to dry.)

3. Wait 1 to 2 minutes for your horse's skin to air-dry.

4. Proceed with your injection.

STEP 4: GIVING AN INJECTION

1. Fill the syringe with the appropriate dose.

2. With a firm twist, remove the needle from the syringe and uncap it. In a single, smooth motion, insert the needle into the chosen, disinfected site, advancing it all the way to the hub. (Practice first on an orange or grapefruit, if you're unsure as to how much force will be needed.)

3. Look into the hub for any sign of blood. If there's blood, pull out the needle, get a fresh one, and start over. If there is no blood present, go on to the next step.

4. Attach the syringe firmly to the needle. While steadying needle hub with one hand, pull back slightly on the plunger to confirm that the needle is not accidentally in a blood vessel. If blood appears in the syringe, pull the needle out, get a fresh needle and a fresh dose of medication, and start over. If no blood appears in the syringe, go on to the next step. (Why get a fresh needle? Because there's blood in

RED-ALERT SIGNPOST

What tou see: You've barely given the entire dose when your horse begins to breathe heavily, twitch, act excited, or begin backing up. Before you can remove the needle, he either collapses or rears up and falls over backward.

What's happening:

The medication was inadvertently given into a blood vessel. Get out of harm's way and call your veterinarian NOW.

RED-ALERT SIGNPOST

What you see: Delayed, severe reaction. You've given the entire dose, removed the needle, and up to an hour has gone by when you notice your horse breathing heavily. He has an anxious look, and his skin is riddled with hives.

What's happening: **He's having an allergic-type reaction, called anaphylaxis[G], which occurs occasionally when a horse becomes hypersensitized to certain substances, including penicillin and other antibiotics, vaccines, and vitamins. Call your veterinarian NOW.**

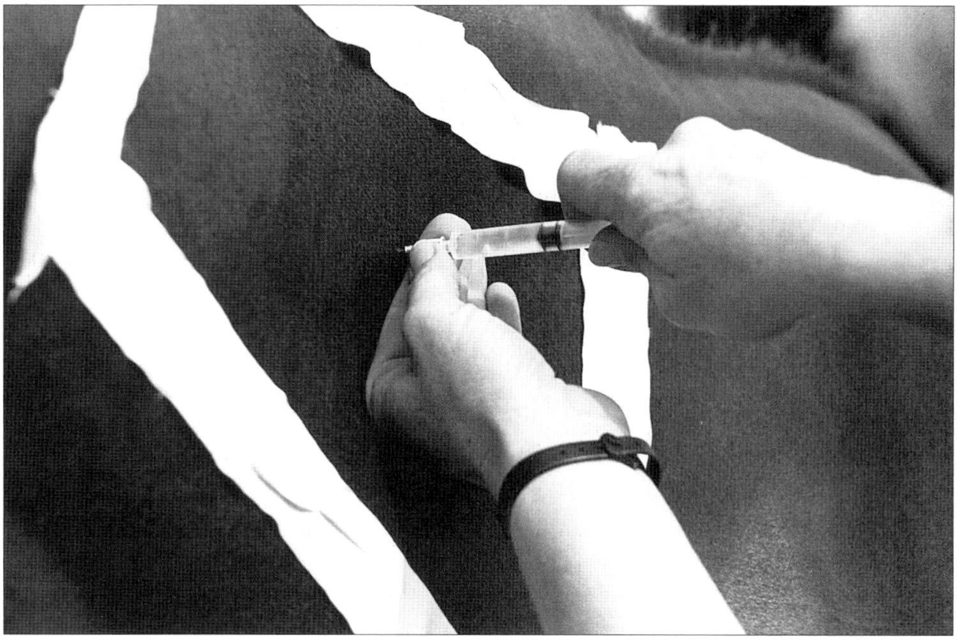

IM shot procedure in neck site.

this one, which can make it difficult for you to determine whether you've hit another blood vessel on your next attempt.)

5. While continuing to steady the hub of the needle, push the plunger steadily (about 1 to 2 cc per second) until the syringe is empty. Wait for 5 seconds so the medication will have time to dissipate away from the tip of the needle.

6. Pull out the needle in a single, smooth motion and immediately massage the injection site with the balls of your fingertips. This will aid in dissipating the medication and will help close the needle hole.

SIGNPOST

What you see. **Swelling at the injection site: A day or two after giving the shot, a palm-sized swelling has appeared. It's hot to the touch, and your horse resents finger pressure there.**

What's happening: **It's one of two things: a non-infected inflammatory reaction, or an infection. If it's an infection, it could be rapidly fatal unless treated with antibiotics and other medications to prevent shock—it depends on the type of bacteria involved. Even though the fatal infection is relatively rare, in the early stages it's virtually indistinguishable from the non-infected inflammatory reaction. To be safe, call your veterinarian at the first hint of swelling, heat, or tenderness/soreness at an injection site, regardless of who gave the injection.**

CHAPTER 13

How to CLEAN A WOUND

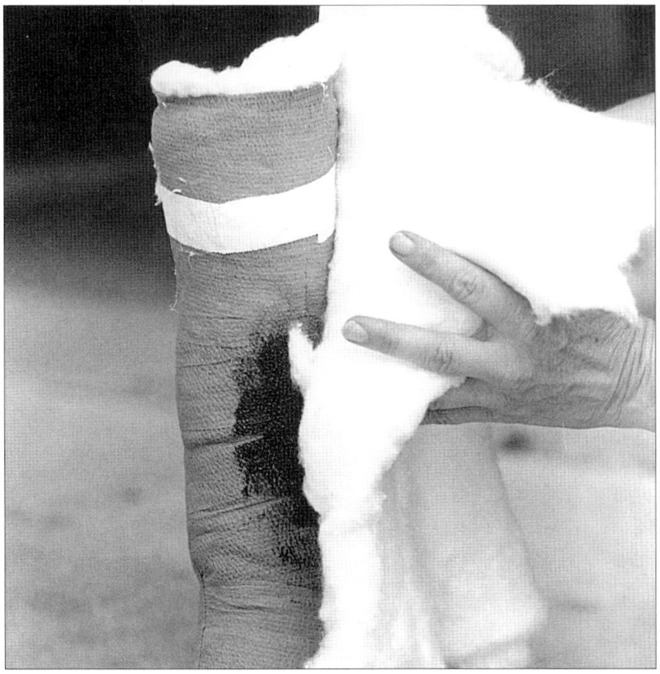

13

How to
CLEAN A WOUND

Every wound has its own special treatment requirements. These are detailed in Section I of this book—find the Action Plan that best describes your horse's wound, and follow the appropriate instructions. What follows are basic guidelines for removing visible dirt and debris, and invisible (bacterial or fungal) contamination.

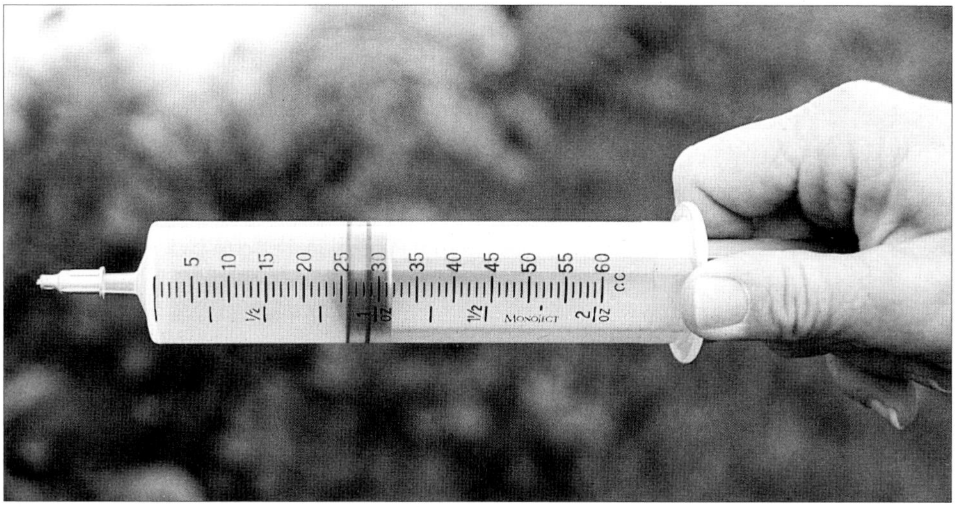

Wound-cleaning tool: Large-dose syringe with a blunted 18-gauge needle.

1. Hose the wound with a standard garden hose. Or irrigate it with saline solution (see page 242), using a trigger-type spray bottle or a large syringe with a blunted 18-gauge needle. Start with a gentle stream, aimed below or adjacent to the wound. Gradually move the water stream onto injured tissues, then gradually increase the intensity of the stream until it mimics the assertiveness of a Water-Pik on full power. This will help dislodge bacteria sticking to tissues. Continue until the wound appears completely clean, or until 5 minutes have gone by, whichever happens sooner.

2. If after 5 minutes of flushing, portions of the wound still appear dirty, lather it with Betadine® surgical scrub, using your clean fingertips or a brand-new infant's toothbrush. Rinse thoroughly, using saline solution for the final rinse.

3. For wounds that still look visibly dirty after Steps 1 and 2, or when cleaning deep wounds or those in which a joint may be involved, take the following steps while you await your veterinarian's arrival:

- Cover it with a thick sanitary napkin or disposable diaper soaked in double-strength saline solution (see page 242). The solution will moisturize tissues and loosen debris; the salt concentration will kill some bacteria and help to draw out contamination that's penetrated deeper layers.

- If the wound involves your horse's lower leg, anchor the saline-soaked pad with a spiral of stretch gauze and secure it, without excessive pressure, with an outer elastic layer, such as Vetrap®.

Budget-wise Bandage Tip...

If your horse needs frequent leg bandaging and you're using disposable materials, you might be able to save a few bucks by using pre-packaged bandages, called Army Surplus bandages or Burn Compresses. Available through veterinary supply catalogs, each kit contains a large (18 inch x 22 inch x 1/2 inch) pad and a 4-inch roll of stretch gauze—for less than the cost of a roll of cotton. They're great for the padding portion of a standing wrap, and can generally be re-used several times.

NOTES

CHAPTER 14

How to ICE AN INJURY

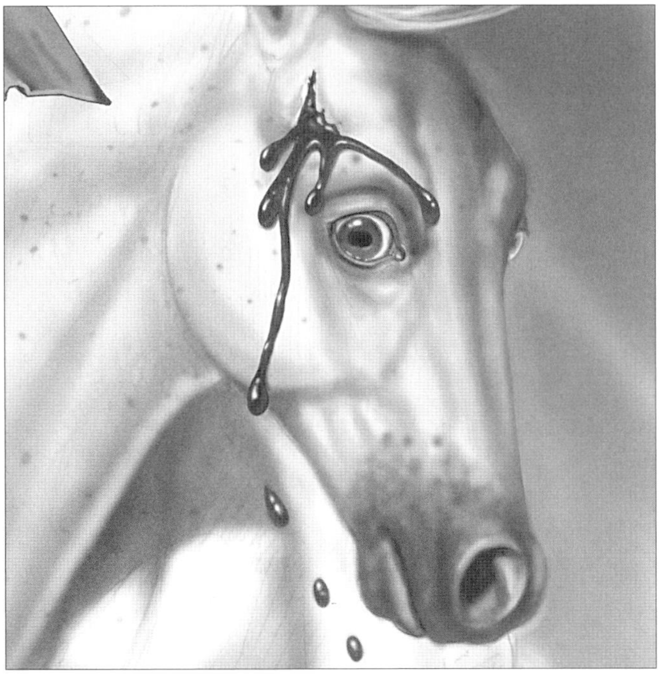

14

How to

ICE AN INJURY

Place a buffer, such as a towel or sheet cotton, between the ice pack and your horse's skin, to protect against tissue damage and help dissipate the cold. The chart at right will tell you which of three types of ice pack would be best to use based on the injury location. It'll also tell you how many layers of buffer to apply, depending on the ice pack and the state of the area being iced. If possible, avoid using chemical cold packs—they can require more protective layers of cloth between pack and skin to prevent frostbite. (However, they're wonderful when you're miles from the nearest freezer and need to ice an injury.) For how long to ice, see Icing Guidelines, below. For how to bandage an ice pack in place, see page 270.

TYPES OF ICE PACKS

• **Rigid:** Waterproof packages containing solid slabs of ice, chemical (e.g., for picnic coolers), or frozen wet cloths.

• **Flexible:** Bags of small, frozen fragments, such as crushed ice, frozen peas, or corn kernels.

• **Chemical:** Padded pouches containing separate chambers which, when mixed, create a super-cold chemical reaction.

ICING GUIDELINES

• For injuries over intact skin, the general rule of thumb is: ICE ON 5 minutes; ICE OFF 15 minutes, one time only.

• If the skin is broken, the rule of thumb is: ICE ON 5 minutes; ICE OFF 15 minutes. Repeat 3 times in a row.

• When at least 1 layer of cloth separates the ice pack from your horse's skin, ice can be left on until it melts and is no longer pulling heat from tissues (usually around 1/2 hour). Be sure to remove the pack when it's no longer cooler than the tissue being iced. Otherwise, it might hold heat in.

INJURY LOCATION	BEST ICE PACK TO USE	METHOD
Eye or other fragile area	Flexible	If using a non-chemical ice pack, place a single layer of cotton cloth between ice and skin. If using a chemical ice pack, place a triple layer of cotton cloth between ice and skin.
Heavily muscled area, such as forearm or hip	Rigid	If using a non-chemical ice pack, place pack directly against unbroken skin. If skin is broken, place a single layer of cotton cloth between pack and wound. If using a chemical ice pack, place a single layer of cotton cloth between the pack and unbroken skin. If skin is broken, place a double layer of cotton cloth between pack and wound.
Bony (e.g., leg or head), or hoof wall	Flexible	If using a non-chemical ice pack, place pack directly against unbroken skin. If skin is broken, place a single layer of cotton cloth between pack and wound. If using a chemical ice pack, place a single layer of cotton cloth between pack and unbroken skin. If skin is broken, place a double layer of cotton cloth between pack and wound.
Joint	Flexible	If using a non-chemical ice pack, place pack directly against unbroken skin. If skin is broken, place a single layer of cotton cloth between pack and wound. If using a chemical ice pack, place a single layer of cotton cloth between pack and unbroken skin. If skin is broken, place a double layer of cotton cloth between pack and wound.

NOTES

CHAPTER 15

How to BANDAGE AN INJURY

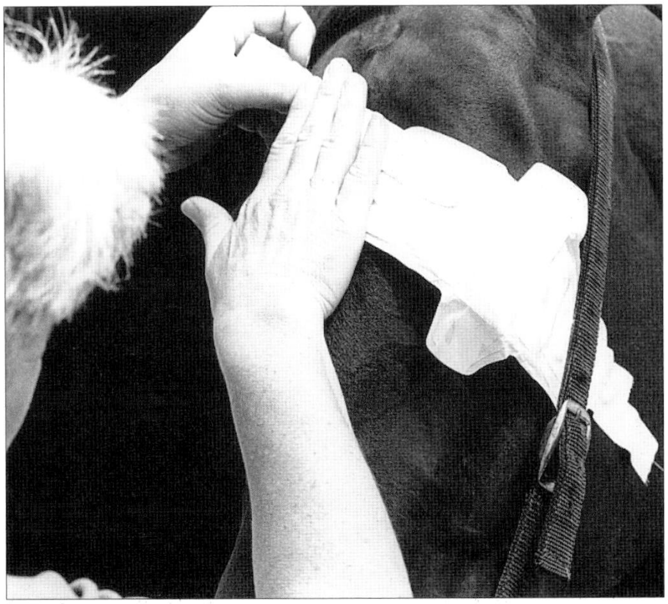

15

How to
BANDAGE AN INJURY

There are four reasons you might want to bandage a wound:

1. To protect it from contamination and/or insects.

2. To hold a medicated dressing or ice pack against the wound.

3. To limit swelling and bleeding.

4. To hold disrupted tissues in their proper positions.

Following are step-by-step instructions for the most common bandages your horse might need due to injury. Included are tips on how to choose appropriate bandaging materials, how to apply them properly, and how to avoid common pitfalls. If your horse's wound requires a variation of these examples, decide your primary reason for bandaging the wound, then use the "Rules of Thumb" (page 269) to help you achieve that goal safely.

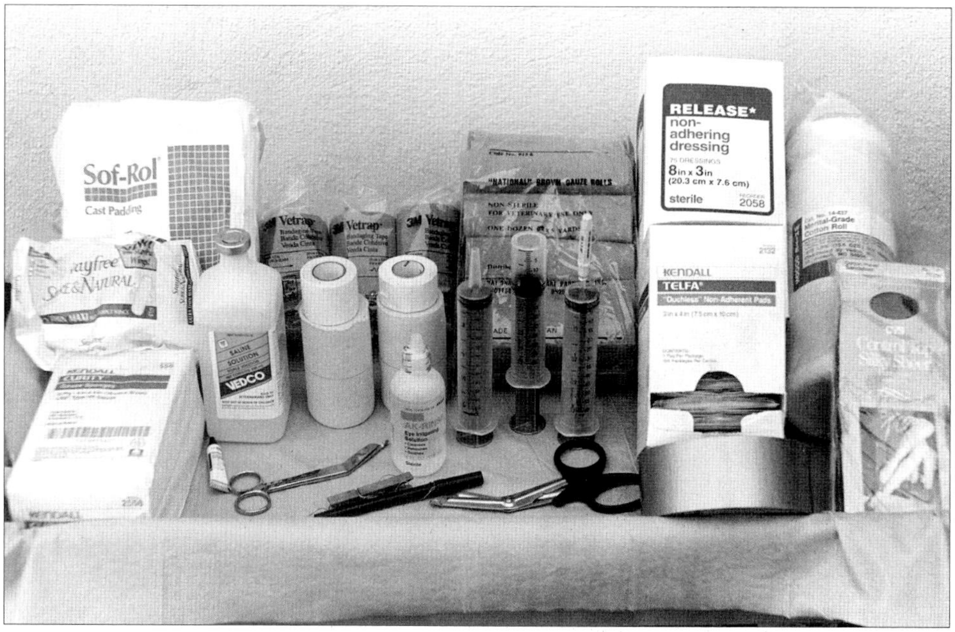

Your equine first-aid kit should include a wide selection of bandaging materials. For what to have on hand, see "Supplies Needed" for the variety of bandages on the following pages.

BANDAGE #1: THE HOOF BOOT

Sample Scenario: Your horse has a wound or abscess on the sole, frog, wall or coronary band of his hoof, or he's thrown a shoe. Your task: Keep the area clean and dressed, and/or protect the hoof against chipping, until your vet or farrier arrives.

SUPPLIES NEEDED		
IDEALLY	**WHY**	**WHAT TO USE IN A PINCH**
Padding: roll cotton or sheet cotton.	To hold dressings against the wound, to absorb drainage, and to keep hoof edges from wearing through outer bandage layers.	Disposable diaper; bath towel folded in half; 12 x 12 piece of sweatshirt material.
Elastic bandage: Vetrap® or something similar.	To hold padding in place.	Ace bandage; or this layer can be skipped.
Waterproof barrier: commercial hoof boot.	To protect inner bandage from wear, debris, and moisture.	Duct tape.

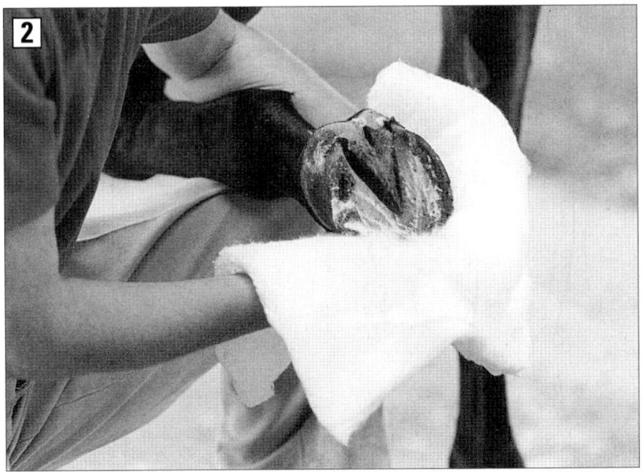

HOW-TO:

Step 1. Clean the hoof. If there's a wound, see pages 13 to 27, for proper care. If you have a hoof boot, apply it now. (Tip: Lubricate the boot with petroleum jelly for easier application.) Otherwise, proceed to Step 2.

Step 2. Center the roll cotton or the absorbent side of a disposable diaper over the sole (above). Bring the edges over the hoof walls. ➤

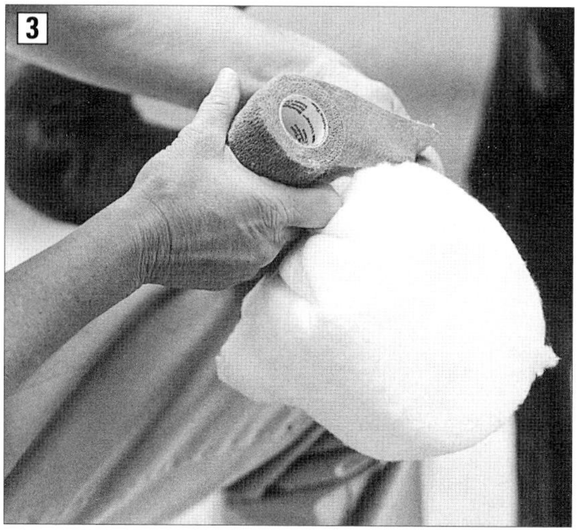

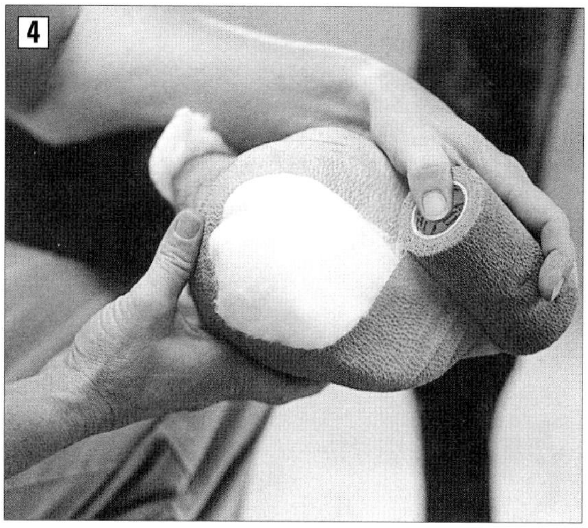

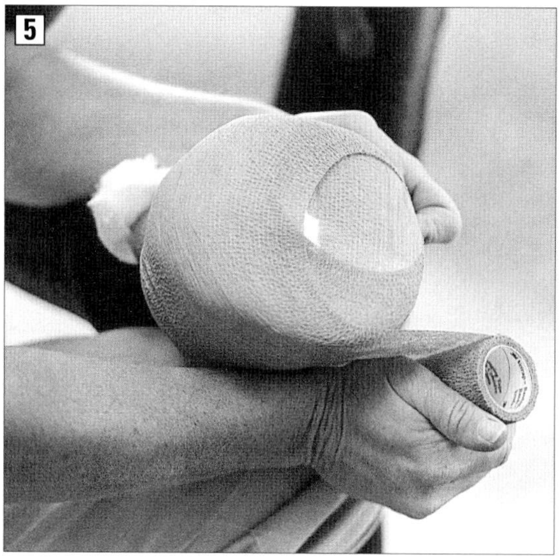

Step 3. Secure it in place with an elastic bandage. Begin by circling the hoof wall and lower pastern once or twice...

Step 4. ... then cover the sole, applying the bandage in a figure-8 pattern. Continue to crisscross the sole...

Step 5. ... to cover any padding still exposed. Take a final wrap around the hoof wall and lower pastern for extra security.

Step 6. Anchor the end with a strip of adhesive tape. Encourage your horse to stand still, by having a helper hold him, or offering him some hay. Pawing or stamping the foot until you've finished Step 8 could result in tears in the bandage.

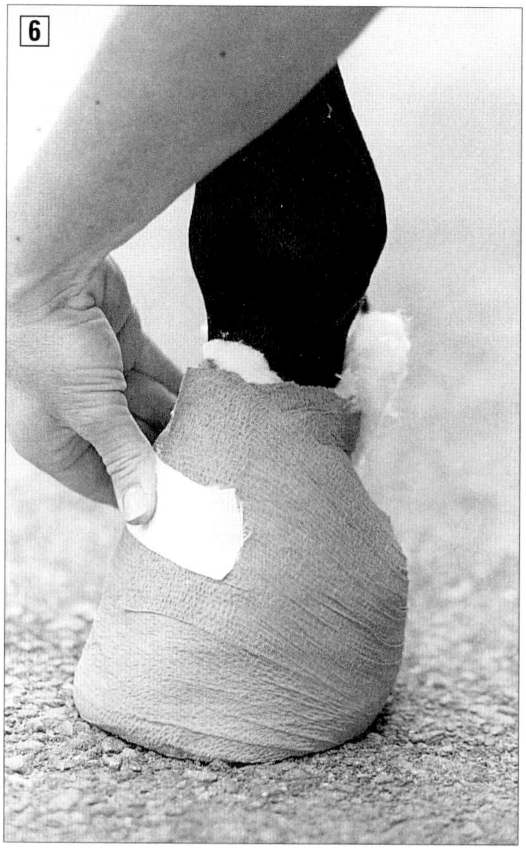

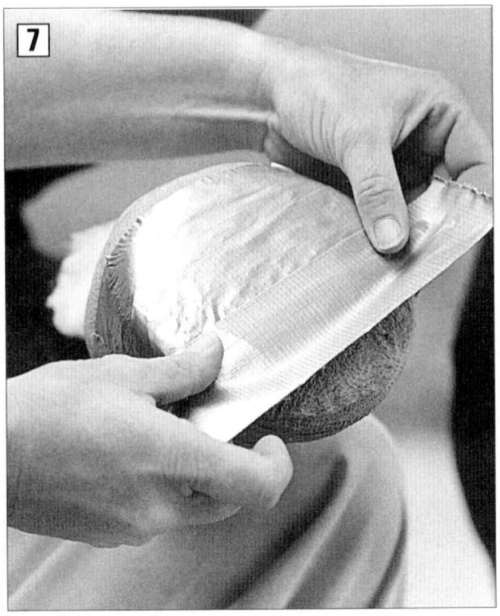

Step 7. Reinforce the wrap by fashioning a waterproof bandage. Apply 10-inch strips of duct tape to the sole, overlapping each strip and the hoof walls.

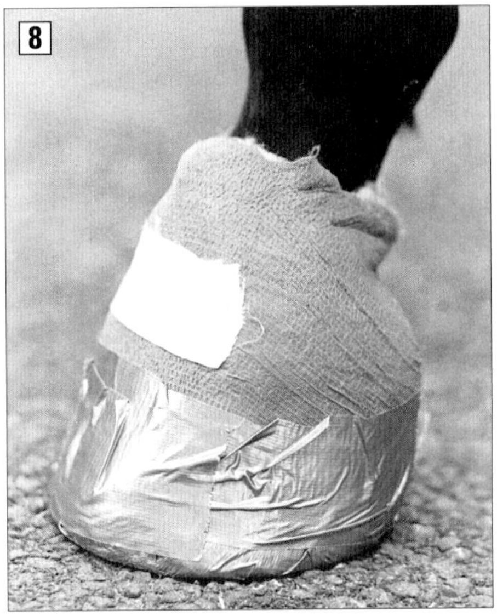

Step 8. Secure it with more duct tape, if necessary. Be careful not to girdle the coronary band, which could cut off the blood supply to the foot. Confine your horse until help arrives.

BANDAGING RULES OF THUMB

1. If your primary goal is to protect the wound from contamination and/or insects:

- Consider applying a chemical barrier, such as petroleum jelly or Swat® (Farnam), instead of a bandage.
- Keep the wound scrupulously clean and free of insect-attracting serum and crust.
- If the wound involves a leg, consider applying a clean track wrap, to keep dust and other contaminants from touching it. If the wound involves your horse's face or an eye, consider applying a fly mask.

2. If your primary goal is to hold a medicated dressing or ice pack against the wound:

- Choose a light elastic bandage with no adhesive, preferably with 100 percent or greater stretchability (a 4-inch section can be stretched to 8 inches or more). The stretchier the bandage, the better it will conform to the contours of your dressing or ice pack, and the less pressure it will exert on your horse's leg.

3. If your primary goal is to limit swelling and bleeding:

- Use a minimum of 2 layers of padding to help distribute pressure evenly over fragile tissues such as tendons.
- Whenever possible, secure the padding layer in place with stretch gauze or a suitable substitute, such as a rolled-up strip of cheesecloth or nylon stocking.

(CONTINUED ON PAGE 271)

BANDAGE #2: THE ICE WRAP

Sample Scenario: Your horse has suffered an injury to soft-tissue structures in his leg. You anticipate (or have already detected) swelling and heat in the injured area. Your task: Chill the tissues in and around the injury to slow the metabolism of adjacent, uninjured tissues that might otherwise die because of decreased circulation through swollen tissues.

SUPPLIES NEEDED

IDEALLY	WHY	WHAT TO USE IN A PINCH
Flexible ice pack filled with crushed ice.	To chill tissues.	Bag of frozen peas.
Elastic bandage: Vetrap®; Elastikon®; or something similar.	To hold the ice pack in place.	Ace bandage and masking tape.

HOW-TO:

Step 1. If the skin is unbroken, place the ice pack directly over the wound. If the skin is broken, separate pack from skin with a protective layer, such as a clean washcloth or one layer of sheet cotton. For more information on choosing an ice pack and deciding whether to use a protective buffer between pack and skin, see page 262.

Step 2. Secure the ice pack to your horse's leg using the elastic bandage. Make it tight enough to hold securely, but loose enough to slip two fingers between it and the leg. (Use a spiral or figure-8 pattern, rather than a closed circle, so as not to cut off blood supply or damage a tendon.) Anchor the end with surgical or masking tape.

Step 3. Leave the ice on for 5 minutes, then off for 15 minutes. (This is appropriate even for broken skin, because you'll have applied a layer of protective buffer between the pack and your horse's skin.)

BANDAGING RULES OF THUMB (CONTINUED FROM PAGE 269)

This will help prevent bunching and wrinkling when you compress the padding with an outer elastic layer.

- **When in doubt about how much padding to apply, apply more. Extra padding layers help protect blood vessels and tendons from pressure.**
- **Choose an elastic bandage with 25 percent to 50 percent stretchability (a 4-inch section can be stretched to 5 to 6 inches). The less stretchy a bandaging material is, and the heftier the fabric it's made of, the greater is its ability to compress tissues (to slow or stop bleeding and swelling) and provide mechanical support. For highly moveable and hard-to-bandage areas, choose adhesive-backed elastic bandage materials for greater security and less slippage.**
- **If blood soaks through the bandage, don't remove it. (This would disturb any tentative clots that may have formed, and the bleeding would start anew.) Instead, apply additional padding and elastic (compression) layers over the existing bandage.**

4. If your primary goal is to hold disrupted skin edges in their proper positions:

- **Gently press the skin edges in place with your fingertips, then tape a clean, dry wound dressing, such as a 1/2-inch stack of gauze sponges or a Kotex sanitary napkin, directly over the wound. Follow with padding and elastic (compression) layers as outlined above for bandaging a swelling/bleeding wound.**

BANDAGE #3: THE STANDARD LEG BANDAGE

SUPPLIES NEEDED		
IDEALLY	**WHY**	**WHAT TO USE IN A PINCH**
Padding: Roll-cotton; sheet cotton; cast padding; leg quilts.	To spread compressive forces evenly under the bandage, hold dressings against external flesh wounds, and absorb drainage.	Thick sanitary napkin; disposable diaper; terrycloth dishtowels or handtowels.
Security layer: Stretch gauze.	To hold padding in place.	Nylon stocking or cheesecloth cut into a strip, 3 in. wide and 3- to 4-feet long, or this layer can be omitted.
Elastic bandage: Vetrap®; Elastikon®; or something similar.	To hold the padding in place and compress it.	Ace bandage and masking tape.

➤

How To Apply a Standard Leg Bandage:

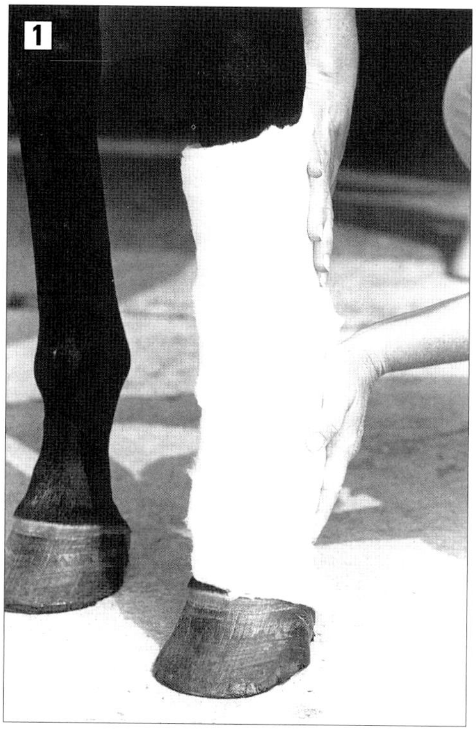

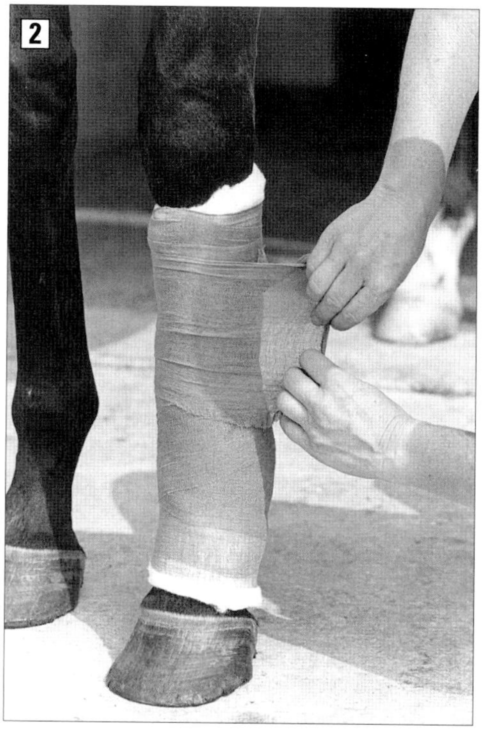

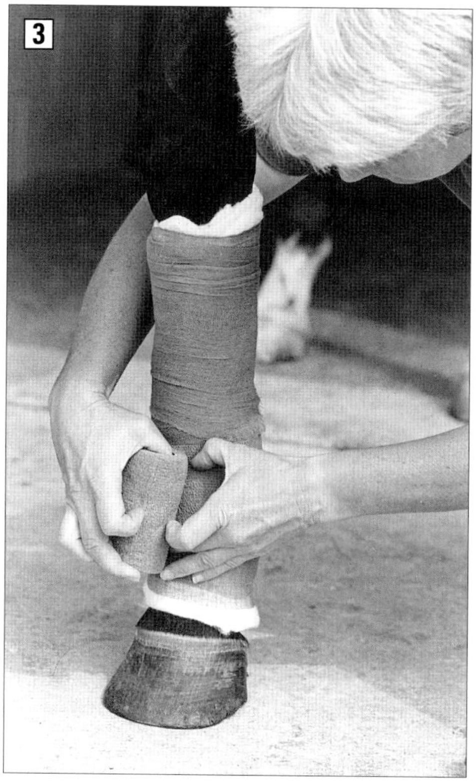

Step 1. Apply 1 inch of padding to the shin (cannon bone), extending from below the fetlock joint to the top of the cannon bone, as shown.

Step 2. Hold the padding in place with a layer of stretch gauze or substitute (see "Supplies Needed", page 271), beginning 1/2 inch above the lower edge of the cotton and spiraling upward. Overlap each previous round by half the width of the bandage material. Continue spiraling upward until 1/2 inch of padding is exposed at the top. Secure the end by tucking under previous rounds.

Step 3. Apply the elastic bandage, using the same pattern as in Step 2, exerting just enough stretch...

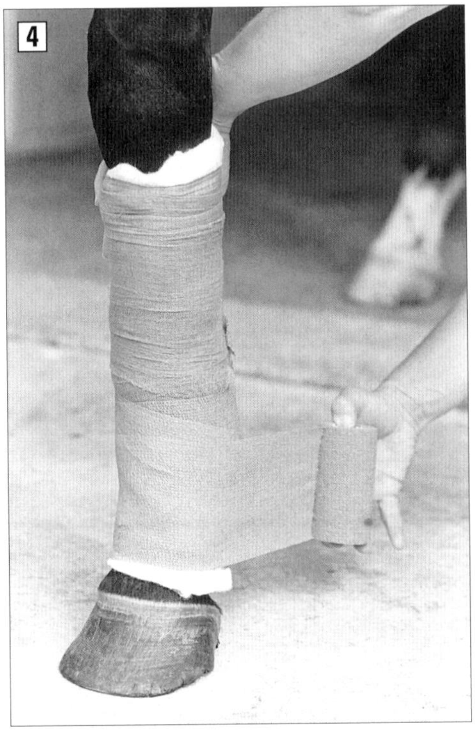

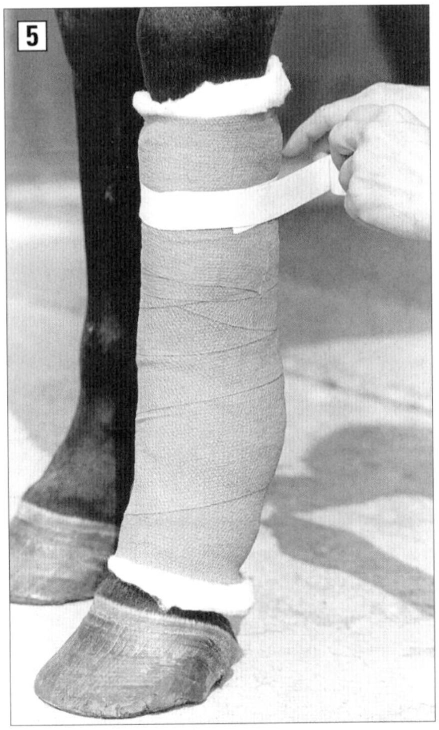

Step 4. ...to make the bandage snug and secure, but not so tight that you're unable to admit one finger between the leg and bandage at any point around the top or bottom.

Step 5. Loosely anchor the end with a strip of adhesive tape. (This also will serve as the anchor portion of the hock or knee bandage, shown on page 274 and 276.)

Did You Know...

When DMSO (dimethylsulfoxide) is mixed with water (or applied to wet skin), the resultant emulsion undergoes a chemical reaction and releases an impressive amount of heat. This could irritate your horse's skin, particularly if he's sensitive.

BANDAGE #4: THE HOCK OR KNEE WRAP

Sample Scenario: Your horse's hock or knee joint is hot, swollen, and/or sporting a visible flesh wound. Your task is to cover any wounds and limit swelling and/or joint movement until your vet arrives.

SUPPLIES NEEDED		
IDEALLY	**WHY**	**WHAT TO USE IN A PINCH**
Padding: Roll-cotton; sheet cotton; cast padding; leg quilts.	To spread compressive forces evenly under the bandage, hold dressings against external flesh wounds, and absorb drainage.	Thick sanitary napkin; disposable diaper; terrycloth dishtowels or handtowels.
Security layer: Stretch gauze.	To hold padding in place.	Nylon stocking or cheesecloth cut into a strip, 3 in. wide and 3- to 4- feet long, or this layer can be omitted.
Elastic bandage: Vetrap®; Elastikon®; or something similar.	To hold the padding in place and compress it.	Ace bandage and masking tape.

Hock Portion

Step 1. Apply "Standard Leg Bandage", page 271, as an anchor.

Step 2. Apply 1 inch-thick padding to the hock, smoothing out all wrinkles and folds so it lays flat against the skin (right). The lower margin of the bandage should overlap the anchor bandage by 2 inches; the upper margin should extend halfway between hock and stifle, as shown in Step 3.

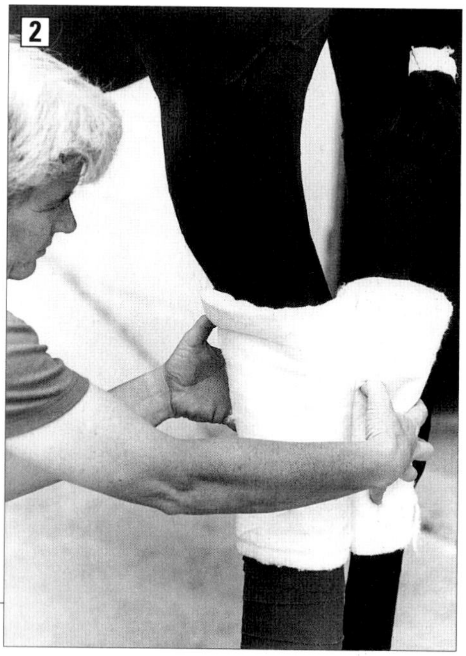

Step 3. Hold the padding in place with a layer of stretch gauze or substitute. Begin on the anchor bandage, below the lower margin of the hock portion as shown at right...

Step 4. ...and spiral upward, forming a figure-8 pattern around the point of the hock to avoid excessive pressure there. Continue spiraling upward until 1/2 inch of padding is exposed at the top.

Step 5. Spiral back down the leg, once again forming a figure-8 around the point of hock, until you reach the end of the gauze roll. Secure the end by tucking under previous rounds.

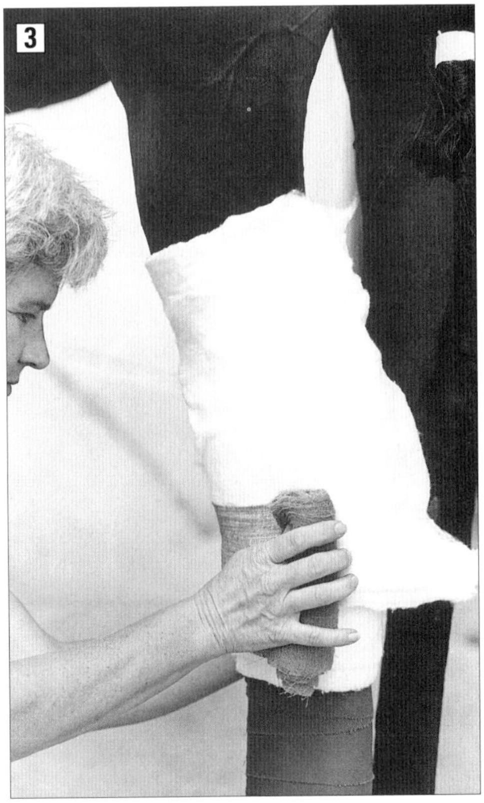

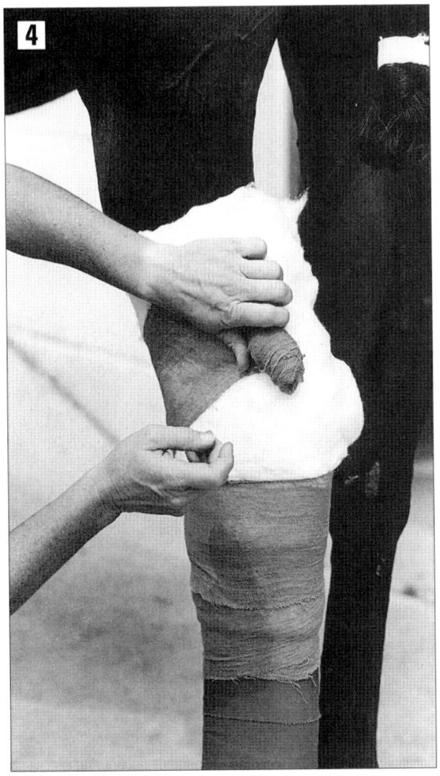

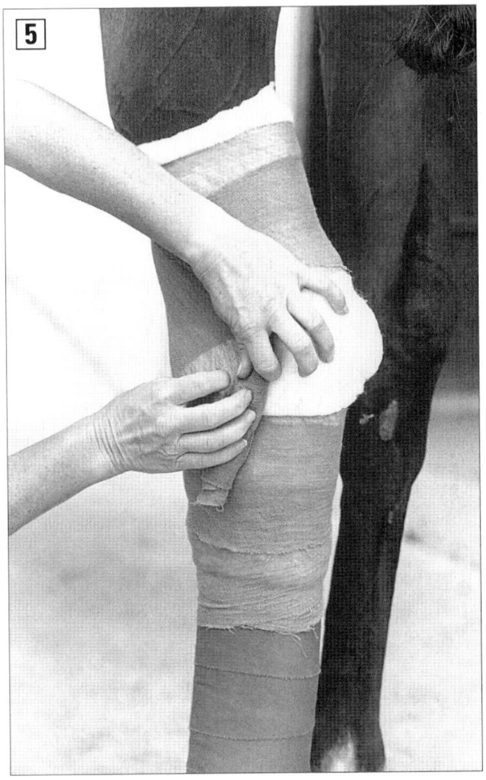

➤

Hock Portion, continued

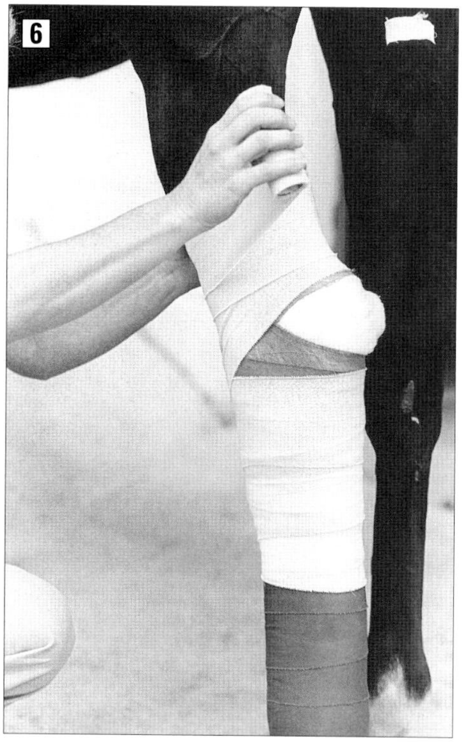

Step 6. Apply a layer of elastic bandage, using the same pattern as in Steps 3 to 5. Exert half-maximum stretch (if a 4-inch length of your elastic bandage can stretch to a maximum of 6 inches, stretch it half that amount, to 5 inches).

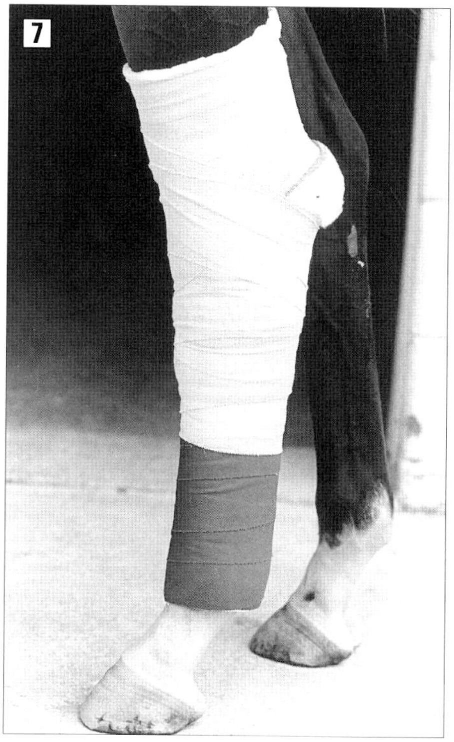

Step 7. Check your hock bandage as often as you can for slippage, preferably every hour. Bandages in this location are difficult to keep up even under the best of circumstances.

Knee Portion

Step 1. Apply "Standard Leg Bandage," page 271, as an anchor.

Step 2. Now make upper anchor (right): Apply a 1-inch layer of roll cotton over the upper foreleg, from just above the knee to just below the elbow.

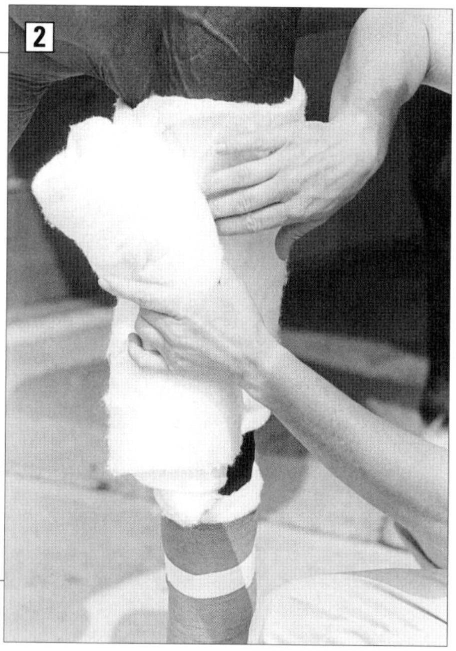

Step 3. Secure the padding with stretch gauze. Start above the bottom edge, then spiral up to 1/2-inch below the upper edge, and back down again. Overlap each round by half the width of the gauze.

Step 4. Follow with a layer of elastic bandage (Elastikon® or Vetrap®), using the same pattern as for the gauze layer, applying at half-maximum stretch. (If a 4-inch length of your elastic bandage can stretch to a maximum of 6 inches, stretch it half that amount, to 5 inches.)

Step 5. Loosely anchor the end with a piece of adhesive tape.

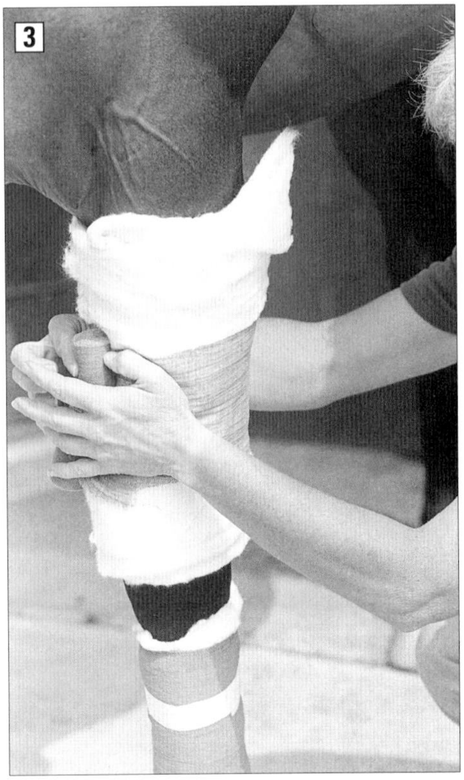

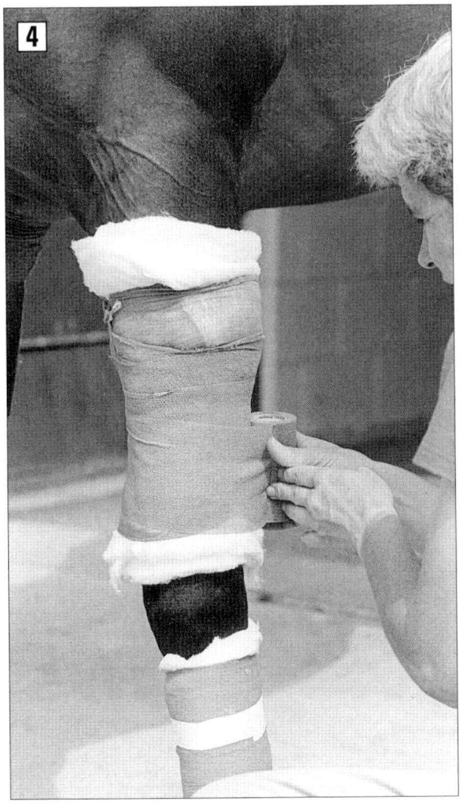

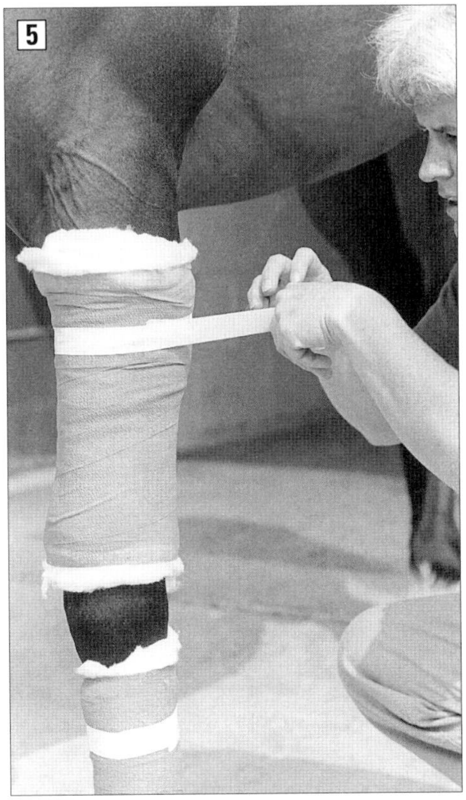

Step 6. Apply 1 to 2 inches of padding to the knee, beginning at the center of the lower-leg anchor bandage and ending at the center of the upper-leg anchor bandage, halfway between the knee and elbow.

Step 7. Hold the padding in place with a layer of stretch gauze or substitute, applying it in a spiral pattern from bottom to top.

Step 8. Apply a layer of elastic bandage (such as Vetrap®), using the same pattern as in Step 7 and applying half-maximum stretch. (If a 4-inch length of your elastic bandage can stretch to a maximum of 6 inches, stretch it half that amount, to 5 inches.)

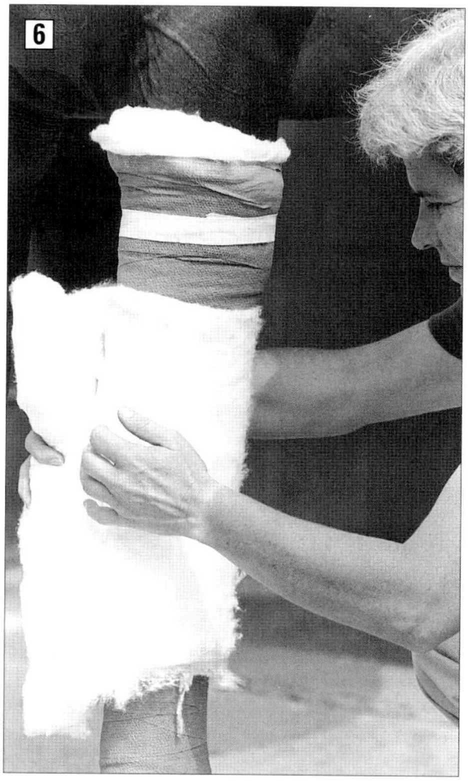

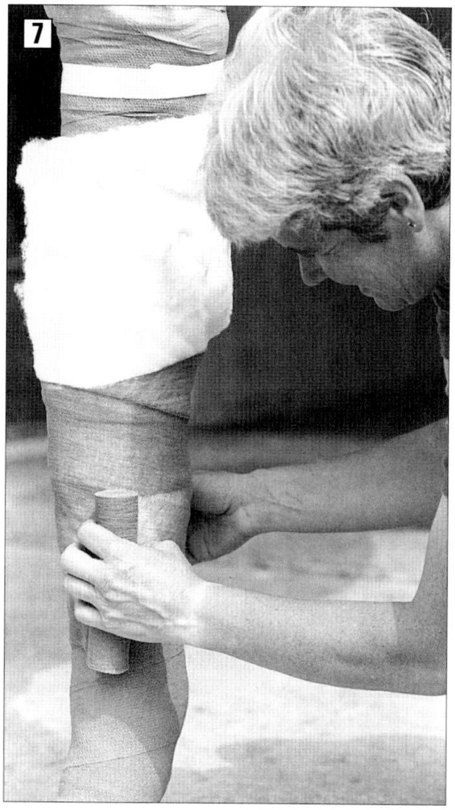

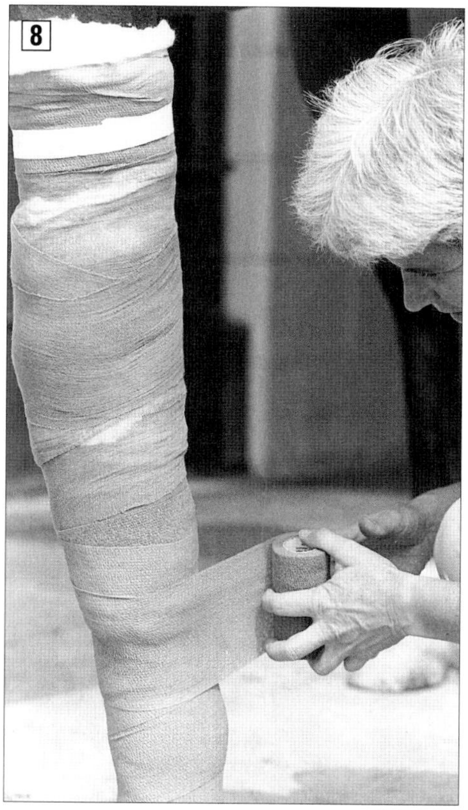

Step 9. Loosely anchor the end in place with adhesive tape. Confine your horse to minimize movement. Check on him frequently (at least every hour), to be sure no bandage slippage has occurred.

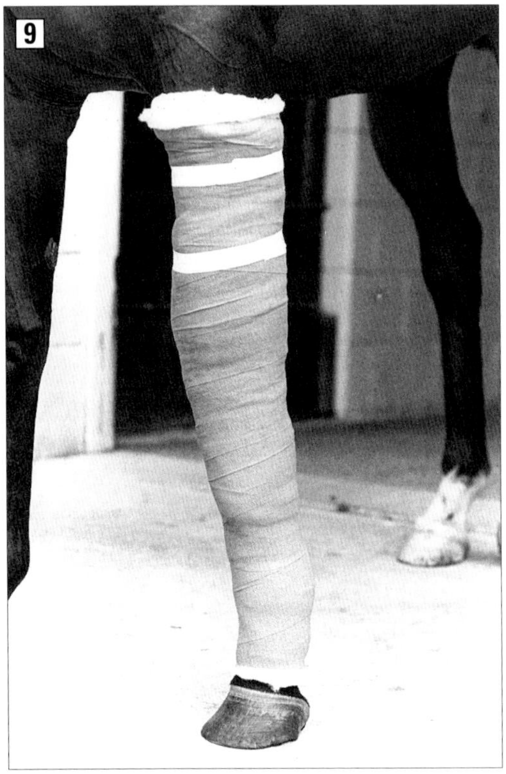

BANDAGE #5: THE PRESSURE WRAP

Sample Scenario: Your horse has a flesh wound, and what looks like a lot of blood is rushing from it (1/4 cup or more per minute). Your task: Get the bleeding stopped while you wait for your veterinarian.

Supplies Needed

IDEALLY	WHY	WHAT TO USE IN A PINCH
Padding: Several layers of roll cotton.	To press against the source of the bleeding, to spread compressive forces evenly over the leg, and to absorb drainage.	Thick sanitary napkins; disposable diapers; folded washcloths or towels.
Security layer: Stretch gauze.	To hold padding in place.	Nylon stocking or cheesecloth cut into a strip, 3 inches wide and 3- to 4-feet long. Or this layer can be omitted.
Elastic bandage: Vetrap®; Elastikon®; or something similar.	To compress the bleeding tissues and stop the blood flow so clotting can occur.	Ace bandage and masking tape.

➤

The Pressure Wrap, continued

How-To:

Step 1. Center padding material over the wound. Choose a pad that's large enough to completely cover it; see chart on previous page. Here, we used a sanitary napkin on a pastern wound (left) and one on the cannon bone (inset).

Step 2. Secure with a layer of stretch gauze.

Step 3. Apply a 1-inch layer of padding around the leg. For a pastern wound, extend it to the coronary band, then up to the knee. For a wound on the cannon bone, extend it from below the fetlock to the knee.

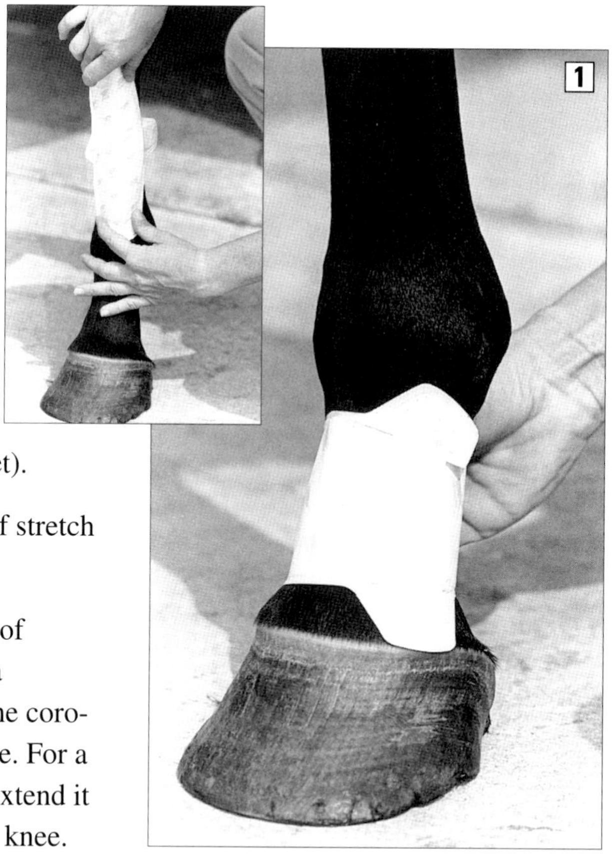

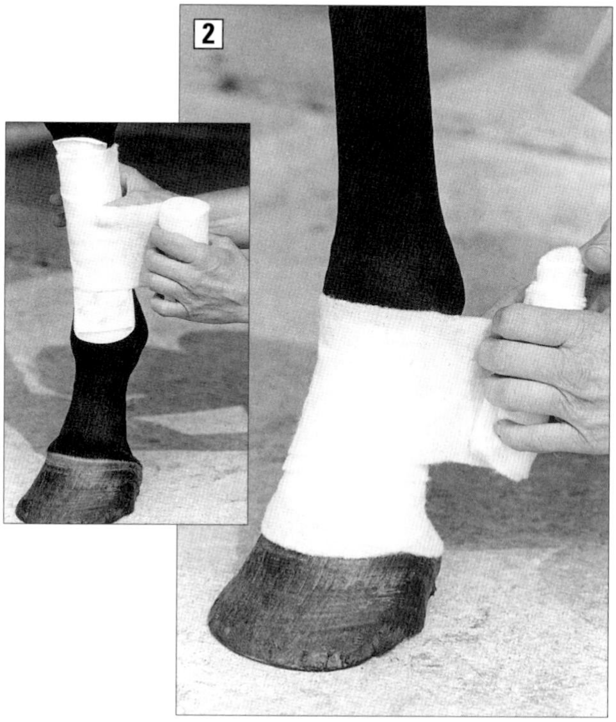

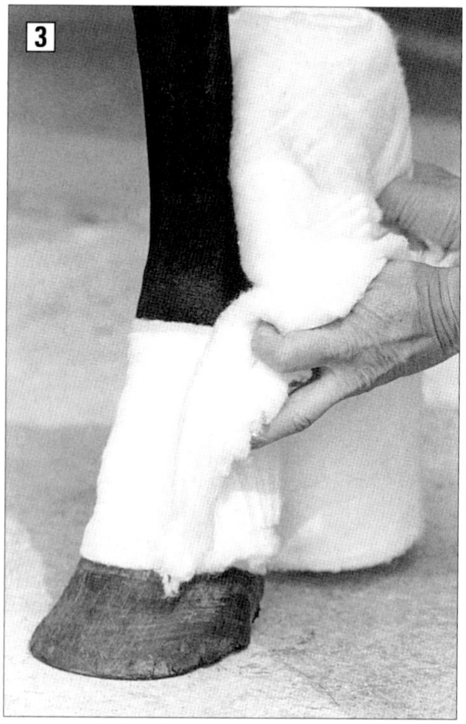

Step 4. Hold the padding in place with a layer of stretch gauze or substitute. Apply it in a spiral or figure-8 pattern to avoid girdling vulnerable nerves and tendons. Loosely anchor the end with adhesive tape.

Step 5. Tightly apply a layer of elastic bandage, leaving enough room to admit only your pinky finger between padding and leg. Start with an anchor loop directly over the wound, spiral down to below the coronary band, onto the hoof wall (for a pastern wound). Then spiral upward, overlapping each round by half the bandage material's width, until all but the top 1/2-inch of padding is covered. Secure with adhesive tape.

Step 6. If blood should soak through the bandage, repeat Steps 3 through 5 over the existing wrap. If you were to remove it, you'd risk disturbing blood clots that may have formed.

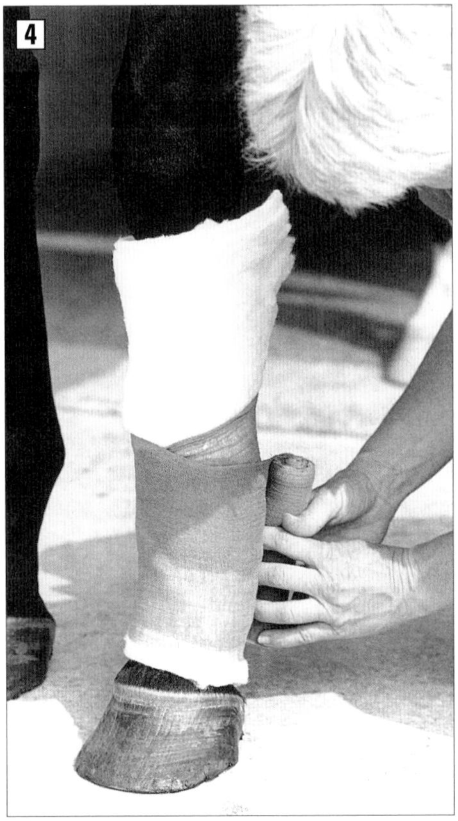

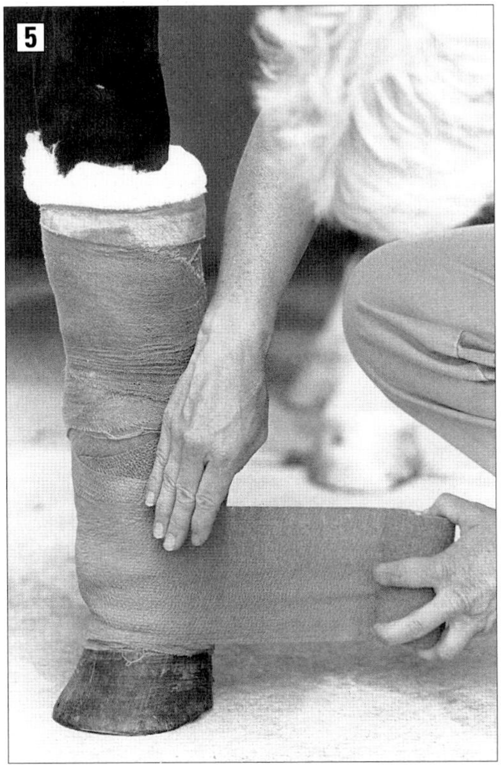

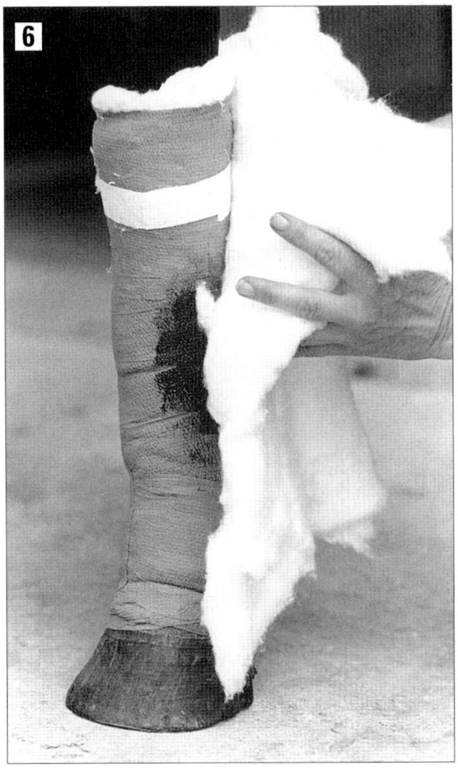

BANDAGE #6: THE BOWED TENDON BANDAGE

Sample Scenario: Your horse has bowed a tendon[G] in his fore leg. A palm-sized swelling is appearing at the back of his cannon bone. Your task: Arrest the swelling and protect the tendon from further damage while you wait for your veterinarian.

SUPPLIES NEEDED		
IDEALLY	**WHY**	**WHAT TO USE IN A PINCH**
Padding: Several layers of roll cotton.	To spread compressive forces evenly over the leg, thereby reducing swelling and bleeding within torn tendon fibers.	Disposable diapers; folded dish towels.
Security layer: Stretch gauze.	To hold padding in place.	Nylon stocking or cheese-cloth cut into a strip, 3 inches wide and 3- to 4-feet long; or this layer can be omitted.
Elastic bandage: Vetrap®; Elasti-kon®; or something similar.	To compress bleeding tissues and stop the blood flow so clotting can occur.	Ace bandage and masking tape.

HOW-TO:

(For visual how-to guidelines, see Bandage #3: The Standard Leg Wrap, page 271.)

Step 1. Ice the leg (see Bandage #2, page 270). While the tissues chill, gather materials for the bowed tendon bandage.

Step 2. Apply a minimum of 1-inch of padding over the leg, extending from below the coronary band to just below the knee. This should take several layers, depending on the padding material you're using.

Step 3. Hold the padding in place with a layer of stretch gauze or substitute, applied in a spiral or figure-8 pattern to avoid girdling the already damaged tendon. Anchor the end with surgical or masking tape.

Step 4. Apply the elastic bandage tightly, leaving enough room to admit your pinky finger between padding and leg. Start with an anchor loop above the injured area, spiral down to below the coronary band onto the hoof wall, then spiral upward. Overlap each round by half the bandage material's width, until all but the uppermost 1/2-inch of padding is covered. Secure the end with surgical or masking tape.

How to Sweat a Leg

You can use a sweat in lieu of a poultice, to help reduce lower-leg swelling in a benign condition such as stocking up, or when your veterinarian directs you to "sweat" an injury. Here's how to do it:

- Apply the leg-sweat preparation according to label or veterinary instructions (or make your own—see recipe on page 242).
- Cover the area loosely with plastic kitchen wrap (such as Saran®), smoothly conforming the plastic to your horse's leg.
- Apply a standard bandage over the site. (For how to apply a standard bandage, see page 271.)
- As a rule of thumb (unless directed to do otherwise by label instructions or your vet), leave the sweat on for 12 hours. Then unwrap and rinse the leg(s), allow it to "rest" for 12 hours, then re-apply a sweat for another 12 hours. Repeat as needed or directed.

BANDAGE #7: THE EYE WRAP

Sample Scenario: Your horse has a wound on his eye. (This wrap also can be used on a head wound.) You're worried that he'll worsen the injury by rubbing it. Your task: To protect injured tissues against contamination, drying, and further trauma.

SUPPLIES NEEDED		
IDEALLY	**WHY**	**WHAT TO USE IN A PINCH**
Wet dressing: A stack of gauze sponges or a compound bandage pad soaked in sterile isotonic saline.	To moisturize tissues, keep them pressed into place, protect them from contamination and trauma, and minimize swelling.	Thick sanitary napkins; disposable diapers; folded washcloths or towels. Wet with homemade saline solution (see page 242), or commercial eyewash.
Elastic bandage: Vetrap®; Expandover®; stockinette; or something similar.	To press the moist dressing over the wound and protect injured tissues from trauma by rubbing.	Seat portion from queen-size pantyhose or tights; Ace bandage and masking tape.

HOW-TO:

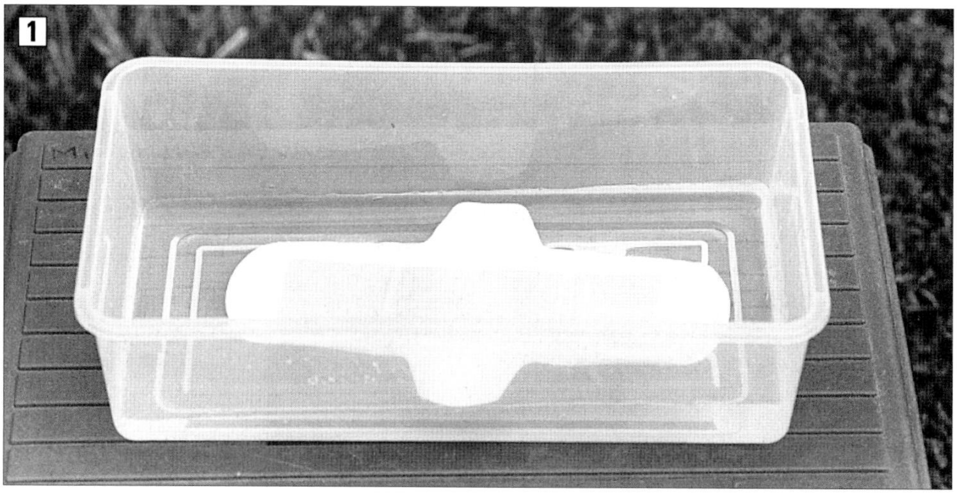

Step 1. Choose a pad that's large enough to cover the eye completely. Moisten it with saline solution so it's wet but not dripping. (We used a sanitary napkin.)

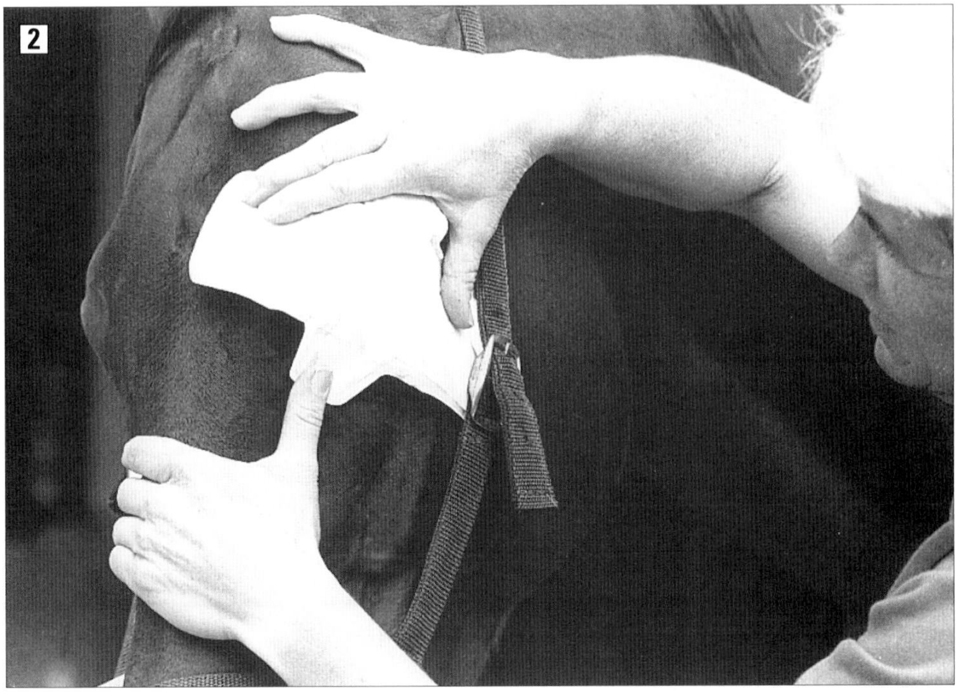

Step 2. Center it over the eye.

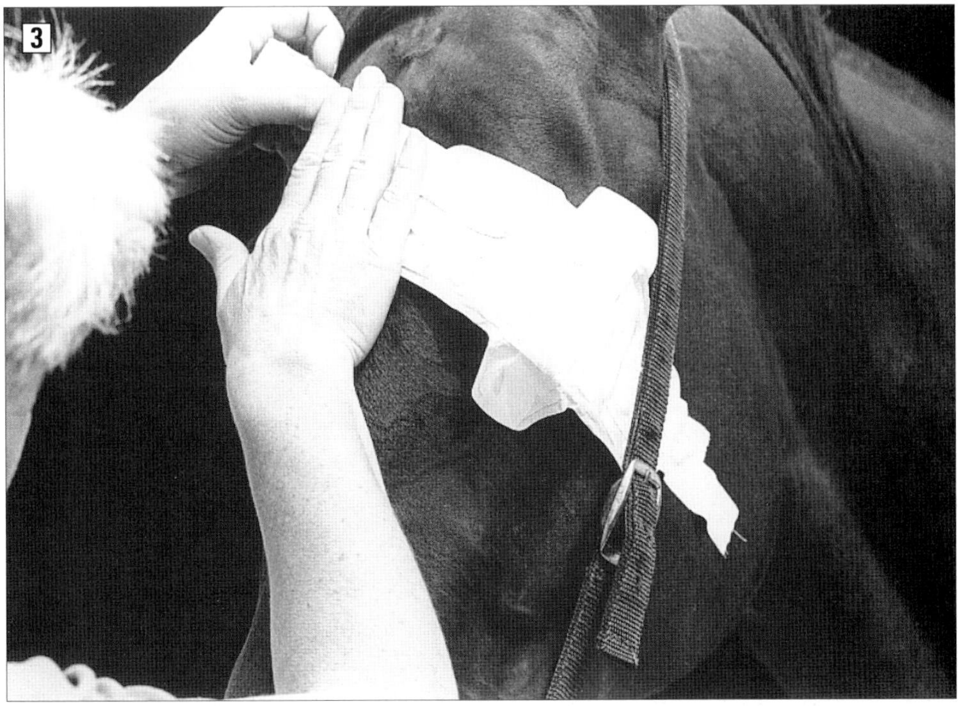

Step 3. Hold the pad in place temporarily, using tape. Secure it by applying a custom-made mask or a wrap, as shown on the next page. ➤

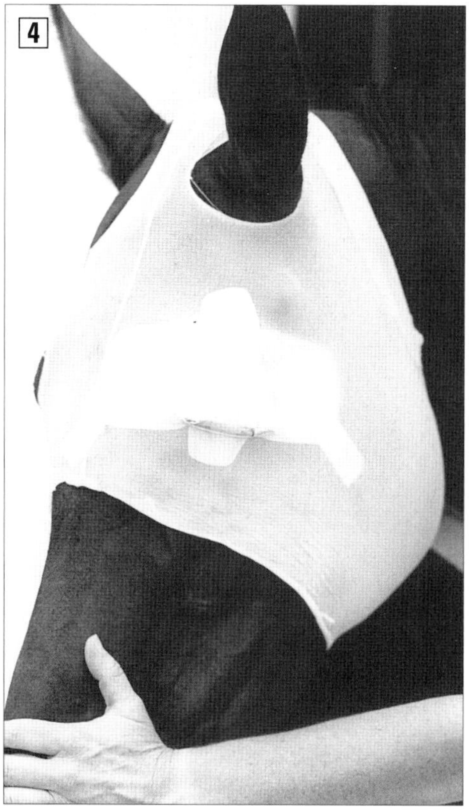

Step 4. *If using pantyhose:* Cut off both legs, to form a single large hole. Measure, mark, and cut 3 holes in the seat itself, just below the waist band. These will accommodate your horse's ear and good eye. Roll up the seat to form a ring. Slip the ring (waist first) over your horse's muzzle, advancing it past his nostrils, to the bony part of his nose. Begin unrolling the ring over his face, carefully adjusting the holes for his eye and ears, as necessary. (Slit a portion of the mask at the throatlatch so it's not tight there. You'll want the large bones of his lower jaw, rather than his throat, to support the bottom part of the mask.) Slip your horse's halter over the mask. Secure the lower edge of the mask to the halter's nose-band with tape.

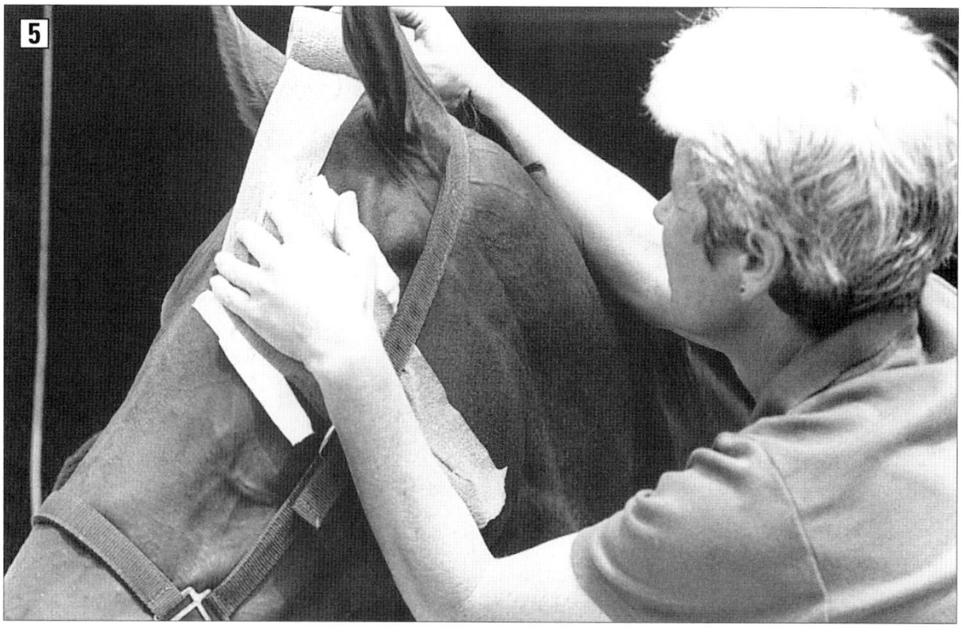

Step 5. *If using a bandage:* Secure the pad by applying the elastic bandage between your horse's ears, and under his jaw. Here's how: Hold the bandage in place over the eye with a strip of tape, as you wrap over your horse's head, between his ears.

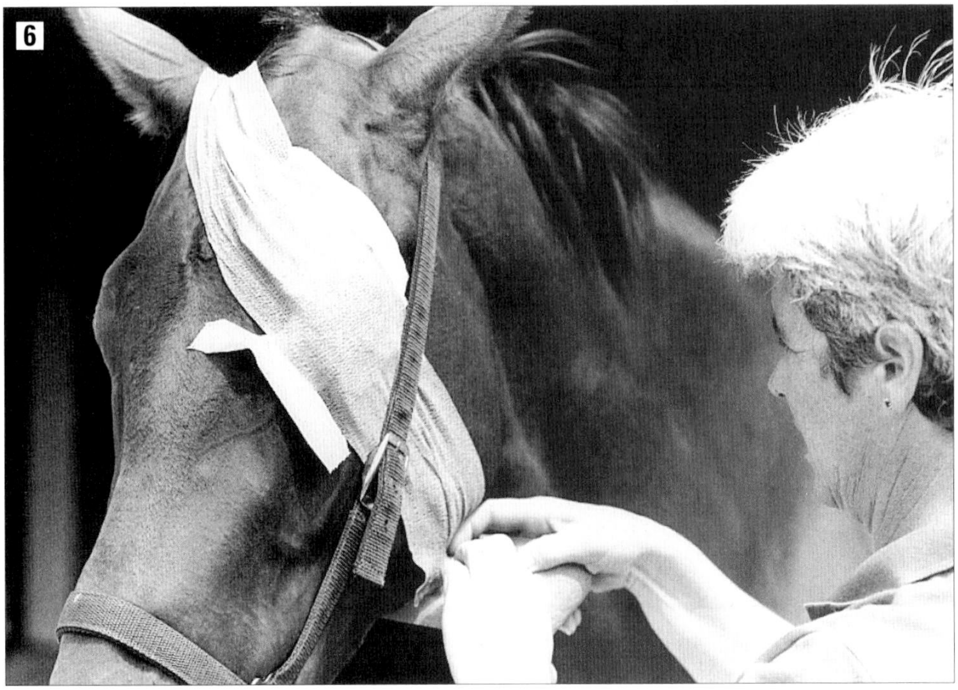

Step 6. Bring the wrap under his jaw bones.

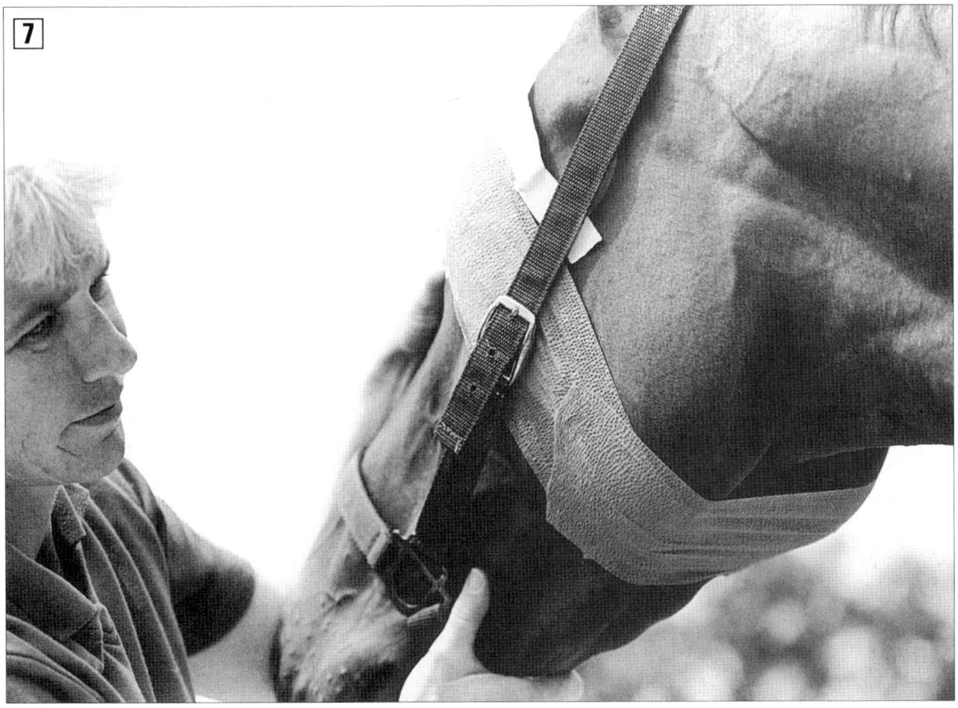

Step 7. Anchor the bandage in place, using tape.

NOTES

CHAPTER 16

How to examine and TREAT YOUR HORSE'S EYES

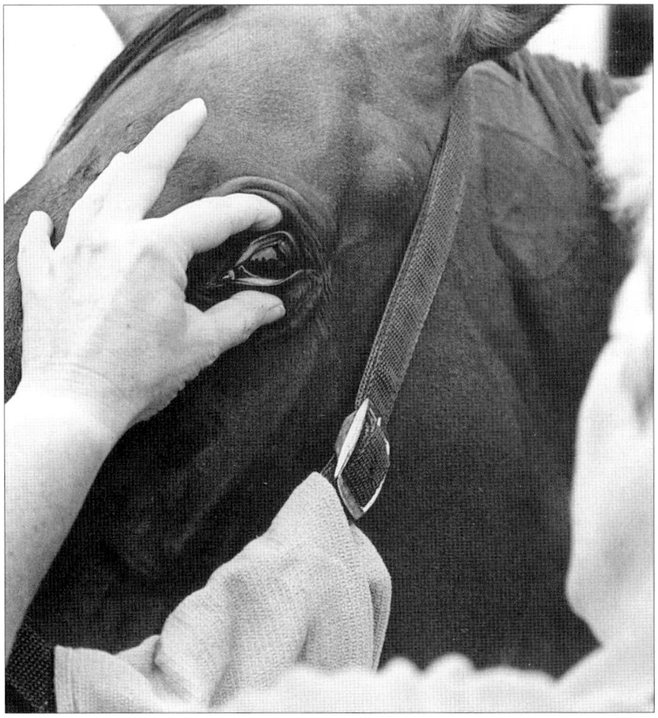

16

How to examine and

TREAT YOUR HORSE'S EYES

Unfortunately, a lot of serious eye problems look exactly the same as minor ones: You see squinting, watering, redness, and/or rubbing. Nine times out of 10, however, mild to moderate eye discomfort is the result of something simple, such as dust in the eye. This you can resolve quickly and easily with minor first aid—if your horse will allow it. The more serious cases that'll require veterinary intervention reveal themselves by failing to improve within a few minutes of home-treatment.

If your horse won't allow you to check an eye problem without a fight, don't engage him. There are eye problems that leave the eyeball weak and vulnerable to rupture. The added pressure of an eyelid tightly clenched against your efforts to force it open could actually damage the eyeball itself. However, if your horse will allow you to examine and treat his sore eye, there are techniques you can use to help you achieve the task without doing harm. Following are guidelines for examining an eye, rinsing it, and applying ophthalmic ointment.

EXAMINING AN EYE

TIP: If you're experienced in the use of a twitch for restraining your horse, you might find it useful to use it while treating your horse's irritated eye. Even if he doesn't strenuously resist your treatments, any sudden movement on his part could increase the risk of injury to you or his eye. A twitch might decrease the likelihood of such movement. If you're not experienced using a twitch, ask your veterinarian to give you a hands-on lesson.

Symptoms that say, "Stop! Call the vet now!" are marked with an asterisk.*

Step 1. Stand at a distance (as close as you can get without stimulating an anticipatory increase in squinting). How widely your horse holds the eye open, and whether or not it's watering, are crude but relatively accurate measures of

Step 3, the exam.

how painful it is. Make your observations, and refer to them later to determine whether your treatments have helped.

Step 2. Halter your horse. Stand to the side of the eye, out of striking range. Without touching his face, take a close look, and make the following observations:

- If there's a discharge, is it watery, thick, or colored? Is his face crusted with it, telling you it's been going on for more than just a few minutes?
- Is there evidence that he's been rubbing at it? (You'll see raw, hairless places on the bony protrusions of his face, and/or swollen eyelids*.)
- If he holds the eyelids at least partially open, aim a penlight into the eye (don't hold it any closer than 1 foot away) and look for breaks* and/or cloudy spots* on the clear portion of the eyeball.
- Look also at the pupil, which is a horizontal oval in the horse: Memorize its size, then examine the pupil in your horse's good eye so you can compare the two. Is the pupil in the sore eye smaller than the one in the good eye*?

Step 3. Place one hand under your horse's chin and lift it up. Your horse naturally will roll the eyeball downward, exposing its upper margin. Take advantage of this and get a good look at the "white" of his eye to see if it's got splashes or brushstrokes of bright red*, if it's bloodshot, or has an injury* or foreign material embedded in it*. ➤

Step 4, the exam.

Step 4. Now rest the heel of one hand (the one closest to your horse's muzzle) beside the bridge of his nose so that the fleshy part of your thumb rests at the crease between his upper eyelid and the skin above it. Press and lift gently until your thumb rests against the ceiling of the bony eye socket, to raise the upper lid...

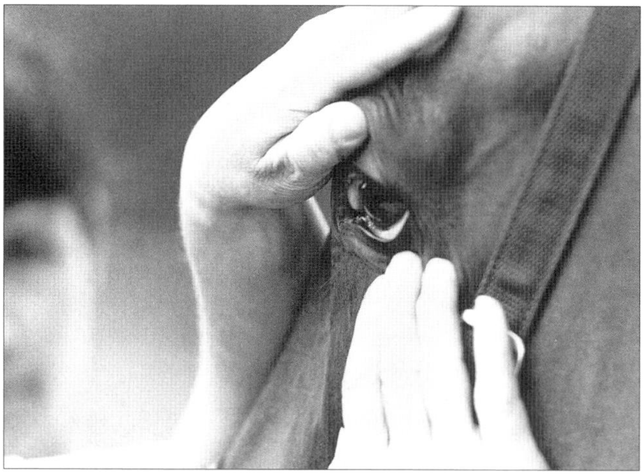

Step 5, the exam.

Step 5. ...while simultaneously pulling down on the lower lid with the fingers of your other hand. Take a quick survey of all the visible parts: cornea (the clear part); pupil; and conjunctiva (the normally pale pink, delicate tissues that connect the eyeball to the skin around it). Call your veterinarian immediately if you notice any of the "call the vet now" symptoms marked. Otherwise, rinse your horse's eye as outlined on the opposite page, to rid it of irritating dust.

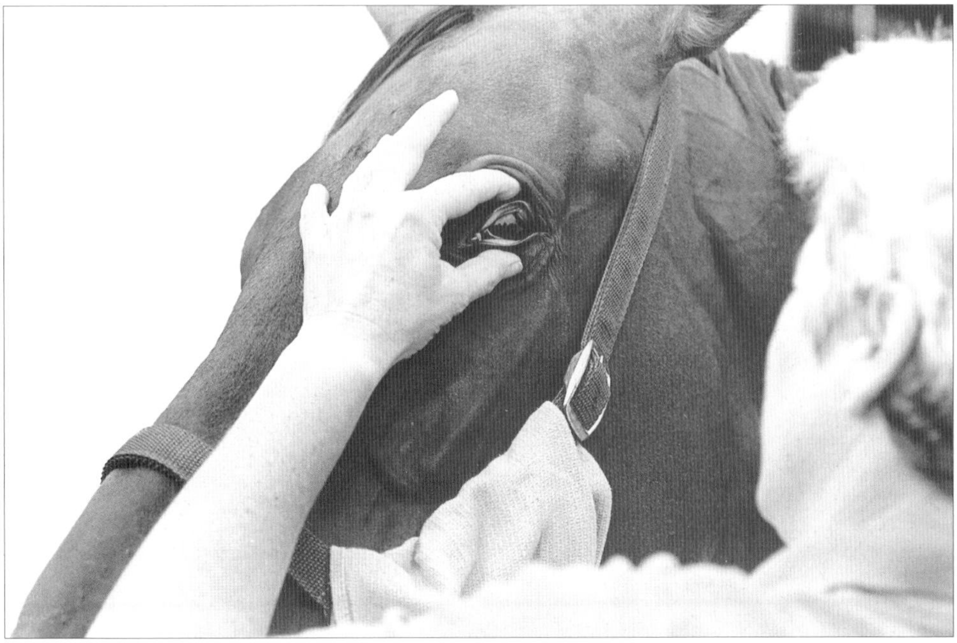

Step 3, eye rinse.

RINSING AN EYE

Step 1. Warm a squeeze bottle of human or veterinary sterile eye-wash solution, by standing it up to its neck in a bowl of warm tap water until a drop of the solution on the underside of your wrist feels neutral.

Step 2. If you have an assistant, ask him/her to hold your horse's lead rope while standing on the good-eye side. Otherwise, drape the lead rope over your horse's neck and position him so solid walls limit any sideways or backward retreat. Stand to the side of his sore eye.

Step 3. Tuck a terrycloth dishtowel or handtowel under the noseband and side-piece of your horse's halter to absorb any solution, should it spill. (If it were to drip onto his muzzle, it could upset his fragile agreement to allow you to perform this treatment.)

Step 4. Rest the heel of the hand closest to your horse's muzzle beside the bridge of his nose. The fleshy part of your index finger should rest in the crease between his upper eyelid and the skin above it, and your thumb on the skin beneath the lower lid. Press and lift gently with your finger until it's against the bony ceiling of the eye socket, to pull the upper lid up. Pull the lower lid gently downward with your thumb. Simultaneously rest the heel of your other hand, holding the squeeze bottle and the halter, on his face just behind the eye. Angle the bottle so it's bottoms-up and aiming slightly toward the eye.

Step 5. Without delay, squeeze the solution onto the eyeball so it runs from the outer corner to the inner corner. First direct the stream upward, toward the pocket under the upper lid, then downward across the eyeball and into the pocket under the lower lid. Do this for 5 to 10 seconds if your horse will allow it.

TIP:

The squeeze bottle's tip should be close to the eye (within 1/2 inch) so the stream of eye-wash solution doesn't pulverize the eyeball.

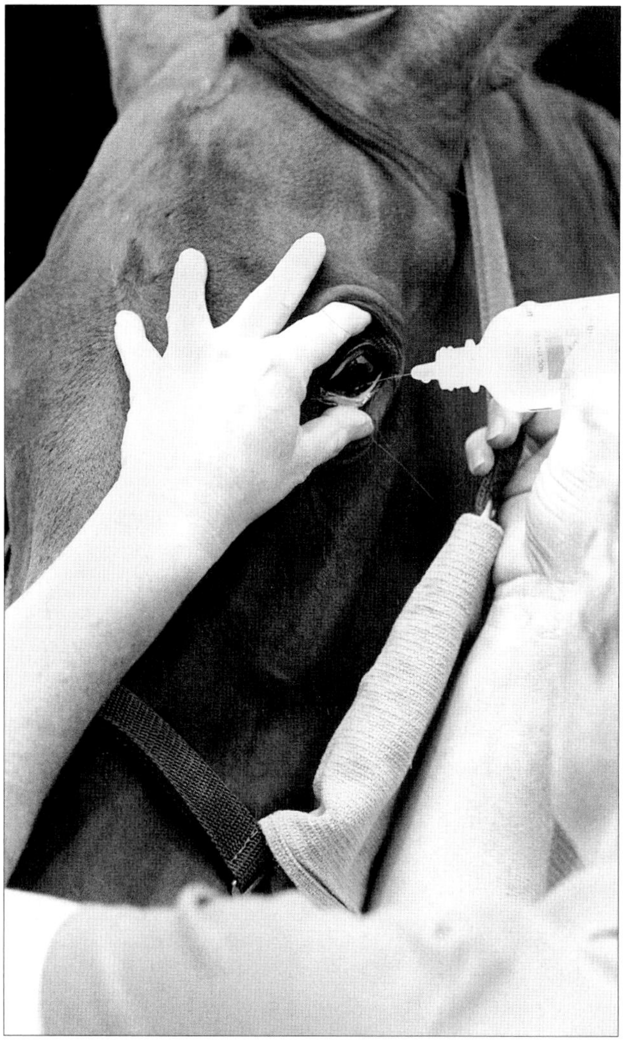

Steps 4 and 5, eye rinse.

TIP: When the solution first touches your horse's eye, he'll probably object by lifting his head and pulling back. Most horses will relax and tolerate this treatment as soon as they realize it doesn't hurt and the treatment has continued despite their reaction.

However, some horses—particularly if in significant pain—will react more violently, by striking with a foreleg or lunging forward. Stay alert, stay out of striking range, and be ready to move out of harm's way.

APPLYING EYE OINTMENT

Step 1. Standing off to the side, rest the heel of the hand closest to your horse's muzzle beside the bridge of his nose, so that your thumb rests on the skin below the edge of his lower lid.

Step 2. Rest the heel of your other hand, holding the tube of ointment between thumb and forefinger, against your horse's face just behind and slightly below the eye. Grasp the halter's cheekpiece with the free fingers of that hand, as shown at right.

Step 3. Gently pull down on the skin below the lower lid with your thumb.

Step 4. Without delay, apply 1/2 inch of ointment into the pocket behind the lower lid. The warmth of the tissues will melt it, and blinking will spread it across your horse's eyeball.

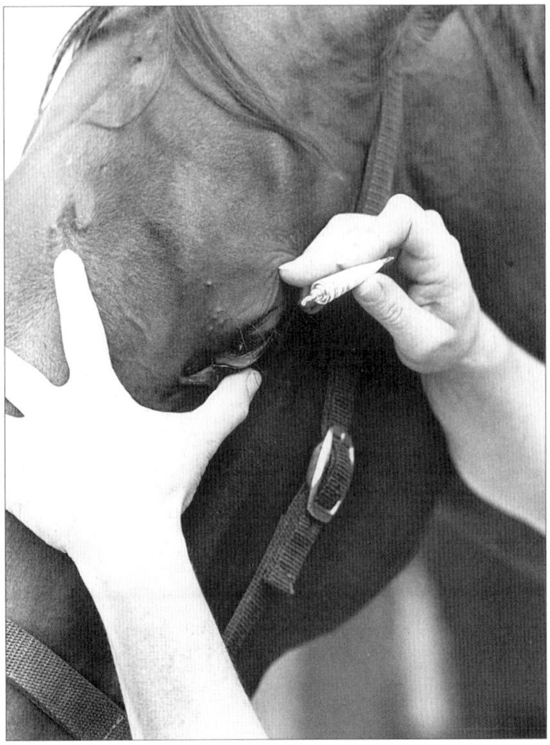

Step 3, applying ointment.

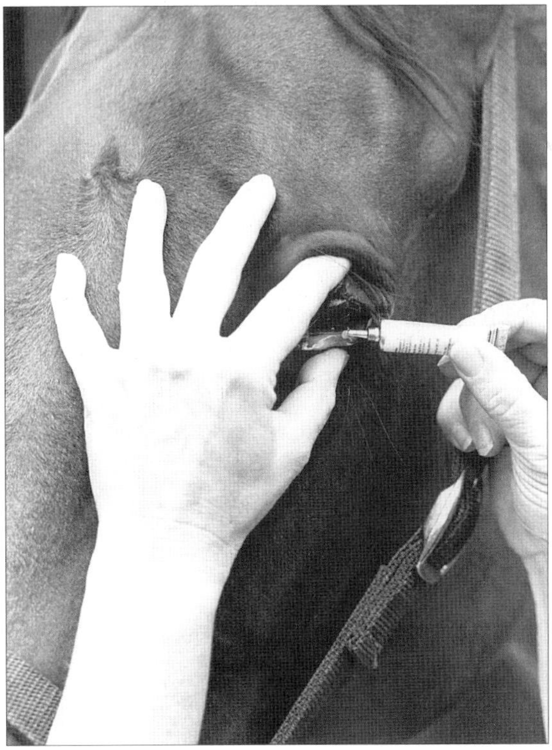

Step 4, applying ointment.

NOTES

CHAPTER 17

How to determine WHICH LEG IS LAME

17

How to determine
WHICH LEG IS LAME

In most cases, recognizing and pinpointing a lameness isn't difficult, if you follow the logical series of steps outlined below. In addition to identifying a lame leg or legs, you also might be able to tell precisely where on that leg the problem is. (Note: If your horse's lameness is obvious and he's reluctant to bear weight on the involved leg or legs, skip these diagnostic steps, which could cause more harm. Instead, follow the advice outlined in Section I of this book, using the Action Plan that best describes his symptoms.)

HOW LAME IS YOUR HORSE?

There are many different methods of defining and grading lameness. We've adopted the classification of the American Association of Equine Practitioners, as defined in their *Guide to Horse Shows*:

Definition: Lameness is a deviation from the normal gait or posture due to pain or mechanical dysfunction.

Classification:
Grade 1: Difficult to observe; not consistently apparent regardless of circumstances (i.e., weight carrying, circling, inclines, hard surfaces, etc.).
Grade 2: Difficult to observe at a walk or trotting a straight line; consistently apparent under certain circumstances (i.e., weight carrying, circling, inclines, hard surfaces, etc.).
Grade 3: Consistently observable at a trot under all circumstances.
Grade 4: Obvious lameness; marked nodding, hitching, or shortened stride.
Grade 5: Minimal weight bearing in motion and/or at rest; inability to move.

What You're Looking For:
Watch for one or more of the following clues.

- **Head-bob:** The head bobs UP when a sore forelimb hits the ground and bears weight. The head bobs DOWN when a sore hindlimb hits the ground and bears weight. (See chart, page 300.)
- **Hip-hike or hip-drop:** The hip on one side raises HIGHER and/or sinks LOWER than the other side.
- **Toe drag:** The toe of the affected hind limb drags on the ground on the forward swing.
- **Shortened stride:** The stride on one leg is shorter than the stride on the other legs.

How to use the clues to locate the lame leg(s)
Follow the steps below while watching for abnormalities. If you find no clues to identify a lameness, but you're still suspicious that something's wrong, call your veterinarian. Some subtle lamenesses might require more experience, more precise tests, and/or nerve blocks to locate them.

Step 1. Examine your horse's legs and feet.
Why: There might be external evidence of his lameness.
How:

- Stand your horse squarely on solid, level ground. From a distance of 5 or 6 feet, look at his legs and coronary bands for bumps, swellings, wounds, discharges, and anything that makes one leg look different from another.
- Feel each hoof wall to judge its temperature. If it feels warm, compare it to the warmth of the other three feet. If they're all warm, if possible compare to the warmth of another horse's feet.
- Check for the strength of his digital pulse in both front legs. (For how-to,

(continued on page 302)

TIPS: The HEAD BOB is easier to see while the horse is trotting toward you. As a general rule, the more pronounced the bob, the more severe the pain.

The HIP-HIKE or HIP-DROP is easier to see when your horse is trotting away from you. You can make it even more visible by sticking a piece of adhesive tape on each hip, to give your eye a frame of reference.

While your horse is moving, listen to the cadence: If the stride on one leg is shortened, you'll hear *dot-dash, dot-dash* instead of *dot-dot-dot-dot* as his hooves hit the ground.

Or, while watching from the side as your horse moves past, look at the placement of each hind hoof relative to its corresponding fore hoof: If a hind leg's stride is shortened on one side, its hoof won't meet the print of the fore hoof (or overlap it as much as the other side does). If a fore leg's stride is shortened, there'll be more overlap of its print by the corresponding hind hoof.

WHICH LEG IS LAME?

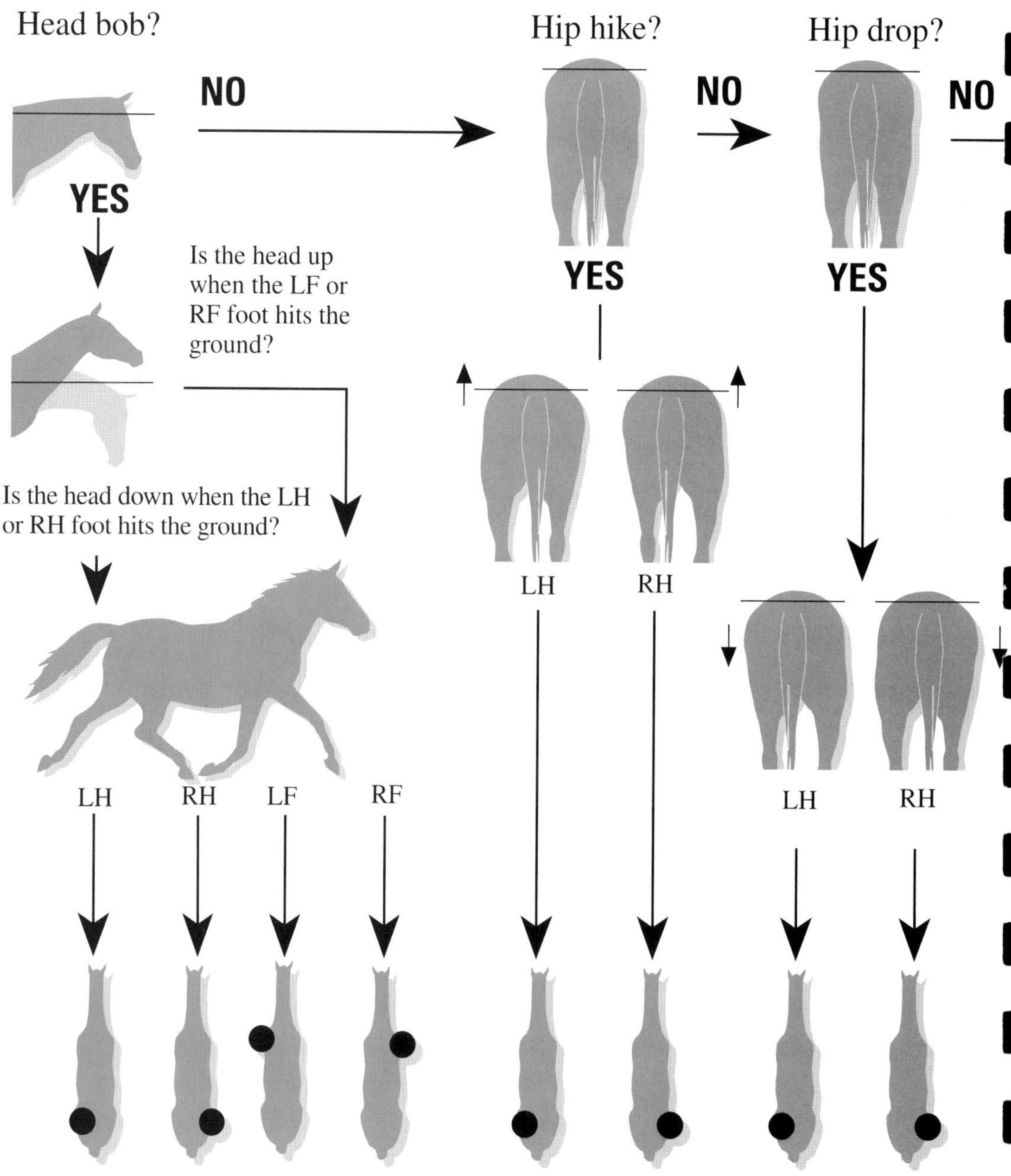

Lame leg

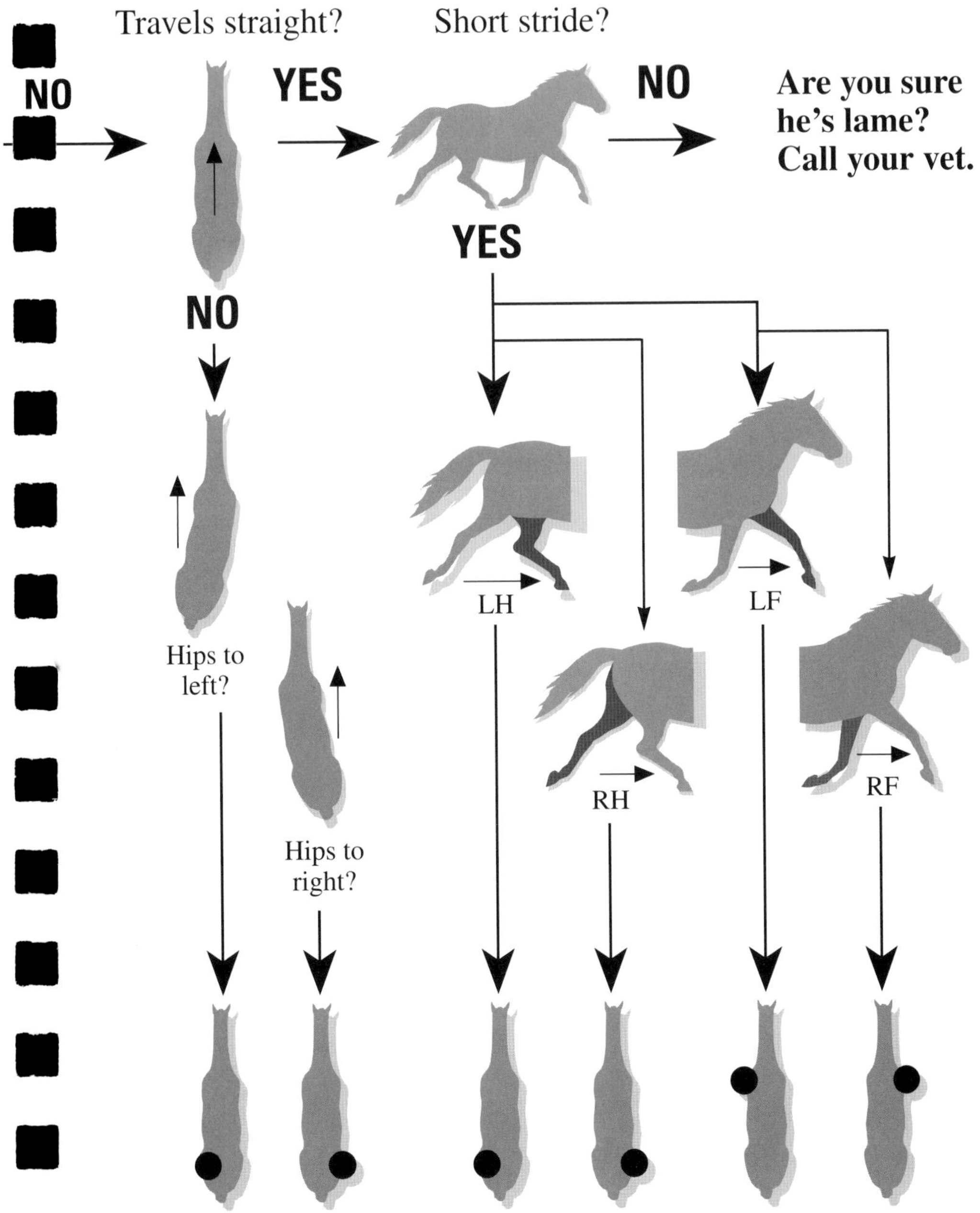

Travels straight?
Short stride?
NO
YES
NO
Are you sure he's lame? Call your vet.
YES
NO
LH
LF
Hips to left?
RH
RF
Hips to right?

Lame leg

Step 2.

see page 202.) If normal, the pulse will feel absent, or present but faint. If abnormal, it'll be stronger than usual (but not necessarily faster).

- Pick up each foot, being sure to notice whether he resists. (This could mean soreness in another foot/feet, resulting in reluctance to increase their load by lifting this foot.) Clean the foot, looking for nails, cracks, bruises, or any abnormality.
- Feel each leg, slowly moving your hands from coronary band to top of leg, in search of swellings, pain, and/or excess heat.

Step 2. Watch your horse trot a straight line.
Why: Lamenesses can be invisible or barely perceptible at the walk, but become evident at the trot.
How:

- Find a flat, smooth area with no obstructions, preferably with solid footing (not a deep-footed arena), such as a driveway turnaround, or a closely cropped yard.
- Recruit a helper, equip him/her with a crop or buggy whip, if necessary, to get your horse trotting in-hand.
- Have your helper trot the horse on a straight line away from you. Have

him/her loosely hold the lead so as not to interfere with head-bobbing, and keep about an arm's length away, so your view of the horse is unobstructed.

- When your horse has trotted about 50 feet, have your helper trot back toward you.
- Now have the pair trot past you, while you watch from each side.

Repeat this exercise two or three times. If you haven't found a lameness after the third trip, one of three things is happening:

1) Your horse isn't cooperating. Either he's too fresh to go straight on a loose lead, or he's too uncomfortable and/or lazy to jog in-hand.

2) The lameness is bilateral or too subtle to show up when going straight.

3) There's no lameness.

Step 3. Observe your horse on a longe line, or trotting in circles in-hand.
Why: Some lamenesses are more evident when the horse is executing a turn, which places uneven stress on joints, tendons, ligaments, and bones. As a general rule, the tighter the turn, the more pronounced the lameness.
How: Have your assistant longe your horse in both directions, starting with a large circle and gradually shortening the line so the circle becomes smaller, thereby tightening the turn. Call your veterinarian if you observe any sign of injury or lameness in Steps 1, 2, or 3.

Maturity Matters...

As your horse enters the realm of senior citizenship, he'll be more prone to injury and illness, due to a decrease in flexibility and a gradual decline in immune system competence. And, he may lose status within his social circle. When age starts encroaching on well-being, a horse's social niche can erode and lower herd members sense it. This sets the stage for conflict (and injury) as younger horses increasingly issue challenges in an attempt to improve their social status. If you see your horse becoming involved in such conflicts, separate him from any top-dog wannabes before somebody gets hurt.

NOTES

CHAPTER 18

How to PULL A LOOSE SHOE

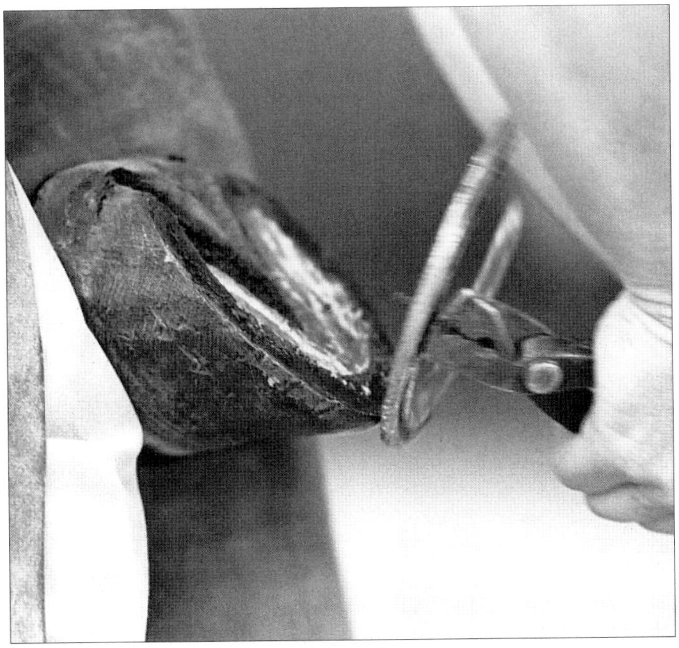

18

How to

PULL A LOOSE SHOE

WHAT YOU NEED:

1. Gloves to protect your hands (optional).

2. Either a low-slung hoof boot, or materials to make a hoof slipper (right). These will protect the hoof from chipping.

3. Clinch cutters; hammer; and shoe pullers.

MATERIALS TO MAKE A HOOF SLIPPER

- **1 square foot of padding: (a single layer roll cotton; 4 layers of sheet cotton; trimmed bath towel; discarded sweatshirt; or a disposable diaper)**
- **1 yard of elastic bandage: (Vetrap®, Ace bandage, Co-Flex, or something similar)**
- **Duct tape**

HOW TO DO IT:

Step 1. Straighten the nail ends so they'll pull through the hoof without damaging it. Place the narrow, tomahawk-like blade of the clinch cutters against the bend in the clinches. Bend them open, or straight, by tapping on the cutter with the hammer. Or, cut clinches off as shown.

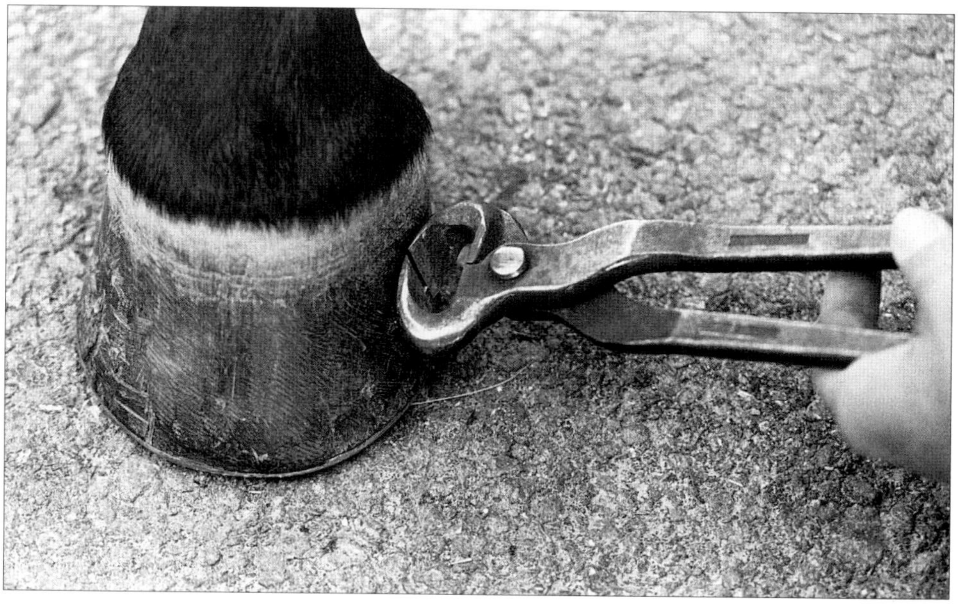

Step 1.

Step 2. Pick up your horse's hoof. If you can get a grip on them, pull the nail heads out with the shoe pullers. Odds are, though, that you'll be able to get some of the nails, but not all of them. That's okay—get the ones you can. (Be sure to discard the nails in a safe place, where they won't be stepped on.)

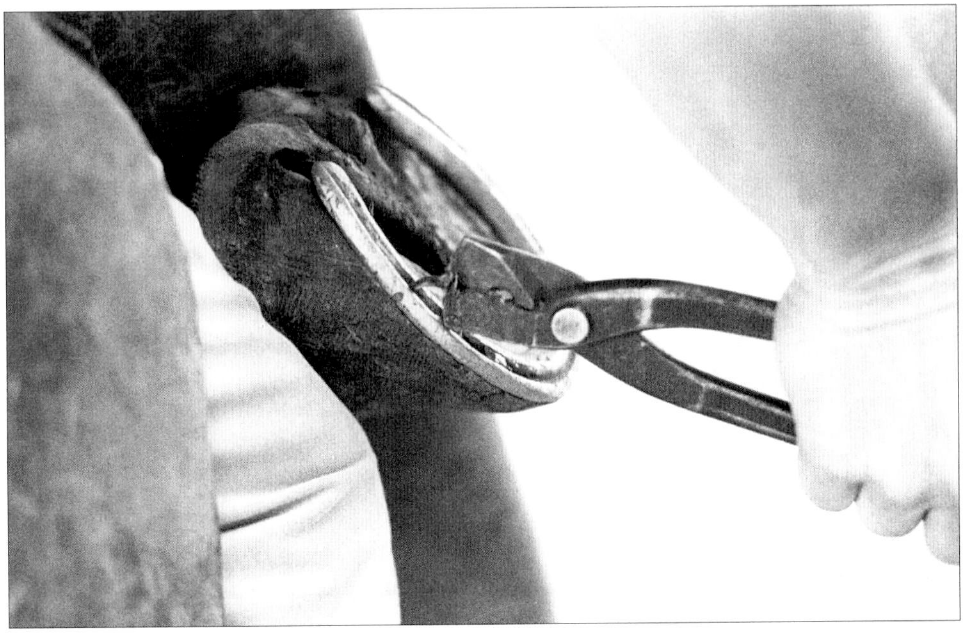

Step 2.

Step 3.

Step 3. Loosen the shoe heels by slipping the shoe puller's jaws between the shoe and the buttress of the hoof's heel. Push the tool's handle inward, toward the center of the sole. (It's important that you resist the urge to pry outward—this could rip off a substantial chunk of the hoof wall.) ➤

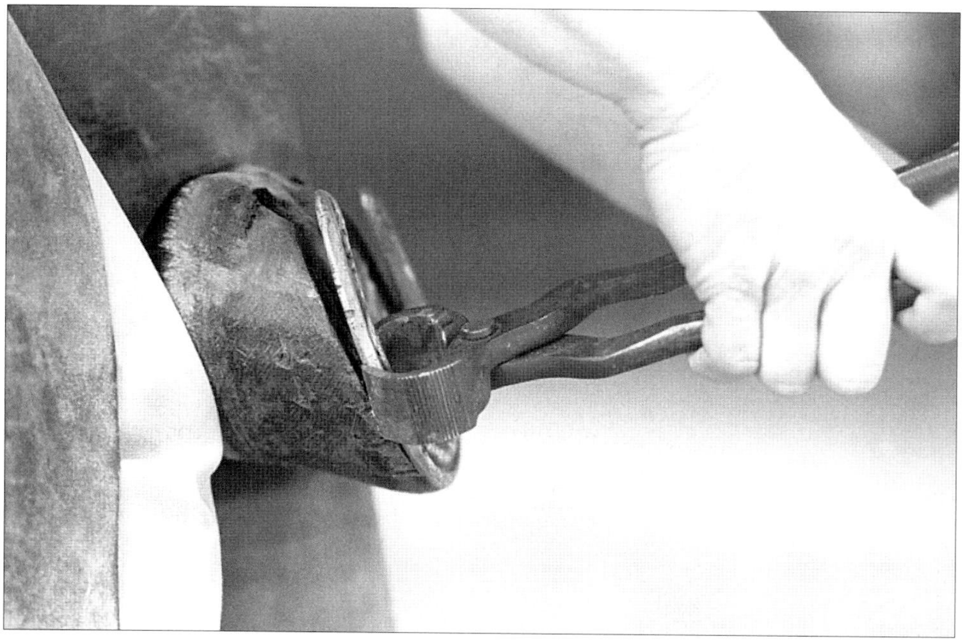

Step 4.

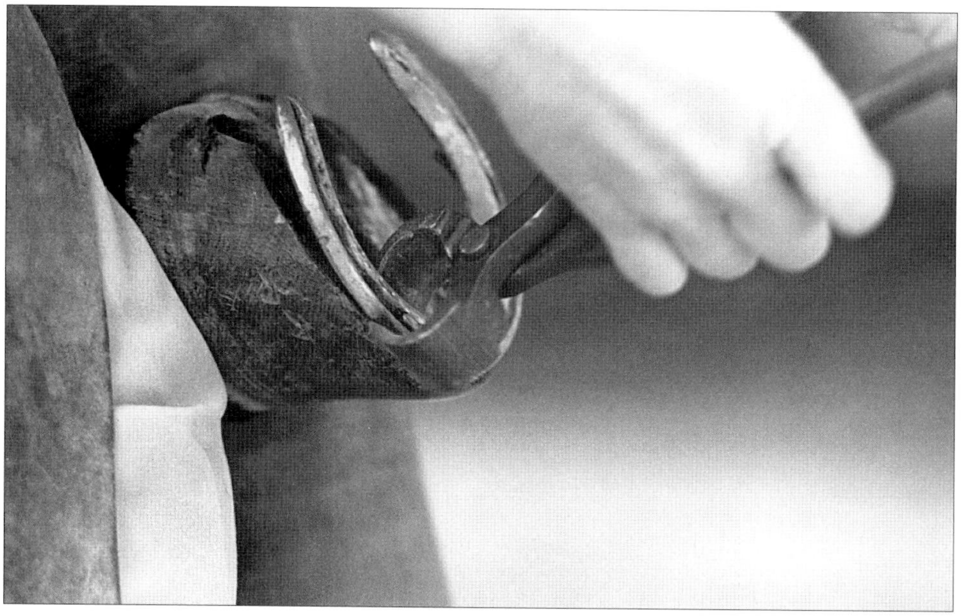

Step 5.

Step 4. After you've loosened both heels, pry the shoe's toe loose in the same manner, by pulling the handle of the shoe pullers inward, toward the center of the sole.

Step 5. Repeat this motion wherever the shoe is still nailed, until it comes off. If any nails remain in the hoof wall, pull them out with the shoe pullers.

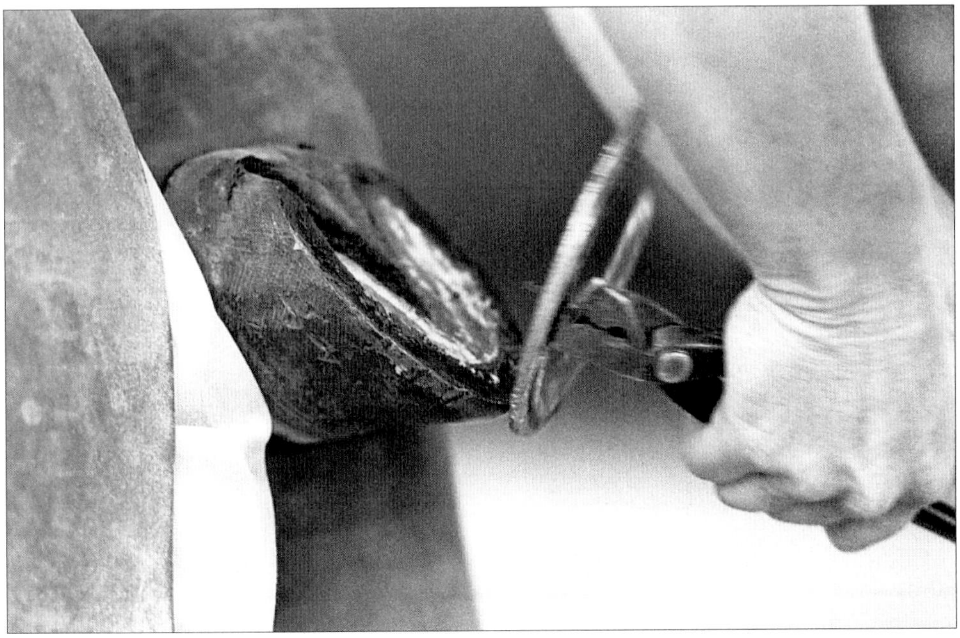

Step 6.

Step 6. Remove the shoe.

Step 7. Apply the hoof boot, or make a hoof slipper: Center the padding over the sole, bringing the edges up around the hoof wall. Secure it there with the elastic bandage; cover the bandage with strips of duct tape to keep the hoof edges from wearing through. (For complete how-to instructions, see page 267.)

Step 8. Confine your horse and schedule a farrier visit today.

Did You Know...

If you're considering giving your horse a nutritional biotin supplement to strengthen his hooves, select one that includes the amino acids dL-methionine and lysine, for optimal effectiveness. When in doubt, read the label.

NOTES

CHAPTER 19

Guide to COMMON TOXIC PLANTS & AGENTS

19

Guide to

COMMON TOXIC PLANTS & AGENTS

Following is a chart of toxic plants that are common throughout North America and known to cause illness in horses. Learn which of these plants is endemic in your area, and make a habit of checking your pastures and paddocks at least once a month during growing season.

Plant or Substance	Location	Symptoms	Toxin	Treatment/ Prognosis
Black walnut shavings	Throughout U.S.	Laminitis and vasculitis of lower legs when shavings used as bedding.	Unknown.	Removal from source; supportive and symptomatic; full recovery depends on prompt treatment.
Blister beetles	Can infest alfalfa stands and hay throughout the U.S.	Colic; depression; sweating; jerky movement of chest and diaphragm.	Cantharidin.	Symptomatic; fatal shock can set in after eating only a few beetles.
Blue-green algae	Water tanks in warm sunny weather.	Colic; diarrhea; trembling; dyspnea; staggering; jaundice; sensitivity to sunlight; seizures.	Microcystin.	Symptomatic and supportive care; fatal if liver is unable to regenerate.
Bracken fern and **Horsetail**	Throughout North America. Horsetail: moist or sandy areas. Bracken fern: boundaries between forests and open fields.	Weight loss; weakness; staggering; trembling; paralysis.	Thiaminase.	Injections of thiamine (vitamin B_1); complete recovery if treated before brain damage becomes permanent.

A VISUAL GUIDE TO TOXIC PLANTS

(When available, several views are provided.)

Azalea

Bracken Fern

Buttercup

Castor bean

Choke cherry

Death Camus

Elderberry Flower

Elderberry Fruit

Foxglove

Dutchman's breeches

Fescue

Horsetail, leafy stage

(continued on page 315)

Plant or Substance	Location	Symptoms	Toxin	Treatment/ Prognosis
Buttercup (must eat fairly large amount)	Throughout U.S. in moist areas, toxic only in fresh form.	Blisters on lips and mouth; slobbering; colic; diarrhea.	Proto-anemonin.	Symptomatic; usually a full recovery with supportive care treatment.
Castor bean (beans mixed in grain products)	Subtropical climates.	Colic; diarrhea; labored breathing.	Lectin.	Symptomatic; often fatal.
Fungus-infested red or white clover	Throughout U.S.	Slobbering; sweating.	Slaframine, a toxin produced by the mold *Rhizoctonia* that can infest clover and other plants.	Remove from source; usually recover completely within 24 hours.
Fungus-infested rye; wheat; barley; bahia; or **wild grasses**	Throughout North America.	Nose, ears, tail, and feet die and fall off; seizures.	Ergot.	Symptomatic; prognosis for survival is guarded; survivors are permanently disfigured and may have gangrene.
Fungus-infested tall fescue	Throughout U.S.	Delayed birthing; abortion; stillbirth; weak foals; no milk.	Fungus *(Acremonium coenophialum)* infesting the grass.	Remove from source and administer neurotransmitter domperidone; if done within 60 days of foaling can salvage pregnancy.
Hoary alyssum	Northern U.S.	Fever; depression; laminitis; leg swelling; death.	Unknown.	Removal from source; symptomatic and supportive; full recovery depends on prompt treatment.

VISUAL GUIDE, continued from page 313

Horsetail, late summer

Jimsonweed

Jimsonweed, in bloom

Larkspur

Laurel

Lily-of-the-valley

Lupine

Milkweed

Milkweed, in bloom

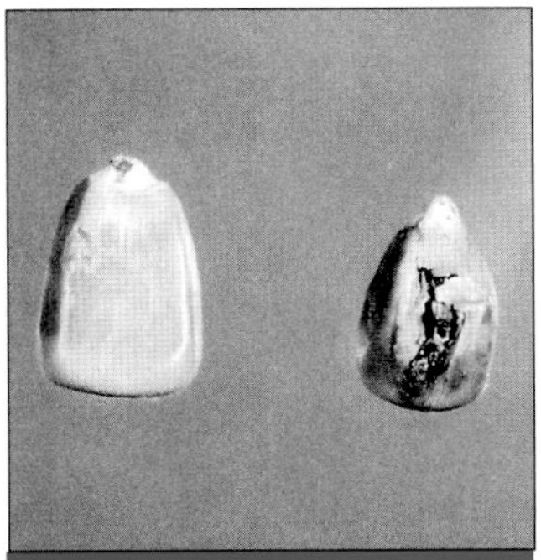
Moldy Corn

Morning Glory

Morning Glory, in bloom

(continued on page 319)

Plant or Substance	Location	Symptoms	Toxin	Treatment/ Prognosis
Japanese Yew	Throughout U.S.; ornamental	Trembling; staggering; diarrhea; collapse; cardiac arrest.	Alkaloid.	Cardiac crash drugs; almost always fatal; treatment is rarely possible, rarely effective.
Jimsonweed	Throughout U.S.	Thirst; blindness; flushed skin; aimless wandering; convulsions; death.	Alkaloids.	Symptomatic; death usually occurs within minutes to hours.
Larkspur	Midwestern and Western U.S.	Trembling; collapse; seizures.	Alkaloids.	Symptomatic and supportive; often fatal.
Lead	Contaminated water or soil, batteries, lead paint, used motor oil or grease.	Weakness; staggering; blindness; trembling; circling; head pressing; seizures.	Lead.	Chelation therapy; symptoms of brain damage may be permanent.
Lily-of-the-valley; oleander; laurel; azalea; rhododendron; foxglove; death camas	Throughout U.S.	Usually found dead; otherwise see colic; seizures.	Cardiac glycosides, which cause heart attack.	Cardiac crash drugs; almost always fatal; treatment is rarely possible, rarely effective.
Locoweed	Western North America.	Depression; staggering; blindness; trembling; difficulty swallowing; panic; inability to eat or drink.	The alkaloid swainsonine.	Symptomatic and supportive. Victims may survive, but never completely recover.

Plant or Substance	Location	Symptoms	Toxin	Treatment/ Prognosis
Lupine (bluebonnet)	Western U.S. naturally; throughout U.S. as cultivated ornamentals.	Labored breathing; snoring; depression; trembling; convulsions; coma.	Quinolizidine alkaloids present in plant and especially in seeds.	Symptomatic; death usually occurs within 24 hours of eating large amount in small period of time.
Marijuana	Throughout U.S.	Staggering; sensitive skin; depression; labored breathing; trembling; salivation; sweating; coma.	Tetrahydrocannabinol (THC).	Good prognosis with symptomatic treatment; protect from injury until recovery.
Milkweed	Throughout North America.	Depression; weakness; staggering; irregular heart beat; seizures; coma.	Cardenolides.	Symptomatic; recovery is rare.
Moldy corn	Wherever corn is grown, processed, or stored.	Aimless wandering; head pressing.	Fumonisin B.	None; nearly always fatal; survivors often have residual neurological effects.
Monensin	Cattle feeds; horse feed contaminated with cattle supplement.	Loss of appetite; sweating; rapid breathing; colic; depression; staggering; collapse.	Ionophores.	Symptomatic and supportive care; usually death within 48 hours.
Morning glory	Throughout North America.	Weight loss; depression; delirium.	Lysergic acid amines (like "LSD").	Protect from injury until recovery from hallucinogenic "trip".

➤

Plant or Substance	Location	Symptoms	Toxin	Treatment/ Prognosis
Mustard weed (seeds mixed in grain products)	Throughout U.S.	Salivation; colic; diarrhea.	Mustard oils (thiocyanates).	Digestive tract protectants such as mineral oil; often fatal.
Nightshade	Throughout U.S.	Drowsiness; salivation; labored breathing; trembling; weakness; paralysis; coma.	Solanine.	Medications such as mineral oil to coat the digestive tract and stimulate rapid movement; death usually occurs within 48 hours.
Oak buds in spring; **acorns** in fall.	Throughout U.S.	Colic; constipation; thirst; black diarrhea; frequent urination.	Tannins.	Symptomatic and supportive care; death by kidney failure if large volume of acorns is eaten.
Onions	Throughout U.S.	Brown urine, weakness, icterus.	S-methylcysteine sulfoxide	Transfusion; support; recover if treated early.
Phenothiazines	The tranquilizers acepromazine, promazine, and fluphenazine; and the dewormer phenothiazine.	Within 24 hours, see depression; weakness; loss of appetite; colic; fever; icterus; brown urine; dyspnea; collapse; and death.	Phenothiazine in sensitive individuals.	Transfusion; support; often fatal in sensitive individuals.
Pine needles and bark	Throughout U.S.	Proven to cause abortion in late-term cows; speculated to affect pregnant mares similarly but not yet proven.	Isocupressic acid.	Removal from source at third trimester; no treatment is effective once poisoning has occurred.

VISUAL GUIDE, continued from page 315

Mustard

Nightshade species

Nightshade species

Nightshade species

Oak Buds/Acorns

Oleander

Poison hemlock

Red Maple

Rhododendron

Rhododendron, in bloom

Sorghum

St. John's-wort

(continued on page 322)

Plant or Substance	Location	Symptoms	Toxin	Treatment/ Prognosis
Poison hemlock	Throughout U.S. and southern Canada.	Salivation; excitement; severe colic.	Alkaloids.	Symptomatic; almost always fatal.
Pyrethrins	Insecticidal products.	Salivation; diarrhea; trembling; hyperexcitability; depression; seizures.	Pyrethrin.	Good prognosis with symptomatic treatment; protect from injury until recovery.
Red Maple (wilted leaves)	Throughout U.S.	Rapid breathing; jaundice or muddy gums; weakness; brown urine.	Unknown.	Transfusion and support; often fatal.
Selenium	Feed supplement; also present in certain plants in geographic areas where selenium content of soil is high.	Blindness; staggering; paralysis; coronary band erosion; weight loss; rough hair coat; joint stiffness; lameness.	Selenium.	Removal from source; symptomatic and supportive treatment; complete recovery unless damage to liver and nerve tissue is severe; can cause death within 48 hours if large dose taken in short time.
Sorghum; sudan grass; spring buds or wilted leaves of fruit trees; elderberry; choke-cherry	Throughout U.S.	Usually found dead; otherwise see excitement; trembling; labored breathing; seizures; collapse.	Cyanide.	Rapid administration of antidote (sodium nitrite); usually fatal.

Plant or Substance	Location	Symptoms	Toxin	Treatment/ Prognosis
St. John's-wort; buckwheat; bishop's weed; Dutchman breeches	Throughout U.S.	Severe ulceration of light-colored exposed skin.	Hypericin or liver toxins.	Symptomatic; not fatal, but sun-sensitivity can be permanent.
Tansy ragwort; groundsel; hound's tongue; fiddleneck and **rattlebox**	Throughout U.S., mostly Western.	Weight loss; rough hair coat; depression; anorexia; jaundice; head pressing.	Pyrrolizidine alkaloids.	Symptomatic and supportive care; fatal if liver is unable to regenerate.
Water hemlock	Throughout U.S.	Violent, rapid course: within 20 minutes of ingestion, see tremors; convulsions.	Cicutoxin.	None, almost always fatal within 1 hour of onset of symptoms.
White snakeroot	Eastern and Southwestern U.S.	Stiffness; staggering; dysphagia; sweating; cardiac arrest.	Tremetone.	Removal from source; supportive and symptomatic; lethal dose is 2 to 10 pounds of the plant.
Yellow star thistle, Russian knapweed	Western U.S.	Inability to hold or chew food or drink water; tense upper lip; bars of lips held back in a grimace; jaw champing; yawning; head tossing; submerging lips and muzzle in water.	Unknown.	No treatment; brain damage is permanent and usually necessitates euthanasia.

➤

VISUAL GUIDE, continued from page 319

St. John's-wort in bloom

Water hemlock

White snakeroot

White snakeroot, in bloom

Wild onion

Photos of Buttercup, Castor bean, Choke cherry, Elderberry, Foxglove, Dutchman's breeches, Horsetail, Jimsonweed, Larkspur, Lily-of-the-valley, Lupine, Milkweed, Morning glory, Nightshade, Poison hemlock, Red Maple, Rhododendron, St. John's-wort, Water hemlock, White snakeroot, and Wild onion © M. Williams. Used with permission. All others courtesy of Robert D. Linnabary, DVM, MS.

SECTION III

REFERENCE INFORMATION

GLOSSARY

Abscess
An infection around which the body has constructed a wall of fibrous tissue, to isolate it. Treatment with antibiotics is more likely to be effective if drainage of the abscess can be established, eliminating accumulated pus and debris.

Abscess, in brain
Most often the result of bacteria carried in the bloodstream to the brain from infection elsewhere in your horse's body. Can result from such bacterial invaders as *Corynebacterium* (or *Rhodococcus*) in lung or intestinal infections, or *Streptococcus equi* (strangles[G]). Signs depend on area of the brain affected. Treatment is difficult because of a natural barrier in the brain's circulation preventing the entrance of many substances, including some antibiotics, and because by definition abscesses are walled off from the body's usual defenses.

Acute
Referring to disease: An acute disease is a disease of short, sharp course.

Alar folds, excessive; excessive alar folds
An excess of tissue inside the nostril folds, causing respiratory noise and, rarely, decreased performance. In horses that are not strenuous athletes, it's unlikely to be a problem. Treatment may include the surgical removal of the extra tissue.

Alimentary lymphosarcoma
Cancer of the lymphatic system which has invaded the intestinal tract, often interfering with normal digestion and absorption of nutrients. This can cause profound weight loss, despite normal or increased appetite. Treatment choices may include surgical removal and/or chemotherapy; prognosis generally is poor.

Alkali disease, chronic selenium poisoning
Chronic[G] selenium poisoning due to ingestion of mildly toxic amounts of this essential mineral over a period of weeks to months. Signs may include gradual weight loss, "bobtail disease" (loss of mane and tail hair), and tender feet with cracked and broken hooves. Liver damage occurs; there's a 50 percent chance of recovery with treatment, depending on whether the liver is able to regenerate adequately.

Allergy
Increased sensitivity to specific substances or agents. Your horse's body develops an allergy after prior exposure, which sensitizes his immune system. Subsequent exposure brings a disproportionate "overreaction," either locally or body-wide. There's disagreement over why an allergy develops: some say it's a genetic predisposition, others say it's cumulative based on chronic exposure.

Anaphylaxis
An allergic-type hypersensitivity reaction to a substance or agent to which there has been prior exposure. After becoming sensitized (which may follow years of exposure with no evidence of any problem), a particular exposure brings a body-wide overreaction that can include the formation of hives, edema[G] in the respiratory tract, circulatory shock[G], and death.

Anemia
A decrease in red blood cell population due to bleeding, red blood cell destruction (from diseases such as equine infectious anemia[G]), or from decreased production of new red blood cells to replace those that die after their normal life span. This can result from disease of the bone marrow, where red blood cells are manufactured.

Anhidrosis
Loss of the ability to sweat (your horse's primary mode of cooling). Most often a problem of horses in hot, humid climates. Your anhidrotic horse may suffer a loss of performance ability (because he'll overheat); have a higher than usual heart rate when exercising

(and takes longer than usual to recover); flare his nostrils even when at rest; and have an elevated rectal temperature. Some anhidrotic horses retain the ability to sweat only in selected areas: around the mane; axillary areas (armpits); and groin. Hair follicles adjacent to the defunct sweat glands can deteriorate, leading to hair loss on his head and neck. Some feed supplements have shown promise recently in treating anhidrosis, but the universally recommended treatment is management: move the horse to a cooler, less humid climate; train only when temperatures are cool; and use water rinses and fans to help your horse stay cool.

Antibiotics, and diarrhea
By killing "good" bacteria normally present in your horse's intestines, antibiotics can allow disease-producing bacteria to flourish and can cause colitis[G], diarrhea[G], and endotoxemia[G]. In severe cases, death by endotoxemia can occur before diarrhea is seen.

Antibiotic sensitivity
A laboratory test to determine what antibiotics, if any, are effective against bacteria cultured from an infected patient. Small paper discs impregnated with specific antibiotics are placed on a culture plate. Bacteria that are sensitive to the antibiotic won't grow near the disc.

Antitoxin, and serum sickness
Serum sickness is a rare, poorly understood liver disease that's often fatal. It can occur several months after your horse has been given certain serum-containing treatments such as anti-endotoxin and tetanus antitoxin. Icterus[G] is a common symptom. Treatment is supportive.

Aortic thrombosis
This condition occurs when a blood clot (thrombus) travels through your horse's bloodstream and becomes lodged in the rear portion of the aorta, completely or partially shutting off the blood supply to one or both hind limbs. Signs can include weakened or absent pulse in the affected limb(s), cold limb(s), and weakness. Treatment, which requires removal of the offending clot, is difficult and often unsuccessful.

Arsenic poisoning
Arsenic is present in several chemicals commonly found at horse facilities, including certain herbicides, ant baits, and medications. The poison can cause damage to your horse's intestinal tract, kidneys, and lungs, producing symptoms such as: intense abdominal pain; diarrhea; drooling; staggering; trembling; weakness; collapse; and death. Survival is possible if diagnosed and treated promptly and vigorously. Treatment may include intensive support, intestinal protectants, and administration of specific chemicals to bind the arsenic in your horse's system so it can be eliminated.

Arytenoid chondropathy, chondrosis, chondritis
Inflammation of the cartilage at the back of the throat (the arytenoid cartilage) which becomes thickened, ulcerated, deformed, and possibly paralyzed, all as a result of the inflamation. The free passage of air is affected, thereby decreasing performance in strenuous athletes. No single cause has been identified. Surgery may be required to widen the airway.

Aspiration pneumonia
Lung disease resulting from feed, saliva, or regurgitated stomach contents entering the respiratory tract and reaching your horse's lungs, creating inflammation, cell damage, and infection. Common causes of aspiration pneumonia can include: choke[G]; injury or disease interfering with your horse's ability to swallow; administration of medication via oral drench[G]; and administration of medication by a stomach tube accidentally placed in the windpipe (trachea) rather than the esophagus.

Aural hematoma
Accumulation of blood in the space between your horse's skin and the cartilage of his ear flap, causing the flap to appear puffy and pillow-like instead of flat. Without proper treatment, an aural hematoma can result in a bunched, misshapen ear.

Avermectin
A class of dewormer products. The equine product ivermectin is a member of this class.

Bacterial folliculitis
Infection of the hair follicle, usually after the skin has been damaged by injury, insect bites, and/or chronic filth. Most often occurs during warm weather. Signs can include pimples which break open to form hairless, crusted sores. Diagnosis is suggested by the appearance of the lesions, and can be confirmed by biopsy. Treatment usually includes clipping and cleaning the affected area, keeping it scrupulously clean and dry, and applying topical antiseptic medications. For deep folliculitis that can't be reached by topical treatments, bacterial culture to determine the appropriate antibiotic is done; the antibiotic is given systemically.

Balling gun
A device used for administering large pills orally to livestock, usually cattle. Use of a balling gun in a horse can lead to throat injury[G] and can deposit the pill down the windpipe (trachea), rather than the esophagus.

Belly tap, abdominal paracentesis
A diagnostic procedure most commonly used when attempting to determine the severity of, and best course of action for, a particular case of colic. After clipping and disinfecting a patch of skin on your horse's lower belly, a large needle is inserted into his abdominal cavity. A sample of abdominal cavity fluid is collected and analyzed for color, clarity, and protein content: amber-colored, clear, low-protein fluid is considered favorable. Blood-tinged or manure-contaminated, cloudy, and high-protein fluid may indicate that the colic is severe and/or advanced.

Benign
Referring to a cancerous growth: Not invasive or destructive, and not tending to spread to other areas of the body.

Bighead disease
A nutritional disorder due to inadequate calcium and excessive phosphorus content in the diet, causing loss of bone density. Bones become thicker to compensate for their weakness, and the result is seen first in the bones of the face: they're enlarged, but symmetrical. Horses heavily supplemented with high-phosphorus feeds such as grain concentrates and wheat bran, and horses with high calcium demands (broodmares) are most often affected. If the dietary imbalance is not corrected, bone fractures and/or heart failure can occur. Correction of the diet is usually curative, but the facial abnormality can be permanent.

Bile stones
Stones formed within your horse's bile ducts (tubes which carry bile–a digestive fluid–from the liver to the intestines). Signs can include: depression; icterus[G]; and intermittent colic[G]. Diagnosis is confirmed by viewing the stones with ultrasonography[G]. Surgery to remove the stones is complex, but usually curative unless extensive liver damage has occurred.

Black walnut shavings toxicosis
An as-yet unexplained poisoning from skin contact with wood shavings made from the black walnut tree, most often the consequence of unknowingly using them to bed a stall. (Anecdotal evidence suggests that other walnut varieties may also be toxic.) Vasculitis[G] and laminitis[G] are virtually guaranteed and usually severe. Treatment involves removing the walnut shavings, and treating the resultant vasculitis and/or laminitis.

Bladder, infection of
Bacterial onslaught in your horse's bladder. Common signs can include: frequent urination; painful urination; and blood-tinged urine. After identifying the causative organism by bacterial culture, treatment with an appropriate antibiotic is usually curative unless there's a persistent underlying problem. These can include: the presence of a bladder stone which constantly irritates the bladder lining; or the presence of a tumor within the bladder, which intermittently bleeds and provides food for bacterial growth.

Bleeding disorder
Any disorder that interferes with blood clotting in a wound. Causes can include: congenital diseases such as hemophilia; bone mar-

row diseases that interfere with the formation of blood clotting cells (called platelets); a rare complication after severe infection that causes depletion of platelets (called disseminated intravascular coagulation, or DIC); red clover poisoning; and poisoning with products containing the chemical warfarin or coumadin.

Blind staggers
Poisoning by the essential mineral selenium, due to ingestion of moderately toxic levels. Signs can include: blindness; straying from the herd; aimless wandering; and eventually paralysis and death. Treatment is often unsuccessful once symptoms are evident.

Blister beetle poisoning, cantharidin poisoning
Poisoning due to ingestion of a beetle, typically 1/2 inch long, solid black or black with yellow stripes. It inhabits some alfalfa fields and other forages, and contains a powerful stomach irritant called cantharidin. Most poisonings occur when the beetle is killed and baled into your horse's hay, then ingested. The toxin can cause severe colic due to burning of the stomach lining. Ingestion of only a few beetles can be fatal to a full-grown horse and treatment is symptomatic and supportive. Prognosis is guarded: As many as half of all patients die despite vigorous therapy.

Bog spavin
Spavin infers a hock joint injury due to wear and tear, which comes on gradually after repeated hard work. The different types of spavin are based on what's seen from the outside, but the internal problem is not always revealed by external signs. Bog spavin is a swelling of the upper part of the hock joint resulting in a water-balloon-like protrusion on both the inner and outer sides. The swelling can be pushed from one side to the other with your fingers. Depending on the underlying cause, bog spavin is not necessarily accompanied by lameness, pain, or heat. Treatment is aimed at the underlying cause.

Bone scan, nuclear imaging
See Nuclear scintigraphy, nuclear imaging, bone scan.

Bone spavin
(See definition of "spavin" under "Bog spavin.") Bone spavin is arthritis of the lower portion of the hock. Most commonly, bone spavin appears as a hard swelling on the inner (joint) surface, where the hock meets the cannon bone. It also can occur in the lower aspect of your horse's hock joint without visible enlargement. Lameness is common but can be difficult to detect because both hind limbs are often affected. Pain is often associated with flexing and advancing the affected limb(s), causing your horse to carry the leg(s) abnormally and/or drag his toe, as revealed by unusual wear patterns there.

Botulism, forage poisoning
Disease caused by the nerve-poisoning toxin of the bacteria *Clostridium botulinum* which live in certain soils, wounds, and in decaying organic matter. The first signs in adult horses can include loss of tongue, tail, and eyelid tone, resulting in subtle changes in the face and tail carriage that often go unnoticed. As the disease progresses, swallowing can become difficult, resulting in quidding[G], drooling, tongue lolling, and/or bad breath, followed by weakness, gait instability, collapse, and death by respiratory paralysis. Intensive-care treatment, including administration of botulism antitoxin, is successful in approximately 70 percent of cases.

Bowed tendon
Sprain and/or tearing of one or both flexor tendons that run along the back of your horse's lower leg. The result is swelling, heat, pain, and lameness. In older, healed bowed tendons, the only remaining sign is enlargement of the area. Bowed tendon is a serious threat to a horse's performance career because the healed tendon is weaker and less elastic than the pre-injury one, and therefore is prone to re-injury.

Bows are most common in the superficial digital flexor tendon, resulting in swelling at the cannon bone's midsection. When the deep digital flexor tendon is bowed, swelling is located in the tendon's lower half, below the fetlock joint. Treatment usually is aimed at limiting damage from bleeding and swelling between tendon fibers, and protecting against further tearing. After bleeding and inflammation have subsided, physical therapy may be prescribed to prevent and/or break down adhesions.

Bracken fern poisoning, "bracken staggers"
Poisoning by a perennial fern likely to occur at margins of forests and open fields, which is toxic in both fresh form and when dried (in hay). Signs can occur within about 30 days of eating hay with 20 percent bracken fern, and can include: weight loss; weakness; staggering; paralysis; and death. Bracken fern inactivates vitamin B_1 and causes brain swelling due to severe B_1 deficiency. The horse can be cured dramatically if B_1 injections are given before brain damage is permanent.

Bronchitis
Inflammation of the lining of your horse's bronchial tubes. It can result from infection, allergy, lungworms, or chronic irritation from inhaling dust and molds.

Bronchoalveolar lavage, BAL
A diagnostic procedure to confirm a tentative diagnosis of pneumonia. Also used to help identify the causative bacteria and the antibiotic that will be most effective against it. While your horse stands under light sedation, a thin tube is inserted into his nostril and advanced as far as possible toward the lungs. Approximately 1/2 to 1-1/2 cups of a sterile solution is infused under low pressure, then withdrawn into special test tubes for laboratory analysis.

Brucellosis
Infection by bacteria of the *Brucella* family, which can infect damaged cartilage in the withers area and cause fistulous withers[G], and also can invade the reproductive tract and cause infertility and abortions. Because *Brucella* bacteria can infect several species, including cattle, housepets, and humans, extreme care should be taken when handling a horse suspected of harboring this bacterial strain. Diagnosis is confirmed by laboratory culture of infected tissues and/or blood test; treatment can include antibiotic therapy and aggressive wound management with removal of affected cartilage.

Bucked shins
Tiny cracks in the cannon bone's front surface, usually occurring in the front legs of a young horse in too-strenuous training. These tiny fractures may not be visible on standard x-rays and can require special, high-detail x-rays if the diagnosis is to be confirmed. Most cases resolve with 4 to 6 weeks of rest, support bandaging, and adjustment of the training routine.

Bursitis
Inflammation of the bursa, a small fluid-filled sac that cushions large tendons as they course over major joints. The most common sites of bursitis in your horse are at the point of his elbow and at the point of the hock. Bursitis at the point of the hock results in the unsightly blemish known as capped hock[G].

Buttercup poisoning
Poisoning by this yellow-flowered perennial, well established throughout North America, can cause blistering of your horse's lips, mouth, and intestinal tract, and signs of salivation, colic, and diarrhea. The fresh plant must be ingested; dried buttercup does not cause these symptoms. Treatment is usually symptomatic: Remove the horse from access to the plant, then work to relieve his pain, and coat his stomach and intestines with a protectant such as mineral oil.

COPD, chronic obstructive pulmonary disease, heaves
See Heaves, chronic obstructive pulmonary disease, COPD.

Calcinosis circumscripta
A benign tumor containing calcium deposits that look like bone on x-ray. The tumor, which lies beneath normal skin and can be as large as 6 inches in diameter, forms a hard, painless lump adjacent to a major joint, most often just below the stifle joint on the outer side. Surgical removal is usually curative but unnecessary unless the location of the mass

interferes with normal leg function, or if its presence is disturbing aesthetically.

Canker
An infection of the frog that can spread to the adjacent sole and hoof wall. The affected frog grows thick folds and ridges, and a foul-smelling, cottage-cheese like exudate oozes from the crevices. Affected feet usually are lame. Canker is most often caused by long-term hoof neglect and wet, filthy footing. Because infection is often quite deep, successful treatment might require surgical debridement[G] and systemic antibiotics.

Cannon keratosis
A skin disorder that causes scaly, crusty, hairless patches on the fronts of the hind limb cannon bones, sometimes accompanied by heat, swelling and pain. The cause is unknown but some clinicians believe it may be a congenital condition. If there's inflammation, it can be alleviated with topical anti-inflammatory medications such as over-the-counter cortisone creams. The scale and crust can be controlled with human or equine anti-seborrheic shampoos and gels that contain benzoyl peroxide. There is no cure.

Cantharidin poisoning
See "Blister beetle" poisoning.

Capped hock
Enlargement and swelling of a fluid-filled pouch (see "Bursitis") at the point of your horse's hock, forming a cosmetically unappealing, golf-ball-sized, floppy cap that tends to persist even after the underlying problem has been resolved. Capped hock is rarely associated with lameness. It is most often caused by too-tight hock bandages or by repetitive trauma to the hocks, such as from kicking stall walls, or kicking in a trailer.

Capsulitis
A painful joint condition due to inflammation and thickening of the joint capsule (a fibrous tissue layer enveloping the joint). Any movement that wrinkles or tugs the inflamed joint capsule is painful; a horse with capsulitis voluntarily limits movement to avoid pain. As scar tissue infiltrates the healing capsule, what began as voluntary limitation of movement becomes compulsory. The scar tissue, which is not elastic, restricts his joint's range of motion. Treatment is aimed at relieving inflammation and addressing the underlying cause (which can be joint infection, injury, or wear and tear). Controlled exercise and physical therapy during the healing process are often used to prevent future range of motion limitations due to scarring of the joint capsule.

Cartilage, injury within joint
Injury from trauma or wear and tear can involve the cartilage, which covers your horse's bone ends with a smooth, concussion-absorbing coating. Inflammation within the joint causes thinning of its lubrication, increasing friction against cartilage, and stimulating production of caustic chemicals that literally eat away at it, causing pitting and cracking. Because cartilage has no blood supply of its own, it has a limited ability to heal and regenerate. Pain-killing medications that encourage your horse to use his joint while it continues to degenerate can accelerate cartilage destruction. Direct treatment of cartilage injury or disease usually includes: addressing the underlying cause; resting the joint to prevent further concussion; restoring depleted joint fluid by injecting hyaluronan (a.k.a. sodium hyaluronate, hyaluronic acid) into the joint and administering chondroprotective (cartilage-protecting) medications intramuscularly or into the joint.

Cataract
Loss of transparency of an eye lens. Once a lens becomes clouded, there is no treatment to restore it. If the cataract is large enough to block vision, the lens may be removed surgically, which permits the horse to see, but not to focus.

Cathartic
A laxative given to quickly purge your horse's bowels of their contents. Examples include Epsom salt solution, mineral oil, or psyllium.

Cattle grub, myiasis
Migrating fly larvae (grubs) tunneling beneath

skin. Normally affecting cattle, the eggs are deposited on the bovine's legs. Resultant larvae penetrate the skin and migrate to the back or throat region, where they punch through the hide, fall to the ground, sprout wings, and fly away. Horses that commingle with cattle occasionally are infested with grubs, which invariably get lost during the migratory phase through the wrong host, forming marble-sized nodules where they stop, usually on the withers, shoulder, or back. If the grub is still alive, it'll form a breathing pore (hole) in your horse's skin. When it dies, the nodule becomes a permanent, hardened grave. Treatment may include administration of the dewormers avermectin (ivermectin) or milbemycin (moxidectin), which kill grubs wherever they're located in a horse's body. If the resultant nodule is cosmetically unacceptable, it can be surgically removed using local anesthetic. Prevention: Don't let your horses commingle with cattle and/or cattle manure, where flies breed.

Cauda equina syndrome, polyneuritis
A degenerative nerve root disorder (the first branches of nerves from your horse's spinal cord). In cauda equina syndrome, nerve roots at the spinal cord's tail end are involved. Signs can include paralysis of the tail and anal sphincter and weakness of the hind limbs. In polyneuritis, the condition spreads to nerves in other areas. There is no known treatment.

Cauterize, cauterization
To congeal, burn, or obliterate tissue by applying heat.

Cellulitis
Inflammation of cells and connective tissue, usually associated with deep skin conditions such as scratches[G] or greasy heel[G].

Chickens, and itchy skin
Chickens can be infested with stick-tight fleas. If horse and chicken habitats overlap, the fleas can hop onto your horses and create or worsen itchy skin. To eliminate this problem, chickens and their territory can be treated with chicken-safe appropriate insecticide for stick-tight fleas.

Choke
An object or wad of feed lodged in your horse's esophagus. Muscles around the obstruction clench in response, prolonging the choke and increasing the odds of damage to esophageal lining, which can lead to narrowing of the esophagus due to scar tissue. (A narrowed esophagus is prone to repeated chokes.) During a choke, food, water, and saliva are regurgitated through one or both nostrils, and your horse may cough and/or retch. Encouraging the choked horse to keep his head lowered can help prevent regurgitated material from spilling into the windpipe (trachea), which can cause aspiration pneumonia[G].

Treatment can include: gentle irrigation and suction of impacted feed with warm water or saline through a stomach tube, removal of any lodged foreign matter with an operating endoscope or by surgery (a last resort) if it can't be removed endoscopically, and/or diagnosis and treatment of any underlying problem that caused the choke. Anti-inflammatory medications usually are given to soothe tissues inflamed by the choke and treatment. Treatment for aspiration pneumonia is administered, if necessary.

Cholinergic pruritus
A rare skin disorder that causes intense itching when exercise, a warm bath, or anxiety causes your horse's core body temperature to rise. Affected horses have no lumps, bumps, or other skin lesions, but begin to scratch, rub, and bite at their skin as soon as they become warm enough to break a sweat. Cool baths relieve the itch. For some patients, regular antihistamine use can lessen or eliminate the itchy episodes. There is no cure.

Chronic
A disease or condition of long duration.

Chronic obstructive pulmonary disease, COPD, heaves
See Heaves, chronic obstructive pulmonary disease, COPD.

Cicatricial alopecia
A smooth, hairless scar from a healed injury with permanently damaged hair follicles.

Circulatory shutdown (shock)
A shift in the flow of blood which causes it to pool in your horse's veins rather than flow to his heart and lungs. Blood that does circulate is shunted to selected tissues, leaving parts of the body without adequate supply. Signs of circulatory shutdown can include depression; pale, blue-tinged, or mud-colored gums; and rapid but weak pulse. Treatment usually focuses on trying to increase blood volume (therefore increase blood pressure) by administering massive amounts of intravenous fluids and giving medications that can alter blood distribution. There is a definite point of no return, beyond which no amount of treatment will save the patient.

Ciliary apparatus
Hair-like structures lining the respiratory tract which, by their rhythmic movement, sweep debris up and out of the tract.

Clostridial myositis, malignant edema
An infection in the muscle due to bacteria of the *Clostridium* family being carried in via intramuscular injection through contaminated skin. Clostridial myositis results about once every 100,000 injections. The bacteria can proliferate rapidly, destroying muscle tissue, causing painful swelling and lameness within two days, and liberating massive amounts of toxins. Without prompt treatment, the affected horse absorbs those bacterial toxins, often with fatal outcome within three or four days of the initial injection. In addition to severe pain and swelling, signs can include: loss of appetite; weakness; depression; recumbency; coma; and death. *Clostridium* species ordinarily are sensitive to antibiotics. If treated early, stricken horses usually recover quickly. Many horses lack prompt treatment as the swelling is mistaken for a local inflammatory reaction that will resolve on its own.

Coffin bone, fractured
A fracture that usually is associated with a misstep or fall; commonly seen on the inside (and more consistently stressed) leg of racehorses. Symptoms usually include sudden-onset lameness, heat that can be felt on the hoof wall, and increased digital pulse[G]. Treatment depends on the fracture's location and on how unstable it is. Some cases heal well with 12 months' rest and application of a bar shoe to limit hoof flexion. Others require surgery and stabilization of the fracture with bone screws.

Coggins test
A blood test to detect infection with the virus that causes Equine Infectious Anemia (EIA[G]). The disease is spread by biting insects that feed on infected horses, then carry the virus to other horses. Many events such as shows and rodeos require recent (6 to 12 months) negative Coggins tests on all participants, and most states require negative Coggins test in horses crossing their borders. Horses testing positive become subject to state law that requires quarantine away from biting insects and other horses, or euthanasia. There is no known cure, and no vaccine.

Cold splint
A hard knob on the inside surface of your horse's cannon bone. Can be due to concussive forces irritating the connective tissue around the splint bones; external trauma (a kick, or interference from the opposite leg); or as a normal part of the maturing process in young adult horses. When not accompanied by swelling, heat, or pain, this knob is referred to as a cold splint and is considered a cosmetic blemish. Treatment usually is not necessary. However for cosmetic purposes, the cold splint can be surgically removed.

Colic
Non-specific abdominal pain, usually due to intestinal problems and/or gas buildup. Also can be caused by abdominal disorders such as: internal bleeding; liver disease; kidney disease; reproductive problems; and ulcers. In addition, other diseases can cause signs that mimic colic even though they don't involve the abdomen, such as: laminitis[G]; tying-up[G] syndrome and other muscle disorders; weakness; heart problems; nervous system disorders; and pleuritis[G]. Treatment usually focuses on relieving pain, preventing shock, and diagnosing and resolving the underlying problem. Surgery is required in a minority of cases.

Colic, involving large bowel

Although there are exceptions, significant problems in the large bowel can cause only mild, dull colic pain when compared to the more severe pain exhibited in similar problems in the small intestines. The underlying problem might be life-threatening in both cases. Therefore, severity of pain should not be used to gauge the severity of the problem.

Colitis X

Severe, acute[G] inflammation of the colon often responsible for sudden death before any telltale signs of intestinal trouble are seen. The disease is believed to be due to an infectious bacterium, but its identity has yet to be proven (hence the name X). If the patient survives long enough to show signs and be treated, treatment usually focuses on relieving the symptoms of fever and colic pain, and fighting shock[G] and dehydration[G] by administration of massive volumes of intravenous fluids and electrolytes.

Colitis

Inflammation of the colon, usually due to infection (such as *Salmonella*, Potomac horse fever, and *Clostridium*). Diarrhea, colic pain, and rapidly progressing dehydration are usually the result. Other causes can include: administration of nonsteroidal anti-inflammatory medications such as bute (phenylbutazone); administration of antibiotics such as tetracycline, tylosin, neomycin, and lincomycin; intestinal lymphosarcoma[G]; inorganic arsenic poisoning; and granulomatous enteritis. Treatment focuses on relieving symptoms and preventing dehydration and shock while identifying and treating the underlying cause, if possible.

Compartmental syndrome

Pressure damage to major nerves and blood vessels between muscle compartments that are swelling because of injury. Signs can progress from soreness to numbness to paralysis as the bleeding and swelling continue within the injured muscles, and pressure on nerves increases. Treatment usually focuses on slowing bleeding and swelling and, if necessary, relieving pressure surgically.

Congestive heart failure

Loss of the heart's efficient pumping ability due to valve leakage allowing blood to reflux backward, into the lungs. This causes lung congestion and decreases the volume of blood delivered to your horse's extremities. The heart compensates by pumping harder, which can worsen lung congestion and damage heart muscle. In your horse, congestive heart failure can result from heart damage due to viral or bacterial disease, or from poisoning with the livestock supplement rumensin[G]. Symptoms can include: weakness; decreased performance; nosebleed during exercise; delayed recovery from workout; and/or cough. Treatment is usually focused on identifying and treating the underlying cause, relieving lung congestion, and improving the heart's efficiency with various medications.

Conjunctivitis

Inflammation and/or infection of the tissues around the eye. Symptoms can include reddening, itching, watering, and swelling. Causes can include irritants such as dust or flies; trauma; and infection. Treatment usually includes gentle cleaning, addressing the underlying cause, and medicating with ointments containing appropriate antibiotics and/or anti-inflammatory medications.

Contusion, muscle

Bruising due to blunt trauma, resulting in broken blood vessels and bleeding under the skin. Severe muscle contusion can lead to compartmental syndrome[G]. Despite the fact that a contusion's external appearance is less disturbing than an injury with external bleeding, blunt trauma can damage much more tissue than sharp trauma because it can affect a wider area, resulting in massive tissue death and decay. Treatment usually includes: first aid to limit the spread of tissue damage from swelling and hemorrhage; establishment of surgical drainage[G] if necessary; and physical therapy to minimize adhesions that would otherwise deform tissues and limit their range of motion.

Corn, hoof

An injury to your horse's sole, near his heels,

due to pressure there from the heels of a shoe that has been pulled forward as his hoof grows, usually the result of waiting too long before resetting a shod horse's shoes. Symptoms can include lameness and bruise-like discoloration of the sole in the heel area. (Corns may be easier to see when pared with a hoof knife.) The discolored area might be moist and cracked. Treatment usually involves shoe removal and corrective trimming to balance the hoof. If the injured sole is infected, it's treated the same as a sole abscess[G].

Cornea
The transparent, domed portion of the eyeball.

Corneal abscess
An infection between the onion-like layers of the cornea, most often associated with a penetrating wound. The condition is painful and, if unresolved, can result in blindness. Treatment is challenging because the location of the infection between corneal layers makes it difficult for topical or systemic medications to penetrate to the site. Treatment usually is similar to what is prescribed for corneal ulcer[G]; in nonresponsive cases surgery may be needed to remove corneal layers and expose the abscess. (If the infection is resolved, the cornea will heal.)

Corneal ulcer
A defect in the cornea, most often associated with injury and subsequent infection. The condition is painful and, if unresolved, can result in blindness. Treatment usually includes antibiotics and other medications to combat the infection, inflammation, and pain, and facilitate repair of the damaged cornea. In most cases, topical treatment is used.

Corpora nigra
Nodular structures overhanging the pupil in the normal eye, believed to serve as an awning to protect the eye's interior from the sun. Usually the same color as the iris, these nodules can be mistaken for abnormal growths in the eye.

Cortical fissure fracture
A severe form of bucked shins[G], often the consequence of too-strenuous training resulting in incomplete fractures on the front/outside surface of the cannon bones on your horse's forelimbs. A cortical fissure fracture is visible on x-ray and usually is associated with localized pain, swelling, and lameness. Treatment usually includes 4 to 6 months of rest, support bandages, and a gradual return to training that has been adjusted to reduce bone stress. In many cases, placement of a bone screw is needed to stabilize the fracture.

Crash helmet
A padded head device, usually made of dense-cell foam (similar to what's used in backpackers' foam mattresses), used in equine hospitals for horses recovering from anesthesia. Some horse farms have crash helmets for use on horses with severe colic pain to protect the head and eyes from injury during thrashing.

Cryosurgery
Obliteration of tissue by freezing with liquid nitrogen or carbon dioxide. This technique is often used to treat certain skin cancers such as squamous cell carcinoma[G], and to remove sarcoids[G].

Culture
The cultivation of a sample of tissue or body fluid in a laboratory growth medium in order to identify infectious bacteria or fungi present.

Curb
Soft swelling due to ligament strain, located on the outer, rear surface of your horse's hind limb where the hock joint meets the head of the lateral splint bone (at the top of the cannon bone). Horses with excessively angled hocks (cow hocks or sickle hocks) are more likely to have this injury. Signs can include sudden onset of the characteristic swelling, with pain, heat, and lameness made worse with a hock flexion test. Over time the swelling becomes hard and painless. Treatment usually includes: first aid to reduce heat and swelling; rest; pressure bandaging to limit swelling; and physical therapy to prevent or limit adhesions.

Cushing's disease
A hormonal disease due to a pituitary gland tumor (pituitary adenoma[G]). It causes a variety

of problems which can include a diabetes-like syndrome; weight loss; chronic laminitis[G]; and a long, shaggy, curly hair coat that fails to shed. There is no cure, but in some cases the signs can be lessened by administration of medications to suppress overproduction of certain hormones, and stimulate production of the neurotransmitter dopamine.

Cutaneous lymphosarcoma
A form of cancer that causes the formation of multiple nodules under the skin. Affected horses often suffer weight loss; anemia[G]; edema[G]; swollen lymph nodes; and internal tumors. The condition is diagnosed by biopsy. Tumor removal is feasible only if the nodules are few in number. Some patients go into temporary remission if treated with cortisone-like medication. Affected mares often go into remission when they become pregnant.

Cyst
An enclosed, smooth lump with a solid or liquid center produced by the cells lining the cyst's wall. A sebaceous cyst contains oil produced by oil glands in the cyst's lining. A serous cyst contains serum. A dentigerous cyst, usually located beneath one ear, is lined with cells that were present when the horse was an embryo, became "lost in the shuffle" when the embryo was becoming organized into distinct parts, and usually contains one or more teeth and bits of hair. Cysts generally do not cause problems unless their location and size are in the path of tack or interfere with function of adjacent parts. Treatment options for cysts can include: surgical removal; cryosurgery[G]; cauterization[G]; or obliteration by laser. When a fluid-filled cyst is simply drained, it usually refills within a few days.

Cytology
The study of cells on a smear or smudge of tissue placed on a slide and viewed under a microscope.

DMSO, dimethylsulfoxide
A solvent by-product of the paper industry, which has anti-inflammatory effects when administered topically, orally, or via injection. When used topically, it's absorbed through your horse's skin. Care must be taken to avoid applying DMSO to skin that is tainted with anything that could be toxic–DMSO might carry the toxin into the horse's bloodstream and cause poisoning. Similarly, when you apply DMSO to your horse, you probably absorb it yourself. It's advisable to wear non-porous gloves. When DMSO is mixed with water, the resultant emulsion undergoes a chemical reaction and releases an impressive amount of heat. If applied to wet skin, it can cause irritation.

Debridement
Removal of dead or contaminated tissue and foreign matter from a wound.

Degenerative joint disease, DJD
A progressive breakdown of joint components, beginning with injury or inflammation within the joint. This causes breakdown and thinning of the joint fluid, which normally is a viscous lubricant, and culminates in cartilage destruction. Treatment can include: resolving the underlying cause; breaking the degenerative cycle by restoring volume and thickness of joint fluid; providing materials the joint needs to rebuild damaged components; and tailoring your horse's activity level so circulation is maximized, scar tissue is minimized, and no further joint trauma occurs during the healing process.

Degenerative suspensory ligament desmitis, DSLD
A degenerative disease of the hindlimbs. Seen most often (but not exclusively) in Peruvian Paso horses between the ages of 3 and 8, after they've entered into full training or performance. DSLD often is mistaken for simple ligament stress/injury. It's bilateral, so detecting and diagnosing the lameness is sometimes tricky. In initial stages, pain and swelling usually occur at the back of the hind cannon bones, about 2/3 of the way down from the hock. This is where the main body of the suspensory ligament splits into inner and outer branches. As the disease progresses, which it seems to do in spite of treatment, swelling

can spread down to the fetlock joint and beyond.

As it tries to heal, damaged parts of the ligament are replaced by granulation tissue[G] and cartilage, which make a poor substitute for normal, elastic, strong ligament tissue. The fetlocks progressively sink toward the ground, giving the limb an L-shape in later stages. It can be extremely painful; affected horses have been known to lie down and moan. Selected cases have been salvaged by surgically fusing the fetlock joint, which relieves pain, but the horse is no more than pasture sound.

Dehydration
Decrease in the body's normal water content due to inadequate water intake and/or increased water loss, such as via sweat or diarrhea.

Dentigerous cyst
A benign[G] growth, usually located at the base of an ear and covered with normal skin and hair. A sticky, amber-colored discharge may be noticed coming directly from the cyst or from a drainage hole nearby. Unless it has become infected and inflamed, the cyst is usually painless. Present at birth, it might be overlooked until discovered to lie in the path of the halter or bridle headstall. The cyst, which is a firm cluster of tissues that "got lost" during the horse's development as an embryo, usually contains hair and one or more teeth. Surgical removal is the treatment of choice.

Dewormer, anthelmintic
Medication given to eliminate intestinal parasites, or "worms." (For a partial listing of products, see page 221.)

Diarrhea, acute
Abnormally wet stool (semi-solid to watery) passed at least twice as often as normal, for a rapid, short course of less than a week. Treatment usually is aimed at the underlying cause, if known, and at supporting the horse by replacing lost fluids and electrolytes.

Diarrhea, chronic
Abnormally wet stool (semi-solid to watery) passed up to 1-1/2 times more often than normal, for an extended duration of days to months. Sometimes occurs with longer, intermittent periods of cow-pie or semi-solid stool. Treatment usually is aimed at identifying and correcting the underlying cause.

Diarrhea, infectious causes of
Infections with *Ehrlichia* (Potomac horse fever), *Salmonella*, or *Clostridium* species are the most common infectious causes of acute or chronic diarrhea in adult horses. Long-term and/or severe infestation with strongyles[G] (intestinal parasite) also can cause this condition.

Diarrhea, medications as cause of
Antibiotics that can cause diarrhea include tetracycline, erythromycin, sulfamethoxazole/trimethoprim, lincomycin, neomycin, and tylosin. Nonsteroidal anti-inflammatory medications that can cause diarrhea include bute (phenylbutazone), flunixin meglumine (Banamine), ketoprofen, and naproxen. Treatment generally involves removal of the medication, and support.

Diarrhea, sand as cause of
Horses fed on sandy ground can accidently ingest sand, which accumulates in the colon and irritates it, causing chronic colitis[G] and diarrhea. Treatment usually focuses on removing the sand, either through bulk laxatives or via surgery.

Digital pulse
Rhythmic pulsing of the digital artery behind your horse's pasterns, with each heart beat. The digital pulse is subtle but can be felt in a normal horse. (For how-to information, see page 202.) With certain disorders, it can become stronger and easier to feel.

Dimethylsulfoxide, DMSO
See DMSO, dimethylsulfoxide.

Dorsal displacement soft palate, DDSP
During such strenuous exercise as racing, the soft palate of some horses becomes displaced upwardly and lodges there, where it interferes with breathing. Affected horses may make a gagging sound and significantly slow their pace as they struggle for air. Diagnosis is

usually confirmed by endoscopic exam and by demonstrating that the problem does not occur when the horse's tongue is tied down during racing. There are many different surgical approaches that claim a variety of success rates.

Drainage, surgical
Surgical creation of an opening for accumulated blood, serum, pus, and/or debris to drain from a wound.

Draining tract
An opening formed by your horse's body for accumulated blood, serum, pus, and/or debris to drain from an internal wound that's healed as much as it's going to without outside help. The constant trickle of accumulated liquid along a path between muscle and connective tissue can prevent the tract from healing. Treatment can include resolving the underlying problem that's causing the wound to ooze, such as infection, or the presence of a foreign body[G] or sequestrum[G]. The draining tract is debrided[G] so it can heal.

Dry eye
Inadequate tear production, leading to irritation of the eye's cornea. Treatment usually is aimed at identifying and correcting the underlying cause, if possible, and protecting the eye with artificial lubrication.

DSLD, degenerative suspensory ligament desmitis
See Degenerative suspensory ligament desmitis, DSLD.

Duodenitis/jejunitis (D/J); proximal enteritis; anterior enteritis
Inflammation of the first part of the small intestine (the duodenum and a portion of the jejunum). The affected horse usually shows signs of moderate to severe colic. When a stomach tube is inserted, stomach fluid is retrieved, often flowing out under pressure. D/J is difficult to distinguish from a colic that requires surgery. In severe cases, treatment must continue for weeks, and can include: removing accumulated stomach fluids by stomach tube several times daily; soothing the stomach and intestinal tract with protectants such as mineral oil or Pepto-Bismol®; administering medication to control colic pain; and administering massive amounts of intravenous fluids to replace the gallons of liquid removed from the stomach. The cause is unknown. Roughly half the patients hospitalized and treated for D/J survive.

Dysphagia
Difficulty swallowing, which can be due to pain, obstruction (choke), or a problem with the nerves that govern throat muscles. The most common signs of dysphagia are slobbering of food from the mouth and/or drainage of chewed food and saliva from nostrils. Treatment usually is aimed at identifying and resolving the underlying cause, and adjusting feeding methods (e.g., feeding by stomach tube) to avoid aspiration pneumonia[G].

Ear canal, infection of; otitis externa
Infection of the ear canal outside your horse's ear drum, often secondary to damage from *Otobius megnini* (ear tick), or foreign matter such as grass awns. Symptoms can include head shaking and holding the ear drooped to one side. Treatment usually is aimed at the underlying cause, and at cleaning the ear of wax and debris that resulted from the inflammation. (Sedation may be needed to accomplish this).

Ear mites
Infestation by parasites that have invaded your horse's ear canal, causing inflammation, itching, and increased wax formation. Signs can include head shaking and holding the ear drooped to one side. Treatment generally is aimed at killing the mites with insecticides, and cleaning the ear of wax and debris that resulted from inflammation. (Sedation usually is needed to accomplish this).

Ear, inner, inflammation of; otitis interna
Inflammation within the ear canal beyond the ear drum. Causes can include: trauma to the poll with internal bleeding; certain poisons such as Ryegrass staggers; infection; or idiopathic vestibular syndrome[G]. Signs may include staggering; leaning against walls or

fences; holding the head tilted toward the affected side; and rapid sideways movements of the eyeballs (nystagmus). Treatment usually is aimed at identifying and addressing the underlying cause, if possible, and can include systemic antibiotics if bacterial infection is suspected. Anti-inflammatory medications are administered to reduce irritation of the nerves and balancing mechanisms within the inner ear.

Eastern equine encephalomyelitis, EEE
Viral infection of your horse's brain and spinal cord, which can infect horses, humans, and selected birds; it's transmitted by mosquitoes. Signs can include behavioral changes, loss of appetite, and fever. These can progress in 12 to 24 hours to dementia with head pressing, teeth grinding, circling, and often blindness. The disease is fatal in up to 90 percent of cases. Surviving horses (commonly referred to as "dummies") often have residual mental dullness. Treatment generally is supportive.

Edema
Swelling due to leakage of clear fluid (serum) from the bloodstream into tissues.

EDM, equine degenerative myeloencephalopathy
See Equine degenerative myeloencephalopathy, EDM.

EHV-1, equine Herpesvirus-1
See Equine Herpesvirus-1, EHV-1, respiratory rhino.

EHV-4, equine Herpesvirus-4, rhinoabortion
See Equine Herpesvirus-4, EHV-1, rhinoabortion.

EIA, equine infectious anemia
See Equine infectious anemia, EIA.

EIPH, exercise-induced pulmonary hemorrhage
See Exercise-induced pulmonary hemorrhage, EIPH.

Electrolytes, imbalance of
Any variation from normal balance of electrolytes in your horse's body. Electrolyte imbalances can cause heart arrhythmias, fluttering of the diaphragm, weakness, muscle cramping, collapse, and death.

Encephalitis
Inflammation of the brain, usually due to infection.

Endometritis
Inflammation of the uterine lining, usually due to infection.

Endoscopy
Use of an instrument called an endoscope, which is a rigid or flexible fiberoptic device that can be inserted into natural (nostril, urethra, uterus) or man-made (surgical incision) openings to diagnose and/or treat internal problems.

Endotoxemia, endotoxic shock
Blood poisoning that can occur with such serious conditions as: Potomac horse fever[G]; colitis-X[G]; grain overload[G]; severe colic[G]; Salmonella infection[G]; respiratory tract infection; or uterine infection. As bacteria die a natural death, they release a miniscule amount of toxin that has no effect on your horse unless the bacteria are present in larger-than-usual numbers. In such a case, the dose of toxin your horse absorbs can cause endotoxemia. This condition is the biggest killer of horses from non-traumatic causes, and is the cause of death in most fatal colics. See Circulatory shutdown[G].

Endotoxin
A substance produced by bacteria that, when absorbed into your horse's body, can cause endotoxic shock. See Endotoxemia, endotoxic shock[G].

Enterolith
A "stone" in your horse's intestinal tract, made of minerals present in his feed and/or intestinal secretions, and usually formed around a foreign body, such as a small piece of debris. Small, pebble-like enteroliths can be

swept out with his manure, or they can remain in the intestinal tract where they grow large enough to interfere with manure passage. Although enteroliths occur in horses all over the world, there is a higher incidence in California. Treatment often includes removal by surgery. If the enteroliths are small enough, removal by the regular administration of a bulk laxative can be used. Dietary changes might also be prescribed, if laboratory analysis of the stones reveals that they're composed of minerals that are present in excessive amounts in your horse's diet. (Example: some enteroliths contain phosphorus, from horses regularly fed wheat bran, which is high in that mineral).

Entrapped epiglottis
A condition in which the epiglottis (a valve-like flap at the back of your horse's throat that closes the windpipe during swallowing) becomes tucked behind a fold of tissue adjacent to it, partially closing off the horse's airway. In horses afflicted with this condition, the entrapment occurs during strenuous exercise, such as racing, and can profoundly affect the horse's performance as he struggles for air. Treatment usually is surgery to alter the size of the epiglottis and/or the fold that entraps it.

Eosinophilic granuloma (EG)
A common skin disease that causes firm, smooth nodules that don't itch or cause hair loss. The cause is unknown, but some researchers believe EG can be triggered by a hypersensitivity to insect bites. If there are only a few lesions, treatment usually is surgical removal or injection of each lesion with a cortisonelike medication. If there are too many lesions to treat this way, systemic treatment with antihistamines and/or a cortisonelike medication may be given. Warning: Systemic treatment with corticosteroids increases the risk of laminitis[G].

Epiphora
Watery eye; spilling of tears.

EPM (equine protozoal myeloencephalitis)
See Equine protozoal myeloencephalitis, EPM.

Equine Degenerative Myeloencephalopathy, EDM
A progressive degenerative disease of the nervous system, often mistaken for a lameness problem. The cause is unknown but in some cases a congenital vitamin E deficiency is suspected. (Certain pedigree lines appear to be deficient in vitamin E when fed the same diet that provides adequate vitamin E to other lines.) When walking, the affected horse may lift his hind feet too high, then slap them down with excessive force. He may step on himself when backing, and sit like a dog. The inner surfaces of the hind fetlocks often have sores from the horse accidentally kicking himself while walking. There is no known treatment. Breeding horses with a high incidence of EDM in their pedigree are believed to have a better chance of producing normal offspring if supplemented with vitamin E.

Equine Herpesvirus-1, EHV-1, rhino abortion, equine rhinopneumonitis
A viral infection that can cause a common cold-like upper respiratory disease and is the most commonly diagnosed infectious cause of late-term abortion in the horse (usually after 7 months of pregnancy). Affected mares abort within 2 weeks to 4 months after showing mild signs of upper respiratory disease. As many as 15 percent of all diagnosed abortions have been attributed to EHV-1. Vaccination with killed EHV-1 virus, containing both strains 1P and 1B, is recommended at the 5th, 7th, and 9th month of pregnancy to help prevent rhino abortion, although no vaccine is considered to be fully protective.

Equine Herpesvirus-4, EHV-4, respiratory rhino, neurologic rhino, equine rhinopneumonitis, rhino abortion
A viral infection that can cause a common cold-like upper respiratory disease and, rarely, paralysis due to disease of the brain and spinal cord. Sporadic abortion has been reported rarely in association with this virus. Signs of the respiratory disease can include: fever; depression; dry cough; and an initially thin nasal discharge that becomes thicker as the disease runs its course and resolves, usually

within 1 to 2 weeks. Generally, little or no treatment is required. Signs of the neurologic disease can include: sudden onset of weakness; staggering; weak tail muscles; and/or loss of urine control; any or all of which appear within a few weeks of recovering from respiratory disease. Horses that are unable to stand are not likely to survive. Those that are less severely affected usually improve with supportive treatment; the likelihood of residual deficits increases with increased severity of the initial symptoms.

Vaccine containing EHV-4 virus provides short-lived but cumulative protection against respiratory symptoms but may not keep the virus from invading. In other words, a horse may still become infected with the virus but not show signs of illness. This may be how the virus spreads. There is speculation that the neurologic form of the disease is associated with an aberrant immune response. Some investigators advise against giving the vaccine to a horse during an outbreak of the respiratory disease, speculating that it might increase the risk of neurologic disease.

Equine infectious anemia, EIA

A viral disease that causes a progressive decrease in the number of red blood cells. As it progresses, affected horses become increasingly weak. The disease is spread by biting insects. Diagnosis is made through a Coggins test[G]. There's no treatment and no vaccine. Owners of horses with confirmed positive Coggins tests may be required by state officials to prevent spread of the disease by lifelong quarantine or euthanasia.

Equine influenza

A contagious viral disease of the upper respiratory tract. Symptoms can include: cough; fever; muscle soreness; and nasal discharge. This discharge usually starts out thin and watery then becomes thicker as the disease runs its course. Treatment generally is supportive. Rest until at least 2 weeks after the cough has resolved is an important component of successful treatment, because premature return to work can prolong cough. Prevention by vaccination is the most effective means of controlling influenza in horses.

Equine protozoal myeloencephalitis, EPM

Infection of the brain and spinal cord by a protozoan called *Sarcocystis falcatula*. It's believed that the organism is carried in the fecal matter of opossums. Horses can become infected by picking up eggs when eating where opossum droppings are present. Signs can vary widely, from the obscure to the profound, and can include weakness, staggering, head tilt, dysphagia[G], and/or seizures. Diagnosis is based on symptoms and analysis of cerebrospinal fluid taken by spinal tap. Treatment can include anti-inflammatory medication and a specific antibiotic combination given for several months, until laboratory tests for the infectious agent are negative.

Equine viral arteritis, EVA

A contagious viral disease spread by casual contact (moisture droplets in the air via cough, sneeze, or tears), or by breeding with a previously infected mate. If mares are infected while pregnant they usually abort. Affected horses are sick and contagious for a week to 10 days with flu-like symptoms. With good nursing care, most victims recover completely (but can spread the disease to others after recovery, via sexual contact). When first coming down with EVA, your horse might have a fever, act depressed and off-feed, and/or have swelling in his legs due to vasculitis[G].

Ergot poisoning

Poisoning from eating fresh and/or dried grass and/or grain tainted with the fungus *Claviceps*, which produces the toxin ergot. Affected horses may be depressed, become blind and deaf, stagger, and/or have convulsions within only one or two days of eating the toxin. With treatment, including removal from the toxin source and supportive nursing care, recovery can occur within a week.

Exercise induced pulmonary hemorrhage, EIPH

Bleeding in the lungs during strenuous exercise such as racing. Signs can include a bloody nose. Or, there might be no blood visible from the outside, with affected horses showing a decrease in performance due to compromised breathing, as a result of blood in their respiratory tracts. Severity of bleeding can vary widely, from a trickle to a fatal hemorrhage. A specific cause has not been identified, so there is no specific treatment. Medications that increase urine output—thus causing a decrease in blood pressure—have been used prior to racing to decrease the incidence or severity of bleeding in affected horses.

Exploratory surgery
Surgery for the purpose of determining a diagnosis.

Eyelid, laceration of
A common injury associated with sharp protruding objects such as nailheads: Horses scratch their faces in doorways and on feeders, catching an eyelid on the protrusion, then pull away abruptly, slicing the eyelid. In some cases, a peninsula of eyelid tissue, including a portion of the row of eyelashes, dangles across the eye and curls into a spiral due to contraction of muscles, making the flap appear too small for a cosmetically appealing repair. However, the flap usually re-assumes its normal anatomy when properly stitched in place. First aid should focus on protecting the flap from further injury and/or drying out by applying an eye bandage soaked in saline solution. (For how-to information, see page 284.) Most eyelid lacerations can be repaired with the horse sedated (mainly so his head will be lowered), and with the injured eyelid numbed and paralyzed by local nerve blocks[G]. Care must be taken to reposition the flap properly so eyelashes are oriented correctly and so the cut ends of the stitches don't rub on the horse's cornea.

Fasting, and icterus
Fasting (not eating) normally causes mild icterus[G] (yellow discoloration of the gums, eyelid rims, and whites of the eyes).

Fibrous and ossifying myopathy (fibrotic myopathy)
A muscle disorder in which the affected hind leg is advanced normally, and then slapped down to the ground at the end of the stride. Often mistaken for stringhalt because the gait abnormality looks similar, this disorder usually is the result of repeated and/or severe stress damage to the muscles at the back and outer surface of a horse's thigh due to sudden sliding stops and direction changes in Western performance and rodeo horses, or aggressively kicking back and missing the target. Upon healing, torn muscle fibers are replaced with scar tissue, which shrinks as it matures. In severe cases, scar tissue can become encrusted with calcium deposits. Successful treatment might require surgery, followed by exercise and physical therapy to stretch muscles and prevent adhesions during healing. In fresh and/or less severe cases, physical therapy can be effective without surgery.

Fistulous withers
A deep infection at the withers, possibly due to a contusion-type injury from poor-fitting tack, followed by a break in the skin through which damaged tissues become contaminated. In true fistulous withers, bacteria causing the resultant infection are members of the *Brucella* family, which can infect humans. Signs can include: swelling; heat; pain; and discharge of pus and debris through draining tracts[G]. Treatment, which is done cautiously to avoid human infection, generally focuses on debridement[G] and disinfection of contaminated tissues. In some cases, administration of systemic antibiotics is performed.

Flexor tendons
Generally refers to the tendons that run along the back of your horse's cannon bones and fetlock joints. Their function is to support the weight transmitted down through his leg, and to propel him forward.

Floating the teeth
Filing of sharp points worn into your horse's cheek teeth that threaten to cut the soft tissues of his mouth. For some horses, an experienced operator using patient, gentle technique can float teeth with nothing more than minimal restraint (no twitches, no tranquilizers).

Fluoroscein dye and blacklight
A diagnostic technique used for determining whether an eye problem includes injury to the cornea. A fluorescent green dye is applied to

the eye by touching a dye-impregnated strip of paper to the eye's surface, then rinsing off with eye wash solution. The dye seeps into any breaks in the cornea, glowing bright green (especially if the eye is viewed with a battery-powered ultraviolet light). This technique also can be used to assess whether tear ducts are clogged: within 10 minutes of applying dye to an eye, a trickle of fluorescent green discharge usually appears in the nostril on the same side.

Fly hypersensitivity
An allergic skin condition triggered by biting flies and/or gnats. Affected horses react to fly bites more severely than do normal horses, often developing nodules at bite sites and rubbing itchy skin so much that they cause bald patches. During cold weather, when flies are dormant, skin irritation ceases.

Forage poisoning
See Botulism, forage poisoning.

Foreign body, interfering with healing
The presence of a foreign body, such as a wood splinter, gravel, or piece of metal, will prevent a wound from healing, even if it's scrupulously cleaned and antibiotics are given. Treatment usually is removal of the foreign body, and debridement[G] and disinfection of contaminated, damaged tissues.

Founder, laminitis
See Laminitis, founder.

Frostbite
Tissue damage due to exposure to extreme cold. Mild cases can cause swelling, redness, and pain. Severe cases actually kill tissues, which slough off or become infected with gangrene. The most common site of frostbite injury in horses is the ear tip, which sloughs off, leaving a rounded "bat-ear."

Fungal infection of hoof horn
Fungal invasion causing a crumbly, weak hoof wall that can't hold horseshoe nails. Occurs most often in moist, humid climates. Cold weather doesn't kill the infective fungus (several different species have been implicated). The fungus enters the hoof at its weak points—cracks, nail holes—and feeds on the insensitive portion of the hoof wall, hollowing and weakening it. Treatment usually is: removal of all affected hoof horn; exposing infected tissues so they'll dry; applying a strong disinfectant; and providing clean, dry housing.

Grain overload
Ingestion of a large amount of grain, as would happen if your horse broke into a grain storage area. The first consequence usually is colic, which might occur immediately, due to overfilling of his stomach, or might be delayed until the grain reaches his large intestine. The second consequence generally is endotoxemia[G] and diarrhea, which occur within 72 hours due to bacteria that flourish in the high-carbohydrate environment. The third consequence often is laminitis[G]. Treatment is most effective when given before signs appear: The stomach generally is pumped of its contents, then treated with mineral oil or other cathartics[G]. Preventative treatment often is given to help protect against endotoxemia[G] and laminitis[G].

Granulation tissue
Tissue formed during healing of a wound, to fill defects and form a nourishing base upon which new skin can grow. Made of tangled masses of tiny blood vessels and immature scar tissue, granulation tissue is pink, slightly lumpy, has virtually no nerve supply (and thus no feeling), and bleeds easily. Overgrowth by granulation tissue is known as proud flesh[G].

Granulomatous gastrointestinal disease
Broad regions of proud flesh[G]-like thickening in affected small intestine, dramatically interfering with digestion and absorption of nutrients. Although the horse's manure might appear normal (abnormal manure usually results when the problem is in the *large* intestine), affected individuals can be "poor doers"; show edema and other signs of abnormally low protein in the blood; and/or have skin lesions including hair loss, itching, and flaking/scaling. Treatment usually involves resolving any underlying causes that might be determined, and removing the affected tissues surgically or attempting to restore them with medications. Prognosis is guarded and depends on the severity and extent of the lesions.

Greasy heel, grease heel
A severe, deep skin infection on the backs of your horse's pasterns. The bubbly-looking skin growth creates deep crevices for the infective organism to escape topical treatments. This condition usually involves two or more feet, most often (but not exclusively) the hind feet. Whether the infection is a cause or a result of tissue inflammation and damage is controversial, but once started, the condition is self-perpetuating. Successful treatment generally requires aggressive debridement[G], with twice-daily cleansing and disinfection of remaining tissues. The horse must be housed in an area that's dry and clean. Systemic antibiotics may be warranted if the specific infective bacteria are identified via culture[G].

Grub worms, breathing hole
See Cattle grub, myiasis.

Guttural pouch infection
Infection in one or both of the guttural pouches, deep sacs located under your horse's skin behind his jawbone, under both ears. Many important structures run through the guttural pouches, such as facial nerves and branches of major arteries; infection there can adversely affect any or all of these structures. Treatment can include infusion of antiseptic and specific antibiotic or anti-fungal medications, via a catheter inserted into the pouches through the nasal cavity. Surgery and/or systemic medications to fight the infection and protect affected vital structures might also be required.

Guttural pouch mycosis
Guttural pouch infection[G] due to a fungus. A notorious effect of fungal infection here is erosion of a branch of the carotid artery that runs through the pouch, causing hemorrhage that spills from the pouch to the horse's throat, and out his nostril. In many cases the hemorrhage can be fatal. Most fungal infections tend to persist despite medical treatment; surgery usually is needed to prevent fatal hemorrhage.

Habronema
A stomach worm of horses, the larvae of which develop in the maggots of house- and stable flies and can be carried to open wounds by the adult flies. There, they cause a pulpy, persistent ulceration called summer sore[G]. Treatment generally is oral administration of a dewormer[G] such as ivermectin or moxidectin, which kills the larvae. The wound is then treated as any other superficial ulceration, with debridement[G] of damaged tissue, disinfection, and protection against further irritation.

Halitosis
Foul-smelling breath, often due to dental or periodontal disease.

Head shaking, neuritis and
A vigorous, involuntary nodding of your horse's head, which can be dangerous if it occurs during performance. It's been linked to infraorbital neuritis (inflammation of the infraorbital nerve that provides feeling to the muzzle), and causes tingling, itching, and/or electric-shock-like sensations. Inexplicably, in many cases sunlight appears to trigger the response: The signs appear and/or worsen when the horse is led into the sun, and abate when he's taken indoors. This syndrome often follows recovery from a viral respiratory disease and is therefore thought to be caused by residual virus.

Other possible causes include ear infection[G], ear mites[G], dental pain, other neurological diseases, and learned behavior problems. Treatment usually is aimed at identifying and correcting the underlying cause, if applicable, and at reducing signs with anti-inflammatory medications until the neuritis resolves on its own (usually within 12 weeks). In some cases a mask worn over the horse's muzzle lessens or prevents head-shaking. In stubborn cases, bilateral infraorbital neurectomy—surgically severing the nerves—has been used as a salvage procedure.

Heat exhaustion
Increased body temperature due to muscle exertion combined with high environmental temperature and humidity, which interferes with the evaporation of sweat, your horse's main mode of cooling. Signs can include:

depression; lack of interest in eating or drinking; colic pain; muscle cramping; elevated rectal temperature (104 to107.6º F); rapid, shallow breathing; little or no gut sounds; and/or "thumps" (a rhythmic jerking of the belly muscles, like rapid-fire hiccups). Treatment usually focuses on cooling the horse, and bringing body fluid and electrolyte levels back into balance with massive volumes of intravenous fluids. As soon as body temperature and hydration begin to improve, signs tend to disappear.

Heaves, chronic obstructive pulmonary disease, COPD

A hypersensitivity of the smaller branches of your horse's respiratory tree, resulting in asthma-like bronchospasm, difficulty breathing, coughing, and decreased performance. Chronic exposure to dust and molds is the most common trigger for heaves victims. Signs worsen in the winter, when they're brought from pasture into stalls with dusty bedding and dusty hay. A small percentage of cases are worse when in pasture: It's believed these horses have developed hypersensitivity to allergens in their outside environment. There's no cure, but signs can be managed by minimizing the horse's exposure to allergens that trigger respiratory signs, and by administering medications to minimize the airway's overreaction to allergens that can't be eliminated.

Hematoma/seroma

A bruise or contusion, resulting from blunt trauma (e.g., a kick or a collision). The hematoma is a pocket of blood caused when blood vessels have broken under intact skin; it feels squishy, like a balloon full of thin pancake batter, and it's only minimally tender to touch. A seroma is a hematoma which has matured: instead of a blood-filled center, the seroma is filled with amber-colored serum and a shrinking nugget of clotted red blood cells.

Hemolytic anemia

A decrease in red blood cell count due to increased destruction of red blood cells. Signs increase in severity as anemia worsens, and can include: icterus[G]; brownish discoloration of the urine; fatigue; and weakness. Treatment usually focuses on the underlying problem, such as bacterial infection or exposure to certain poisons. Transfusions are given if the blood count is dangerously low. Neonatal isoerythrolysis[G] (NI) is one type of hemolytic anemia.

Hepatic encephalopathy

Disease of the brain due to advanced liver disease and a resultant increase of toxins in the horse's body. Signs can include: depression or excitability; head tilt; head pressing; circling; aimless wandering; blindness; deafness; collapse; coma; convulsions; and death. Treatment usually is aimed at identifying and addressing the underlying disease.

Histopathology

A laboratory procedure in which a biopsied section of tissue is preserved, sliced to a one-cell-thick layer, and affixed to a slide, then studied under the microscope to determine whether any abnormal changes occurred in that tissue before the biopsy was taken.

Hoof, puncture wound of

A penetrating wound in the sole or fleshy frog portion of your horse's hoof, which can carry contamination to vital internal structures, such as bones, joints, cartilages, ligaments, and tendons. Treatment usually includes: removal of the penetrating object and establishment of good drainage; debridement of contaminated and/or damaged tissues; disinfection; protection of remaining tissues against further contamination; and review/renewal of tetanus immunization.

Horner's syndrome

A collection of facial symptoms due to damage to the sympathetic[G] portion of the involuntary nerve supply to your horse's face. Symptoms will occur on one or both sides of his face, depending on the location of the nerve damage. These can include: upper eyelid droop; pupil contraction; protrusion of the third eyelid[G]; and excessive sweating on the side of his neck and around his ears. Treatment usually is focused on addressing the underlying nerve damage problem, and applying protective eye ointment to the drooping-eyelid eye to keep it from drying.

Horsetail poisoning

Poisoning by the perennial horsetail plant, which is likely to be found in moist fields, meadows, and roadsides. It's toxic in both fresh form and dried (in hay). Signs can occur after about 30 days of daily ingestion, with horsetail comprising less than 10 percent of the overall forage eaten. These can include: weight loss; weakness; staggering; paralysis; and death. Horsetail inactivates vitamin B_1 and causes brain swelling due to severe B_1 deficiency. Poisoning victims can be cured if treated early with B_1 injections, before permanent brain damage occurs.

Hygroma, "blown knee"

Technically, hygroma refers to thickening and swelling of tissues outside the knee (carpal joint) due to repetitive trauma to the area, without involvement of the knee joint itself. However, some people use the term interchangeably with "blown knee," which is swelling of the knee due to joint injury.

Depending on the severity of the injury, swelling in a "blown knee" can result from increased production of joint fluid by irritated synovial cells[G], and/or blood from injured and bleeding joint parts. Whether swelling is accompanied by pain, stiffness, and/or lameness depends on the severity of the injury to internal joint parts. Even after the injury has healed, severe knee swelling can remain and produce a cosmetically unappealing "big knee" that fills back up after being surgically drained. For best success in restoring the knee's appearance after treating the underlying cause, pressure bandages are applied for a minimum of 1 week, then gradually loosened.

Hyperkalemic periodic paralysis, HYPP

An inherited disorder of certain lines of Quarter Horses, most noticeably those related to the late halter stallion *Impressive.* It causes a derangement in the chemical pathways that govern muscle activity. Affected horses seem normal between attacks. These can be mild or severe, last from a few minutes to several hours, and seem to be triggered by work stress, anxiety, cold, and/or eating a diet high in potassium. Signs can include: occasional skin rippling; localized muscle twitching; violent body-wide tremors; sweating; panting; passing loose manure; hindlimb weakness; and collapse. Severe episodes can be fatal due to heart failure. Diagnosis is confirmed by a genetic blood test. There's no cure, but frequency and severity of attacks can be reduced with careful management and diet adjustment to reduce potassium levels.

Hypersensitivity to sunlight, photosensitization

A skin disorder due to a photoactivating substance in the skin that produces skin-damaging chemicals when triggered by the absorption of ultraviolet light. The photoactivating substance can include certain toxic plants or drugs, or it can be a chemical by-product of liver disease. Signs can include: redness; blistering; ulceration; and crusting of exposed skin that's pale colored and not protected by hair, such as muzzle and eye tissues. (Another form of photosensitization is photoactivated vasculitis[G], for which the photoactivating substance hasn't been identified.) An effort to determine the type and source of the photoactivating substance must be made so treatment can address the underlying cause. Other preventative steps may include sunblocks, masks, or keeping the horse indoors until dusk. Skin lesions are treated as any other superficial ulceration, generally with debridement[G] of damaged tissue, disinfection, and protection against further irritation.

Hypoproteinemia

Low protein in your horse's blood, due to abnormally low protein intake in his diet, poor digestion and/or absorption of dietary protein in his intestines, or excessive loss of protein in his manure and/or urine. Signs can include: loss of muscle mass; weakness; fatigue; edema[G] (swelling) in the legs and/or lower abdominal wall; and depression. Treatment usually is focused on identifying and addressing the underlying cause.

Hypothyroidism

Diminished production of thyroid hormones.

In horses, hypothyroidism often is secondary to a tumor of the pituitary gland, called pituitary adenoma[G]. It also can be the result of oversupplementation with iodine, due to feeding kelp-based supplements. Signs of hypothyroidism can include general weakness; fatigue; dullness; obesity; and/or shaggy haircoat. Treatment usually focuses first on any underlying causes, then on relieving signs with oral supplementation with a thyroid hormone.

HYPP, hyperkalemic periodic paralysis
See Hyperkalemic periodic paralysis, HYPP.

Icterus
Yellow discoloration of skin and mucus membranes (gums, eyelid rims, inner surface of vulva) due to accumulation of pigments normally metabolized by your horse's liver. Causes can include: liver disease; hemolytic anemia[G]; snakebite[G]; ingestion of certain potential toxins, such as red maple leaves[G], onions[G], or phenothiazine[G] drugs; and fasting[G]. Treatment usually is focused on addressing the underlying problem.

Idiopathic vestibular syndrome
Inflammation of your horse's inner ear (beyond his ear drum), where balance is regulated, with no discernible underlying cause. (Viral infection is suspected by some researchers.) Signs usually are the same as with other inner ear infections[G].

Impaction colic, and cold weather
Lack of water intake can lead to impaction colic. Horses generally consume less water in cold weather, increasing their risk of impaction. In a recent cold-weather study, horses drank 40 percent more if offered water that was warmed to 120º F; they did most of their drinking within 3 hours of being given the warm water. Some horses refuse warm water, so always offer a choice. In this study those that preferred the warmer water drank significantly more water overall than those that refused it.

Impaction colic, exercise and
Lack of exercise, particularly in horses that have been stall-confined for one reason or another within the past 2 weeks, can be a contributing factor to impaction colic. Inactivity is believed to lead somehow to slower movement of manure through your horse's intestines.

Impaction colic, slow intestinal transit and
The slower the movement ("motility") of manure through the large intestine, the more water is absorbed from it. Manure transit time is influenced by the amount of fiber in your horse's diet: the less roughage in his diet, the slower his manure moves, and the drier it'll be. Example: lush, juicy spring grass is loaded with moisture, but lacking in the fiber department, so it can be the cause of excessively dry manure. Some medications will also affect gut motility.

Impression smear
A smudge on a slide made when the wet surface of a lesion or biopsy section is pressed against the slide for microscropic inspection.

Infection, inner ear
See Ear, inflammation of, otitis interna.

Infection, in wound
A wound becomes infected when bacteria and/or fungi contaminating it begin reproducing in an organized fashion, causing a disproportionate increase in one species over the others. Effective treatment usually focuses on improving the horse's own defenses (e.g., providing drainage, removing dead tissue), and directly attacking the infection with an antibiotic to which the bacteria are sensitive.

Infection, in blood; septicemia
Disease caused by the spread of infectious organisms and their toxins in your horse's bloodstream. See Septicemia[G].

Infection, muscle
Invasion of muscle tissue by an infectious organism, usually by contamination of a wound or by intramuscular injection with a contaminated needle, syringe, and/or medication. (See Clostridial myositis[G].) Treatment

can include: debridement and disinfection of damaged and/or contaminated tissues; establishment of drainage; administration of anti-inflammatory medications; and/or systemic administration of antibiotic or antifungal medications shown to be effective against the infective organism.

Influenza
A viral infection that causes a highly contagious upper-respiratory disease. Signs can include: fever; dry cough; watery nasal discharge; decreased appetite; muscle soreness; enlarged lymph nodes; and swollen legs. If your horse's resistance is decreased at the time of infection, secondary bacterial pneumonia can result. Rest and nursing care are important for recovery. The disease causes a temporary hyper-reactivity of the respiratory tract, which can prolong the cough if your horse is returned to work too early. The rule of thumb is to rest a minimum of 3 weeks, or 1 full week for every day the horse had a fever, whichever is longer. Influenza vaccine, containing current flu strains, is usually recommended up to four times per year, depending on the incidence of the disease and your horse's exposure to other horses.

Injection, local reaction to
Inflammation in tissues where an intramuscular injection was given, due to caustic or irritating characteristics of the injected substance (e.g., certain vaccines), and/or failure of injected substances to dissipate (as when injecting into a level, horizontal area, such as the croup). Symptoms can include swelling, heat, tenderness, and stiffness of the affected muscle tissue, and reluctance to use or stretch it. Treatment may include: application of warm, moist compresses; massage of affected muscle; administration of anti-inflammatory medication; and (if the injection was given in the neck muscles) adjustment of feed and water sources so your horse can eat and drink without stretching his neck.

Insect sting
Bee, wasp, and ant stings can be toxic, due to nerve-poisons and caustic chemicals in their venom, causing painful skin lesions and occasionally generalized reactions. If your horse is especially sensitive to a toxin, or if multiple stings occurred, hemolysis (see Hemolytic anemia[G]), difficulty breathing (due to swelling within the respiratory tract), collapse, and even death can occur. For local reactions, treatment may include application of a poultice[G] to soothe and draw out swelling and venom. (For how-to information, see page 102.) For generalized reactions, treatment usually is focused on halting and reversing respiratory distress and neutralizing the body's reaction to the toxin with such medications as antihistamines, anti-inflammatories, and corticosteroids.

Iodine toxicity
Most often due to feeding of supplements containing high-iodine ingredients such as seaweed (kelp), or in horses receiving sodium iodide as treatment for "thrush" or cough. Iodine toxicity can result in a hacking cough, runny eyes, patchy hair loss, and the formation of an enlarged thyroid gland at the throatlatch (goiter). Recovery is usually prompt and complete with removal of the excessive iodine from the diet (or stopping the sodium iodide treatments).

Ivermectin
A dewormer[G].

Jack spavin
"Spavin" infers a hock injury due to wear and tear, which came on gradually after repeated hard work. The different types of spavin are based on what's seen from the outside, but the internal problem is not always revealed by external signs. Jack spavin, also referred to as bone spavin, is a large, hard swelling on the inner (medial) surface, where the hock joint joins the cannon bone. It usually affects both hind limbs, causing severe lameness. Because pain is associated with flexing and advancing the affected limb, the horse might carry that limb lower than usual and drag the toe, causing tell-tale wear there.

Jaundice
See Icterus[G].

Jaw, pain in
Can be due to injury or illness, and can affect your horse's ability to eat.

Joint capsule
Thick tissue encasing joints in your horse. The joint capsule is richly endowed with blood vessels and sensory nerves, so any inflammation of this tissue (capsulitis[G]) can be associated with significant pain.

Joint tap, arthrocentesis
Sampling joint fluid by inserting a needle into the joint.

Joint, penetrating injury of
Any time a wound enters a joint, the resultant contamination can lead to infection and severe arthritis that persists even after the infection has been resolved. Most clinicians recommend aggressive treatment of penetrating joint wounds by joint irrigation with the horse either heavily sedated or anesthetized, then treatment with anti-inflammatory medication and systemic antibiotics.

Juvenile warts
Pink or brown, fleshy, hairless growths, usually on the muzzle or elsewhere on the face of young (less than 3-year-old) horses. Believed to be caused by a contagious virus, juvenile warts tend to run their course and disappear suddenly, after being present a few weeks to several months. It's believed that the positive response to various home remedies is merely coincidence—the warts were going to resolve anyway.

Kidney disease
Includes several syndromes, including the formation of kidney stones, kidney infection, and a number of disorders that can impair the kidney's ability to function as a filter of toxins and conserver of proteins, minerals, and water. Causes can include infection: kidney stones (formed due to excessive calcium intake); impaired blood circulation to the kidneys; and/or overmedication with drugs such as certain antibiotics and non-steroidal anti-inflammatory medications. Treatment usually includes identifying and addressing the underlying cause and administering of intravenous fluids and medications to affect urine output.

Kissing spines, overriding dorsal spinous processes
A touching or overriding of the vertical (dorsal) spinous processes of the vertebrae. The primary sign generally is pain on palpation over the backbone and the long muscles beside it. Depending on the location and extent of the problem, the horse's gait may be restricted. Treatment options may include: rest; injection of the area with medications to block inflammation and pain; acupuncture; ultrasound; or surgery.

Lactation tetany
Painful muscle contractions and cramps due to low blood calcium levels, resulting from loss of calcium via lactation and inadequate intake. Signs can include: depression; rapid, shallow breathing with flared nostrils; trembling of jaw muscles; signs of colic; sweating; extreme fever; and, in severe cases, thumps[G], collapse, convulsions, and death. Treatment usually is slow, cautious administration of an intravenous solution of calcium, magnesium, and phosphorus. If given too fast, cardiac arrest can occur.

Laminitis, founder
A disease process causing reduced blood flow to your horse's foot and subsequent breakdown of the attachments of the hoof. Several causes have been identified, including: grain overload[G]; acute endometritis[G]; endotoxemia[G]; walnut shavings toxicosis[G]; Potomac horse fever[G]; or obesity. Many cases of laminitis occur without any readily identifiable cause. Treatment of acute laminitis generally is aimed at arresting the breakdown process, resolving the underlying cause, and restoring circulation to the foot. The sooner in the disease process these efforts are made, the better the outcome. Acute laminitis is that which has occurred within several days; chronic laminitis has been going on for longer than several days. The term founder signifies chronic laminitis.

Laryngeal hemiplegia
Paralysis of one side of your horse's larynx,

due to malfunction of the nerve that supplies the muscle on that side. This causes a fold of tissue to drape over the opening to his windpipe, reducing that opening by as much as 100 percent. Symptoms result from the reduction in airflow, and can include decreased performance and a roaring or snoring sound while breathing. (Hence the term "roaring.") Treatment usually is one of several surgical techniques to open that drape and affix it in the open position.

Lead poisoning
Poisoning by ingestion of lead. Sources include used motor oil, lead-based paint, or soil or water contaminated by lead from automobile exhaust or from silver mine tailings. The classic sign of lead poisoning is a roaring or snoring sound when breathing, due to laryngeal hemiplegia[G]. Other signs can include: weakness; knuckling of the fetlocks; incoordination; joint enlargement; and stiffness. Treatment usually includes: removal of your horse from the lead source; intravenous administration of specific medication to bind the lead and render it inactive; and general support as needed.

Leeches, phycomycosis, gulf coast disease, swamp cancer
A skin condition characterized by a red, oozing sore that forms when a larval form of the parasite *Phycomyces* invades your horse's skin through a previous wound. The parasite normally resides in stagnant pools of water in perennially warm parts of the country, such as Florida, Louisiana, and coastal Texas, but there have been reports of the disease in more temperate zones as well. Presence of the parasite in tissue creates an exuberant, angry, fast-growing lesion that appears tumor-like and ulcerated. Treatment is usually aggressive surgical removal.

Leg mange
A skin condition of the lower legs near the fetlocks, due to infestation with a microscopic mite called *Chorioptes*. Signs can include: intense itching (exhibited by foot stomping, ankle chewing, or slipping the feet between fence boards and rasping back and forth); hair loss; swelling; redness; and crusting of the skin at the backs of the pasterns and fetlocks. Treatment may include: clipping away hair over affected skin; bathing with an antiseborrheic shampoo to dissolve and lift scabs; and killing the mites with at least two applications of insecticide at 2-week intervals.

Leptospirosis
Infection by bacteria of the *Leptospira* family, which can infect your horse's kidneys and reproductive tract, and also can invade tissues of the eye. Because *Leptospira* bacteria can be carried by several species, including pigs, cattle and wild deer, and can be spread in common water sources, horses at facilities with confirmed Leptospirosis cases should be kept isolated from other species and provided separate water. There is no "Lepto" vaccine approved for use in horses. Use of vaccines made for other species may or may not be safe and effective. The bacteria are sensitive to many antibiotics.

Leukoencephalomalacia, fumonisin poisoning, fusarium toxicosis, leucoencephalomalacia, moldy corn poisoning
Disease of the liver and/or nervous system of horses that have eaten corn contaminated with the mold *Fusarium moniliforme,* which produces toxins called fumonisins. Affected corn may or may not appear obviously moldy, and not all molds produce the toxin. If a horse's nervous system is affected, the toxin causes specific areas of the brain to soften and liquefy, resulting in permanent damage.

Neurological signs can include: blindness; staggering; head pressing; depression; and/or anxiety. If the liver is affected, signs can include icterus[G] in addition to the neurologic signs. Treatment is supportive only; there is no antidote. Damaged or broken corn kernels are more likely to harbor molds; corn can become moldy at any stage of development—in the field, during processing, or in storage.

Lice
Infestation by biting or blood-sucking lice. Signs can include itching and scratching, patchy hair loss, skin reddening, abrasions, and scaling. Treatment options may include at least two applications of insecticide (spray,

dip, or powder) at 2-week intervals, and/or administration of ivermectin or moxidectin dewormer[G] at the standard dose on the label, twice at 2-week intervals.

Ligament, injury
Sprain or rupture of a ligament, the tough band of tissue that holds the bones of a joint in alignment. Ligament injury usually occurs when a joint is stressed while the muscles and tendons around it are passive, weak, or fatigued. The result of the injury is an unstable joint that's prone to re-injury and likely to develop arthritis. Treatment depends on the injury's severity and ranges from rest and anti-inflammatory medications, to surgical repair.

Light eruption
See Hypersensitivity to sunlight[G], photosensitization[G].

Linear foreign object, eating of
Most commonly the accidental or mischievous ingestion of baler's twine. When any linear foreign object is eaten, the intestine may have trouble moving it along, causing obstruction and colic that's likely to require surgery.

Linear alopecia
A rare condition, most often found in Quarter Horses, in which lesions first appear between the ages of 1 and 5 years. Lesions consist of linear bands of skin thickening, resembling long, hairless calluses, arranged over the neck and lateral aspect of the horse's body. Some scaling may be present. It's believed to be a developmental problem, and there's no known treatment.

Liver disease
The liver is the body's toxic waste dump. Its main job is to detoxify and package toxins for elimination. When liver disease progresses to the point that the organ's function is impaired, a variety of problems can appear, which can include weight loss; dermatitis of unpigmented skin (see Hypersensitivity to sunlight[G]); icterus[G]; and hepatic encephalopathy[G].

Liver biopsy
Sample of liver tissue, usually taken through a small flank incision in a horse that's lightly sedated but standing. A special biopsy tool is inserted through the incision, and takes a small punch sample in a matter of seconds. There's a risk of internal bleeding, but most liver biopsies cause no problems.

Locoweed poisoning
Poisoning by locoweed, a perennial member of the pea family, causing brain damage with signs that can include: depression; staggering; muscle tremors; dysphagia[G]; hyperexcitability; blindness; weakness; inability to eat or drink; and death. Once a horse gets accustomed to the taste of locoweed, he may seek it out. Affected horses never recover; there's no treatment.

Long toe-low heel, LTLH
A common configuration of trimmed and/or shod horses, based on the belief that it delays breakover and causes the horse to lift his leg with more impulsion, therefore improving movement. Many chronic lamenesses and leg blemishes may result from, or be exacerbated by, this tendency, including: navicular disease[G]; windpuffs[G]; stocking up of the lower legs; flexor tendinitis[G]; osselets[G]; and degenerative joint disease[G].

Lung abscess
One or more pockets of infection within your horse's lungs, caused by a bacterial invasion via the respiratory tree, or spread of infection elsewhere in the body through his blood. Affected horses might show no abnormal signs until one or more abscesses breaks open, liberating pus, debris, and millions of bacteria into the lungs to cause an acute flare-up of pneumonia[G] and/or pleuritis.

Lungworms
Parasites of the *Dictyocaulus* family that infect a horse's lungs, causing signs of decreased performance and cough during exercise. Treatment is administration of a deworming agent labeled effective against *Dictyocaulus.*

Luxation
Dislocation of a joint or other body part, away from its normal position.

Lyme disease
Infection with the spiral-shaped bacteria *Borrelia burgdorferi*, spread by the bite of an infected tick. Signs vary widely and can include: recurrent lameness that shifts from one leg to another and for which no other cause can be found; arthritis; stiffness; and reluctance to move. Treatment usually is administration of antibiotics from the penicillin or tetracycline family.

Lymphangitis
Inflammation of the lymphatic vessels due to deep skin infection, most often occurring on your horse's lower limbs. Signs may include: fever; swelling; pain; blisters; pustules; and ulcerations of the skin in the affected area. Treatment can include: clipping hair; debriding[G]; cleansing and disinfecting of raw tissues; bandaging; hand walking; and systemic antibiotics.

Lymphosarcoma
Cancer of the lymph nodes.

Malignant
Referring to a cancerous growth: Locally invasive and destructive, and/or tending to spread to other areas of the body.

Malignant edema
See Clostridial myositis[G].

Malignant hyperthermia
Sudden onset of high fever and rigid muscles due to drug reaction or to abnormally low blood calcium levels. (See Lactation tetany[G].)

Malignant lymphoma
One of the most common internal forms of cancer in the horse (although its incidence of less than 0.1 percent means it's very rare). A variety of tissues can be affected, but the most common site is the lymph nodes along the intestinal tract, resulting in impaired digestion. The lymph nodes adjacent to the heart and lungs also can be affected. Signs may include: weight loss; fever; swollen lymph nodes; impaired vision; signs of respiratory disease; colic; diarrhea; loss of appetite; edema; and depression. There is no cure, although cancer chemotherapy has been reported to bring temporary remission in about half the cases treated. Mares have been reported to go into spontaneous, temporary remission in pregnancy.

Manure, hard/dry, and cold water intake
Abnormally hard, dry, small manure balls can be a result of dehydration due to inadequate water intake, a commonly reported problem when seasonal weather changes cause an abrupt drop in temperature. Horses that are reluctant to drink cold water during this time often will drink significantly more when warm water is provided, decreasing the risk of impaction colic.

Manure, hard/dry, and gut hypomotility
The longer your horse's manure remains in his colon, the more water is absorbed from it, possibly resulting in abnormally hard, dry, small manure balls. Transit time through his intestines is affected by water and fiber content of his diet: an inadequacy of either can cause slow movement and hard, dry, small manure balls, increasing the risk of impaction colic.

Manure, hard/dry, and partial intestinal obstruction
Anything that impedes the movement of manure through your horse's intestines will result in its drying. (See Manure, hard/dry, and gut hypomotility[G].) Swellings, growths, or foreign bodies that impinge on his intestines and narrow the lumen can delay manure passage.

Manure, hard/dry, and risk factors leading to large colon obstruction
Any influence that causes manure balls to be hard, dry, and small can increase the risk that manure will become impacted in the large colon. The risk of impaction is further heightened when your horse has been stressed, stabled, subjected to changes in management, or trailered. Treatment for mild to moderate impactions may include: medication with stool softeners; water and/or laxatives via stomach tube and/or via high enema; and administration of intravenous fluids to help

rehydrate intestinal contents and stimulate gut motility. Severe or long-standing impactions might require surgery.

Manure, hard/dry, exercise, and water intake

Inadequate water intake, coupled with increased water loss via heavy breathing and/or sweating, increases the risk of dehydration and hard, dry, small manure balls. See Manure, hard/dry, and cold water intake[G], and Manure, hard/dry, and risk factors leading to large colon obstruction[G].

Manure, loose

Manure with increased water content, but passed at a normal or only briefly increased frequency.

Manure, mucus in

See Mucus, in manure.

Melanoma

Usually firm, smooth, hairless black nodules relatively common in gray horses, most often found under a horse's tail, around his ear, and on his face near the main joint of his jaw. Some can grow aggressively, causing erosions and spreading to adjacent lymph nodes and lungs, but most melanomas grow slowly and are benign (don't tend to spread to other organs).

Treatment is seldom recommended, as external melanomas often return after surgical removal. Some studies have shown decreased size and number of melanomas when high doses of the anti-ulcer medication cimetidine (Tagamet®) were given, but the melanomas returned when medication was withdrawn.

Mercury poisoning

Leg blisters containing mercury are still used by a few horsepeople, resulting in severe skin inflammation. If a horse licks the blistered skin and ingests mercury, or if his skin is treated with DMSO[G] either prior to or after application of the blister, sufficient mercury can gain entry into his body to cause mercury poisoning. Signs can include colic and blood- or brown-tinged urine. Only with prompt treatment aimed at removing the toxin from his body will the horse have a chance of recovery; most cases are fatal.

Midges, no-see-ums

Tiny flies of the *Culicoides* family, considered responsible for the warm-weather skin allergy called Sweet itch[G].

Milkweed poisoning

Poisoning by milkweed, a perennial weed likely to occur when pastures are thin and grazing options are limited. It's toxic in both fresh form and dried (in hay). Signs occur within 1 to 2 days of eating the plant, and may include: depression; weakness; dizziness; collapse; convulsions with muscle rigidity; coma; heart attack; and death. There's no specific treatment; most cases are fatal.

Moldy corn poisoning, fumonisin poisoning, fusarium toxicosis, leukoencephalomalacia, leucoencephalomalacia

See Leukoencephalomalacia, fumonisin poisoning, leucoencephalomalacia, moldy corn poisoning.

Monensin® toxicosis, rumensin toxicosis

See Rumensin toxicosis[G], Monensin® toxicosis[G].

Moon blindness, periodic ophthalmia, recurrent ophthalmia, uveitis

A disease of the uvea (the colored iris) inside the eyeball. The uvea becomes inflamed (uveitis), which causes its muscles (ciliary muscles) to spasm, thereby constricting the pupil. Eye pain from uveitis is severe and can cause squinting, tearing, excessive blinking, and dangerous eye-rubbing (increasing the risk of eye trauma). Initially, uveitis can result from eye trauma and injury, infection within the eye, body-wide disease, and/or aberrant immune reaction within the eye. In moon blindness, uveitis recurs without warning and with no apparent reason. If not resolved, severe uveitis can result in permanent blindness. Treatment can include topical and systemic medication to relieve pain and inflammation, relax the spasming ciliary muscles, and combat possible infection. Infection by bacteria from the *Leptospira* family is sometimes implicated in uveitis.

Mouth speculum
A device inserted into your horse's mouth to hold it open for examination and/or dental treatment.

Mucus, in manure
A sign of prolonged transit time of manure through the intestines, which occurs when intestinal motility is abnormally slow. Your horse's intestinal lining secretes mucus to protect itself from irritation. The appearance is similar to white, translucent worms on the seams between individual manure balls.

Multiple myeloma, plasma cell myeloma
See Plasma cell myeloma, multiple myeloma.

Myiasis, cattle grub
See Cattle grub, Myiasis[G].

Narcolepsy
A progressive, incurable brain disorder, causing a horse to fall asleep abruptly at inappropriate times, such as while exercising or eating. Signs usually are obvious: the horse literally falls asleep while standing; some actually fall to the ground. Though the disease can't be cured, it can be managed by administration of a drug that affects the neurotransmitters in his brain.

Nasal cavity, growth in
Tumors, abscesses[G], polyps, and proud flesh[G]-like growths can appear in a horse's nasal cavity, causing difficult and/or noisy breathing, and nasal discharge of varied composition. Treatment is aimed at identifying and correcting the underlying condition.

Nasal polyp
An abnormal growth inside the nostril, made of fibrous connective tissue. Nasal polyps are connected to the lining of the nostril by a slender stalk and can vary in size from a small pea to a mass large enough to fill the nostril. Signs include nasal discharge and respiratory noise. Treatment may include surgical removal.

Nasal septal disease
Any of a number of conditions affecting the nasal septum, including thickening or inflammation due to trauma, infection, or cancerous growth. The result is abnormal air movement through the nostrils, nasal discharge, and/or respiratory noise. Treatment generally focuses on resolving the underlying cause.

Navicular disease, navicular syndrome
A chronic degenerative condition that results from derangement of the blood flow to the navicular bone and/or excessive pressure and friction on the navicular bone, the pillow-like sac that cushions it (the navicular bursa), and/or the deep digital flexor tendon that bends around it in the back of your horse's foot.

Signs can include gradual onset of lameness in one or both fore limbs, causing a stilted or choppy gait. The condition can be initiated or made worse by a long toe/low heel configuration. (See Long toe/low heel, LTLH[G].) There's no cure, but treatment can reduce the signs and restore the horse's usefulness in many cases, and may include: corrective farriery; weight reduction if the horse is obese; controlled exercise; the judicious use of pain-killing and anti-inflammatory medications; and medications to dilate blood vessels in the foot (during the acute phase).

Needle aspiration
A sampling of fluid and suspended bits of soft tissue from a lesion, abscess, or tumor by inserting a needle and pulling back on the syringe's plunger to obtain contents for laboratory examination.

Nerve, damage to, leg buckling because of
Whether due to direct injury or to illness of the nerve itself, nerve damage can cause the muscles of your horse's leg to malfunction, allowing the leg to buckle or bend the wrong way. Treatment usually is aimed at identifying and correcting the underlying cause, and at protecting the limb from further damage by artificially stabilizing affected joints with splints, support bandages, or casts.

Nerve block
Injection of local anesthetic in the vicinity of a specific nerve to deaden the region for which that nerve provides sensation and motor function. Nerve blocks are used to: diagnose lameness

(numb the area suspected to be the source of the lameness, and the lameness goes away—diagnosis confirmed!); to allow pain-free surgery on an awake patient; to paralyze specific body parts (e.g., to paralyze a wounded eyelid so it'll hold still for repair); and to relax internal muscles (e.g., a spinal nerve block can stop uterine contractions so a foal's malposition can be corrected). Depending on the local anesthetic used, effects can last from 20 minutes to 8 hours.

Nervous, loose stool
Abnormally wet stool (semi-solid to watery) passed at a variable frequency, for an hour or less. Example: a nervous, herd-bound horse might pass several sloppy piles during the first half hour of a trail ride, due to anxiety.

Neuritis
Inflammation of a nerve.

Neurological rhino, equine Herpesvirus-4, EHV-4
A viral infection that can cause a common cold-like upper respiratory disease and, rarely, paralysis due to disease of the brain and spinal cord. Signs of the neurological disease can include sudden onset of weakness, staggering, weak tail muscles, and/or loss of urine control, any or all of which appear within a few weeks of recovering from respiratory rhino disease. Horses that are unable to stand are not likely to survive. Those that are less severely affected usually improve with supportive treatment. The likelihood of residual deficits increases with increased severity of the initial signs. There is speculation that the neurological form of the disease is associated with an aberrant immune response. Some investigators advise against giving the respiratory (EHV-4) vaccine to horses during an outbreak of that disease, speculating that it might increase the risk of developing the neurological condition.

Neuroaxonal dystrophy, NAD
A specific type of Equine Degenerative Myeloencephalopathy (EDM[G]), appearing within the first 2 years of life. NAD occurs more often (but not exclusively) in the Morgan Horse breed. Affected horses generally have a jerky hindlimb gait, lifting the limbs too high then slapping them down to the ground. The horse may appear dizzy because of difficulty moving his hind limbs properly through complex movements, such as tight turns, walking on slopes, and backing. There's no known treatment.

Nictitating membrane
The "third eyelid," a pink membrane normally folded out of sight in the inner corner of your horse's eye, covering the eyeball when the upper eyelid closes. If the nictitating membrane is visible while the eye is open, something's wrong—either the eye is irritated, or nerve supply to the membrane isn't working right.

Night blindness
An inherited vision problem that, although present at birth, might not be noticed until later in life. (In general, the more severe it is, the earlier it's recognized.) Signs can include reluctance to move when it's dark; head cocking as though trying to hear what can't be seen; star gazing; and a cross-eyed appearance when viewed from the front. Most cases have visual deficits during the daytime too, but they're virtually blind at night. This disorder occurs most often in horses with Appaloosa blood in their pedigrees, but other breeds have been affected as well. There's no known treatment.

Nuclear scintigraphy, nuclear imaging, bone scan
A diagnostic technique for determining whether a particular area of your horse's body (most often musculo-skeletal) is functioning normally. A radioactive substance is injected, given orally, or infused into his body, then tracked by a sort of medical Geiger counter called a gamma camera, which shows whether his body is dealing normally with the substance. This high-tech procedure is a valuable adjunct to traditional imaging techniques, such as x-ray and ultrasound, when diagnosis is difficult.

Onchocerca
A worm that's carried to your horse in the bite of tiny *Culicoides* flies (also known as midges[G] or no-see-ums). Adult worms live along the crest of a horse's neck in the broad,

band-like ligament called the ligamentum nuchae. The worms' tiny offspring migrate through the connective tissue to the skin of his lower chest, lower abdomen, head, neck, and withers, and also can invade his eyeballs. Signs can include itching, patchy hair loss, and crusting and scaling in the middle of the forehead. If the eye is affected, signs can include uveitis[G] and conjunctivitis[G]. Treatment involves killing the worms and their offspring with ivermectin or moxidectin dewormer[G]. It can cause an initial worsening of symptoms due to the presence of the dead parasites in your horse's tissues, but improvement is seen within a week.

Onions
Both wild and cultivated onions are toxic to horses, causing hemolytic anemia[G]. Signs can include icterus[G], brownish-colored urine, and weakness and loss of stamina as the anemia progresses. Treatment usually is supportive. Prevention of further ingestion of onions is key. If the anemia is severe, a transfusion may be needed.

Optic nerve, injury to
Injury to the optic nerve—the large nerve that connects your horse's eye to his brain—can cause temporary or permanent blindness, depending on the severity of the injury. The most common cause of optic nerve injury is flipping over backward and landing on the poll: at the moment of impact, inertia jerks the brain backward, which tugs on the optic nerve.

Oral drench
A means of administering a liquid medication, by squirting or pouring it into the back of your horse's mouth with a large syringe or long-neck bottle. Although drenching was a common way of medicating horses in early times and is still used in the cattle industry, it has fallen into disfavor in the treatment of horses because of the risk the liquid will go down the windpipe (trachea) rather than the esophagus, and cause aspiration pneumonia[G].

Osselets
Thickening of the joint capsule at the front of your horse's fetlock joint due to repeated trauma. Signs may include lameness; puffiness of the fetlock joint; and the appearance of a soft tissue mass that can be felt at the front of the joint. Treatment may include surgical removal of the mass if associated with lameness.

Ossifying fibroma, equine juvenile mandibular ossifying fibroma
A benign[G] tumor of the front portion of the lower jaw bone (mandible), most often seen in young horses (3 years and under). Surgical removal may be the treatment of choice.

Paralytic rhino
See Equine Herpesvirus-1[G].

Paraphimosis
Entrapment of, and rubber-band-like constriction on, an extended penis by the sheath's opening. The most common cause is prolonged extension of the penis, which causes it to swell (due to the effects of gravity) until the sheath's opening becomes too tight. Treatment generally focuses first on treating any external wounds on the penis, then on replacing it into the sheath so the swelling will subside. Treatment is then aimed at identifying, and resolving if possible, the underlying cause for prolonged penile extrusion. Penile paralysis[G], which often is permanent, is a cause of this problem. Depression, weakness, and long-acting sedatives can cause temporary relaxation of the penis.

Parasitic diarrhea
Intestinal parasites, most notably members of the *Strongyle* family, cause tiny sores in your horse's intestinal tract as they move about. With heavy and/or long-standing parasite infestation, the amount of tissue damage and inflammation can affect intestinal function and cause chronic diarrhea. Treatment may include: killing the parasites with an appropriate dewormer[G]; soothing the inflamed intestines with medications given systemically; and feeding a bland but nutritious diet. Management changes focus on reducing exposure to parasite eggs and larvae. Options can include: diligent bi-weekly removal of manure from the environment; purge deworming[G] on the basis of

regular fecal egg counts, using products to which the resident parasite population is not resistant; or switching to a program that includes daily deworming with pyrantel tartrate (Strongid-C®).

Parasitism, and dull shaggy coat
The damage done to your horse's intestinal lining by parasites can affect digestion and absorption of nutrients, leading to nutritional deficiencies even if his diet is adequate. A dull haircoat is one external sign of undernourishment.

Parotid sialocele
The accumulation of brown, stringy liquid and/or cheesy material along the side of your horse's face or under his jaw, where the salivary duct has been ruptured due to injury. Treatment may include cleaning out of accumulated material and debriding[G] contaminated tissues, then resolving the underlying problem by repairing the damaged duct; removing or chemically obliterating the salivary gland; or redirecting what's left of the duct to deliver saliva into his mouth at a different location.

Patella, upward fixation of, upward patellar fixation
Locking of the hind limb in an extended, stretched-out position due to the medial patellar ligament (which holds the kneecap in place) getting hung up on a notch at the end of the thigh bone (femur). In affected horses, the locking occurs suddenly and without warning. It's not usually associated with lameness, but can be dangerous if it occurs while the horse is performing. Factors believed to contribute to this problem can include: loss of body fat; lack of muscle strength; neurologic disease; conformation; or injury.

Horses that are thin may have a smaller fat pad over the femur's notch, thereby allowing the ligament to fall deeper into the notch and get caught. Horses with inadequate strength or stamina might have weak quadriceps muscles, which normally pull the kneecap up out of the notch before allowing it to slide down to permit knee bending. If neurological disease and traumatic injury have been ruled out, initial treatment may include anti-inflammatory medication on the assumption that the ligament and/or tissues adjacent to it are inflamed and swollen, and so are more likely to get hung up on nearby protrusions. Muscle-building exercise such as hill work is often recommended to improve strength of the quadriceps muscles, and dietary adjustment is used if necessary to improve body condition. If these measures fail, stifle injections can be considered, or the ligament may be severed surgically.

Pemphigus foliaceus
A skin disorder caused by the body's immune system mistakenly attacking some of its own cells involved in skin production. Signs tend to wax and wane, and include the formation of blisters and pustules that break open and form crusted sores. Lesions generally start on a horse's face and limbs, eventually spreading to the rest of his body. There's no cure, but treatment can control the lesions and cause the disorder to go into remission. Some reports indicate that the younger a horse is, the greater the chance that the condition will go into long-term remission. Treatment may involve suppression of the immune system by administration of systemic corticosteroids (which can cause increased risk of infection and laminitis[G]).

Penile paralysis
Paralysis of the muscle which normally retracts the penis into its sheath. It can be caused by injury or illness of the nerve that governs the muscle, or by drug reaction. Drugs most commonly implicated are members of the phenothiazine[G] family, which include certain dewormer[G] medications and certain tranquilizers. The presence of the hormone testosterone increases the risk that these drugs will cause penile paralysis, so their use is avoided in stallions. There's no cure, and paralysis often is permanent. This usually necessitates surgical amputation of the penis and creation of a new opening, just beneath the anus, through which the horse can urinate.

Percussion
A diagnostic technique to judge the contents of

body cavities by tapping on them while listening with the naked ear or a stethoscope. A condition commonly diagnosed by percussion is infection of the facial sinuses, which fill with pus and no longer sound hollow when percussed.

Periodontal disease
Disease of the gums and connective tissue around your horse's teeth. Incidence of this condition increases as your horse ages and his teeth become narrower, leaving spaces between them where food and debris can become lodged. The most common sign of periodontal disease is foul-smelling breath (halitosis[G]), most often smelling like moth balls.

Pharyngeal cyst
A fluid-filled cyst around the tissues at the back of your horse's throat. If the cyst impinges upon his airway, signs can include abnormal respiratory noise and decreased performance. Treatment usually is surgical removal by one of many available techniques.

Pharyngeal lymphoid hyperplasia, PLH, follicular pharyngitis
Abnormal enlargement of pimple-like lymph structures normally present at the back of the throat, sometimes occurring in concert with a lower respiratory infection. If the structures become large enough to obstruct the normal movement of air through your horse's throat, respiratory noise and/or decreased performance will result. The condition is diagnosed by viewing the enlarged structures via endoscopy[G]. Treatment may include rest; administration of medications to reduce inflammation; vaccination with flu and/or rhino vaccines, and/or immunostimulants; antibiotics; and/or obliteration of the enlarged lymphoid follicles by freeze-treating or cauterization.

Phenothiazine poisoning
Legitimate drugs from the phenothiazine family, including the tranquilizers promazine and acepromazine, are poisonous to a small percentage of horses. Signs, seen within hours, can include: depression; pale gums due to rapidly developing anemia; loss of appetite; colic; fever; penile paralysis; icterus[G]; brownish discoloration of the urine; labored breathing; collapse; and death. Treatment usually is symptomatic and, if anemia is severe, may include transfusion.

Photoactivated vasculitis, white leg disease
Extensive, painful edema (swelling) on white limbs only, often accompanied by skin reddening, erosions, and the formation of scabs and crust. Affected horses are most often, but not exclusively, sorrel or chestnut in color. The underlying cause is a hypersensitivity to sunlight, called photosensitivity[G], which can be the result of liver disease or ingestion of such toxic weeds as goatweed (St. Johnswort, klamath weed) or alsike clover. Treatment usually is aimed at resolving the underlying cause, and at reducing signs by providing sun protection and administering anti-inflammatory medications.

Photosensitivity
See Hypersensitivity to sunlight[G].

Pigeon fever
Infection with bacteria of the *Corynebacterium* family, causing one or more lumps beneath the skin in your horse's brisket and lower abdominal area. Seen primarily in California and to a lesser degree in other Western states, in the summer months when biting flies (which deposit the bacteria in the skin) are present. Lumps are filled with creamy to cheesy pus. If there are several abscesses, or if the infection spreads to internal organs, signs often include those of general illness (off feed, fever, depression) in addition to skin lumps. Treatment may include the application of hot-packs and/or poultices to draw out infection, and/or lancing the abscesses. Antibiotics may be prescribed after abscesses have been lanced.

Pinworms
Intestinal parasites of the *Oxyuris* family that reside in your horse's lower intestine and deposit their eggs in the tissues of his anus, causing intense anal itching. The most common external sign of pinworm infestation is a rubbed-out tail, due to attempts by your horse

to scratch his anus. Treatment is administration of an appropriate dewormer[G] medication.

Pituitary adenoma

The pituitary gland, located at the base of your horse's brain, has the vital role of secreting hormones that regulate a multitude of body functions. A portion of the pituitary gland may become cancerous and begin releasing overdoses of hormones. The result: a condition called Cushing's Disease, generally characterized by one or more of the following: laminitis[G]; muscle wasting; excessive sweating; excessive water drinking and urinating; and a long, shaggy haircoat that won't shed out. A series of blood tests yield the diagnosis; treatment is mainly symptomatic.

Plasma cell myeloma, multiple myeloma

A form of leukemia resulting from cancer within the bone marrow. Signs can include: weight loss; loss of appetite; swollen lymph nodes; staggering; weakness; and edema. There is no cure, although some horses have gone into temporary remission with cancer chemotherapy.

Pleuritis

Inflammation and/or infection of the pleural cavity (the space between your horse's lungs and his chest wall). Pleuritis is painful, making it difficult to expand the chest to breathe. Affected horses are deeply resentful of any pressure on their chest—even the touch of a stethoscope might bring evasive action and/or a grunt of pain. Ultrasound examination of the pleural cavity can reveal the presence of fluid (pus) and can be used to gauge whether the horse is responding to treatment. Treatment can include administration of antibiotics that the causative bacteria are sensitive to; and if there's pus accumulated within the pleural cavity, installation of a drain. (In severe cases, several gallons of pus can be retrieved.)

Pleuropneumonia

Combined infection involving the lungs (pneumonia[G]) and the pleural cavity (pleuritis[G]), often associated with the stress of a recent long-distance shipment. Signs can include fever; depression; lack of appetite; labored breathing; and a soft cough (which is painful because of chest movement). Treatment generally includes administration of antibiotics that the causative bacteria are sensitive to. If the pleural cavity contains accumulated pus, a drain probably will be installed to remove it.

Pneumonia

Infection in the lungs, sometimes occurring after a viral upper respiratory infection, due to bacteria that take advantage of your horse's weakened resistance. Other contributing factors can include: stress; aspiration; the stress of pneumonia[G]; long-distance shipment; and exposure to powerful bacteria that can cause pneumonia even in horses that are otherwise healthy and unstressed. Signs may include fever; lack of appetite, cough; discharge of pus from nostrils; depression; and rapid and/or labored breathing. Treatment usually includes support and administration of appropriate antibiotics that the causative bacteria are sensitive to.

Pneumothorax

The presence of air or gas in the pleural cavity (the space between your horse's lungs and his chest wall), usually the result of a penetrating wound. Because his lungs can't expand properly, it's difficult for the horse to get enough oxygen. Signs usually include anxiety and preoccupation with breathing. Treatment generally is surgical repair.

Poison, causing blood "thinning"

The ability of the blood to clot can be impaired by certain poisons, including moldy sweetclover hay or pasture, and rodent poisons that contain coumarin or dicumarol. Signs can include external evidence of a clotting problem, such as a wound that bleeds more, and for a longer time, than might be expected. Or, if the bleeding is internal, symptoms can include: pale gums; depression; weakness; rapid shallow breathing; and death. Treatment can include vitamin K_1 injections and blood transfusion.

Poisoning, causing bright pink gums

Poisons containing cyanidelike substances

prevent normal oxygenation of tissues, essentially suffocating their victims. Plants containing cyanide include fresh or baled sorghum/sudan grass, and parts of fruit trees. Signs may include: anxiety; general muscle tremors; labored breathing; drooling; convulsions; and death. Treatment generally is supportive; intravenous administration of a chemical (sodium nitrite and/or sodium thiosulfate) that can remove cyanide from the blood may be used. However, in most cases the patient dies before there's time to administer treatment.

Polyneuritis
A disease of the nervous system. The affected horse moves stiffly, as if all joints and all four feet hurt. Although he has no fever and his appetite is unaffected, he tends to lose weight and muscle mass, especially over his shoulder blades and upper thighs. He trembles as he becomes progressively weaker, lifting his head only when alerted, then lowering it to his knees when at rest. There's no known treatment.

Potomac horse fever, PHF,
Ehrlichia risticii
Protozoal infection of the intestinal tract usually causing diarrhea; fever; depression; and colic. Treatment generally is supportive and administration of appropriate antibiotics, along with preventive measures to avoid the development of laminitis[G], a common sequel to PHF.

Poultice
A soft, mushy dressing, made of a mixture of dry, absorbent substances with liquid or oil, applied to wounds or swellings to soften, relax, or stimulate the tissues, or reduce swelling.

Progressive ethmoid hematoma, PEH
A mass of tangled capillaries growing from the tissues inside your horse's nasal cavity. The cause is unknown, but previous infection and/or injury are often reported. Signs can include intermittent blood-tinged discharge from one nostril, unrelated to exercise. If the mass is large enough, abnormal respiratory noise and distortion of the face can occur. Treatment generally is removal or destruction of the mass, by surgery; cauterization[G]; cryosurgery[G]; laser surgery; injection, or a combination.

Protein deficiency
See Hypoproteinemia[G].

Proud flesh,
exuberant granulation tissue
An overgrowth of pink, bubbly-looking tissue during healing of certain flesh wounds, particularly those involving wounds to the lower legs where there's no muscle beneath the skin. It can protrude from the injury site like a tumor, preventing new skin from covering the wound. Treatment depends on location and severity, and usually will include one or more of the following: topical applications of various medications designed to melt away the excessive tissue; pressure bandages; and/or surgical removal of proud flesh.

Psyllium
The dried ripe seed of the common plantain plant. Used as a bulk laxative.

Purge dewormers
Dewormer[G] medication used to wipe out susceptible adult worms and some immature forms. There are no residual protective effects—re-infection commences as soon as your horse picks up eggs and larvae from infested ground.

Purpura hemorrhagica
A form of vasculitis[G] that occurs several weeks after recovery from a respiratory illness such as strangles[G] or influenza[G]. The affected horse generally has severe, warm, painful edema[G] at several locations on his body, including legs, lower abdomen, and muzzle. The swelling can cause his skin to stretch so much that it can split and ooze serum and blood. Gums and delicate tissues around his eyes may have tiny red splotches where blood vessels have broken. Edema also can occur within the respiratory tract and can make breathing difficult. Treatment generally is aggressive intensive care and intravenous corticosteroids to reduce the swelling; antibiotics if bacterial infection of damaged tissues is suspected; and nursing care as detailed in

vasculitis[G]. Even with aggressive treatment, purpura hemorrhagica is fatal for some of its victims.

Pyramidal disease
Inflammation (and, in severe cases, fracture) of the extensor process of your horse's coffin bone (a triangular protrusion at the bone's front edge where the extensor tendons attach). It generally occurs due to strain from a misstep or repeated over-extension, or due to abnormal development. Signs can include sudden onset of moderate to severe lameness, with swelling and pain over the coronary band at the front of the foot. If there's no fracture, treatment usually is rest; ice; bandaging of the swollen coronary band; and administration of anti-inflammatory medications. If there is a fracture, surgery often is indicated to remove the fracture fragment.

Pythiosis
See Leeches[G].

Quicked
A horse is "quicked" when a hoof is trimmed too short or when a horseshoe nail is driven into the quick, or sensitive lamina of his hoof. In many cases the horse flinches or pulls back when the quick occurs. Within a few days, some cases develop tenderness and mild to moderate lameness due to developing infection in the area. Treatment involves removal of the offending nail, if applicable; cleansing the hole; and application of a poultice to draw out remaining contamination.

Quidding
The spitting out of partially chewed wads of food. Quidding is a sign of a dental problem and/or difficulty swallowing.

Rabies
A fatal viral infection of the central nervous system spread by the saliva of an infected animal. Signs can vary widely and can include colic; lameness; bizarre gait; slobbering due to difficulty swallowing; depression or excitability; convulsions; and death within days of onset of signs. There's no treatment. Suspected cases should be quarantined. Euthanasia and definitive diagnosis using laboratory test of brain tissue should be considered in all cases of suspected rabies, so any other animals (human or otherwise) that were exposed can be treated and/or quarantined.

Rainrot
A crusting skin disorder affecting your horse's saddle area, with tufts of crusted-together hair easily pulled out, leaving a raw crater. The causative organism, which has characteristics of both bacteria and fungi, tends to thrive in wet weather when the skin is waterlogged and less capable of fighting infection. It can be spread to other horses by contaminated grooming tools. Treatment usually is: softening and removal of scabs; disinfection of affected area with iodine- or chlorhexidine-based shampoos or rinses; strict hygiene and provision of dry shelter; and disinfection of grooming tools. Severe or persistent cases might also be treated with systemic antibiotics.

Rebreathing bag
A diagnostic technique to make it easier to evaluate your horse's lung sounds when listening to his chest with a stethoscope, because your vet can't ask your horse to "take a deep breath." A bag is held over the muzzle so that exhaled air is re-used (and gradually becomes high in carbon dioxide and low in oxygen). Your horse naturally breathes more deeply when this occurs.

Recumbent, recumbency
Lying down, reclining.

Red maple tree leaf poisoning
Poisoning by ingestion of the wilted leaves of the red maple tree (*Acer rubrum*), causing hemolytic anemia[G].

Respiratory tree
The branched airways of your horse's respiratory tract, comprised of his windpipe (trachea), bronchi, and bronchioles.

Retinal degeneration
Gradual, progressive deterioration of the retina (the neuroreceptive tissues of the eyeball), most often associated with advanced age.

Rhabdomyolisis
See Tying up[G].

Rhino
See Equine Herpesvirus-1[G], Equine Herpesvirus-4[G].

Ringbone
A condition causing gradual lameness in one or more of your horse's legs due to external trauma (such as hoof-contact injuries), or strain on tissues adjacent to the pastern and coffin bone. The result is the formation of new, ragged-edged bone around the front and sides of the upper (high ringbone) or lower (low ringbone) pastern bones. Signs can include lameness and firm thickening of the pastern region. If the problem is caught before excessive bone growth occurs, treatment generally is 3 to 4 months of rest with support of the affected leg(s) to minimize movement of the area. If new bone growth already has occurred, rest and anti-inflammatory medications can help control signs, but there's no cure.

Ringworm
A fungal infection of your horse's skin, contagious to other horses and to other animals (including humans). The main sign of ringworm is patchy hair loss without itching. Treatment can include: clipping hair from affected areas; daily bathing with iodine-based shampoo; possible application of topical anti-fungal preparations after each bath; strict maintenance of dry shelter; and exposure to sunlight whenever possible. For severe cases, oral administration of anti-fungal medications may be necessary.

Roaring
An abnormal respiratory noise in your horse, most often noticed during exercise when breathing is heavy. Possible causes can include: laryngeal hemiplegia[G]; the presence of a mass in the horse's upper respiratory tract; or abnormal position of normal tissues within the upper respiratory tract (from the nostrils to the windpipe [trachea]). Treatment generally is aimed at identifying and resolving the underlying cause.

Rumensin toxicosis, Monensin® toxicosis
Poisoning of horses with this livestock supplement, either by accidentally giving cattle feed to horses, or by residual rumensin contaminating horse feed at the feed mill. Signs can include: loss of appetite; sweating; rapid, shallow breathing; colic; depression; incoordination; and death within hours to a few days after eating less than an ounce of rumensin.

Ruptured diaphragm
A tear in the muscular sheet that separates your horse's chest from his abdomen. It usually is the result of severe blunt trauma to the chest or abdomen, as from a kick or from being hit by a vehicle. Signs can include: signs of colic; labored breathing; decreased exercise tolerance; and resentment (and sometimes collapse) when a girth is tightened. Treatment generally is surgical repair; prognosis is guarded.

Russian knapweed poisoning
Poisoning from eating the fresh or baled Russian knapweed, a perennial weed that causes permanent brain damage similar to that seen with yellow star thistle poisoning[G]: A specific region of the brain becomes softened and liquefied. Signs generally include sudden onset of paralysis of the mouth, making it impossible for the horse to hold or chew food or drink water. The upper lip becomes tense, with the corners of the mouth held partially open in a grimace, and the tongue moving awkwardly in a futile attempt to hold and move food. The horse champs his jaw; yawns; tosses his head; and may submerge his head in water up to his eyes in order to drink. Brain damage is permanent; there's no treatment.

Salivary duct stone
The formation of a stone in your horse's salivary duct, causing a hard lump on the side of his head behind his jawbone, below his ear, or just behind the corner of his mouth. If the duct is completely blocked by a stone, there generally will be heat, swelling, and pain along the side of his head below the ear, due to inflammation in the salivary gland. Treatment usually is surgical removal of the stone.

Salmonellosis, *Salmonella* infection, *Salmonella* enteritis
A contagious intestinal infection by *Salmonella* bacteria, causing severe acute diarrhea[G] or chronic diarrhea[G]. Acute diarrhea is usually accompanied by fever and abdominal pain; horses that recover often fall victim to laminitis[G]. Treatment usually requires aggressive intensive care; quarantine; pain management; stress management, and may include antibiotics and transfaunation[G].

Sarcoid
A skin condition caused by invasion of skin tissues by an unidentified virus. Lesions usually are tumor like, sometimes ulcerated, spreading locally or to other areas of your horse's body. Some reports suggest that sarcoid tends to run in lines of horses; others suggest certain premises have a higher incidence of sarcoid among resident horses, whether they're related or not. Choice of treatment is debated by veterinarians. Some advocate surgical removal; others advocate freezing (cryosurgery); still others believe they get the best results from immunotherapy (injecting one or more lesions with a commercial immunostimulant). Some believe "quiet" sarcoids might be stimulated to grow and spread when sarcoids elsewhere on the body are treated. For each case, optimal treatment usually is chosen on the basis of individual characteristics, such as location; aesthetics; and aggressiveness of growth. It's not uncommon for sarcoids to return after removal.

Schirmer tear test
A test for quantity of tear production. A strip of specially prepared, absorbent paper is inserted between the lower eyelid and the eyeball and left in place for a precise length of time while it absorbs the moisture produced by tear glands. Upon removal, the paper is examined and the length of the wet portion is measured and compared to a chart of normal findings.

Scratches, eczematoid dermatitis
A hot, swollen, raw, painful inflammation of the skin on the backs of your horse's pasterns, usually involving two or more feet. Most often occurs in the hind feet. Lesions are often infected, but whether infection is the cause or effect of the condition is controversial. Regardless, once the problem gets started, it becomes self-perpetuating. Successful treatment requires diligence and strict hygiene, and generally includes gentle daily or twice daily cleansing of the area; removal of scabs; application of an antiseptic dressing; and housing in an area that's dry and clean. Treatment failure occurs when the inflammation and/or infection are too deep to be reached topically, requiring systemic medication and/or surgery to remove affected tissue.

Selenium poisoning, acute
Poisoning from overdose of this essential mineral. Unfortunately there's a narrow margin between the amount needed for health, and the amount that can make a horse sick—or worse. When a dose is mildly toxic, chronic selenium poisoning (alkali disease[G]) occurs. When the dose is moderately toxic, subacute selenium poisoning (blind staggers[G]) occurs. When the dose is highly toxic, acute selenium poisoning occurs. Symptoms can include depression; labored breathing; diarrhea; collapse; and death within 24 hours of ingestion of the mineral.

Septicemia
Blood poisoning due to bacteria and their toxins in your horse's bloodstream. Symptoms usually include: loss of appetite; fever; and depression. Treatment generally includes support and administration of antibiotics to which the causative bacteria are sensitive.

Sequestrum
A loose, dead fragment of broken bone, often causing local infection.

Seroma
The result of blunt trauma causing bleeding under the skin. A seroma is a hematoma[G] in which accumulated blood has separated into serum and clotted red blood cells.

Shivers
A trembling disorder of the hind limbs and, in severe cases, other body parts. Signs are seen

most often when the horse is at rest, backing, or when asked to pick up a hind foot. The horse flexes an affected hind limb to an extreme, and the leg trembles violently. Trembling also can occur in his tail, forelimbs, eyes, and ears. Musculoskeletal pain in the affected limb can make shivering worse. In some cases, shivers has occurred after recovery from general anesthesia; in other cases, particularly in draft horses, it appears when a horse is worked strenuously enough to become rapidly fatigued. The condition tends to worsen over time, and there's no specific treatment. Some cases respond well to anti-inflammatory medication.

Shock
See Endotoxic shock[G].

Sinusitis
Inflammation and/or infection of the membrane lining a sinus. Signs usually include nasal discharge and/or asymmetrical swelling of your horse's face. Treatment usually is: drainage of material accumulated in the sinus and administration of appropriate antibiotics. Depending on which sinus is involved and the nature of the material accumulated in it, drainage might require opening a hole into the sinus through a bone of the horse's face.

Skin cancer
The most common type of skin cancers causing external tumors in horses are melanoma[G], lymphoma[G], sarcoid, and squamous cell carcinoma[G].

Slaframine
A toxin present in a soil fungus that infests certain legumes, such as clover, when climate conditions are favorable (warm and humid). It can cause excessive salivation and slobbering, and in some cases epiphora[G]. Removal from the pasture containing infested clover is curative within a few days. The fungus retreats to soil when conditions become dry and/or cool.

Snakebite
The bite of certain venomous snakes can cause illness in horses, including swelling and bruising at the bite site, and potentially dangerous swelling of the respiratory tract. (This is a common problem with horses because they are often bitten on the muzzle.) Treatment generally is: administration of anti-inflammatory medications to minimize swelling; tracheotomy[G] and/or supplemental oxygen if necessary to aid in breathing; antibiotics; and administration of specific antivenin if the type of snake is known and diagnosis is made very soon after the bite.

Sole abscess, gravel
Infection within your horse's hoof, due to invasion by bacteria via imperfections in the hoof horn, or via puncture wound. Pain and/or lameness are the result of pressure from the festering infection; profound relief usually is seen when drainage of pus and debris is accomplished. Treatment generally focuses on establishing drainage, either by opening a tract through the sole, or by drawing the infection out via a draining tract forming at the coronary band. Without drainage, antibiotics generally aren't effective.

Sorghum poisoning
See Poison, causing blood thinning.

Sprain, tendon or ligament
Stretching and/or tearing of tendon or ligament fibers due to excessive strain. The injury is worsened by swelling and bleeding within the torn tendon or ligament, and by additional strain. Treatment may include ice and pressure bandaging; prevention of further stress by limiting movement of the affected limb with a splint, cast, or heel wedge; administration of anti-inflammatory medications; and physical therapy to prevent adhesions that would limit future range of motion.

Squamous cell carcinoma
Cancer of a specific type of cells present in skin and mucus membranes lining internal organs such as the bladder, intestines, and uterus. Squamous cell carcinoma of the skin is commonly associated with ultraviolet rays on unpigmented, hairless skin adjacent to a white-coated area (which reflects sun onto the vulnerable skin for a double dose of ultraviolet rays). When lesions are few and accessible,

treatment generally is removal and/or obliteration by surgery and/or cryosurgery[G]. When too extensive or inaccessible, often the only treatment option is chemotherapy.

Stone, bladder
A stone formed within the bladder from minerals normally dissolved in urine. The minerals come out of solution and coalesce into a progressively growing stone. Symptoms can include frequent urination; blood-tinged urine; and, if the stone has blocked the passage of urine, posturing to urinate but failing to pass urine. Treatment generally is surgical removal of large or obstructing stones, and administration of appropriate antibiotics for underlying infection.

Strangles
Contagious upper respiratory tract infection by bacteria called *Streptococcus equi*, that can cause fever; loss of appetite; watery-to-thick nasal discharge; cough; and swelling and eventual drainage of pus from the lymph nodes under your horse's lower jaw. Treatment generally is supportive. Hot packs and/or poultices are used to encourage drainage of abscessed lymph nodes. Administration of systemic antibiotics may be indicated. Some horses develop a potentially fatal condition called purpura hemorrhagica[G] after recovering from strangles.

Stringhalt
A muscle and/or nerve disorder, affecting one or both hind limbs. The affected horse often lifts his affected hindlimb(s) too high, sometimes so high that he kicks himself in the belly, holds the leg elevated for a moment, then slaps it sharply down. It can develop at any age; the cause is unknown. Stringhalt usually is treated with muscle relaxants and/or surgical removal of a section of the culprit muscle and its tendon, the lateral digital extensor. Without treatment, the condition rarely improves.

Stroke
A brain disorder that occurs when a loose blood clot travels through your horse's bloodstream and becomes lodged in a blood vessel in his brain. This can result in loss of blood supply, leakage of loose blood (which is inflammatory) into the brain tissue, and/or brain swelling. Signs depend on the area of the brain affected. Treatment generally is support and aggressive administration of anti-inflammatory medications.

Strongyles
Common intestinal parasites that can cause widespread tissue damage during their migration through your horse's intestinal walls, liver, pancreas, and the walls of his major intestinal artery, on their way to his large intestine.

Strychnine poisoning
Poisoning from eating strychnine, a chemical usually found in commercial rodent baits. Symptoms occur within 10 minutes to 2 hours of eating it and can include: excitability; muscle tension; "saw-horse" stance; violent seizures triggered by external stimuli such as touch or sound; and death. Treatment generally is symptomatic: anti-seizure medications; and intravenous fluids to speed elimination of poison from the body.

Summer sores
See Habronema[G].

Swamp cancer, Pythiosis, Gulf coast fever
See Leeches[G].

Sweet itch, queensland itch, culicoides hypersensitivity
Hypersensitivity to the bites of tiny members of the Culicoides fly family called midges[G] or "no-see-ums." An affected horse rubs the crest of his neck until mane hairs break off and the skin becomes thickened. There is no cure. Treatment can include increasing pest-control efforts, and, in severe cases, administration of systemic corticosteroids to soothe inflamed tissues. (Caution: Systemic administration of corticosteroids has been linked with increased incidence of laminitis[G].)

Sympathetic system
The portion of your horse's involuntary ner-

vous system involved primarily with enhancing bodily functions that support "flight or fight," such as dilating the pupils, widening his eyes, raising the blood pressure, increasing heart rate, and dilating his nostrils and respiratory tree.

Synovial cells, synovial membrane
Thin, flexible tissue lining most joints in your horse. The synovial membrane is comprised of synovial cells, which manufacture a viscous fluid (synovial fluid) that fills and lubricates the joint.

Synovitis
Inflammation of the soft, pliable membrane lining a joint. Often the first in a series of events that can lead to degenerative joint disease[G].

Tendinitis
Inflammation of a tendon, usually due to injury. Signs generally include: swelling and heat over the inflamed tendon; pain on finger pressure; lameness; and a protective stance to limit tendon stress. Treatment usually includes: aggressive first aid to limit swelling and hemorrhage between tendon fibers; enforced rest; immobilization of the tendon (e.g., with a cast); administration of anti-inflammatory medications; and physical therapy to limit formation of adhesions.

Tendon, damage, leg buckling because of
Injury from stress, or due to external trauma, can partially or completely sever a tendon, leaving it incapable of supporting your horse's leg. Such injuries are most common in his lower limbs, where load-bearing forces are great and where there's little padding to protect tendons against injury from external trauma. Injuries that sever the extensor tendon on the front surface of a leg will allow the leg to buckle forward, onto the front of its fetlock. Injuries that sever one or both flexor tendons on the rear surface of a leg will allow the fetlock to sink toward the ground. Treatment generally is rest and support of the leg.

Tetanus antitoxin
Antitoxin is a product made from blood serum containing antibodies against a specific toxin (poison). Tetanus antitoxin is made of equine serum and contains antibodies against the tetanus toxin. See Antitoxin, and serum sickness[G].

Tetanus toxoid
A toxoid is a vaccine made of toxin (poison) that has been altered chemically so that it has no toxic effects, but is able to stimulate an immune response. Tetanus toxoid is a vaccine that stimulates your horse's body's production of antibodies against the toxins that cause tetanus.

Tetanus
A disease resulting from toxins produced by bacteria of the *Clostridium* family, usually resulting when they infect a wound, particularly (but not exclusively) a deep puncture wound, where oxygen is scarce. *Clostridium* species are natural soil inhabitants. Because they're present in horse manure, they're ubiquitous in the soil on a horse property. Signs of tetanus may include: elevation of both nictitating membranes[G] when the horse's face is tapped gently below the eye; spasms of the muscles in his jaw, making it difficult or impossible to eat or drink; a "sawhorse" stance with rigid legs; convulsions triggered by noise or other stimuli; profuse sweating; and death. Treatment usually is aggressive debridement of the infected wound to prevent further toxin absorption; intravenous administration of tetanus antitoxin; administration of anti-seizure medications, sedatives and muscle relaxants; and intensive supportive care including intravenous fluids and feeding a gruel via stomach tube.

Thermography
A diagnostic technology that detects variations in tissue temperatures. It may be useful in localizing the source of an obscure lameness.

Third eyelid
See Nictitating membrane[G].

Throat injury
Injury to the back of your horse's throat, often the result of rough passage of a stomach tube

or use of a balling gun[G]. It can cause symptoms that include: difficulty swallowing and, if swelling is severe, difficulty breathing; visible swelling in the throatlatch area; and nasal discharge. Treatment usually includes rest and anti-inflammatory medications.

Thrush
A bacterial infection of the frog and/or adjacent crevices of the foot's sole, causing a blackish discharge and foul odor. Treatment generally includes trimming and debridement[G] of affected tissues; disinfection with copper sulfate, tincture of iodine, strong (7 percent) iodine, or merthiolate; provision of dry, clean environment; good hygiene; and daily foot care.

Thumps
Rhythmic jerking of the walls of your horse's chest or abdomen, appearing to coincide with breathing but actually due to spasm of the diaphragm each time his heart beats. The cause is a profound imbalance of minerals and electrolytes, usually the result of massive fluid loss by sweating during strenuous endurance work. Treatment usually is cautious administration of intravenous fluids, calcium, magnesium, and glucose while monitoring the heart for cardiac arrest (which can occur if calcium is given too quickly).

Tongue, injury to
Your horse's tongue can be injured by harsh bits, overzealous tongue-tying (see Tongue, tying, and DDSP[G]), or a sharp object in his feed or feed tray. Depending on the injury's severity, treatment can include surgical repair or amputation, although many severe tongue injuries heal well without stitches. Approximately half the tongue can be amputated if necessary, with little effect on your horse's ability to function.

Tongue, tying, and DDSP
Tying a horse's tongue to his lower jaw during strenuous exercise, such as racing, is used in some instances as a diagnostic procedure and/or a way of managing the condition called dorsal displacement of the soft palate, or DDSP (see Dorsal displacement of the soft palate, DDSP[G]). Injury to the tongue can occur if it's tied too tightly.

Toxoplasmosis
Infection with a member of the *Toxoplasma* family, a protozoal organism. What was formerly called Toxoplasmosis is now called Equine protozoal myeloencephalomyelitis, or EPM[G].

Tracheotomy
An artificial opening made in the windpipe (trachea) when a problem in your horse's nasal cavity or throat has blocked the passage of air, making it impossible to breathe. Usually an emergency procedure.

Transfaunation
Administration of beneficial bacteria to a horse suspected of intestinal disease due, at least in part, by disruption of the normal bacterial population in the gut.

Transtracheal wash
A diagnostic procedure used to confirm a tentative diagnosis of pneumonia and to help identify the causative bacteria, and thus the antibiotic that will be most effective against it. While the horse stands with minimal restraint, a small area at the front of his neck (over the windpipe) is clipped and disinfected, then numbed with a local anesthetic. A small incision is made through the numbed skin into the windpipe, through which a long, sterile catheter is inserted and directed toward the lungs. Sterile saline is infused through the catheter into the bronchial tubes, sucked back out into a syringe, and analyzed at a laboratory.

Tying up
A muscle disorder known as rhabdomyolysis, causing stiffness, hardening, and breakdown of the major muscle masses. There is a variety of causes.

Ultrasonography
A diagnostic imaging technique used to image soft, deep tissues by sending ultrasonic sound waves to and/or through them, and forming a live image with the sound waves that bounce back. Ultrasound examinations

are used commonly in reproduction; diagnosing and/or monitoring healing of tendon, muscle, and ligament injuries; and in detecting structural abnormalities in the liver, spleen, kidney, heart, umbilicus, and eye.

Upward fixation of the patella
See Patella, upward fixation of [G].

Urethra, blockage of
A blocked urethra stops the flow of urine from your horse's bladder to the outside and is, therefore, an emergency situation. Urethral blockage can be caused by passage of a bladder stone or blood clot, or by pressure on the urethra from an adjacent mass. Symptoms generally include frequent posturing and straining to urinate with sporadic or minimal output. Treatment usually is identifying and treating the underlying cause.

Urethra, infection of
A problem in breeding stallions causing blood to be discharged into the ejaculate, and possibly infecting mares bred by natural cover or by artificial insemination without added antibiotics. Signs of urethral infection can include frequent urination; blood-tinged urine; and frequent posturing and straining to urinate with only dribbles coming out. The stallion's fertility can be affected by urethral infection because blood in the ejaculate is toxic to sperm.

Uveitis
Inflammation and/or infection of the uvea, the colored iris of your horse's eye. Several potential causes exist, including trauma to the eye; infection with *Leptospira* bacteria; infestation with eyeworms; and abnormal immune activity within the eye. However, the cause of most cases of uveitis is never determined. Signs can include: constricted pupil; watery eye; squinting; and rubbing. If allowed to progress, uveitis can lead to breakdown of the eye's internal structures; detachment of the retina; and blindness. Treatment includes frequent application of pupil-dilating ophthalmic medications as well as anti-inflammatory preparations such as dexamethasone or prednisone on the eye and/or systemically; systemic administration of nonsteroidal anti-inflammatory medications; and detection and treatment of the underlying problem, if possible.

Vasculitis
Inflammation of small blood vessels and capillaries which, because of damage to their walls, leak serum into the tissues and cause swelling, most often in your horse's lower legs. Vasculitis is a symptom of an underlying, body-wide problem, most often a viral respiratory infection. Swelling can progress to the point that your horse's skin splits and oozes serum and blood. In addition to addressing the underlying cause, treatment generally is aimed at cooling and soothing the swollen legs with gentle cold-water irrigation, and supporting the skin with padded compression bandaging to prevent splitting. If skin has already split, the affected area usually is treated as a laceration.

Vasomotor rhinitis
Congestion of the lining of your horse's nasal passages, without infection.

Venezuelan equine encephalomyelitis, VEE
A viral disease of the central nervous system of horses, mules, donkeys, and man, spread by infected mosquitoes and found in parts of South America, Panama, Trinidad, and Mexico, with outbreaks occasionally occurring in the southern Unites States near the Mexican border. Signs can include: fever; diarrhea; depression; and central nervous system signs that are mild (when compared to Eastern[G] or Western Equine Encephalomyelitis[G]), consisting primarily of dizziness and head-pressing. Prognosis is guarded to good with symptomatic and supportive treatment.

Vertebral body osteomyelitis
Inflammation and/or infection of the spinal vertebrae.

Vesicular stomatitis, VS
Viral infection causing blisters and sores on the lips and gums, sometimes accompanied by swelling and blistering of the coronary bands, blisters on the udder of lactating mares, and

blisters on the tip of the penis. VS is a reportable disease, meaning that your state and/or federal veterinarian should be notified if it's diagnosed. Affected horses should be quarantined until they've recovered. Treatment generally is supportive and symptomatic.

Warts

Viral-induced growths in your horse's skin that are hairless, not itchy or crusty, and can occur anywhere on his body. Treatment options can include: no treatment; surgical removal or obliteration; or administration of a vaccine made of material from the horse's own warts. For information on warts on the muzzle of young horses, see Juvenile warts[G].

Wave mouth

Undulating surface of the grinder teeth due to uneven wear.

Western equine encephalomyelitis, WEE

Viral infection of the central nervous system of horses, mules, donkeys, and humans, spread by infected mosquitoes. Signs can include: loss of appetite; fever; excitability with overreaction to external stimuli such as lights and sounds; depression; aimless wandering; head-pressing; staggering; paralysis; and death. Most horses recover if given extensive supportive treatment, but many have residual mental changes and are commonly referred to as "dummies."

Windpuffs

Synovial effusion[G], with or without involvement of the adjacent tendon sheath, in the fetlock joint. This causes puffiness of the joint that might extend partway up your horse's cannon bone. Windpuffs may or may not be associated with lameness. Causes can include excessive stress on joint soft tissues and tendons due to poor conformation, poorly balanced farriery (see Long-toe/low-heel, LTLH[G]), heavy training, and/or sudden stall confinement after a period of regular training. Treatment generally focuses on identifying and correcting the underlying cause; rest; ice; and pressure wraps to limit inflammation and swelling.

Wolf teeth, newly emerging

Wolf teeth, which are first premolars, are located toward the back of the space between your horse's front teeth and his grinders. They're commonly found only in the upper arcade, and can range in size from 1/4 inch nubs to almost as large as the canine teeth (located in the front half of the space between front teeth and grinders). When present on the lower jaw, wolf teeth are small and needle-like. When the presence, position, and/or size of wolf teeth interfere with acceptance of the bit, the teeth are removed, usually with the horse awake and sedated.

Yellow star thistle poisoning

Poisoning from eating the fresh or baled perennial weed causes permanent brain damage. A specific region of the brain becomes softened and liquefied. Signs include sudden onset of paralysis of the mouth, making it impossible for the horse to hold or chew food or drink water. The upper lip is tense, the corners of his mouth held back in a grimace, and his tongue moves awkwardly in a futile attempt to hold and move food in his mouth. The horse may champ his jaw, yawn, and toss his head, and may submerge his head in water up to his eyes in order to drink. Brain damage is permanent; there is no treatment.

REFERENCES

Aleman M, Spier SJ, Wilson WD et al. *Corynebacterium pseudotuberculosis* infection in horses: 538 cases (1982-1993). *Journal of the American Veterinary Medical Association* 209:4(1996):804-808.

Andrews FM. Acute rhabdomyolysis. In: Veterinary Clinics of North America, Equine Practice 10:3 (Dec 1994): 567-574. Phila: W. B. Saunders.

Baker GJ. Dental morphology, function, and pathology. In: *Proceedings of the 37th Annual AAEP Convention* (1991): 83-94.

Bassage LH II, Parente EJ, Krotec KL et al. Sterile nodular panniculitis associated with lameness in a horse. *Journal of the American Veterinary Medical Association* 209:7(1996):1242-1244.

Baxter GM. Acute laminitis. In: Veterinary Clinics of North America, Equine Practice 10:3 (Dec 1994): 627-642. Phila: W. B. Saunders.

Baxter GM. Management of proximal splint bone injuries in horses. In: *Proceedings of the 38th Annual AAEP Convention* (1992): 419-428.

Beard W. Upper respiratory causes of respiratory intolerance. In: Veterinary Clinics of North America, Equine Practice 12:3(1996):435-456. Phila: W. B. Saunders.

Beech J. Chronic obstructive pulmonary disease. In: Veterinary Clinics of North America, Equine Practice 7:1(1991):79-92. Phila: W. B. Saunders.

Beeman GM. The clinical diagnosis of lameness. *Compendium on Continuing Education* 9:11(1987): 1124-1135.

Bernard WV. Leptospirosis. In: Veterinary Clinics of North America, Equine Practice 9:2(1993):435-444. Phila: W. B. Saunders.

Bertone AL. Infectious tenosynovitis. In: Veterinary Clinics of North America, Equine Practice 11:2(1995):163-176. Phila: W. B. Saunders.

Bertone AL. Management of exuberant granulation tissue. In: Veterinary Clinics of North America, Equine Practice 5:3(1989):551-562. Phila: W. B. Saunders.

Bertone AL. Principles of wound healing. In: Veterinary Clinics of North America, Equine Practice 5:3 (1989): 449-464. Phila: W. B. Saunders.

Bertone AL. Tendon lacerations. In: Veterinary Clinics of North America, Equine Practice 11:2(1995):293-314. Phila: W. B. Saunders.

Bertone JJ. Critical care in adult horses: restraint, analgesia and anti-inflammatory support. *Veterinary Medicine* 88(1993):1066-1085.

Black JB. Hindlimb lameness of the western working stock horse. In: *Proceedings of the 37th Annual AAEP Convention* (1991): 393-404.

Blythe LL, Watrous BJ, Pearson EG et al. Otitis media/interna in the horse. In: *Proceedings of the 36th Annual AAEP Convention* (1990):517-528.

Booth L. Early wound management in the horse. *Equine Practice* 14:7 (1992):24-33.

Boyd JS. Selection of sites for intramuscular injections in the horse. *Veterinary Record* 121:9(1987):197-200.

Brillig Hill, Inc. Lyme disease in horses. *Equine Practice* 18:5(1996)29-32.

Brown CM. Acquired cardiovascular disease. In: Veterinary Clinics of North America, Equine Practice 1:2(1985):371-382. Phila: W. B. Saunders.

Buechner-Maxwell V. Airway hyperresponsiveness. *Compendium on Continuing Education* 15(1993):1379-1383.

Carr EA, Spier SJ, Kortz GD et al. Laryngeal and pharyngeal dysfunction in horses homozygous for hyperkalemic periodic paralysis. *Journal of the American Veterinary Medical Association* 209:4(1996):798-802.

Chaffin MK, Schumacher J, McMullan WC. Cutaneous pythiosis in the horse. In: Veterinary Clinics of North America, Equine Practice 11:1(1995):91-104. Phila: W. B. Saunders.

Chambers TM, Holland RE, Lai ACK. Equine influenza—Current veterinary perspectives, Part 1. *Equine Practice* 17:8(1995):19-23.

Cohen ND. Neurologic evaluation of the equine head and neurogenic dysphagia. In: Veterinary Clinics of North America, Equine Practice 9:1(1993):199-212. Phila: W. B. Saunders.

Collatos C. Clinical conditions associated with endotoxemia. In: *Proceedings of the 41st Annual AAEP Convention* (1995):103.

Cook WR. Headshaking in horses part 4: Special diagnostic procedures. *Equine Practice* 2 (1980):7-15.

Craig TM, Courtney CH. Epidemiology and control of parasites in warm climates. In: Veterinary Clinics of North America, Equine Practice 2:2(1986):357-366. Phila: W. B. Saunders.

Dabareiner RM, White II NA. Large colon impaction: A retrospective study in 147 horses. In: *Proceedings of the 40th Annual AAEP Convention* (1994): 121-122.

Dabareiner RM, White NA II. Large-colon impaction: retrospective study in 147 horses. In: *Proceedings of the 40th Annual AAEP Convention* (1994):121-122.

Dean PW. Upper airway obstruction in performance horses: differential diagnoses and treatment. In: Veterinary Clinics of North America, Equine Practice 7:1(1991):123-148. Phila: W. B. Saunders.

DeBowes RM, Yovich JV. Penetrating wounds, abscesses, gravel, and bruising of the equine foot. In: Veterinary Clinics of North America, Equine Practice 5:1(1989):179-194. Phila: W. B. Saunders.

Derksen FJ, Woods PSA. Chronic lung disease in the horse: role of aeroallergens and irritants and methods of evaluation. *Equine Practice* 16:5(1994):11-13.
Dik KJ, Dyson SJ, Vail TB. Aseptic tenosynovitis of digital flexor tendon sheath, fetlock, and pastern annular ligament constriction. In: Veterinary Clinics of North America, Equine Practice 11:2(1995):151-162. Phila: W. B. Saunders.

DiPietro JA, Todd KS. The role and control of internal equine parasites in colic. In: Equine Acute Abdomen; *Proceedings of the Veterinary Seminar at the University of Georgia* (1986):15-20.

Divers TJ, Mohammed JO, Cummings JF. Equine motor neuron disease. In: Veterinary Clinics of North America, Equine Practice 13:1(1997):97-106. Phila: W. B. Saunders.

Doran R. Field management of simple intestinal obstruction in horses. *Compendium on Continuing Education* 15:3(1993):463-471.

Drudge JH, Lyons ET. Large strongyles: recent advances. In: Veterinary Clinics of North America, Equine Practice 2:2(1986):263-280. Phila: W. B. Saunders.

Dwyer RM. Disinfecting equine facilities. *Rev. sci. tech. Off. int. Epiz* 14:2(1995):403-418.

Dwyer RM. Practical methods of disinfection and management during outbreaks of infectious disease. In: *Proceedings of the 38th Annual AAEP Convention* (1992):381-388.

Dyson SJ, Denoix JM. Tendon, tendon sheath, and ligament injuries in the pastern. In: Veterinary Clinics of North America, Equine Practice 11:2(1995):217-234. Phila: W. B. Saunders.

Easley KJ. Recognition and management of the diseased equine tooth. In: *Proceedings of the 37th Annual AAEP Convention* (1991):129-140.

English M, Pollen S. Pastern dermatitis and unguilysis in two draft horses. *Equine Practice* 17:8(1995) :25-30.

Evans AG. Urticaria in horses. *Compendium on Continuing Education* 15:4(1993):626-631.

Evans DL. Cardiovascular adaptations to exercise and training. In: Veterinary Clinics of North America, Equine Practice 1:3(1985):513-532. Phila: W. B. Saunders.

Fadok VA. An overview of equine dermatoses characterized by scaling and crusting. In: Veterinary Clinics of North America, Equine Practice 11:1(1995):43-52. Phila: W. B. Saunders.

Fadok VA. Overview of equine papular and nodular dermatoses. In: Veterinary Clinics of North America, Equine Practice 11:1(1995):61-74. Phila: W. B. Saunders.

Fadok VA. Overview of equine pruritus. In: Veterinary Clinics of North America, Equine Practice 11:1(1995):1-10. Phila: W. B. Saunders.

Fessler JF. Hoof injuries. In: Veterinary Clinics of North America, Equine Practice 5:3 (1989):643-664. Phila: W. B. Saunders.

Fessler JF. Hoof injuries. In: Veterinary Clinics of North America, Equine Practice 5:3(1989):643-664. Phila: W. B. Saunders.

Firth EC. Vestibular disease, and its relationship to facial paralysis in the horse. *Australian Veterinary Journal* 53(1977):560-564.

Fischer D, Easley J. Proper restraint. *Large Animal Veterinarian* Nov/Dec 1993:14-33.

Foil L, Foil C. Parasitic skin diseases. In: Veterinary Clinics of North America, Equine Practice 2:2(1986):403-438. Phila: W. B. Saunders.

French DA. Soft tissue emergency in adult horses. In: Veterinary Clinics of North America, Equine Practice 10:3 (Dec 1994):575-590. Phila: W. B. Saunders.

Gaughan EM. Skeletal origins of exercise intolerance in horses. In: Veterinary Clinics of North America, Equine Practice 12:3(1996):517-536. Phila: W. B. Saunders.

Green S. Equine tetanus: A review of the clinical features and current perspectives on treatment and prophylaxis. In: *Proceedings of the 38th Annual AAEP Convention* (1992): 299-306.

Green SL. Equine rabies. In: Veterinary Clinics of North America, Equine Practice 9:2(1993):337-348. Phila: W. B. Saunders.

Hall JO, Buck WB, Coté LM. Natural poisons in horses (1993). Urbana: National Animal Poison Control Center, University of Illinois.

Haussler K. Bad backs. *Large Animal Veterinarian* 6(1996):22-23.

Herd RP. Epidemiology and control of parasites in northern temperate regions. In: Veterinary Clinics of North America, Equine Practice 2:2(1986):337-356. Phila: W. B. Saunders.

Herd RP. Vacuuming horse pastures: A nonchemical approach to the control of horse parasites and colic. In: *Equine Colic Research; Proceedings of the Second Symposium at the University of Georgia* (1986):11-13.

Hintz HF. Commonly asked questions about nutrition and colic. *Equine Practice* 16:10(1994):10-15.

Hormanski CE. Management of anaphylactic reactions in the horse. In: *Proceedings of the 37th Annual AAEP Convention* (1991): 61-70.

Hulbert LC, Oehme FW. Plants poisonous to livestock, Third edition (1968). Manhattan, KS: Kansas State University Printing Service.

Jackson SG, Pagan JD. Equine nutrition: a practitioner's guide. In: *Proceedings of the 37th Annual AAEP Convention* (1991):409-432.

Kawcak CE, Stashak RS, Norrdin RW. Treatment of ossifying fibroma in a horse by hemimaxillectomy. *Equine Practice* 18:7(1996):22-25.

Keegan KG, Baker GJ, Boero MJ et al. Measurement of suspensory ligament strain using a liquid mercury strain gauge: evaluation of strain reduction by support bandaging and alteration of hoof wall angle. In: *Proceedings of the 37th Annual AAEP Convention* (1991):243-244.

Klei TR, Turk MAM, McClure JR et al. Natural and acquired resistance to Strongylus vulgaris: its associated lesions and colic. In: *Equine Colic Research; Proceedings of the Second Symposium at the University of Georgia* (1986):14-17.

Kristula M, McDonnell S. Effect of drinking water temperature on consumption and preference of water during cold weather in ponies. In: *Proceedings of the 40th Annual AAEP Convention* (1994):95-98.

Lane JG, Mair TS. Observations on headshaking in the horse. *Equine Veterinary Journal* 19(1987):331-336.

Lindsay WA. Equine bandaging techniques. In: Veterinary Clinics of North America, Equine Practice 5:3(1989):513-538. Phila: W. B. Saunders.

MacKay RJ. Equine protozoal myeloencephalitis. In: Veterinary Clinics of North America, Equine Practice 13:1(1997):79-96. Phila: W. B. Saunders.

Marks D. Back pain. In: Current Therapy in Equine Medicine 4(1997):6-12. Phila: W. B. Saunders.

May SA, Wyn-Jones G. Identification of hindleg lameness. *Equine Veterinary Journal* 19:3(1987):185-188.

McCall JP. Controlling fear in the horse. In: *Proceedings of the 38th Annual AAEP Convention* (1992):81-84.

Mitten LA. Cardiovascular causes of exercise intolerance. In: Veterinary Clinics of North America, Equine Practice 12:3(1996):473-494. Phila: W. B. Saunders.

Modransky P, Welker B, Pickett JP. Management of facial injuries. In: Veterinary Clinics of North America, Equine Practice 5:3(1989):665-682. Phila: W. B. Saunders.

Moore BR. Lower respiratory tract disease. In: Veterinary Clinics of North America, Equine Practice 12:3(1996):457-472. Phila: W. B. Saunders.

Morgan SE. Feeds, forages, and toxic plants. *Equine Practice* 18:1(1996):8-12.

Moyer W, Fisher JRS. Bucked shins: effects of differing track surfaces and proposed training regimens. In: *Proceedings of the 37th Annual AAEP Convention* (1991):541-548.

Murphy MJ. A field guide to common animal poisons (1996). Ames: Iowa State University Press.

Murray MJ. Diarrhea in adult horses. *Journal of Equine Veterinary Science* 13(1993):374-376.

National Research Council (U.S.), Subcommittee on Horse Nutrition. Nutrient requirements of horses, Fifth Revised Edition (1989). Washington, D.C.: National Academy of Sciences.

Naylor JM. Hyperkalemic periodic paralysis. In: Veterinary Clinics of North America, Equine Practice 13:1(1997):129-144. Phila: W. B. Saunders.

Nickels FA. Diseases of the nasal cavity. In: Veterinary Clinics of North America, Equine Practice 9:1(1993):111-122. Phila: W. B. Saunders.

Ostlund EN. The equine Herpesviruses. In: Veterinary Clinics of North America, Equine Practice 9:2(1993):283-294. Phila: W. B. Saunders.

Pagan J. Advancing the science of equine nutrition. *The Horse* 12:7(1995):12-19.

Palmer JE. Potomac Horse Fever. In: Veterinary Clinics of North America, Equine Practice 9:2(1993):399-410. Phila: W. B. Saunders.

Pool RR. Pathogenesis of navicular disease. In: *Proceedings of the 37th Annual AAEP Convention* (1991):709-710.

Powell DG. Viral respiratory disease of the horse. In: Veterinary Clinics of North America, Equine Practice 7:1(1991):27-52. Phila: W. B. Saunders.

Powell DG. Viral respiratory disease of the horse. In: Veterinary Clinics of North America, Equine Practice 7:1(1991):27-52. Phila: W. B. Saunders.

Reed SM. Potomac horse fever update. *World Equine Veterinary Review* 1:1(1996):19-22.

Reinemeyer CR. Small strongyles: recent advances. In: Veterinary Clinics of North America, Equine Practice 2:2(1986):281-312. Phila: W. B. Saunders.

Rose PL. Villonodular synovitis in horses. *Compendium on Continuing Education* 10:5(1988):649.

Ross WA, Kaneene JB. Evaluation of outbreaks of disease attributable to eastern equine encephalitis virus in horses. *Journal of the American Veterinary Medical Association* 208:12(1996):1988-1996.

Rosser EJ Jr. Infectious crusting dermatoses. In: Veterinary Clinics of North America, Equine Practice 11:1(1995):53-60. Phila: W. B. Saunders.

Scrutchfield WL, Schumacher J. Examination of the oral cavity and routine dental care. In: Veterinary Clinics of North America, Equine Practice 9:1(1993):123-132. Phila: W. B. Saunders.

Sellon DC. Equine Infectious Anemia. In: Veterinary Clinics of North America, Equine Practice 9:2(1993):321-336. Phila: W. B. Saunders.

Severin GA. Equine ophthalmology seminar. In: *Proceedings of the 39th Annual AAEP Convention* (1993):21-28.

Smith JM, DeBowes RM, Cox JH. Central nervous system disease in adult horses. Part II. Differential diagnosis. *Compendium on Continuing Education* 9:7(1987):772-780.

Smith JM, DeBowes RM, Cox JH. Central nervous system disease in adult horses. Part III. Differential diagnosis and comparison of common disorders. *Compendium on Continuing Education* 9:10(1987):1042-1054.

Spier SJ. Salmonellosis. In: Veterinary Clinics of North America, Equine Practice 9:2(1993):385-398. Phila: W. B. Saunders.

Spirito MA. Capped hocks. *The Horse* 13:8(1996):70.

Sprouse RF, Garner HE, Green EM. Carbohydrate-induced endotoxemia in horses. In: *Equine Colic Research; Proceedings of the Second Symposium at the University of Georgia* (1986):329-332.

Timoney JF. Strangles. In: Veterinary Clinics of North America, Equine Practice 9:2(1993):365-374. Phila: W. B. Saunders.

Timoney PJ, McCollum WH. Equine viral arteritis. In: Veterinary Clinics of North America, Equine Practice 9:2(1993):257-282. Phila: W. B. Saunders.

Traub-Dargatz JL, Jones RL. Clostridia-associated enterocolitis in adult horses and foals. In: Veterinary Clinics of North America, Equine Practice 9:2(1993):411-422. Phila: W. B. Saunders.

Traub-Dargatz JL. Bacterial pneumonia. In: Veterinary Clinics of North America, Equine Practice 7:1(1991):53-62. Phila: W. B. Saunders.

Trent AM, Cox V. Pressure wraps: a comparison of surface pressure peaks and durations. In: *Proceedings of the 37th Annual AAEP Convention* (1991):245-246.

Trotter GW. Principles of early wound management. In: Veterinary Clinics of North America, Equine Practice 5:3(1989):483-498. Phila: W. B. Saunders.

Turner TA, Wolfsdorf K, Jourdenais J. Effects of heat, cold, biomagnets and ultrasound on skin circulation in the horse. In: *Proceedings of the 37th Annual AAEP Convention* (1991):249-258.

Uhlinger C. Leukoencephalomalacia. In: Veterinary Clinics of North America, Equine Practice 13:1(1997):13-20. Phila: W. B. Saunders.

Underdal RG, Park BJ, Yates CS. A comparative report on the support characteristics of bandaging products (unpublished paper). C. Steven Yates, Head Athletic Trainer, Bowman Gray School of Medicine, Wake Forest University, Post Office Box 7329, Winston-Salem, NC, 27109.

Valberg SJ. Muscular causes of exercise intolerance in horses. In: Veterinary Clinics of North America, Equine Practice 12:3(1996):495-516. Phila: W. B. Saunders.

Watrous BJ. Head tilt in horses. Veterinary Clinics of North America, Equine Practice 3(1987):353-370.

Wescott RB. Anthelmintics and drug resistance. In: Veterinary Clinics of North America, Equine Practice 2:2(1986):367-380. Phila: W. B. Saunders.

Whitson TD, Ed. Weeds of the West, Fifth Edition (1996). The Western Society of Weed Science; PO Box 963, Newark, CA.

Wilkins PA, Ducharme NG, Lesser FR. Headshakers: a diagnostic dilemma. In: *Proceedings of the 39th Annual AAEP Convention* (1993):263-264.

Wilson TM, Ross PF, Nelson PE. Fumonisin mycotoxins and equine leukoencephalomalacia: an overview. In: *Proceedings of the 38th Annual AAEP Convention* (1992):581-582.

Wilson WD. Equine Influenza. In: Veterinary Clinics of North America, Equine Practice 9:2(1993):257-282. Phila: W. B. Saunders.

Wyn Jones G. Equine Lameness (1988):3-9. Oxford: Blackwell.

Zamos DT, Honnas CM, Parson EM et al. Effects of three immobilization techniques on strain of superficial and deep digital flexor tendon in equine cadaver hindlimbs. In: *Proceedings of the Veterinary Orthopedic Society 20th Annual Conference* (1993):1-2.

INDEX

H

SECTION IV

USEFUL HORSEKEEPING FORMS

STALL CARD

Horse's name ______________________

Breed ______________________ Age __________

Veterinarian's name ______________________

Phone number(s) ______________________

Mortality insurance

Company ______________________

Policy# ______________ Emergency # __________

Major medical insurance

Company ______________________

Policy# ______________ Emergency # __________

Owner's name ______________ Home phone __________

Work phone ______________ Cellular phone __________

Allergies known or suspected

____

____

____

____

Special health/management issues?
(Example: "Tends to colic on rainy nights," "has a retained testicle," or "tends to get hot painful swellings after flu shots.")

____

____

____

____

Feeding instructions:

Hay: a.m. ________ noon ________ p.m. ________ **Grain:** a.m. ________ noon ________ p.m. ________

STALL CARD

Horse's name ______________________

Breed ______________________ Age __________

Veterinarian's name ______________________

Phone number(s) ______________________

Mortality insurance

Company ______________________

Policy# ______________ Emergency # __________

Major medical insurance

Company ______________________

Policy# ______________ Emergency # __________

Owner's name ______________ Home phone __________

Work phone ______________ Cellular phone __________

Allergies known or suspected

____

____

____

____

Special health/management issues?
(Example: "Tends to colic on rainy nights," "has a retained testicle," or "tends to get hot painful swellings after flu shots.")

____

____

____

____

Feeding instructions:

Hay: a.m. ________ noon ________ p.m. ________ **Grain:** a.m. ________ noon ________ p.m. ________

VACCINATIONS/ MEDICATIONS RECORD

Horse's name ____________________

Date	Vaccination/Medication	Dose	Administered by	Next dose due	Comments

VACCINATIONS/ MEDICATIONS RECORD

Horse's name ______________________

Date	Vaccination/Medication	Dose	Administered by	Next dose due	Comments

DEWORMING RECORD

Horse's name ______________________________

Date	**Product type** brand/active ingredient	**Dosage**	**Administered by**	**Next due**	**Comments**

DEWORMING RECORD

Horse's name ____________________

Date	Product type brand/active ingredient	Dosage	Administered by	Next due	Comments

HOOF CARE RECORD

Horse's name ______________________________

Date	Front		Rear		Pads/ type	Shoe style	Comments	Next due	Farrier
	Trim	Reset	Trim	Reset					

HOOF CARE RECORD

Horse's name ______________________

Date	Front		Rear		Pads/ type	Shoe style	Comments	Next due	Farrier
	Trim	Reset	Trim	Reset					

EXPENSE RECORD

Horse's name ______________________

Date	Board	Feed/ bedding	Farrier	Vet	Lessons/ training	Tack/ equipment	Transport	Horse shows	Misc.	Total
TOTALS										

EXPENSE RECORD

Horse's name ____________________

Date	Board	Feed/ bedding	Farrier	Vet	Lessons/ training	Tack/ equipment	Transport	Horse shows	Misc.	Total
TOTALS										